Epistemology and Logic in the
New Testament

Epistemology and Logic in the
New Testament

Early Jewish Context and Biblical Theology
Mechanisms that Fit Within Some
Contemporary Ways of Knowing

Douglas W. Kennard

WIPF & STOCK · Eugene, Oregon

EPISTEMOLOGY AND LOGIC IN THE NEW TESTAMENT
Early Jewish Context and Biblical Theology Mechanisms that Fit Within Some Contemporary Ways of Knowing

Copyright © 2016 Douglas W. Kennard. All rights reserved. Except for brief quotations in critical publications or reviews, no part of this book may be reproduced in any manner without prior written permission from the publisher. Write: Permissions, Wipf and Stock Publishers, 199 W. 8th Ave., Suite 3, Eugene, OR 97401.

Wipf & Stock
An Imprint of Wipf and Stock Publishers
199 W. 8th Ave., Suite 3
Eugene, OR 97401

www.wipfandstock.com

PAPERBACK ISBN: 978-1-5326-0815-5
HARDCOVER ISBN: 978-1-5326-0817-9
EBOOK ISBN: 978-1-5326-0816-2

Manufactured in the U.S.A.   NOVEMBER 16, 2016

This book is dedicated to
Janet Sue Kennard
Faithful partner in life, curiosity, and joy.

Contents

1 Introduction | 1
2 Epistemology and Logic of Jesus as Presented in Matthew and the Other Synoptic Gospels | 10
3 Lukan Historiography and the Epistemology of Gospel Proclamation | 86
4 Petrine Epistemology of Testimony, Prophecy as Proclamation and Evidentialism | 121
5 Epistemology and Logic of the Apostle Paul | 128
6 Johannine Empirical Epistemology with Revelation and Early Jewish Perspectivalism | 163
7 James' Wisdom Epistemology of Empiricism and Evidence | 200
8 Hebrews Epistemology of Prophecy as Rhetorical Proclamation that Christ is Supreme | 215
9 Putting the N. T. Epistemology Together | 222

Select Bibliography | 225
Author Index | 253
Subject Index | 261
Scripture Index | 263

1

Introduction

THE UNIVERSE OF THE philosopher and the universe of the biblical exegete rarely cross the same landscape. These disciplines rarely talk with each other. Their distinctive methodologies are rarely shared. This book is an attempt to bridge this rift. Hopefully, if the reader comes from one side of these disciplines they will be encouraged when their side of the conversation is engaged and they can see connections into the other side, exegetes with philosophers and philosophers with exegetes.

As an exegete, I try to keep abreast with biblical issues to inform my teaching graduate students and to contribute in the field of mostly New Testament and biblical theology among the Society for Biblical Literature, Institute for Biblical Research and Evangelical Theological Society.[1] The author is aware that sermons and comments in the gospels and Acts are authorial summaries that retain language consistent with the speaker but are selectively reduced for purposes fitting the written text. Within this spectrum of societies, the progressives will date the composition of the New Testament to mostly the second century produced by communities of redactors, while the conservatives and patristics tend to consider that the New Testament is composed during the mid-first century and finished in a repeatedly transmitted version by the end of the first century. The author's perspective is toward the conservative side and will be argued for within the chapter on Luke's historiography. Also within this spectrum of societies is the recognition that mid-twentieth century exegesis tended to be dominated by Hellenistic patterns in the wake of Bultmann but with the broad accessibility of early Jewish (and especially Qumran) manuscripts since the nineteen eighties, the Jewish side of N. T. exegesis has risen to a more dominant emphasis in the wake of Weiser, Schweitzer, Davies, Sanders, Dunn,

---

1. Kennard, *Messiah Jesus*; *Biblical Covenantalism*, three volumes; "The Reef of the O.T.," *SwJT* 56:1(2013): 227–57; "Evangelical Views on Illumination," *JETS* 49(Dec. 2006): 797–806; "Petrine Redemption," *JETS* 30(1987): 399–405; and with Pate, *Deliverance Now and Not Yet*.

and Wright. This book reflects this dominant interpretation on the Jewish side of N. T. interpretations. Therefore, the epistemic comments in the N. T. books reflect the epistemological concerns of the early Jewish context that surround the speakers and authors of the books. So much of this book explains authorial features engaged with and modifying early Judaism into its younger sister emerging Christianity. In fact, this book could be read as a development of how early Judaism affects biblical Christianity of the N. T.

As a philosopher of religion and one who teaches and writes on religious epistemology and theological method, I try to keep abreast in these fields and to contribute to my graduate students and writing among American Academy of Religion, American Theological Society, Society of Christian Philosophers, and Evangelical Philosophical Society.[2] I was asked to write this book in the wake of presenting an earlier expression of the chapter "Epistemology and Logic of the Apostle Paul" to philosophers in the American Academy of Religion, philosophy of religion section. The philosophical community in the twenty-first century has methodology that represents some of these N. T. epistemic methods but many of these methods must be modified to fit more accurately the early Jewish and biblical theology perspectives. My hope is that this book can start a conversation between these two very different worlds to enrich them both.

This book is not an attempt to explain the epistemology of contemporary hermeneutics. I have done that elsewhere positioning myself in the wake of Thiselton and Ricoeur.[3] Others have done the similar epistemic engagement for contemporary hermeneutics.[4] This book is an attempt to explore a biblical theology topic of the epistemology of Jesus and the N. T. authors in their context to the extent that they explain it within their biblical books. The authors who have accomplished this task before do so reflecting

---

2. Kennard, *A Critical Realist's*, 9–121 the author critiques many of the philosophers not aligned with here such as Plato, Philo, Aristotle, Kant and others; *The Relationship Between Epistemology*.

3. Kennard, *Critical Realist's*, 175–287; *The Relationship Between Epistemology*, 117–52; Thiselton, *The Two Horizons*; Ricoeur, *Essays on Biblical Interpretation*; *Interpretation Theory*; *The Symbolism of Evil*; *The Conflict of Interpretations*; *Time and Narrative*. three volumes; *Hermeneutics & the Human Sciences*; excellent summaries of Ricoeur's hermeneutic are presented by: Vanhoozer, *Biblical Narrative in the Philosophy of Paul Ricoeur* and Stiver, *Theology After Ricoeur*; Thiselton, *New Horizons in Hermeneutics*.

4. Gadamer, *Truth and Method*; Brueggeman, "Impossibility and Epistemology in the Faith Tradition of Abraham and Sarah (Gen 18:1–15)" *ZAW* 94:4(1982):615–34; Osborne, *The Hermeneutical Spiral*; Vanhoozer, *Is There Meaning in this Text?*; Ochs, Peirce, *Pragmatism and the Logic of Scripture*; Mathies, "Reading the Moral Law" *The Conrad Grebel Review* 23:3(2005): 74–84; Selby, *The Comical Doctrine*; Miller, "Divided by Visions of the Truth," *AUSS* 47:2(2009): 241–62 and many more.

their strength of either exegetical or philosophical awareness[5] but do not show the familiarity or interact with the other discipline sufficiently. That is, the unique niche this work is trying to fill is deep engagement with exegesis of biblical authors, early Judaism, and precise epistemic strategies in their respective contexts.

Each chapter draws out an epistemology positioned within testimony of a communal faith or language game of a Christian Pharisaic-Rabbinic worldview. Many of the chapters provide an oral *torah* that surrounds or extends the written *torah* of the Pentateuch into a new written tradition through which the early Church understood their Christ centered Trinitarian perspective. Each biblical testimony has its own character and hue. No one chapter pretends to be everything that a biblical author believed or everything by which they operated within life. The goal of each chapter is to reflect what these biblical authors have expressed from within the credible biblical material affiliated with each of them. Since these testimonies are concerned for vivid clarity one might position them within collective memory of Maurice Halburachs and Werner Kelber, and testimony of Paul Ricoeur.[6] For example, Paul Ricoeur identified that testimony is valid if 1) it agrees with other testimonies about the same event, 2) if it is obtained by means other than violence or corruption, 3) there is no reason to suppose that the witness produced the information for her own agenda, and 4) the testimony fits with the other verifiable information that we possess about the event.[7] Each chapter works within this framework, appreciating that this material engages the rabbinic language and thought forms of early Judaism, especially the chapters on Jesus, Paul, and Hebrews. Some might consider this a proto-rabbinic oral tradition since Rabbinic Judaism and Jesus' Christianity

---

5. A few others have done this task including the following but most are discussed in each chapter, but from the exegetical side: Healy and Parry, *The Bible and Epistemology*; Scott, *Paul's Way of Knowing*; all theological wordbooks; and from the philosophical side: Moser, *Jesus and Philosophy*. Many more are engaged in the respective chapters.

6. Clement of Alexandria, *Strom.* 7.106.4; Eusebius, *Hist. eccl.* 2.1.4; 1QS 6.6–8); 2 *Apoc. of James* 36.15–25; Halbwachs, *On Collective Memory*; Assmann, *Das kulturelle Gedächtnis*; Kelber, "The Case of the Gospels," *Oral Tradition* 17(2002): 55–56, 65; "The Words of Memory," in *Memory, Tradition, and Text.* ed. Kirk and Thatcher, 222– 23, 226, 238– 39; "The Generative Force of Memory," *BTB* 36(2006): 15–22; Dunn, *Jesus Remembered*, 239–243; Ricoeur, *Memory, History, Forgetting*; Bauckham, *Jesus and the Eyewitnesses*, 296, 310-57; Silberman, *Orality, Aurality and Biblical Narrative*; Dewey, *Orality and Textuality in Early Christian Literature*; Draper, *Orality, Literacy, and Colonialism in Antiquity*; Thatcher, *Jesus, The Voice, and the Text*; Kelber and Byrskog, *Jesus in Memory*.

7. Ricoeur, "Toward a Hermeneutics of the Idea of Revelation," In *Essays on Biblical Interpretation*, 101–107; Pokorny, *From the Gospel to the Gospels*, 38.

develop during the same time.[8] Most scholars consider that the New Testament writings were produced before the early forms of Rabbinic Judaism were written down. However, because both Judaism and Christianity are developing concurrently in the same oral context this author considers that there is likely substantial influence from the dominant Pharisaic-Rabbinic Judaism on the developing minority community of Christianity. Additionally, Jewish rabbinics refer to oral tradition presenting a rabbi's comments prior and concurrent to the development of the written New Testament. Furthermore, all the chapters explore aspects of Jewish-Christian *midrash*, re-appropriating Old Testament quotes and narrative in a new performative *pesher* manner to present Jesus as the Christ. The rhetorical emphasis in this volume will emphasize the rising field of rabbinic rhetoric (reflecting the heritage of Weiser, Schweitzer, Davies, and Sanders) rather than through Hellenistic philosophy and rhetoric (following Greco-Roman philosophers, Bultmann, and Conzelmann and their ilk, though these approaches of form and rhetorical criticism are engaged throughout the chapters primarily in the notes). Therefore, these authors utilize prominent roles for inspired biblical revelation, mystical vision, dream or audible divine voice, which all possessed a significant authoritative place in Pharisaic-Rabbinic Judaism. Biblical epistemologists will be extensively engaged in this book but they tend to approach the field through word studies of "knowledge" rather than philosophical categories or approaches. The treatment in this book attempts to accomplish both to foster the conversation between the exegetes and philosophical epistemologists.

Perhaps the thought forms of William Alston help the philosopher to engage these mystical aspects, through envisioning empirical senses occasionally presenting miracle and mystery beyond what the senses normally provide.[9] Some grant that these surprising empirical sensations accurately

---

8. B. Qidd. 66a; 2 Bar. 48.18-24; Dunn, *Jesus Remembered*, 197-254; Gerhardsson, *The Gospel Tradition*; *Memory and Manuscript*; Bailey, "Informal Controlled Oral Tradition and the Synoptic Gospels," *AJT* 5 (1991): 34-54; "Middle Eastern Oral Tradition and the Synoptic Gospels," *ExpTim* 106(1995): 363-67; Bauckham, *Jesus and the Eyewitnesses*; Walton and Sandy, *The Lost World of Scripture*, 97-101, 105-8, 110, 152-66.

9. Alston, *Perceiving God*, 14-35; Pharisaic categories of mystical revelatory knowledge: 1) Angels as revelatory messengers: *Jub.* 1.27-29; 10.10-14; *1 En.* 4.19, 21-26; 7; 8; 17-36; 89.61-77; 90.14-20; *T. Levi* 9.6; *T. Reub.* 5.3; *T. Jos.* 6.6; 2) Authoritative heavenly voice: b. *'Abot* 6.2; *B. Bat.* 73b, 85b; *Mak.* 23b; *'Erub.* 54b; *Šabb.* 33b; 88a; *Soṭa* 33a; p. *Soṭa* 7.5, sect. 5; *Pesiq. Rab Kah.* 15.5; *Lev. Rab.* 19.5-6; *Deut. Rab.* 11.10; *Lam. Rab.* Proem 2, 23; *Lam. Rab.* 1.16 sect. 50; *Ruth Rab.* 6.4; *Qoh. Rab.* 7.12, sect. 1; *Pesq Rab Kah.* 11.16; 3) Authoritative Dreams: LXX additions to Esther; *1 En.*; *2 En.*; *2 Bar.*; *4 Ezra*; *Apoc. Ab.*; *T. Levi*; *T. Job*; *Bib. Ant.*; *Jub.*; *Life of Adam and Eve* and several at Qumran, Flannery, "Dreams and Vision Reports," In *The Eerdmans Dictionary of Early Judaism*. ed. Collins and Harlow, 550.

communicate a perceiver's truth on a new experiential and existential level. Jesus, Paul, and John actively use this mystical approach. That is, emerging from a Jewish root the thought forms tend to be more Jewish than Hellenistic. Such Jewish mysticism fits into the *merkabah*[10] pattern in which reality is encountered empirically on both earthly and the heavenly levels. Within this biblical mysticism, epistemic approaches suggest ways of knowing that are available within a family or immediate relationship such as characterized within Paul Moser's filial knowledge concept.[11]

However, the Lukan historiography extensively engages Greco-Roman historiographic method and the concept of "witness." Such historiography grounds Luke's historical precision. The shift in the concept of witness within Roman culture provides a rationale for why gospel writing began mid-first century instead of upon Jesus' departure. Historiographic issues and the concept of witness will be explored in chapter three.

For the most part the biblical contributors express an oral stage of engaging Christianity from within a Wittgensteinian communal language game or Plantinga properly basic communal faith system of a Christian-rabbinic worldview.[12] Warrant is provided for those who remain consistent within this communal faith language game, and thus the need in this book to explain the perspectival views of each biblical author considered. This approach is similar to a communal application of Thomas Reid's more individual common sense realism,[13] though instead of common sense resisting Humean and Kantian idealism, the biblical authors within their language

---

10. Divine throne/chariot mysticism where God is real on a heavenly throne as in Isa 6 and simultaneously real in an earthly tabernacle Exod 40:34-37; Pate and Kennard, *Deliverance Now and Not Yet*, 98-99, 102-3, 130, 134-35, 222, 421, 483, 491-93, 499, 509-10.

11. Moser, *The Elusive God*, 46-7, 98, 113-123 framed within his empirical commitment (*Empirical Knowledge*).

12. Plantinga, *Warrant and Proper Function*, 6; *Knowledge and Christian Belief*, 25-44; These Plantinga basic belief statements reflect his communal turn evolving beyond his concept of individual basic belief (in "Reason and Belief in God," In *Faith and Rationality*. ed. Plantinga and Woltersdorf, 16-93) through his interaction with Sacks, *The Man Who Mistook his Wife for a Hat*; Wittgenstein, *Philosophical Investigations*, 11e-12e, 15e-16e, paragraphs 23 and 32; Matthews, "Jesus and Augustine," In *Jesus and Philosophy*. ed. Moser,109, 111, a view hinted at through a medieval approach to the psalms by Martin, "The Word at Prayer" and Rae, "Incline Your Ear," In *The Bible and Epistemology*. ed. Healy and Parry, 51, 57, 59, 166.

13. Reid, *Thomas Reid*. ed. Brookes; *Essays on the Intellectual Powers*. ed. Brody, especially essays 2 and 6; Grave, *The Scottish Philosophy of Common Sense*; Jones, *Empiricism and Intuitionism in Reid's*; Abraham, "The Epistemology of Jesus," In *Jesus and Philosophy*. ed. Moser, 158-9; Brueggeman, *A Pathway of Interpretation*, 115; Reid's common sense philosophy reflects Bacon's *Advancement of Learning*; Allen, "Baconianism and the Bible," *CH* 55:1(1986): 65-80.

game simply frame the world from within their collective memory of oral tradition. This non-foundational realism was engaged through dialog within a collective memory of an oral tradition as was practiced among synagogue and the rabbinics, a communal resilient tradition over generations.

When multiple interpretations occur (as with miracles and close rivals), the biblical authors' epistemology shows nuance as an epistemological dualistic non-foundational collective memory expressing a Lockean epistemology where miraculous signs induce an interpretation that contributes to the authority of the testimony conveyed by the perspective of the individual or group.[14] This Lockean approach recognizes that the biblical author's interpretation in context goes beyond the appearance in the original context and thus enters into the complexity of epistemic dualism. Both an inference and confirmation of the meaning of a miracle is made by the biblical author while others who see the same miracles may disagree with a different inference. One side says God is at work while the other side may say it is of Satan. Each perceiver is responsible for the conclusions that they make concerning a miracle. The biblical author's interpretation recognized Jesus is the authority to be understood and heeded based on these miracles. Occasionally, this Lockean epistemic dualism also adds an internal transformation much as Jonathan Edwards modified Locke to set forth his religious affections as a sixth spiritual and moral transformative sense.[15] These religious affections are often caused by God to fund a divine virtue ethic but in the synoptic gospels the emphasis is more on human responsibility so the virtue ethic is presented there as the responsibility of the disciple traveling on the narrow way unto kingdom.[16] These two compatibilist strands of divinely caused and humanly responsible virtue ethic come together especially in Peter, Paul, and Hebrews. At times, these authors try to confirm whether their readers

---

14. Locke, *Concerning Human Understanding* 1.1.15; 2.11.8–9; 2.32.6; 3.3.6–8; "A Discourse of Miracles," In *Works*, 9:256–65; "The Reasonableness of Christianity," In *Works*, Vol. 6; Mouw, "John Locke's Christian Individualism," *Faith and Philosophy* 8:4(1991): 448–60; pre-modern empiricism is apparent in Lactanius, *Workmanship of God*, 9–10.

15. Edwards, *Religious Affections*; YE6:342–3 and *Miscellanies* number 267 and 547; "A Divine and Supernatural Light," Imp., Thirdly, 2, and Doc. 1, sec. 2; Jenson, *America's Theologian*, 15–17, 29, 33; Brown, "Edwards, Locke, and the Bible," *JR* 79:3(1999): 361–84.

16. Kvanvig, *Intellectual Virtues*; Adams, "The Problem of Total Devotion," In *Rationality, Religious Belief, and Moral Commitment*. ed. Audi and Wainwright, 94; Nygren, *Agape and Eros*, 216; Wainwright, *Reason and the Heart*; "Obedience and Responsibility," In *The Wisdom of the Christian Faith*. ed. Moser and McFall, 68; Zagzebski, *Virtues of the Mind*; Wood, *Epistemology*. Virtue ethics are expressed by contemporaries like Philo, *Abr.* 52–54; *Jos.* 1; *Mos.* 1.76; *Praem.* 24, 51.57–66; *Sobr.* 65; *Congr.* 34–38; *Mut.* 12.88; *Somn.* 1.168.

are authentic in the narrow way and when this occurs, the Edwardsian religious affection is appropriated through a Peircean pragmatic move. Charles Peirce proposed that an empirically grounded proposal could be tested and verified in reality empirically.[17] Thus, an empirically framed Edwardsian virtue ethic confirms both the believer's faith and God's supernatural work guaranteeing kingdom now and eschatologically. Therefore, I frame this pragmatism through Peirce rather than the more expansive forms of pragmatism of James or Dewey, even though the life concerns into which the biblical authors are pressing pragmatism are closer to William James' concerns. Occasionally, Peircean pragmatism occurs elsewhere to increase the credibility of the Lockean evidence, as in how Peter takes Christ's transfiguration to pragmatically increase his confidence for the coming kingdom. This internal knowledge with its self-referential confirmation for a personal relationship participates within the range of filial knowledge or relationship with God as developed by philosopher Paul Moser. That is, one's knowledge of the other in relationship is a full-orbed experience of action and response in relationship that permeates far beyond merely cognitive data. For example, my relationship with my wife and my relationship with God work on several levels. Any action a person does in relationship effects what that person knows and how they know it and who they are in the knowing of it. This knowledge is not limited to empirical sensations but the full experience that a person has with the other. As such, filial knowledge is communal, with any part of the relationship affecting the whole relationship.

As a biblical theologian I wish to identify that, I am careful not to be in danger of Schweitzer's warning concerning historical Jesus scholars seeing themselves in the N. T. authors. My epistemology[18] is already developed and more nuanced than the epistemologies present in any chapter in this book. None of the biblical contributors studied adds a critical realist or a post-modern aspect in the wake of Kant and Kierkegaard, so they are all pre-modern thinkers in ways that the realist moderns (like Thomas Reid or John Locke) sometimes reflect. However, the biblical authors express things more through a collective memory reflective of their oriental communal culture.

Much has happened since these authors showed their epistemologies, so that they might not be the last word for the reader's consideration and constructing of one's own epistemology. However, in the same manner

---

17. Peirce, *The Collected Papers*. ed. Hartshorne and Weiss, vol. 5 paragraph 9; "The Fixation of Belief," *Popular Science Monthly* 12(Nov., 1877): 1–15; "How to Make Our Ideas Clear," *Popular Science Monthly* 12(Jan., 1878): 286–302; Ochs briefly mentions in passing that he was motivated to do his study because Kaplan analyzed rabbinic thinking through Peirce's logic (Peirce, *Pragmatism and the Logic of Scripture*, 3).

18. Kennard, *A Critical Realist's*, 1–121.

as biblical authors fund much of the content of Christian faith, they might suggest aspects of epistemology to be considered for inclusion within the reader's own epistemology. Further, since most of these biblical authors also are perspectival in their epistemology, the development of the emphasis of their perspectives provides the surrounding contexts that may also orient the reader to a deeper engagement, contextualization, and worldview perspective. A Christian-Rabbinic-Judaism provides the perspectival framework for Matthew's Jesus, Paul, Peter, and Hebrews. Luke is a Christian hybrid of this rabbinic Judaism as filtered through Hellenistic Greco-Roman historical canons. Qumran sectarian Judaism provides a closer perspectival framework for John to reflect Christ. Finally, James expressed a Christian appropriation of creation theology within an ancient Near Eastern wisdom tradition.

Most of the biblical authors develop an aspect of virtue epistemology, which also funds a disposition, and ethic that can be transferrable onto the reader's own epistemology and ethic. However, rarely are the biblical authors strictly expressing epistemology or ethics, so often this virtue epistemology expresses a facet of the narrow way unto kingdom salvation within a two ways salvation approach.[19]

19. Two ways teaching of the church: *Did.* 1.1.1–4; 4.14b; *1 Clem.* 34–35; *2 Clem.* 6.8; 8.4; Polycarp, *Phil.* 10; Ignatius, *Phil.* 5.1; *Eph.* 3.1; *Barn.* 16.7–8; 18.1–2; 19; Justin Martyr, *Dial.* 3.4; *1 Apol.* 16.8–9; *2 Apol.* 9; Irenaeus, *Haer.* 3.1.10 maintained this as the universal teaching all Christians held at the time; *Herm. Mand.* 2.7; *Herm. Sim.* 3.8.6–11; Clement of Alexandria, *The Strom.* 4.6; Quis div.; Commodianus, *Instructions* 28; Origen, *Comm. Matt.* 14.10–13; *Fr. Prin.* 2.9.7–8; 3.1.12; Cyprian, *Fort.* 12–13; Dionysius of Alexandria, *Exegetical Fragments* 7 Reception of Lapsed; Methodius of Olympus, *The Banquet of the Ten Virgins* 9.3; *Oration Concerning Simeon and Anna* 8; Lactantius, *Inst.* 3.12; 6.3–7; 7.10; *Epitome of Divine Inst.* 73; *Constitutions of the Holy Apostles* 7.1.1–2; *The Clementine Homilies* 18.17; Eusebius, *Hist. eccl.* 2.19; 3.20.6–7; 5.1.10, 48; 5.8.5; 5.13.5; *Council of Sardica Lengthy Creed*: Socrates Scholasticus, *Hist. eccl.* 2.19=Athanasius, *Syn.* 26; 351=Hilary of Pointers, *On the Councils* 34 and 359 A.D. *Sirmium Creed*: Socrates Scholasticus, *Hist. eccl.* 2.30=Athanasius, *Syn.* 27=Hilary of Pointers, *On the Councils* 38; *Synod at Ariminum Creed*: Socrates Scholasticus, *Hist. eccl.* 2.37; 359 A.D. *Seleucia Creed*: Socrates Scholasticus, *Hist. eccl.* 2.40=Athanasius, *Syn.* 8; 359 A.D. *Confession at Niké* and 360 A.D. *Constantinople Creed*: Athanasius, *Syn.* 30; 359 A.D. *Ariminum Creed* and modified for the 381 A.D. Council at Constantinople: Socrates Scholasticus, *Hist. eccl.* 2.41; Athanasius, *Inc.* 57; Cyril, *Catechetical Lectures* 15.1, 24–25, 33; Gregory Nyssa, *On Pilgrimages*, paragraph 1; *The Great Catechism* 40; Gregory Nazianzen *Letter 4 to Basil*; Ambrose, *Duties of the Clergy* 1.16.59; Augustine, *Conf.* 1.11.17; *Civ.* 13.8; 14.25; 19.11; 20.1–8, 12, 14, 22; 21.1; *Trin.* 8.7–8; *Enchir.* 15; 31–32; 55; 107; 113; *Doctr. Chr.* 1.12.10; *Perf.* 42–44; *Ennarat. Ps.* 31.25; 112.5; *Tract. Ev. Jo.* 124.5; Hilary of Poitiers, *On the Trinity* 12.45; Leo the Great, *Sermons* 46.3; 49.2, 5; 63.2, 7; 67.5–6; 72.1; 95.1–9; Vincent of Lérins, *The Commonitory* 23.57–59 where he claims everyone held this teaching at that time 23.4–6; John Cassian, *Cassian's Conferences* 1.1.5; 1.6.3, 8; 1.40.9; 2.13.13, 18; 2.14.3, 9; *Seven Books of John Cassian* 3.13–14; Leo the Great, *Sermons* 23.5; 24.1–5; 26.2; 66.7; 90.2; 95.1–9; John Climacus, *The Ladder of Divine Ascent*, 9.1; summary on step 30; Thomas a Kempis, *Of the Imitation of*

Therefore, when a two ways virtue salvation occurs in the N. T. the reader should consider deepening their virtues beyond epistemology to a level of Paul Moser's concept of filial relationship with Father, Christ and the Spirit.[20] One's existential relationship could also be cultivated on a N. T. mystical level, which is not philosophical mysticism (beyond a human ability to know). Rather, biblical mysticism is a personal intimate relationship in close proximity or internally penetrated (as in *perichorises* or *merkabah* mysticism) with divine persons. Such biblical mysticism cultivates the relationship of being in Christ and allowing the Spirit to empower our corporate and personal life from inside out. In fact, Paul and John urge their readers to be fully within each of the Trinitarian members in such a manner that these persons of God are also within each of our community and us as well. Therefore, for these epistemologies to implement an intimate personal relationship with each of the persons of the Trinity, they should maintain a vibrant prayer life and attempt to reflect Trinitarian character and commitments beyond each of our believing communities to include vulnerable persons. Thus, the filial knowledge reflects a person's whole being and community life. Enjoy the journey as we travel with God and others. In such a journey, the conversation has begun but is never complete provided we are traveling together.

Christ, esp. 1.23; 2.7; 3.44, 56; Bunyan, *The Pilgrim's Progress*, esp. 18, 187; Willard, *The Divine Conspiracy*; Yinger. *Paul, Judaism, and Judgment*, 285 summary but argued through the book; Dunn, *The New Perspective on Paul*, 72–73; "If Paul Could Believe both in Justification by Faith and Judgment According to Works, Why Should That be a Problem for us?" and "Response to Schreiner" in *Four Views on the Role of Works at the Final Judgment*. ed. Gundry, 135, 106–8. However, this view can be granted from outside the two ways tradition, such as from the Reformed tradition: Calvin, *Institutes* 3.15.8; 3.16.1 "we are justified not without works, and not by works, since in the participation in Christ, by which we are justified, is contained not less sanctification than justification," 16.3; 18.1; Schreiner, "Justification Apart from and by Works: at the Final Judgment Works will *Confirm* Justification" in *Four Views on the Role of Works at the Final Judgment*. ed. Gundry, 78–9.

20. Moser, *The Elusive God*, 46–7, 98, 113–123.

2

Epistemology and Logic of Jesus as Presented in Matthew and the Other Synoptic Gospels[1]

THESIS: MATTHEW'S JESUS REFLECTS rabbinic teaching of the early Jewish era with a distinct exception that Jesus presents Himself as the authoritative scribe to settle all kingdom ethical and spiritual issues. The Jewish religious leaders have problems with Jesus' claims but both sides reflect alternative rabbinic positions within early Judaism. However, Jesus demonstrates that He is a superior scribe and thus authoritative in rhetoric, answers, and judgments that reflect patterns utilized among early Judaism. Jesus provides a new oral *torah* through which His Jewish audience might know and apply the Law in a new covenant internal manner, and Matthew has written down this oral *torah* of Jesus so that his Jewish-Christian audience might likewise know and apply the Law.

Everything that is known of Jesus historically is filtered through the authorial process to compose the biblical and extra-biblical gospels and letters. This chapter considers Matthew's presentation of Jesus primarily with other gospels contributing within this perspective. There is no grammatical means to indicate direct quotation in Koine Greek, so Jesus is filtered through the vocabulary and style of the different authors. Jesus' sermons in Matthew are summaries composed of Jesus' characteristic language,[2] similar to the oral stage of rabbinic writings, which captured characteristic oral discussions.[3] Partly this is because Aristotle argues that ancient

---

1. Parts of this chapter were re-appropriated and re-arranged from Kennard, *Messiah Jesus*, 23–151, used by permission from Peter Lang.

2. This is the pattern of historical writing in that day: *Rhetorica ad Herennium* 4.52.65; Quintilian, *Inst.* 3.8.51; Thucydides, 1.22.1; Dionysius of Halicarnassus, *Rom. ant.* 7.66.2–3; 11.1.3–4.

3. Dunn, *Jesus Remembered*, 197–254; Gerhardsson, *The Gospel Tradition*; *Memory*

witnesses are known broadly by many humans, so that uncharacteristic speech would render accounts less credible.[4] The next chapter examines the historiographic process for Luke's compositions of the Gospel of Luke and Acts gospel proclamations.

The eschatological expectations among the Prophets and Qumran were for a Messianic teacher, "the interpreter of the Law" (Isa 42:4).[5] Joel Marcus argues that such eschatological expectation frames Jesus epistemology in apocalyptic directions.[6] *Messianic Apocalypse* (4Q521) presents the character of the hoped for Messianic teacher as echoing Isaiah 61:1.

> [for the heav]ens and the earth will listen to his anointed one, [and all] that is in them will not turn away from the precepts of the holy ones. Strengthen yourselves, you who are seeking the Lord, in his service! Will you not in this encounter the Lord, all those who hope in their heart? For the Lord will consider the pious, and call the righteous by name, and his spirit will hover upon the poor, and will renew the faithful with his strength. For he will honor the pious upon the throne of everlasting kingdom, freeing prisoners, giving sight to the blind, and in his mercy…the Lord will perform marvelous acts such as have not existed, just as he sa[id for] he will heal the badly wounded and will make the dead live, he will proclaim good news to the poor.[7]

Such a Messianic expectation hoped for a Jewish King who is a healer, a spiritual teacher of the Law and a rescuer of the needy.

When Jesus announced His ministry in His home town, Nazareth, He identified that this hoped for expectation was realized in Him by citing Isaiah 61:1-2 (Luke 4:18-19).

---

and Manuscript; Bailey, "Informal Controlled Oral Tradition and the Synoptic Gospels," *AJT* 5 (1991): 34-54; "Middle Eastern Oral Tradition and the Synoptic Gospels," *ExpTim* 106(1995): 363-67; Bommershine, "Jesus of Nazareth and the Watershed of Ancient Orality and Literacy" in *Orality and Textuality*. ed. Dewey, 7-11, 16-17; Bauckham, *Jesus and the Eyewitnesses*; Walton and Sandy, *The Lost World of Scripture*, 97-101, 105-8, 110, 152-66.

4. Aristotle, *Rhet.* 1.15.13, 15.

5. 4Q174 (4QFlor) 1.11-12 (different from the "branch of David" but possibly identified with the priestly Messiah); CD 6.7; 7:18 (identified with the star but different than the Davidic Messiah).

6. Marcus, "Mark 4:10-12 and Marcan Epistemology," *JBL* 103:4(1984): 558, 560-63.

7. 4Q521, frag. 2, col. 2, vs. 1-12; overlap with Isa 35:5-6 and 61:1, and Luke 7:21-22.

> The Spirit of the LORD is upon me, because He anointed me to preach the gospel to the poor. He has sent me to proclaim release to the captives, and recovery of sight to the blind, to set free those who are downtrodden, to proclaim the favorable year of the LORD.

Jesus identified that this very Jubilee reality was being realized in His own ministry. Later when John the Baptist was in prison and needed reassurance about Jesus' ministry, Jesus told John's disciples that the kingdom empirical evidence compellingly identified that Jesus was the coming One with the kingdom.

> Go and report to John the things which you hear and see: the blind receive their sight and lame walk, lepers are cleansed and deaf hear, and dead are raised up, and the poor have the gospel preached to them. And blessed is he who keeps from stumbling over Me (Matt 11:4-6).

Jesus is using a communal nonfoundational form of Lockean empiricism where miraculous observational evidence is induced to form a generalization[8] identifying that Jesus is the Messiah that others claim Him to be (Matt 8:29; 9:27; 12:23; 15:22; 16:16 ; 20:30; 21:9; Mark 3:11; 5:7; 10:47-48; 11:9-10; Luke 4:41; 8:28; 18:38-39; 19:38; 20:41; John 1:27, 34, 41, 45, 49; 12:13).[9] Also operating within an epistemic dualism of perception corresponding to reality, the Jewish people sought such confirming evidence from Jesus even if they did not always believe this conclusion when it was presented to them (Matt 12:38-39; 16:1-4; Mark 8:11-12; Luke 11:16, 29; 23:8; John 2:18; 9:41). In fact, opponents to Christianity, Josephus and the Babylonian *Tamud* left a record believing Jesus to be this kind of miracle worker and thus from their perspective warned the Jewish people of the danger of Jesus leading Jewish people astray if one considered such compelling miraculous evidence from Jesus.[10]

---

8. Locke, *Concerning Human Understanding* 1.1.15; 2.11.8-9; 2.32.6; 3.3.6-8; "A Discourse of Miracles," In *Works*, 9:256-65; "The Reasonableness of Christianity," In *Works*, Vol. 6; pre-modern empiricism is apparent in Lactanius, *Workmanship of God*, 9-10; Keener, *Miracles*, 1:35-208; "Miracle Reports and the Argument from Analogy," *BBR* 25:4(2015): 475-95.

9. Dupont, "Conversion in the Acts of the Apostles," In *The Salvation of the Gentiles*, 61-84 and "La Conversion dans les Actes des Apôtres," *LumVie* 47(1960): 47-70; Black, "The Conversion Stories in the Acts of the Apostles," PhD dissertation Emory University, 1985; Meier, *A Marginal Jew*, 2:509-970; Immanuel, *Repent and Turn to God*; Tovey, "On Not Unbinding the Lazarus Story," In *John, Jesus, and History*. ed. Anderson, Just, and Thatcher, 2:215.

10. Josephus, *Ant.* 18.63-64; *J. W.* 6.312-313; 3.400-402; *b. Sanh.* 107b; 104b; 43a;

Early Judaism expressed a deep commitment to the Mosaic Law as an authoritative covenant document from God, to be understood and obeyed, if Israel was to be blessed. That is, Israel is already in covenant with God, so that they are not trying to obtain this initial blessing. Ryan O'Dowd identified that the epistemology of Deuteronomy is that God revealed the Law and the reader obtains the truth of the Law in the reading of it.[11] Likewise, in Pharisaic and sectarian early Judaisms, Gregory Vall echoes the epistemic authority of the prophets as unpacking divine moral will in a manner that makes cognitively clear that the immoral do not know God.[12] N. T. Wright says it this way, "The Torah was the boundary-marker of the covenant people: those who kept it would share the life of the coming age."[13] Therefore, this covenantal nomism was a primary way Israel had of knowing and maintaining relationship with God, particularly in difficult times. For example, the *Testament of Moses* 9.6 expresses this Jewish attitude from: Mattathias against Antiochus IV to Bar Kokhba against Hadrian, "Let us die rather than transgress the commandments of the Lord of Lords, the God of our fathers." Such commitments reflect the earlier commitments of Daniel and his three friends, who insisted on keeping kosher and not participating in idolatry (Dan 1:1–21 and 3:1–20).

Israel interpreted God as establishing the nation in covenant nomism with the Mosaic covenant such that they must obey the Law or cease to have God's blessing as His people.[14] These Jews saw this passion for the Law as a realization of the new covenant in which God was giving them a "new heart" and a "new spirit."[15] As a result, Israel insisted on circumcision, kosher, and Sabbath keeping as expressions of this purity.[16] Likewise, Tobit, captive in Nineveh, did not eat the Gentile's food.[17] Furthermore, when Judith ingratiated herself with Nebuchadnezzar's general Holofernes so she could kill him, she took all the kosher food to eat through the fourth day

---

67b; *b. Soṭah* 47a; *Sib. Or.* 8.206–7.

11. O'Dowd, "Memory on the Boundary," In *The Bible and Epistemology*. ed. Healy and Parry, 4.

12. Vall, "An Epistemology of Faith," In *The Bible and Epistemology*. ed. Healy and Parry, 22, 27, 30, 34.

13. Wright, *Jesus and the Victory of God*, 301.

14. Jdt 5:17–21; 8:18–23; *Pr. Azar.* 6–14; CD 10.14–11.18; Kennard, *Biblical Covenantalism*, three volumes.

15. As in Jeremiah 31:31–34 and Ezek. 36:24–37:28 so too in: *Jub.* 1:22–25; 1Q3 4, 5; 1QH 4, 5, 18; 4Q Shir Shalb; CD 4Q266 frag. 2 1.6–8; B 19.12–13; 1QpHab 2.3; 11.13; 4Q434 frag. 1 1.4; 4Q437 frag. 1 1.14.

16. *Jub.* 2:17–33; 15:11–34; Jdt 10:5; 12:2.

17. Tob 1.10–12; 4:12–13.

when she carried out the deed.[18] In the LXX version of Esther 4:17, Esther reminds God that she has not eaten food from Haman's table or drunk wine of libations. Furthermore, seven brothers and their mother were tortured and executed on orders of Antiochus IV rather than eat pork.[19] Additionally, the Egyptian Jews kept separate from Gentile's food and worship, which led to hostility between them.[20] Antiochus attempted to force cultural conformity by forbidding aspects of the Law that distinguished Israel from other people, like circumcision and ordering Jews to worship foreign gods.[21] While circumcision was practiced by some other groups, its practice was a strong affirmation of Jewish male identity.[22] Furthermore, many of the Jews abhorred pagan sacrificial meat as evidenced when Antiochus ordered some Jews to eat pork and food sacrificed to idols but Eleazar and others refused and were tortured and killed.[23]

Covenant nomism informed national policy in Israel as well. For example, the Hasmonean John Hyreaus (135–104 B.C.) broke off an important siege because of the coming of the Sabbath year.[24] The *Letter of Aristeas* 139–42 identifies this covenant nomist mindset.

> In his wisdom the legislator (Moses)...surrounded us with unbroken palisades and iron walls to prevent our mixing with any of the peoples in any matter...So, to prevent our being perverted by contact with others or by mixing with bad influences he hedged us in on all sides with strict observances connected with meat and drink and touch and hearing and sight, after the manner of the Law.[25]

Additionally, in 63 B.C. when Pompey hemmed Jews in Jerusalem, he raised the earthworks on Sabbath without firing missiles; the Jews would not fight the Roman troops under their noses because the Jews would only defend themselves on the Sabbath if they were attacked.[26] In fact, the Jews strict

---

18. Jdt 10.5; 12:2, 9–19; 13:8.
19. 2 Macc 7.
20. 3 Macc 3.4–7; 7.11.
21. 1 Macc 1:48 and 2:15–28.
22. Philo, *Migr. Abr.* 89–93; Josephus, *Ant.* 1.10.5.
23. 2 Macc 6:18–31; 4 Macc 5:1–6:30 also *Joseph and Aseneth*.
24. Josephus, *J. W.* 1.157–60; Jews compliance with Sabbath law was well known in the ancient near East (Josephus, *Ant.* 14.10.12; *Ag. Ap.* 2.2, 39; Philo, *Vit Mos.* 2.21; and even more so in sectarian Judaism [CD 10.14–11.18; *Songs of the Sabbath Sacrifice*; *Temple Scroll*=11Q19]).
25. Quoted in Dunn and Suggate, *The Justice of God*.
26. Josephus, *J. W.* 1.145–7.

observance of Sabbath kept Jews from service in imperial armies, for Sabbath became a characteristic feature that identified Jewish communal life.[27]

Jews risked their lives to be faithful to the Mosaic Covenant. For example, in 5 B.C. Herod had erected a golden eagle over the temple as a votive offering, and two learned teachers (Judas and Matthaias) inspired the young men to pull down the image.[28] Herod responded with having many of them arrested, tried and burned alive. Furthermore, Josephus describes instances such as that in 26 A.D. when Pilate introduced Roman standards and a bust of Caesar into Jerusalem. Here Jews were ready to die rather than transgress the Law.[29] A large group followed him to his residence in Caesarea and sat outside his house for five days. When they were summoned to tribunal and troops surrounded them with drawn swords, the Jews fell to the ground extending their necks and exclaiming that they were ready to die rather than to transgress the Law. Pilate was impressed and withdrew the standards. Likewise, in 41 A.D. Caligula ordered Petronius to set up his statue in the Temple, Josephus claims that the protestors said, "slay us first before you carry out these resolutions…we will sooner die than violate our laws."[30] Their hope was that God would intervene and prevail with blessing from the Mosaic Covenant.[31] Presumably, God did since Caligula died before the statue was completed and it never was installed in the Jerusalem Temple. These examples reflect merely a sample of Israel's commitment to Yahweh under the framework of corporate covenant nomism.[32] It is in this framework of sectarian Judaism that the hope for a Messiah, includes that He be a definitive teacher of the Law.[33]

27. Horace, *Sat.* 1.9.69–70; Philo, *Som.* 2.123–24; *Leg. Gai.* 158; Josephus, *Ant.* 13.252; 14.10.12; 14.237. 16.2.3; 16.6.2–4.

28. Josephus, *J. W.* 1.651–5; *Ant.* 17.149–67.

29. Josephus, *J. W.* 2.169–74; *Ant.* 18.55–59.

30. Josephus, *Ant.*18.261–4 and 271.

31. Josephus, *Ant.*18.267.

32. I realize that challenges to this view have been marshaled. Probably Elliott in his *The Survivors of Israel* proposed the most formidable challenge. However, the impact of this work on this question is in my opinion significantly diminished because of the highly selective sectarian selection of documents it surveys and admits it surveys (pp. 13–26). At this point I believe Sanders and Dunn to be presenting a broader reflection of Judaism of this era (1QM; 1QS; CD; Josephus, *J.W.* 1.5.2; 2.8.14; 2.162–3; *Ant.* 13.10.6; 13.172; 13.288; 17.2.4; 18.12–15, *b. Yom.* 19b; *b. Nidd.* 33b; *Life* 12; *Yadayim* 3.7; 4.6; *Makkot* 1.6; *Niddah* 4.2; perhaps *Pss. Sol.* 1.8; 2.3; 7.2; 8.12–13; 17.5–8, 23). Additionally, Biblical texts like James, Matthew and Acts indicate that Jews and Jewish Christians were zealous for the Law.

33. 4Q174 (4QFlor) 1.11 (different from the "branch of David"); 4QpPs (4Q171) 3:13–16; 1QpHab 1.13; 2:2, 8–9; 5:10; 7:4–5; 11:5; CD 1.11; 6.7; 7:18 (identified with the star); 20.1, 28, 32.

In contrast to this sectarian covenant nomism, Israel repeatedly rebelled and brought Israel into covenant curse and Gentile dominance (Deut 9:7; 28:15–30:20; 2 Kgs 17:23; Neh 9:32; Isa 9:1–2; Ezek 21:3; 20:31; Mic 5:3–4).[34] Their precarious condition was confessed by Baruch 1.18–19.

> We have disobeyed Him, and have not heeded the voice of the Lord our God, to walk in the statutes of the Lord that he set before us. From the time when the Lord brought our ancestors out of the land of Egypt to this day.

This rebellion was due to Israel's unfamiliarity and disregard for the Mosaic covenant. Judaism's hope for the kingdom was in part a divine work that would transform Israel into a new covenant people (Deut 30:1–6; Jer 31:33–34).[35] Furthermore, when Israel was dispersed in *diaspora* as in the first century, a Divine re-gathering was the hope of *diaspora* Jews as they anticipated God's covenant blessing.[36] However, this hope did not remove Israel from their obligation to the Law, rather God would enable them to be faithful to the Deuteronomical framework present in the Mosaic covenant (Deut 30:8–18; Jer 31:29–30).[37] So that another part of the possibility of the kingdom was that the Messianic teacher would guide Israel in understanding and complying with the Mosaic covenant. Isaiah 42:4 identifies that the Servant of Yahweh would establish justice upon the earth by bringing Law to the people. Isaiah explains that the people in the kingdom era would be expectantly waiting for His Law.

Early Jewish literature expected the Teacher of Righteousness to teach righteous Jews God's Law and revelation in a new covenant form.[38] Initially, this claim was of the founder of Qumran but after his death these claims took on an eschatological Messianic hope. The Teacher of Righteousness will serve as a rival to the man of the lie, a wicked priest who tried to destroy the Teacher of Righteousness. However, the Teacher of Righteousness (as the

---

34. *1 Esdr.* 8.73–74; *2 Esdr.* 9.7; Bar 1.13, 18–19; 2.6; CD 1.13–21; 1QS 2.4–5; 1QH 2.8–19; 1QpHab 2.1–4; 5.3–8.

35. CD 6.19; 8.21; 20.12; 1QpHab 2.3.

36. *Pss. of Sol.* 8.28; 11.1–4; 17.28; *T. Mos.* 4.9; Philo, *Praem Poen.* 162–63; *2 Bar.* 78.7; *Tg. Isa.* 53.8; *Tg. Hos.* 14.8; *Tg. Mic.* 5.1–3; *Ex. Rab.* 6.4; *Num. Rab.* 5.9; *Deut. Rab.* 8.2; and an allegory to love God through the Law in *Song Rab.*

37. Kennard, "Jeremiah and Hebrews," paper presented at ETS, Mar. 1994; *Biblical Covenantism*, 2:79–89, 3:162–74.

38. 1QpHab 1.11–13; 2.1–3; 7.1–5, 10–11; 8.1–3; 9.9–10; 11.4–8, 13; 4Q165 frag. 1–2; 4Q171 3.14–17; 4.3–4, 26–27; 4Q173 frag. 1 4.

Messiah of Aaron)[39] will prepare those faithful to the Law for eschatological blessing of everlasting life[40] instead of God's judgment on the unfaithful.[41]

M. 'Abot 5.21 describes that as a devout Jewish boy, Jesus would have probably attended some schooling in a Pharisaic synagogue to study the Scriptures from about age five till about twelve. Jesus was educated in *torah* to develop socially and psychologically in belief development as a Pharisee from a rabbi of Nazareth.[42] Jews of Nazareth and Capernaum resisted Hellenization[43] as "separate," extending Judaism into all of daily life (Matt 5:23-26, 33-37) and hoping in resurrection afterlife (Luke 18:12).[44] Jesus grew up within a Judaism that made available rabbinic study to know the Law, especially in synagogue (Luke 4:16-27).

In identifying that Jesus used rabbinic language it is not as though there are rabbinic documents prior to Jesus time or the writing of the N. T. However, when the *Mishnah* is written down around 200 A.D., it and other rabbinic writings show evidence of a continued oral tradition and patterns that develop before and during Jesus' time. Jesus utilized and contributed to this pre-*Mishnaic* rabbinic pattern since they are both within the same Pharisaic-Rabbinic community and lineage. So looking back through the written versions of Jewish oral tradition identifies that Jesus has a place within these patterns.

Jesus utilized an authoritative *mishnahic* method (apodictic laws grouped in lists to aid memorization, perhaps reflected in beatitudes Matt 5:3-12; Luke 6:20-28) and *midrashic* method (focusing on biblical reasons for

---

39. 1QpHab 2.2-9; 4Q171 3.15.

40. CD 3.12-16, 20; *Tg. Onq. Lev.* 18.5; *Tg. Pseudo-Jonathan*; *Sipre Lev.* 193 on Lev 18:1-30.

41. 1QpHab 2.2-10; 5.3-8.

42. Josephus, *Ant.* 13.289; *m. 'Abot* 1.18; 5.17; *b. Šabb.* 17a; *b. Giṭ* 60b; *y. Meg.* 4.74a; *b. Yoma* 28ab; *y. Pe'ah* 2.17a; and Wittgenstein utilizes this game of language acquisition following Augustine to frame a student's worldview thus supporting Wittgensteinian language games as an epistemic lens for a world-view (*Philosophical Investigations*, 11e-12e, 15e-16e, paragraphs 23 and 32; Matthews, "Jesus and Augustine," In *Jesus and Philosophy*. ed. Moser, 109, 111).

43. The archeological remains of reliefs and mosaics in synagogues in these cities show resistance to Hellenization.

44. Josephus, *Ant.* 13. 171-3, 297; 18.12-15; *J. W.* 2.119, 162-3; 4 Macc 5:16-27; Philo, *Dreams* 1.124-5; *m. Yad.* 4.6-8; *B. Qidd.* 66a; Resurrection: 2 Macc 7.9-14, 22-23; 14.43-46; *1 En.* 22; 58.3; 62.14-16; 91.10; 92.2; 104; 108.11-14; *Jub.* 5.10; 10.17; 22.22; L.A.B.; CD 3.11-16, 20-21; 7.5, 9; 13.11; 20.17-20, 25-27; 1QH 11.19-23 [3.18-22]; 19.10-14 [11.7-11]; 1QS 3.7-12; 4.7; 4Q228 frag. 1 1.9; 4Q266, frag. 11; 4Q385 2; 4Q386 1-2; 4QMMT C; 4Q521 2.2.12; 5.2.5-6; *2 Bar.*[Syriac] 30.1-5; 49-51; 4 Macc 7.19; 16.25; *4 Ezra* 7.26-44; *Sib. Or.* 4.180; *T. Benj.* 10.6-8; *T. Levi* 18; *T. Jud.* 24.

action, Luke 4:18–22).⁴⁵ This divides practice into the obligatory *torah* (or *halakhah*, Matt 5) and the narrative story or presentation of nonbinding different positions (*haggadah* or also apparent in parables).⁴⁶ Jesus continues *halakic* appeals through written and oral *torah* as authority, reflecting warrant and obligation from Law (Matt 19:4–5, 17–20).⁴⁷ Such *halakhah* is performative language expressing a Pharisaic Jewish worldview calling disciples to follow in the narrow way unto kingdom.⁴⁸ Such performative language positions Jesus in this narrow way as an example for the disciples to follow.

The Law is the written traditional framework for Jesus' context and the context of Matthew's Jewish-Christian readership.⁴⁹ Matthew is written for a Jewish audience following Jesus.⁵⁰ The other synoptic gospels merely treat the binding nature of the Law as a non-emphasized historical feature of Jesus' ministry⁵¹ while Matthew emphasizes Jesus' binding the Law upon His disciples and his readership. In all the gospels, but especially in Matthew, Jesus' oral tradition radically teaches and lives the Law in three ways.

---

45. Josephus, *Ag. Ap.* 2.175–81; Jerusalem synagogue Theodotus inscription; Philo, *Embassy* 311–3; *Megillat Ta'anit*; *b. Tem.* 14b; *b. B. Meṣ.* 59a–b; *Sifre Deut.* 351; *Iggeret Rav Sherira Gaon* 1–2.

46. *Y. Hor.* 3.5 (48c); Teeter, *Scribal Laws*, 28–33, 189; Alexander, "The Rabbinic Hermeneutical Rules," *PIBA* 8(1984): 96–125; "Quid Athens et Hierosolymis?," In *A Tribute to Geza Vermes*. ed. Davies and White, 153–66; Lieberman, "Rabbinic Interpretation of Scripture," In *Hellenism in Jewish Palestine*, 47–82; Bialoblocki, "Hermeneutik," In *Encyclopaedia Judaica*, 7:1181–94; Jacobs, "Hermeneutics," In *Encyclopedia Judica*, 8:366–72; Maass, "Von den Ursprüngen der rabbinischen Schriftauslegung," *ZThK* 52(1955): 129–61.

47. Gooch, "Paul, the Mind of Christ, and Philosophy," In *Jesus and Philosophy*. ed. Moser, 89.

48. Grice, "Meaning," *Philosophical Review* 66(1957): 377–88; "Utterer's Meaning and Intentions," *Philosophical Review* 78(1969): 147–77; "Utterer's Meaning, Sentence-Meaning, Word-Meaning," In *The Philosophy of Language*. ed. Searle, 54–70; Austin, *How to Do Things with Words*; Ricoeur, *Oneself as Another*, 44; Kennard, *The Relationship Between Epistemology*, 56, 62–65; *A Critical Realist's*, 232.

49. Meier, *A Marginal Jew*, 4:1–477; Saldarini, *Matthew's Christian-Jewish Community*. However, I would date the composition of Matthew as before the destruction of the temple, since Matthew's comments of Jesus on this topic appear to reflect prophecy awaiting fulfillment rather than having been fulfilled, but likely after the Gentile ministry had begun (Kennard, *Messiah Jesus*, 69–155; Overman, *Matthew's Gospel and Formative Judaism*; Levine, *The Social and Ethical Dimensions of Matthean Salvation History*.

50. Irenaeus, *Adv. Haer.* 3.1.1–2; Eusebius, *Hist. Eccl.* 3.24.6; 6.25.4; Epiphanius, *Pan.* 30.3.7; Jerome, *Ep.* 20.5; Augustine, *The Harmony of the Gospels* 1.2–3, 3–6; 1.6.78–79; Hebrew Matthew preserved in fourteenth century text *Even Bohan*; Howard Hebrew Matthew text based on Add no. 26964 (British Library) for Matt 1:1–23:22 and Ms. 2426 for Matt 23:23–28:20.

51. Kennard, *Biblical Covenantalism*, 2:214–47; *Messiah Jesus*, 153–6.

(1) Jesus maintained a more pervasive internalizing of the Law akin to a new covenant internalization of the Law (Jer 31:33).[52] (2) Jesus emphasized the priority of the Law's design over against its permissions. (3) Jesus emphasized the priorities that the Law sets up within itself, such as generosity and compassionate love. Each of these radical extensions is consistent with the Law and a new covenantizing oral tradition of the Law. So that, for Jesus in Matthew, the way of salvation is via the Messiah and a new covenant embracing of Law. Jewish contextual communities' basic belief expected the same thing.[53] In fact, the charge that sectarian Jewish communities would have against a pan-Judaism was that of not being faithful enough to the Mosaic Law.[54] In this way, Jesus could be seen as cultivating and raising up a new sect of peace-making Messianic Judaism, with the same charge against Judaism, they were not faithful enough to the Law (Matt 5:20; 23:23).

Within *torah*, Jesus' utilization of rabbinic method populated a basic belief or language game for Jesus' Jewish worldview based in warrant provided primarily by the written and oral *torah* through which it was interpreted.[55] Basic belief is a good operating framework for Jesus since both knowledge methods and faith are intertwined as overlapping synonyms and one's warrant is provided by being consistent within such a communal worldview.[56]

---

52. Rabbinics saw that there was a continuity of Law into the Messiah's New Covenant ministry and the Kingdom to come (*Gen. Rab.* 98.9; *Eccl. Rab.* 11.1; *Mid. Tanh., Ki Tavo*, par. 4; Midrash fragment, *BhM* 6.151–52; *Halakbot G'dolot*. ed. Hildesheimer, 223 top; Azulai, *Hesed l'Avraham* 13c–14a; Vital, *Sefer haHezyonot*, 160; *Mid. Talpiyot* 58a; *Yemenite Midrash*, 349–50; Yitzhaq, *Imre Tzaddiqim*, ed. Hasid, 10 [5b]. There is no evidence that the Sermon on the Mount was constructed in Hittite treaty form (contra. Law, "The Law of the New Covenant in Matthew," *American Theological Inquiry* [online] 5:2[July 15, 2012]: 27–29), for example: Matt. 5:1–2 is simply a narrative context with no throne names given as occurs in Hittite treaties and Matt 5:3–16 is essential virtues not a historical prologue of the Great King's rescue of the vassal like occurs in a Hittite treaty.

53. Sanders. *Jesus and Judaism*; *Paul, the Law, and the Jewish People.*

54. Elliott, *The Survivors of Israel.*

55. B. *Qidd.* 66a; 2 *Bar.* 48.18–24; Plantinga, *Warrant and Proper Function*, 6; *Knowledge and Christian Belief*, 25–44; Wittgenstein, *Philosophical Investigations*, 11e–12e, 15e–16e, paragraphs 23 and 32; Matthews, "Jesus and Augustine," In *Jesus and Philosophy*. ed. Moser, 109, 111, a view hinted at through a medieval approach to the psalms by Martin, "The Word at Prayer" and Rae, "Incline Your Ear," In *The Bible and Epistemology*. ed. Healy and Parry, 51, 57, 59, 166.

56. Kennard, *Messiah Jesus*, 33–36 explaining the Jewish content within a basic belief of legitimated by Plantinga, *Warrant and Proper Function*; *Knowledge and Christian Belief*; and *Faith and Rationality*. ed. Plantinga and Woltersdorff without a defensive quality of Plantinga, *Warrant: The Current Debate*; *Warranted Christian Belief*; or the Barthian spin of Diller, *Theology's Epistemological Dilemma*.

The miracle healing and forgiving the paralytic shows the overlap of faith and knowledge. Jesus saw the corporate faith of the paralytic's four friends lowering him through the roof and announced that the paralytic's sins were forgiven (Matt 9:2–8; Mark 2:3–12; Luke 5:18–26). To demonstrate that they might know that Jesus has the authority to forgive sins, Jesus healed the paralytic and the healed man walked out carrying his stretcher. Such demonstrations evidence an externalism without epistemic dualism through a practical realistic non-foundational empiricism similar to Thomas Reid's Common Sense Realism.[57] Jesus also utilized knowledge evidentially because the quality of tree is *known* by its fruit (Matt 12:33; Luke 6:44). In fact, the evidence can be internal as the woman with the hemorrhage *felt* the healing within herself (Mark 5:29). However, Matthew also uses "know" in a relational manner indicating the intimacy of the sexual relationship (Matt 1:25).

Pharisaic Judaism was also mystically warranted as developed by William Alston providing direct moments of empirical perceptions from God or angels through vision, dreams, or authoritative audible speech (*bath qol*, Matt 1:20; 2:13; 3:17; 4:1–11; 17:5; Luke 1:11–20, 26–38; 2:9–15; 3:22; 4:1–13; 9:35).[58] Especially statements that identify Jesus as God's Son fit within Pharisaic constructs identified as filial knowledge.[59] Such filial knowledge has God the Father announce His pleasure with His Son Jesus in a manner that continues to support Jesus with special family knowledge and Spirit empowerment for ministry. This Pharisaic Jewish worldview essentially focused on the monotheistic creator God electing Israel and now Jesus' disciples into a covenant relationship and faithfulness unto kingdom blessing (Matt 5:33–35, 45–48; 6:6–13, 28–33).[60] As a disciple expressed the appropriate family response, Jesus confirmed such a filial response (Matt 16:16–18). Such communal knowledge grants Jesus an authoritative place

---

57. Rabbi Gamaliel advocates work and relations along with *torah* study in *m. 'Abot* 2.2; Reid, *Thomas Reid*. ed. Brookes; Abraham, "The Epistemology of Jesus," In *Jesus and Philosophy*. ed. Moser, 158–9; Brueggemann, *A Pathway of Interpretation*, 115.

58. Alston, *Perceiving God*, 14–35; Angels as revelatory messengers: *Jub.* 1.27–29; 10.10–14; *1 En.* 4.19, 21–26; 7; 8; 17–36; 89.61–77; 90.14–20; *T. Levi* 9.6; *T. Reub.* 5.3; *T. Jos.* 6.6; Authoritative heavenly voice: *b. 'Abot* 6.2; *B. Bat.* 73b, 85b; *Mak.* 23b; *'Erub.* 54b; *Šabb.* 33b; 88a; *Soṭa* 33a; *p. Soṭa* 7.5, sect. 5; *Pesiq. Rab Kah.* 15.5; *Lev. Rab.* 19.5–6; *Deut. Rab.* 11.10; *Lam. Rab. Proem* 2, 23; *Lam. Rab.* 1.16 sect. 50; *Ruth Rab.* 6.4; *Qoh. Rab.* 7.12, sect. 1; *Pesq. Rab Kah.* 11.16; Authoritative Dreams: LXX additions to Esther; *1 En.*; *2 En.*; *2 Bar.*; *4 Ezra*; *Apoc. Ab.*; *T. Levi*; *T. Job*; *Bib. Ant.*; *Jub.*; *Life of Adam and Eve* and several at Qumran, Flannery, "Dreams and Vision Reports," In *The Eerdmans Dictionary of Early Judaism.* ed. Collins and Harlow, 550.

59. Moser's attunement to filial knowledge of God providing authoritative evidence for the message communicated (*The Elusive God*, 46–7, 98, 113–123).

60. Sir 17.17–18; 47.22; Jdt 7.30; Sus 16.5; 19.29; *Pss. Sol.* 9.17–18.

to inform His disciples about kingdom knowing and living. Likewise, responses to Jesus that did not fit such a family response provided Jesus with the opportunity to warn his followers that such responses did not know and were at risk (Matt 16:22–23; 13:10–17).[61] This disciple filial relationship also includes being known by Christ (Matt 7:23).

Jesus' filial knowledge of God is evident as a devout Jewish boy of twelve on the yearly Passover trip to Jerusalem. Jesus missed his family's caravan to return home. Discovering Jesus absent, His family went back to Jerusalem, only to find Him on the third day in the midst of the Jewish teachers, listening and asking questions. "All who heard Him were amazed at His understanding, and His answers" (Luke 2:46–47).[62] One example of His wisdom was in His recognition of greater levels of authority and intimacy: such as, God over parents (Luke 2:48–49). Jesus acknowledged that God was His Father in such a manner that Jesus needed His Father's house. This unusual filial knowledge of God identified Jesus purpose with God and the Temple, likely an early expression of Messianic consciousness.[63] Mary treasured these sayings in her heart.

Sermon on the Mount and Plain
(Matt 5–7; Luke 6:20–49)[64]

Jesus' characteristic sermons (the Sermon on the Mount and on the Plain)[65] examined here show Jesus' continuity with rabbinic Judaism and His unique

61. Israel's obduracy: Isa 6:9–10; 28:14–22; 29:9–10; 42:18–20; 43:8; 44:18; 63:17; 1QIsa{a} 6, 2.2–5; 1QH 7.2–3; Matt 13:14–15; Mark 4:12; Acts 28:26–27; John 9:39; 12:40; 1 Cor 2:6–16; 2 Cor 3:14–16; Rom 9–11; Philo, *Spec.* 1.304–7; *Leg.* 2.53–70; ; Isa 6:9–10 in *Targum Jonathan* and in Syriac *Peshitta*; *Melkilta de-Rabbi Ishmael* in Baḥodesh 1 on Exod 19:2; *y. Ber.* 2.3; *b. Meg.* 17b; *b. Roš. Haš.* 17b uniquely rabbi Johanan considers Israel could still repent and *Tanna Debe Eliyyahu* 16.82–83 agrees; Justin, *Dial.* 12.2; 33.1; Tertullian, *Marc.* 3.6.5; 5.19.2; Cyprian, *Test.* 1.3; Origen, *Cels.* 2.8; *Hom. Jer.* 14.12; 20.2; *Comm. Jo.* 29; *Comm. Matt.* 16.9; Hippolytus, *Trad. ap.* 5.16.4; The magisterial study on Israel's obduracy is Evans, *To See and Not Perceive*; Marcus, "Mark 4.10–12 and Markan Epistemology," *JBL* 103(1984): 557–74.

62. There is no hint that he taught the teachers here as the *Infancy Gospel of Thomas* portrays.

63. Moser, *The Elusive God*, 46–7, 98, 113–123.

64. Kennard, *Messiah Jesus*, 69–106.

65. These two sermons are given historically at different times, since the miracle of healing the leper immediately follows the Sermon on the Mount, as Jesus is coming down from the mountain (Matt 8:1–2) and precedes the Sermon on the Plain (Luke 5:12–15; 6:20–49) and Luke identifies that he writes his gospel in consecutive order (Luke 1:3). Additionally, the geography of mount and plain identify different locations (Matt 5:1; Luke 6:17). Any itinerant preacher will use his good material more than once.

supreme scribal authority. Both the sermon on the Mount and on the Plain are addressed to Jesus' disciples (Matt 5:12; Luke 6:20). Of course, the multitude overheard his teaching (Matt 5:1; 7:28) but the thrust was for those already identified with Jesus as His students.

In these sermons, Jesus' set out a two way approach as a basic belief or language game unto the kingdom, much like early Judaism and John the Baptist had before Him (Matt 3:3, 7–10; Luke 3:4–14).[66] Jesus' philosophy becomes a way of life in which choice orients to a form of life warranted in the living of it.[67] Both the sermons follow this Jewish orientation as is apparent especially in the beginning and end of the sermons (Matt 5:3–16; 7:13–27; Luke 6:20–26). However, the clearest development of the two ways approach is in the conclusion of the Sermon on the Mount in which five illustrations portray the two ways: 1) gates and ways, 2) sheep versus wolf in sheep's clothing, 3) trees, 4) claims demonstrated, 5) and builders (Matt 7:13–27). Each way has a goal to which it leads, either that of life and the kingdom (Matt 7:14, 21) or destruction (Matt 7:13, 19, 27; 16:18). Jesus begins His exhortation to enter by the narrow gate[68] and the way that leads to life. Only one of the two-ways saves, the other damns. The narrowness of the strictured way (στενης and τεθλιμμένη) has implications that there are few who find it (Matt 7:13–14; Luke 13:23–25). While the breadth of the way that leads to destruction indicates that many will follow this way (Matt 7:13, 22). The broad way includes those who take advantage of others like: wolves in sheep's clothing and false prophets. The basic way on which a person travels is evidenced by the consistent obedience in following Jesus' and the Father's teaching (Matt 7:21, 24, 26). However, this is not earning one's place in kingdom, it is showing in a natural fruiting manner who has an intimate internalized discipleship relationship with the Son (Matt 7:15, 17–19, 23). The kingdom way is not shown in works like prophecy, exorcisms, or

---

66. Second Temple Judaism develops a two ways view unto kingdom especially from a wisdom and prophetic perspective (Sir 35.11; 48.10; Bar 4.37; 5.5; 2 Macc 1.27; 2.18; *Jub.* 1.15; *Ps. Sol.* 8.34; 11.2; 14.9–10; 15.10; 17.11–12, 28–31, 50; 18.6–9; 1QM 2.2, 7; 3.13; 5.1; 11QT 8.14–16; 57.5; 1QS 3.18–4.26; 4Q228; 4Q473 frag. 2 2–4; *Charter of a Jewish Sectarian Association* 9.21; *Asher* 1.3–5; 6.4–6; Philo, *Rewards* 164; *4 Ezra* 7.6–8; *Sifre Deut.* 53; *Mekhilta of Rabbi Ishmael* on Exod 14:29; *Avot R. Nat.* vers. A.24). Davies and Allison, *Matthew*, 1:439, 442–480 present these beatitudes as entrance requirements into the Kingdom; Plantinga, *Warrant and Proper Function*, 6; *Knowledge and Christian Belief*, 25–44; Wittgenstein, *Philosophical Investigations*, 11e–12e, 15e–16e, paragraphs 23 and 32; Matthews, "Jesus and Augustine," In *Jesus and Philosophy*. ed. Moser, 109, 111.

67. Hadot, *Philosophy as a Way of Life*, 281; Volf, *Captive to the Word of God*, 48–50, 55–58.

68. Luke 13:24 has narrow door instead of gate.

miracles (Matt 7:15, 22). Rather, *the kingdom way is shown in new covenant obedience rather than Lawlessness* (Matt 7:21-24, 26). A good person or tree produces good fruit and generous speech from within her heart (Matt 7:16-20 with vs. 12; Luke 6:43-45).[69] So one's works epistemically show in a common sense realist manner what kind of person that one is.[70] Such a good person builds on the firm rock foundation of obedience to Jesus and the Father (Matt 7:24-27; Luke 6:46-49).[71] *Such strictured but wise living does not remove the troubles of life but enables one to survive them, because one has built upon the foundation of Jesus' teachings.*

Elsewhere, in the two ways soteriology, there is a way of light unto kingdom and a way of darkness resulting in destruction (Matt 7:22-23; Luke 11:34-36).[72] In Judaism, God is seen to dwell in light (Ps 104:2; Dan 3:3-4; Hab 3:3-4)[73] and thus He gives light to His people as an expression of kingdom revelation perhaps within William Alston's mystical perceiving God or Paul Moser's filial knowledge (Job 29:2-3; Pss 4:6; 18:28; 48:3).[74] The eschatological hope is light (Isa 60:20), but those who are God's are even now illuminated by revelation light of life and wisdom (Pss 27:1; 56:13; Hos 10:12 LXX; John 1:4, 9).[75] This illumination even impacts the righteous so that they are described as the people of the light (Isa 42:6; 49:6; Matt 5:14; 6:22; 1 John 1:5-10).[76] These "walk in the light of the Lord" (Isa 2:5). The way of the light sees the issues and allegiances clearly, showing its *sincere allegiance to God* (Matt 6:22; Luke 11:34).[77] The way of the darkness cannot see clearly, it is duplicitous and is deceived, in that it is unaware that it cannot see clearly, rendering it doubly blind, with soul darkened and separated

---

69. A similar good/bad tree comparison occurred in Jewish parables in *m. 'Abot* 3.18; *ARNa* 22.2; *ARNb* 34.

70. Reid, *Thomas Reid*. ed. Brookes; Abraham, "The Epistemology of Jesus," In *Jesus and Philosophy*. ed. Moser, 158-9; there is no need to make an Hellenistic rhetorical "cause and effect" appeal as was done by Lausberg, *Handbook of Literary Rhetoric*, 180 following Quintilian, *Inst.* 5.10.80 because early Judaism makes the same comparisons.

71. *ARNa* 24.1-4, 22 makes similar building materials on rock or sand comparisons in a two ways Jewish salvation.

72. Davies and Allison, *Matthew*, 635-6 develop that the eye in ancient Judaism was viewed as a light source and that they embraced an extramission theory of vision, unlike modern empiricism that embraces an intromission theory of vision.

73. *1 En.* 38.4; Josephus, *Asen.* 6.3.

74. 1QS 11.3; 1QH 9,24; *2 Bar.* 38.1; Alston, *Perceiving God*, 14-35; Moser, *The Elusive God*, 46-7, 98, 113-123; Marcus, "Mark 4:10-12 and Marcan Epistemology," *JBL* 103:4(1984): 558- 59, 567.

75. Sir 8.1; Wis 7.10, 26.

76. *1 En.* 104.2; *T. Levi* 14.3; *LAB* 51.6; *T. Job* 31.5; 53.3.

77. Job 1:1 Aq.; *Barn.* 19.2; *T. Levi* 13.1; *Ps. Phoc.* 50; *CR* col. 3 and 4.

from God (Job 18:5-6; 38:15; Matt 6:23; Luke 11:34-35; 1 John 1:6, 8, 10).[78] Such a condition of Jewish "evil eye" is that of a miser and selfish, signifying intent and leaving one in the dark (Deut 15:9; Prov 23:6; 28:22).[79]

Beatitudes-Similitudes as Jesus' *Mishnahic* Apodictic Laws for His Disciples

Both sermons on the Mount[80] and on the Plain begin with beatitudes, and in Luke the two ways are more explicit by a section of curses following the beatitudes (Matt 5:3–10; Luke 6:20–26). Each of the beatitudes begins with the word "blessed," serving as a repetitive[81] echo of the beneficial condition that a disciple can possess provided he meets the criterion of each verse. This means that the beatitudes are first blessings and show God's grace, rather than requirements.[82] That is, the conditions evidence which disciples of Jesus will be so blessed. Or as Albert Schweitzer said, the beatitudes "define the moral disposition which justifies admission into the kingdom."[83]

The blessed conditions are understood as realized within the kingdom. Matthew's beatitudes begin and end with identifying the blessing with

---

78. *2 Bar.* 48.2-3; *4 Ezra* 12.36-37; *T. Job* 43.5-6; *T. Sol.* 26.7; 1QS 1.19-20; 3.18-21; 9.17; Marcus, "Mark 4:10-12 and Marcan Epistemology," *JBL* 103:4(1984): 560-63.

79. Tob 4.7; Sir 14.8; 26.11; *m. 'Abot* 2.9, 11; 5.19; 1QS 4.9-11.

80. The mountain is treated as location with no development of polemic to Moses' Mount Sinai (Exod 19:3; 24:13, 18), though Jesus does comment on the Law in a new covenant manner.

81. While the O.T. beatitudes do not group more than two together (Ps 84:4-5), the listing of nine beatitudes should not overwhelm the reader, since by early Judaism an occasional list of beatitudes is as long (Matt 5:3-11; five in 4Q525 including purity of heart and faithfulness to the Law; four in Luke 6:20-22). *2 Enoch* 52.1-14 has seven beatitudes and seven curses. Later, *The Gospel of Thomas* has ten beatitudes, some in series (7, 18-19, 49, 54-58, 68-69, 103). Additionally, the Matthew beatitudes may have parallels with Isaiah 61, quoted in Luke 4:18-19; cf. Sir 14.20-27; Davies and Allison, *Matthew*, 1:436-439.

82. Beatitudes found in Jewish wisdom (Sir 14.20-27) and prophetic texts (*2 En.* 52.1-14) are not really Law or covenant, even though these genres possess statements of blessing and curse. Likewise, the Law includes blessing and curse but not in beatitude form (Deut 28-30).

83. Schweitzer, *The Mystery of the Kingdom of God*, 53-54; *The Kingdom of God and Primitive Christianity*, 93-101; Augustine, *Serm. Dom.* 1.1.3; 1.2.4-9; 1.4.12; 1.9; *Serm.* 3.1, 8, 9, 16. Thus the liberal ethical approach (von Harnack, *What is Christianity*; Scott, *The Ethical Teaching of Jesus*; Marshall, *The Challenge of New Testament Ethics*; Harvey Cox, *The Secular City*) has ignored the Jewish eschatological kingdom context for Jesus teaching.

"kingdom" directly (Matt 5:3–10).[84] The *inclusio* (or literary envelope; Matt 5:3, 10; Luke 6:23) of mentioning the kingdom serves to identify the other blessings as kingdom benefits as well. Additionally, some of the benefits are only believably received in the kingdom, such as the meek and gentle inheriting the earth (Matt 5:5).

These kingdom benefits have both present and future benefit in view. Matthew's *inclusio* and Luke's starting point of "theirs *is* the kingdom" evidences by its present tense verb, present kingdom benefits already for those who meet the criteria (Matt 5:3, 10; Luke 6:20). The other beatitudes evidence by their future tense verb a future reward that is not yet received.

Thus the beatitudes must be taken together. No one benefit can be removed from the rest of the kingdom framework, likewise no one beatitude virtue can be lifted to promise kingdom benefits. For example, merely because a person grieves or is gentle does not guarantee her involvement in the kingdom. However, when a disciple of Jesus grieves or is gentle there is an appropriate reassurance that kingdom blessings are hers to meet that need. Robert Adams and William Wainwright describe that in this virtue epistemology, God is the ground and basis for these virtues, however, Matthew emphasizes the Christian's responsibility to love his neighbor as himself (Lev 19:18; Matt 5:43–48; 19:19).[85]

"Blessed are the poor in spirit, for theirs is the kingdom" (Matt 5:3). A recognition of poverty in a disciple's spiritual condition identifies the disciple's trust and dependence upon his Master (Jas 2:5).[86] *As an epistemic virtue having humility within oneself predisposes one's trust and dependence upon Jesus.* So it is not a spiritual benefit for the able and wealthy, but for those who recognize their need. This reverses the popular secular sentiment: "blessed are the rich." Luke 6:20 simplifies the poverty to be material poverty which is more emphasized in Luke than any other synoptic gospel (Luke 1:53; 4:18; 6:20; 7:22; 14:13, 21; 16:20, 22; 18:22; 19:8; 21:3).[87] This

---

84. The kingdom focus of these beatitudes is like the beatitudes of: *Ps. of Sol.* 17.44 or *1 En.* 58.2–3, "Blessed are you righteous and elect ones, for glorious is your portion. The righteous ones shall be in the light."

85. Adams, "The Problem of Total Devotion," In *Rationality, Religious Belief, and Moral Commitment*. ed. Audi and Wainwright, 94; Nygren, *Agape and Eros*, 216; Wainwright, "Obedience and Responsibility," In *The Wisdom of the Christian Faith*. ed. Moser and McFall, 68.

86. Such fiscal poverty was a positive religious designation in Judaism (1QM 11.9, 13; 13.14; 14.7; 1QpHab 12.3, 6, 10; 4QpPs 37 fr. 1, 2.10).

87. This call to the poor is consistent with 4Q88 9.13–14 and the *Passover Haggadah* which calls all the poor (using similar phrases to that of Jesus in Luke) to the Passover feast. *Gos. Thom.* 54 follows Luke on *fiscal poverty* but Matthew on *third person plural* (*their*) with "Blessed are the poor, for theirs is the kingdom of heaven." That is, Luke

Lukan portrait is similar to Qumran's self-designation as the sect of the poor.[88] Whether material poverty shows one to be in need of depending upon God or recognition of one's spiritual nature of inadequacy, the results are the same. Both point to humility and dependence on God, as one admits to one's own spiritual bankruptcy. Within Jewish tradition, such a reference to the poor refers to the meek, humiliated and oppressed people of God (Isa 10:2; 26:6).[89] This sentiment affirms one sense of the Jewish tradition indicated in the *Sibylline Oracles* 8.208 "Blessed are the poor, for they shall be rich." Luke warns those who receive comfort now, that their riches may indicate that they are not depending upon God and thus there are no more benefits to come (Luke 6:24). Jewish tradition indicates that in the kingdom age to come there will be no poverty.[90] Luke later goes on to illustrate this point with Jesus teaching on wealth, in the parable of the rich man and Lazarus (Luke 16:19–31). Abraham in paradise summarized the point for the rich man as "during your life you received your good things and likewise Lazarus bad things; but now he is being comforted here, and you are in agony" (Luke 16:25). However, for those whose dependence is on God, the present reality of the kingdom is their very real possession.

"Blessed are those who mourn, for they shall be comforted" (Matt 5:4; Luke 6:21). Perhaps, picking up the Jewish traditional sentiment from Isaiah 61:1–2, quoted by Jesus as He begins His ministry in the Nazareth synagogue, Jesus provides real comfort in kingdom for the downtrodden and oppressed (Luke 4:18–21).[91] Jewish tradition continued to emphasize that the kingdom should be thought to be broadly comforting to us in our life of mourning (Isa 60:20; 66:10; Jer 31:13; Ps 126:2–6).[92] *As an epistemic virtue, mourning deepens engagement and hope in Jesus throughout one's whole being.* The mourning (Matthew's emphasis) and weeping (Luke's emphasis) that occur in this life are in contrast to the comfort and laughing which will come upon all who are beneficiaries of the kingdom in the

---

personalizes it further by the second person "*yours* is the Kingdom." Additionally, the *Gos. Thom.* 69.2 encourages that these hungry and thirsty will be satisfied.

88. Tob 4.21; 1QpHab 12.2–10; 1QM 11.9, 13; 13.14; 1QH 2.32; 3.25; 5.16, 18, 22; 4QpPs 37 1.9; 2.10; 4Q88 9.13–14; with only the *Damascus Document* using the term in the more common sense of poor people; Dunn, *The Christ & the Spirit, Volume 1 Christology*, 110.

89. *Pss. Sol.* 5.2, 11; 10.6; 15.1–3; 18:2; 5 *Apoc Syr. Ps.* 2:18; 1QpHab 12.3; 1QM 14.7 where such poverty might mean fainthearted; 1QH 5.13–14; 4QpPs 2.9–10.

90. *Sib. Or.* 3.378; *T. Jud.* 25.4; *b. Pesh.* 50 in contrast to *b. Šabb.* 151b and *Sipre* on Deut 15:11.

91. Sir 48.24.

92. *Thanksgiving Scroll* 13.14–15; *Bar.* 4.23; 1QH 18.14–15; 11QMelch 2.20; perhaps also Ps 126:2–6.

future. The mourning refers to a sorrow with the world or one's own poverty of life as it is. Mathew uses "mourning" in one other place to indicate the inappropriateness of mourning when the disciples have Jesus with them, but Jesus reminds them that He will be taken away (Matt 9:15).[93] When Jesus is removed, mourning their loss is quite appropriate. However, this concept of mourning could be much broader, like sorrow for sin in one's life or context (Matt 25:75; Luke 7:38–48; 22:62).[94] This weeping could occur within areas of lack such as hunger or the lack of love (Luke 6:21–22). Mourning can include loss of loved ones and the futility of wasted life (Matt 2:18; Luke 5:38). Jesus grieves over Jerusalem, which is rejecting Him, and urges them to grieve as well (Luke 19:41; 22:28). For those who grieve in any of these ways, real comfort will be theirs in future kingdom benefits. Jesus' present kingdom healing even undoes the cause for grief for some now, in the promise of raising loved ones from the dead (Mark 5:34; Luke 7:13; 8:52). Luke warns those who laugh now and do not take to heart the present context of grief, that they shall mourn and weep in their destruction as they miss future kingdom benefits being poured out (Luke 6:25).

"Blessed are the gentle, for they shall inherit the earth" (Matt 5:5). The quality of πραεις is meekness, absence of pretension and gentleness. As such, this meek gentleness is a synonym to poverty of material and in spirit (Matt 5:3; Luke 6:20). In this statement, Jesus echoes the Jewish tradition[95] evident in 2 *Enoch* 50.2, "In patience and meekness spend the number of your days so that you may inherit everlasting life." This meekness is a quality Jesus displayed in His humble offering of rest for the disciples (Matt 11:29). It is also a quality predicted of Him by Zechariah 9:9, which indicates Jesus peaceful intention in coming to Jerusalem on a colt of a donkey, to offer them the kingdom if they would have Him as King (Matt 21:5). *As an epistemic virtue, gentleness coupled with mercy repositions the perspective of a person to other-orientedness that responds to the other person and her perspective with generosity.* Those, like Jesus, who display this quality in relationship with Him, shall inherit the whole earth, and not merely a part of the land (γης in Matt 5:5, 13). This hope of land inheritance also reflects the Jewish hope for

---

93. While not in inspired Scripture as the earliest, nor the best manuscript, Mark 16:10 shows one example of how mourning and comfort surround the death and resurrection of Christ.

94. Tob 13.14; *Pesiq. R.* 28.3.

95. The praise of meekness and gentleness is also evident in Jewish tradition through (Deut 4:1; Ps 37:11; Tob 4.7–11, 16–19; 2 *En.* 42.7–13; 1QS 4.2–6; Philo, *Vit. Mos.* 2.279; Josephus, *Ant.* 19.330; *m. Soṭa* 9.15; *ARN* 7; *b. Soṭa* 40a, 49b; *b. Šabb.* 30b; *b. Ned.* 38a; 4QPs 2.9–11) and in classical works as well (Plato, *Crit.* 120E; *Rep.* 375C; Lucian, *Somnium* 10; *Ep. Arist.* 257, 263).

the kingdom (Isa 60:21-22; 61:7; Rom 4:13).[96] This eschatological reversal is a common Jewish hope (Luke 1:50-53).[97]

"Blessed are those who hunger and thirst for righteousness, for they shall be satisfied" (Matt 5:6).[98] Jesus sentiment reflects Jewish traditional expectations for communal fairness and righteousness (Pss 42:2; 63:1; 143:6; Amos 8:11).[99] *As an epistemic virtue, such an approach of longing directs the disciple to right affection and action to benefit the entire community, especially the vulnerable.* This longing is the same sentiment as seeking God's kingdom and His righteousness, to which virtue there is real encouragement that Jesus' disciples needs will be met (Matt 6:33). Especially, the Lukan version resonates with the Jewish tradition of eschatological reversal (Pss 37:19; 107:5-9; 132:15; Isa 25:6-8; 32:1, 16-17; 49:10-13; 55:1-2; 65:13).[100]

"Blessed are the merciful for they shall receive mercy" (Matt 5:7). Jesus' teaching reflects the sentiment of rabbis elsewhere.[101] The merciful are the benefactors who attempt to meet other's needs.[102] The dominant expression of mercy in the synoptics is the healing done by the Son of David (Matt 9:27; 15:22; 17:15; 20:30-31; Mark 5:19; 10:47-48; Luke 1:58; 17:13; 18:38-39). Whereas, in Jewish tradition, the primarily merciful One is God (1 Sam 23:21; Ps 72:13; Prov 14:21; Mic 6:8).[103] Mercy is one of the weightier matters of the Law and unfortunately was neglected by the scribes and Pharisees (Matt 23:23). One form of the Jewish neglect of mercy was their restrictiveness to their own Jewish group.[104] Jesus' disciples must have mercy in minis-

---

96. *Jub.* 32.18-19; *2 En.* 5.7; 11QTemple 59.11-13; 4QpPs 2.9-12; 4QPs 37; *2 Bar.* 51.3; *m. Qidd.* 1.10.

97. Sir 35; Wis 5.1-20.

98. *Gos. Thom.* 69.2 takes this beatitude with reference to poverty, hungering and thirsting in need will be satisfied.

99. Sir 39.6-7; Wis 5.15; 4 *Ezra* 14.28-35; *Jub.* 20.1-2; 1QS 4.2-4; Philo, *Poster C.* 172; *Fug.* 139; *Sib. Or.* 3.234-35; *2 En. B* 42.11-12; *T. Benj.* 3.1-5; *b. Sanh.* 100a; *m 'Abot* 2.2; *Sifra A.M.* par. 8.193.1.11; *Sifra Behuq.* pg. 2.262.19; *b. Qidd* 396; *Pesiq. Rab. Kah. Sup.* 2.1; *Deut. Rab.* 7.9.

100. *1 En.* 58.4; 62.14; *2 Bar.* 29.6; *Par. Jer.* 9.20; 1QSa; *T. Levi* 13.5. This theme is continued in 2 Pet 3:13 and *Gos. Thom.* 5.6; 69b.

101. This is parallel in *b. Šabb.* 151b, "He who has mercy on people obtains mercy from heaven;" also *t. B. Qam.* 9.30, "As long as you are merciful, the Merciful One is merciful to you;" *T. Sim.* 4.4; Josephus, *Ant.* 10.41. Additionally, the rabbis identified that God judged the world by two measures: justice and mercy (*Lev. R.* 29.3), so that following a verse about righteousness it is appropriate to develop the theme of mercy. This sentiment continues in early Christendom, *1 Clem.* 13.2; Polycarp, *Ep.* 2.3.

102. *Test. Jud.* 18.3-4; *Epict. Disc.* 1.18.4.

103. *T. Zeb.* 5.1, 3; 7.1-8.6; Philo, *Spec. leg.* 4.72, 76-77.

104. For example, Qumran, the Essenes and other Jews maintained a mercy within the community and a hate to outsiders (1QS 1.4, 10-11; 2.4-9; 9:21-23; 1QM 4.1-2;

tering to sinners and forgiving others without judging them (Matt 6:12-15; 7:1-5; 9:13; 12:7; 18:21-35; Mark 11:25). The good Samaritan exemplifies mercy in meeting his neighbor's and even enemy's needs (Matt 5:44-47; Luke 10:37). This sentiment of showing mercy universally was also a factor in some forms of Jewish tradition.[105] The merciful shall receive mercy (Matt 5:7). The future mercy to be received could be in this life or the kingdom beyond.[106] Praise is given to God for His mercy unfolding in His salvation plan (Luke 1:50, 54, 72, 78). Jesus, through Luke 16:24 warns us that those who do not give mercy, such as the rich man's abuse of Lazarus, will not receive mercy in the afterlife.

"Blessed are the pure in heart, for they shall see God" (Matt 5:8). The pure are the clean that recognize God alone is their hope (Ps 24:3-4; Matt 23:26; 27:59).[107] The kind of purity described is one of whole moral purity. *Such an epistemic virtue of integrity is sincere and not divided against itself.* Examples of internal anger and adultery are developed as contrast to this purity in this context (Matt 5:22, 28). Such a commitment to purity of heart reflects some Jewish tradition (Gen 20:5-6; Ps 24:3-4; Isa 61:1 "broken hearted" as in responsive from one's heart to God).[108] The privilege of the pure in heart in Jewish tradition is to see or know God in the kingdom (Job 19:26; Ps 11:7; 17:15; Isa 52:6; 60:16; Jer 24:7; 31:31-34).[109] Jewish tradition developed that such sight of God at the present tended to be beyond normal expectation,[110] so that it remained an eschatological hope.

"Blessed are the peacemakers, for they shall be called sons of God" (Matt 5:9). The peacemaker is one who reconciles humans into peaceful relationships as is evident in Matthew 5:23-26 and Mark 9:50. Such peacemaking is affirmed by Jewish tradition (Ps 34:14; Prov 10:10).[111] *As an epistemic virtue, peacemaking builds community through dialog and understanding each other.* A peacemaker will not force God's kingdom but will

---

15.6; 1QH 5.4; *b. Ber.* 33a; *b. Sanh.* 92a; Josephus, *J. W.* 2.139).

105. A commitment to universal mercy is present in early Judaism (Tob 4.7-11, 15-19; *Sib. Or.* 3.239-45; 2 *En.* B 42.7-14; 1QS 4.2-6; *Sipra* on Lev 19:18 and *Mek.* on Exod 21:35) and outside the Jewish tradition (Polybius 18.37.7; Hesiod, *Op.* 342-3; Solon, frag. 1.3-5; Plato, *Tim.* 17d-18a; *Rep.* 375c; *Meno* 71e; Tacitus, *Hist.* 5.5-6).

106. 2 Tim 1:18; Jude 21; *1 Clem.* 28.1.

107. *2 Bar.* 9.1; 2 *En.* 45.3.1; *T. Jos.* 4.6; *T. Benj.* 8.2; *T. Isaac*, 64; 4QBeat.

108. *T. Naph.* 3.1; *T. Jos.* 4.6; 1 Tim 1:5; 2 Tim 2:22; Heb 10:22.

109. 4 Ezra 7.98; *b. B. Bat.* 10a; SB 1; *b. Sanh.* 98b; Philo, *Vit. cont.* 11-12; *Abr.* 57-59; *Mut. nom.* 81-82; Matt 16:27; 24:30; 26:64; Mark 13:26; 14:62; 1 Cor 13.12; Heb 12:14; 1 John 3:2; Rev 1:7; 22:4.

110. Exod 3.6; 19:21; 33:20, 23; John 1:18; 1 Tim 6:15-16; *Sipre* on Num 12:8.

111. 2 *En.* 52.11-15; *m. 'Abot* 1.12; *m. Pe'a* 1.1; *Mek.* on Exod 20:25.

humbly wait for it (Isa 25:6–9; 26:8; 30:15, 18; 40:30–31; 49:23; 50:10–11; 57:13; 64:4; Lam 3:22–26; Mic 7:7; Jas 5:7–9). A peacemaker is one who demonstrates that he is a son of the Father by generously loving and praying for his enemies who persecute him (Matt 5:39–45). Such peacemaking may be at significant cost or loss. Such peacemaking may require letting an abuse go, in forgiving one's abuser but it cannot be at the expense of denying Jesus as the Son, that is, the King (Matt 10:34). In maintaining a relationship with Jesus as the Messiah, we should work for peace and thereby identify ourselves as sons of God (Matt 5:9, 45; Luke 6:35; 20:36). A model for sons of God is Jesus, *the* Son of God, who by His mandate in the Davidic covenant, works for peace (1 Chr 22:9–10; Matt 3:17; 4:3; 17:5; 27:9, 40, 43, 54). Being a son of God would identify one as a son of the kingdom in Jesus' teaching (Matt 13:38) and in Jewish tradition.[112]

"Blessed are those who have been persecuted for righteousness sake, for theirs is the kingdom" (Matt 5:10–12; Luke 6:22).[113] The phrase "Those who have been persecuted" is a perfect participle which emphasizes that we are dealing with qualities which in this case we have little control over. This kind of persecution includes: hatred, ostracism, insults, spurning through defamation, excommunicating[114] and saying all kinds of evil against one falsely on account of Jesus (Matt 5:11; Luke 6:22). Such persecution is essentially for those who have identified with Jesus and maintain obedient, righteous character. This is consistent with the Jewish traditional expectation that the righteous will suffer persecution.[115] Such persecution has the potential of devastating a person so that she might fall away (Matt 13:21; Mark 4:17). However, *as an epistemic virtue without being dissuaded from what is right, perseverance contributes resilience to a person's disposition and life.* Such persecutions identify Jesus' disciples with the prophets who were persecuted by the religious leaders before them. This virtually guarantees the certainty of the religious leaders persecuting the disciples (Matt 10:23, 38–39; 16:21, 24–26; 23:34–35; Mark 8:31, 34–38; 10:30; Luke 9:21–24; 21:12). Early Jewish tradition identified that the fate of God's prophets was

---

112. *Ps. Sol.* 17.27; *Sib. Or.* 3.702. Everlasting reward is promised for peacemaking (*m. 'Abot* 2.8; *Pe'a* 1.1; *ARN* 40A).

113. 1 Pet 3:14 and *Gos. Thom.* 68 retain the same sentiment. Cf. Polycarp, *Ep.* 2.3; Clement of Alexandria, *Strom.* 4.6.

114. Perhaps implied by a wooden reading of the text in Matt 5:11 and Luke 6:22, namely, "cast out your name as evil on account of the Son of Man," which probably has beneath it a Semitic expression "to cause an ill name to go out." Davies and Allison, *Matthew*, 1:462.

115. Wis 1.16–5.23.

that of martyrdom.¹¹⁶ In this context it is an evidential bad sign if all speak well of you for this is the way the religious leaders' fathers treated the false prophets (Luke 6:26). To be identified with God's prophets and with His Son in persecution is a cause for rejoicing because it indicates that you will be blessed with life and reward in the kingdom (Matt 5:11-12; 16:24-27; Mark 8:35-38; Luke 9:24-26). This joy in suffering resonates with a Jewish traditional approach,¹¹⁷ but more clearly provides the kingdom rationale for such gladness. In contrast, Luke identifies joy with kingdom (Luke 1:14, 47; 2:10, 13, 20; 10:20; 15:5, 7, 10, 24, 32; 24:41, 52).

"You are the salt of the earth" (Matt 5:13). Salt was gathered from evaporation pools or from the edge of the Dead Sea (Ezek 47:9-11; Zeph 2:9).¹¹⁸ Salt was a primary implement in keeping food from putrefying (Exod 30:35).¹¹⁹ As such, salt was considered one of the valuable staples of life along with oil and wine.¹²⁰ For example, Antiochus IV gave salt, oil and wine to all the Jews who aided him against Ptolemy Philopater (c.a. 170 B.C.). None of the synoptics describe an ethical meaning to this salt description, as though we had a salty task to perform. In fact, since the statement is a descriptive comment of being, "You are salt," there is no exhortation to do some salty purpose like preserving the world. Rather, as a descriptive comment, it recognizes these disciples have beatitude traits but run the risk of losing them in the same way that saltiness can be lost (Matt 5:13; Mark 9:50; Luke 14:34). That is, salt could be leached out leaving a non-productive soil worthy only to be trod upon by feet.¹²¹ This loss of salt (μωρανθῇ) is elsewhere taken as an ethical condition of becoming fools (μωρέ; Matt 5:13, 22; Luke 14:34; Rom 1:22; 1 Cor 1:20).¹²² The exhortation is to stay true to the beatitudes qualities of one's being for in being that way indicates the blessing of the kingdom.

"You are the light of the world" (Matt 5:14). Again, this is a declaration of a quality of being. Jewish tradition developed that people could be light (Isa 42:6; 49:6; Dan 12:3).¹²³ The disciples in their beatitude traits are like

---

116. *Jub.* 1.12; 4QpHos 2.3-6; Josephus, *Ant.* 10.38; *Asc. Isa.* 2.16; 5.1-14; *Par. Jer.* 9.21-32; *Tg.* on Isa 28:1.

117. Jdt 8.25; 2 Macc 6.28-30; 2 *Bar.* 48.48-50; 52.5-7; *b. Sanh.* 101a; Acts 5:41; Rom 5:3-5; Phil 4:10-13; Jas 1:2, 12; 1 Pet 1:6; 4:13-14.

118. Josephus, *Ant.* 13.128.

119. Ignatius, *Magn.* 10; Diogenes Laertius 8.1.35.

120. Sir 39.26; Pliny, *Nat. hist.* 31.102; *m. Sota* 9.15.

121. Pliny, *Nat. hist.* 31.82.

122. This allusion also works in Aramaic and Hebrew, further underscoring that loss of salt and foolishness are related.

123. *1 En.* 104.2; 2 *Bar.* 77.13-16; *T. Levi* 14.3-4; *T. Job* 31.5; *Par. Jer.* 9.14; *Apoc.*

light. Here the emphasis is not on the losing a quality of being (like salt) but on doing what light does. A lit up city is visible at night on a hill, so also lit oil lamps shine light to their whole environment, not to be under a basket (Matt 5:14–15; Mark 4:21; Luke 8:16; 11:33).[124] The disciple is to let this light quality of her life be visible to others *by doing good works reflective of these beatitude virtues* (Matt 5:16). The purpose (ὅπως) of being light is so that others may see our good works and praise the Father as a result.[125]

Jesus' *Halakhah* of Written and Oral *Torah*

Jesus lives the Mosaic Law zealously in a new covenantal manner and mandates a zealous teaching and living of the Law as part of His way for His Jewish followers to head toward the kingdom.[126]

A supreme example of Jesus teaching the Law is Matthew's Sermon on the Mount. The sermon is in a very similar style to that of the rabbis of His day, in a *midrash* (interpretation) style, much evident in the oral *torah* and the later Talmud.[127] Jesus utilizes the *kĕlāl* teaching pattern of a general principle stated first, which is later developed through examples.[128] Similar to Jewish teachers of His day, Jesus teaching goes beyond Law conformity to press application home in the lives of His listeners.[129] Jesus' kingdom teaching to Jews incorporates the Law as the ethic to be lived toward the kingdom, which is the context of Matthew's Jewish-Christian readership.[130]

Adam 83.3-4; *b. Sanh.* 14a; *b. B. Bat.* 4a; *ARN* 25; 1QS 3.3, 19–22; 1QM 13.5-6, 14–15; *Test. Job* 43.6/4; *Sib. Or.* fr. 1.26–27.

124. A similar point is made in *Gos. Thom.* 33b about preaching instead of good deeds.

125. Echoed by rabbinic *Mekhilta deRabbi Ishmael* on Exod 15:2; Young, *Meet the Rabbis*, 67.

126. Matt 4:23; 5:2, 19; 7:29; 9:35; 11:1; 13:54; 15:9; 21:23; 22:16; 26:55; 28:15, 20; Mark 1:21–22; 2:13; 4:1–2; 6:2, 6, 30, 34; 7:7; 8:31; 9:31; 10:1; 11:17; 12:14, 35; 14:49; Luke 4:15, 31; 5:3, 17; 6:6; 11:1; 12:12; 13:10, 22, 26; 19:47; 20:1, 21; 21:37; 23:5; John 3:2; 6:59; 7:14, 28, 35; 8:2, 20, 28; 9:34; 14:26; 18:20; Acts 1:1; Josephus, *Ant.* 18.63. Such a Law emphasis extends rabbinic patterns and resists Locke's dismissal of such theocratic tendency (*A Letter Concerning Toleration.* ed. Tully, 44) as he is advocating for community censure to remove abusive kings.

127. Bokzer, *Judaism and the Christian Predicament*, 194.

128. Davies and Allison, *Matthew*, 1:481–503; Kennard, *Messiah Jesus*, 107–52.

129. Baba Mezia 88a; Mekitta on Exod 18:20; Loader, *Jesus' Attitude Towards the Law*.

130. Saldarini, *Matthew's Christian-Jewish Community*; However, I would date the composition of Matthew as before the destruction of the temple, since Matthew's comments of Jesus on this topic appear to reflect prophecy awaiting fulfillment rather

The other Synoptic Gospels merely treat the binding nature of the Law as a non-emphasized historical feature of Jesus' ministry while Matthew emphasizes Jesus' binding the Law upon His disciples and his readership. In all the gospels, but especially in Matthew, Jesus radically teaches and lives the Law. Jesus' kingdom way incorporates the Law as part of the ethic to be lived in order for His Jewish disciples to obtain kingdom everlasting life. Jesus radically extends the Law in three broad patterns. The first radical extension of the Law is through a more pervasive new covenant internalization of the Law as is evident in Jesus' treatment of: anger, adultery, and seeking God's kingdom and righteousness (Jer 31:33).[131] The second radical extension of the Law emphasizes the priority of design over permission as evident in Jesus' treatment of commitment in marriage, honesty, peacemaking, and Sabbath strictness. The third radical extension of the Law emphasizes the priority of generosity as is evident in Jesus' treatment of legal rights, practical love, judging and Sabbath healing. It is quite clear that Jesus, especially as Matthew portrays Him, requires His Jewish disciples to keep the Law in order to obtain the kingdom, and its everlasting life, which is what the Pharisaic and sectarian Jewish communities would have thought[132] though each version of Judaism would differ on the extent of what this means. In fact, the charge that sectarian Jewish communities would have against a pan-Judaism is that of not being faithful enough to the Mosaic Law (Matt 5:20; 23:13).[133] In this way, Jesus could be seen as cultivating and raising up

---

than having been fulfilled, but likely after the Gentile ministry had begun; Overman, *Matthew's Gospel and Formative Judaism*; Levine. *The Social and Ethical Dimensions of Matthean Salvation History*; Park, "Covenant Nomism and the Gospel of Matthew," *CBQ* 77:4(2015): 668–85.

131. Early Judaism saw that there was a continuity of Law into the Messiah's new covenant ministry and the kingdom to come (Tob 4.5–6; Sir 39.1–8; *4 Ezra* 14.28–35; 4 Macc 5.20–24; Philo, *Dreams* 1.124; *T. Levi* 13.1–6; *T. Iss.* 5.1; *T. Dan* 5.1; *m. 'Abot* 2.8; *Gen. Rab.* 98.9; *Eccl. Rab.* 11.1; *Mid. Tanh., Ki Tavo*, par. 4; Midrash fragment, *BhM* 6.151–52; *b. Ber.* 61b; *Halakbot G'dolot.* ed. Hildesheimer, 223 top; Azulai, *Hesed l'Avraham* 13c–14a; Vital, *Sefer haHezyonot*, 160; *Mid. Talpiyot* 58a; Yemenite Midrash, 349–50; Yitzhaq, *Imre Tzaddiqim*, ed. Hasid, 10 [5b].

132. Sanders. *Jesus and Judaism; Paul, the Law, and the Jewish People*; 1QM; 1QS; CD; Josephus, *J. W.* 1.5.2; 2.8.14; 2.162–3; *Ant.* 13.10.6; 13.172; 13.288; 17.2.4; 18.12–15; *b. Yom.* 19b; *b. Nidd.* 33b; *Life* 12; *Yadayim* 3.7; 4.6; *Makkot* 1.6; *Niddah* 4.2; perhaps *Pss. Sol.* 1.8; 2.3; 7.2; 8.12–13; 17.5–8, 23.

133. 1QpHab col. 8–12 on the wicked priest; 4QoNah 1.6–7; 2.2, 4; 1QM; 1QS; CD; *b. Yom.* 19b; *b. Nidd.* 33b; *Life* 12; *Yadayim* 3.7; 4.6; *Makkot* 1.6; *Niddah* 4.2; perhaps *Pss. Sol.* 1.8; 2.3; 7.2; 8.12–13; 17.5–8, 23. Josephus, *J. W.* 1.5.2; 1.97; 2.8.14; 2.162–3; *Ant.* 13.10.6; 13.172; 13.288; 13.380; 17.2.4; 18.12–15; contrary to Elliott, *The Survivors of Israel*.

a new sect of Judaism (that becomes Jewish-Christianity), with the same charge against Judaism, they were not faithful enough to the Law.

This tension for legitimacy of Jesus' Law teaching among Judaism is responded to by the Jews in two ways: 1) the Jews question Jesus' Law commitment based on: a) His healing on the Sabbath, and b) His permitting Himself to be touched by the unclean and, 2) then the Jewish leadership questioned and tested Jesus' authority as a scribe. These agendas of others are important challenges and must be dealt with after the Sermon on the Mount material to demonstrate Jesus' consistency to His *halakhah*. Especially the second agenda item epistemically shown that *Jesus is the authoritative scribe, Who can teach with authority*.

In Matthew 5:17, "Do not think that" is a rabbinic rhetorical device designed to set aside potential misunderstandings. It does not require there to be a popular opinion in need of polemic, for the phrase is used in Matthew 10:34 with no evidence of a pacifist group in Jesus' disciples. Furthermore, the device does not require an absolute antithesis, for certainly Jesus urged peace as a kingdom virtue (Matt 5:9) in spite of His insistence that conflicts would come (Matt 10:34). So that when Jesus pointed out that His purpose for coming is not to abolish but to fulfill, His insistence on His disciples doing the Law and Prophets can permit teaching consistent with the Law and Prophets but with qualifications not immediately apparent in His brief statement.

The "Law or the Prophets" here mean the O.T. or the Pharisaic Scriptures of Jesus' day (Matt 7:12; 11:13; 12:5; 22:40; Luke 16:29, 31).[134] The disjunctive "or" makes it clear that neither is abolished. The prophets answer the Law, so that the referent does not change when only the Law is mentioned in verse 18.

Jesus calls His disciples to see that their lifestyles need to be about fulfilling the Law and the Prophets. "Abolish" means a destruction or removal from experience (Matt 24:2; 26:61; 27:40). Jesus denies that He will destroy or remove the Law from the experience of His disciples. "Fulfill" (πληρωσαι) means to fill or complete. There is no evidence that πληρωσαι translates the Aramaic קום (*qum*) meaning "establish, validate, or confirm" the Law. The LXX never uses πληρωσαι to render קום (*qum*) or cognates. Instead, the verb πληρωσαι renders the Hebrew מָלֵא (*ml'*), which means "fulfill." Matthew's use of the verb πληρωσαι is to "fill up a pattern," not "a one to one correspondence."[135] In Matthew 5:17 the issue is not Jesus' keeping the Law and the Prophets so that He might be a perfect human able

---

134. 4 Macc 1:34; 2:5–6, 9; 9:2; Josephus *Ant.* 17.151; O'Dowd, "Memory on the Boundary" and Vall, "An Epistemology of Faith," In *The Bible and Epistemology*. ed. Healy and Parry, 4, 22, 27, 30, 34.

135. Matt 1–3 use of "fulfill"; Kennard, *Messiah Jesus*, 17–18.

to die in our place. The issue is that the ethical lifestyle of Jesus' disciples (reflective of His teaching) is to fit within the Law and the Prophets, and contribute toward identifying the disciple with the kingdom.[136]

In Matthew 5:18, "For truly I say to you" emphasizes the connection with the preceding is very important. This "amen faithfully" emphasizes the connection with the preceding, showing why Jesus' disciples need to fit within the Law pattern in identifying themselves with the kingdom.[137]

The Law is still in effect such that even the smallest letters and stroke remain binding (Matt 5:18; Luke 16:17). The smallest Hebrew letter is *yod* or י.[138] The *yod* is the center of much rabbinic discussion as the smallest letter. For example, rabbi Honnah said that rabbi Acha described a tradition from rabbi Hoshaia.

> The letter yod which God took out of the name of Sarai our mother was given half to Sara and half to Abraham. A tradition of rabbi Hoshaia: The letter yod came and prostrated itself before God, and said, 'O eternal Lord, thou has rooted me out of the name of the holy woman.' The blessed God answered, 'Hitherto thou hast been in the name of a woman, and that in the end [viz. in Sarai]; but henceforth thou shalt be in the name of a man, and that in the beginning.' Hence is that which is written, 'And Moses called the name of Hoshea, Yehoshua.'[139]

This Jewish teaching is concluded "So you see not even the smallest letter can pass from the Bible."[140] The name *Yehoshua* is that of Joshua or Jesus, so *yod* matters if you say "Jesus."

When sages declared that Solomon threatened to uproot a *yod* from the Law, God responded that He would instead uproot a thousand Solomons.[141]

Likewise, every stroke (a very small extension on several Hebrew letters which distinguish these from similar ones [ה and ח, or ו and ן or ן, or ר and ד, or כ and ב]) is retained in the Law. Even Luke joins Matthew in identifying that "it is easier for heaven and earth to pass away than for one

---

136. Davies and Allison, *Matthew*, 1:485–487.

137. Davies and Allison, *Matthew*, 1:487–491.

138. I realize that the typeset *yod* is smaller than most instances of manuscript written *yod*, but the argument still holds up as is evident by the following manuscript quotes and second Temple discussion about *yod*.

139. *B. Sanh.* 20.3.

140. *B. Sanh.* 107ab; *p. Sanh.* 2.6.2; *Gen. Rab.* 47.1; *Ex. Rab.* 6.1; *Lev. Rab.* 19.2; *Num. Rab.* 18.21; *Song Rab.* 5.11.3–4.

141. *P. Sanh.* 2.6.2; *Ex. Rab.* 6.1.

stroke of a letter of the Law to fail" (Luke 16:17; Matt 5:18). The rabbis also speak directly to the absolute importance of every stroke in the text.

> It is written (Lev. 22:32) לֹא תְחַלְּלוּ אֶת־שֵׁם קָדְשִׁי "Ye shall not profane my holy name:" whosoever shall change ח into ה, destroys the world (for then לֹא תְחַלְּלוּ written with ה, makes this sense, "Ye shall not 'praise' my holy name.") It is written (Ps 150:6) כֹּל הַנְּשָׁמָה תְּהַלֵּל יָהּ "Let every spirit praise the Lord:" whosoever changeth ה into ח destroys the world. (It would read "Let every spirit profane the Lord.") It is written (Jer. 5:12), כִּחֲשׁוּ בַּיהוָה They lied against the Lord: whosoever changeth ב into כ destroys the world. (It would read "Like the Lord they lied.") It is written (Deut. 6:4) יְהוָה אֱלֹהֵינוּ יְהוָה ׀ אֶחָד The Lord our God is one Lord: he that changeth ד into ר destroys the world. (It would then read "The Lord our God is another [god]."). [142]

Much like the rabbis claiming that the world would be destroyed if strokes were changed, so to Jesus claimed that the strokes of the Law will be preserved until heaven and earth pass away (Matt 5:18). In a parallel construction, the descriptive event that heaven and earth *will pass away* (παρέλθῃ) is mentioned as contrast for not even the slightest letter or portion of a letter from the Law *will pass away* (παρέλθῃ).[143] Jesus affirms that what the Law says about all its minutia being preserved is still applicable for His Jewish disciples. Using the same verb *"pass away"* (παρέλθῃ) Jesus makes the same kind of parallel statement in Matthew 25:35 "Heaven and earth *will pass away*, but My words *will not pass away*." In both these statements, the ethical binding condition is in view and not merely a remembrance or preservation of words. The two "until" (ἕως) clauses in Matthew 5:18 designate the duration of the binding authority of the Law. The first "until heaven and earth pass away" means "until the end of the age" or "never, as long as the present world order persists." The second "until" (ἕως) clause "until all is accomplished" is parallel to the first. The word πάντα ("all" or "everything") probably refers to the prophecies in the Law or the whole O.T. that carry on through the whole eschatological kingdom program. An example of the Law's prophecies that have not happened yet would be that Israel will be re-gathered into the land in a responsive believing condition (Deut 30:3–10). So then until the present order of the world realizes the

---

142. *Tanchum* 1.1 (*Tanchum* is a compilation of midrashic comments which feature the *derashot* of Rabbi Tanhuma Bar Abba, a Palestinian *amora*. His principal teacher in *halakhah* and *aggadah* was Rabbi Huna; Lightfoot, *A Commentary on the New Testament from the Talmud and Hebraica*, 2:102.

143. Echoed by *y. Sanh.* 20c; *Halakhah* 2.6.

complete description of this O.T. program, the Law and the rest of the O. T. are still binding upon Israel.

This doctrine of the immutability of the *Torah* is consistent with the Jewish teaching that understood the *Torah* would in the future be understood better than it had to that point (Jer 31:33).[144] Therefore, Jesus' revisions and intensifications are consistent with the practice of Jewish rabbis affirming the *Torah*.[145]

In Matthew 5:19, "these commandments" refer to ethically binding material in the O. T., especially the Law.[146] In Matthew, ὅς ("this" or "these") never points forward, so Jesus does not include His commands of Matthew 5:20–7:27 within "these commands." However, it is possible that "these commands could include Matthew 5:3–16. Matthew elsewhere uses the verb cognate to "commandments" (ἐντολῶν) of Jesus' teaching in Matthew 28:20 (ἐνετειλάμην) but the noun as used in Matthew 5:19 is never used of Jesus' teaching. Much more likely than referring to the preceding discussion of Matthew 5:3–16, is the immediate context concerning the continued ethical relevance of the Law. Here it cannot be restricted to the Ten Commandments since all the O. T. program is still in effect within this age, even those funded by the minutia of the Law. Furthermore, the kind of commands that Jesus has in mind with regard to the Law, and these commands come from all over the Law, even several minor laws beyond the focus of the Ten Commands.

All these commandments are still binding so that they inform the disciple's life and teaching. The one who by lifestyle or teaching *annuls* or *loosens* (λύσῃ) one of the *least* (ἐλαχίστων) commandments has consequences in his life of being *least* (ἐλάχιστος) in the kingdom. Likewise, the one who keeps and teaches the commandments has the consequences of greatness in the kingdom. Least and greatness refer to gradation with the kingdom ranks as is evident elsewhere in Matthew (Matt 11:11; 18:1–4). Least and greatness probably does not refer to exclusion and inclusion, for Jesus is not placing the disciples under a standard of absolute perfection to be included; there is still a place for poverty of spirit and forgiveness. John Fisher concludes:

> No one can break or set aside even the least of the commands, without jeopardizing his future status (v. 19). As if this were not enough, he concluded this section (v. 20) by emphasizing that his followers needed to be even more observant and devout than

---

144. 1 Macc 4:46; *b. Šabb.* 151b; *Lev. Rab.* on 7:11–12 and 11:2; *Yal.* on Prov 9:2; and *Midr. Ps.* 146.7; Davies and Allison, *Matthew*, 1:492.

145. 11QTemple or Hillel introduction of the prozbul (*m. Seb.* 10.3–4).

146. Davies and Allison, *Matthew*, 1:496.

the Pharisees, going beyond even their exemplary practice of the traditions![147]

Jules Isaac summarizes this as, not only did Jesus "not overthrow the Law... or empty it of its content, but on the contrary I increase that content, so as to fill the Law to the brim."[148] So part of Jesus correct teaching of the Law includes the full implications and complete meaning of the spirit of the commandments. In effect, this new covenant spirit of the commandments is building a "fence around the Law," which would be indicative of the Aramaic for "fulfill" (קוּם/*qum*) and consistent with what earlier sages had done.[149]

Jesus points out that entrance into the kingdom requires a practice of righteousness warranting their place as surpassing the scribes and Pharisees (Matt 5:20). Jesus' criticism here is not that the scribes and Pharisees were not ethically good, but rather that they were not good enough. As the scribes and the Pharisees taught the Law from "Moses seat," they could encourage their society to be good, but their pattern of life did not match their teaching (Matt 23:2–3). They placed a burden upon the people that was too heavy for even them to comply, with such peripheral matters as tithing, clothes, baths, and monuments for the dead (Matt 23:4–36). Later Jesus confronts the negative qualities in the scribes and Pharisees that needed to be transcended. Their fundamental failure was a disregard for the weightier matters of the Law, such as kingdom, the Messiah, justice, mercy, and faithfulness (Matt 23:23; Luke 24:44; John 1:45; 12:34). In the Jewish leaders' radical externalizing of the Law they show themselves to be hypocrites, appearing to be righteous, while they themselves were full of robbery, self-indulgence and lawlessness. Jesus was instead calling for a proper valuing of the Law from the weightier matters down to the minutiae.

The righteousness that is required in the passage is not a past positional righteousness; for the passage is on *doing and teaching the Law*, and *looking ahead* to that which will in the future provide entrance into the kingdom. So to these Jewish disciples, Jesus identified that those who will enter the kingdom identify themselves by a radical practice of righteousness that surpasses the scribes and Pharisees' practice and teaching of the Law. Jesus has already shown Himself to be a practitioner of such righteousness (Deut 6:13–14; 8:3; Matt 4:4, 7, 10). Of course such a radical practice of righteousness is evident in the preceding beatitudes (Matt 5:6, 10) but also in Jesus

---

147. Davies and Allison, *Matthew*, 1:496.

148. Isaac, *Jesus and Israel*, 66.

149. *Pirke Avot* 1.2; cf. Lachs, Montefiore, Finkel, Friedlander, *The Jewish Sources of the Sermon on the Mount*; Lapide, *The Sermon on the Mount*.

subsequent teaching. Probably also the woe side to the Sermon on the Plain indicates what needs to be transcended: the rich, well fed, laughing life, of which all speak well (Luke 6:24-26).

It is in this light that Jesus' comments to the rich young ruler support in a practical manner what has been taught so far in the Sermon on the Mount (Matt 19:16-26; Mark 10:17-30; Luke 18:18-30).[150] Jesus is asked "What good thing shall I do that I may obtain everlasting life?" Here obtaining everlasting life is analogous to entering the kingdom and being saved (Matt 19:16, 23, 24, 25; Mark 10:17; Luke 18:18, 24-25).[151] Jesus' answer for this Jewish ruler is to keep the commandments of the Law. Jesus does not say to try to do the Law until you find out you can't and then throw yourself on the mercy of God; Jesus says keep the Law. This covenant nomism should not surprise us because it is what Jews repeatedly expected and Christian Jews for several centuries tried to live.[152] Since God alone is good, Jesus' answer points to God's commands. Even Mark and Luke (who do not emphasize the keeping of the Law as does Matthew) declare on Je-

---

150. Also corroborated by *Gos. of the Nazareans* 1, as recounted by Origen, *Comm. on Matt.* 15.14.

151. Second Temple sources support this point as well (1QS 4.6-8; CD 3.20; 4Q181 1.3-4; *1 En.* 37.4; 40.9; 58.3; 4 Macc 15.3; *Ps. Sol.* 3.12).

152. Jer 31:31-34 and Ezek 36:24-37:28; Jdt 5:17-21; 8:18-23; 10:5; 12:2, 9-19; 13:8 *Pr. Azar.* 6-14; *Jub.* 1:22-25; 2:17-33; 15:11-34; 1Q3 4, 5; 1QH 4, 5, 18; 4Q Shir Shalb; Tob 1.10-12; 4:12-13; 1 Macc 1:48; 2:15-28; 2 Macc 6:18-31; 7; 3 Macc 3.4-7; 4 Macc 5:1-6:30; *T. Jud.* 26; *Joseph and Aseneth*; Josephus, *J. W.* 1.145-147, 157-60, 651-655; 2.169-74; *Ant.* 13.252; 14.237; 17.149-67; 18.55-59, 261-4, 267, and 271; Wright, *Jesus and the Victory of God*, 301; Sanders, *Paul and Palestinian Judaism*; *Paul, the Law, and the Jewish People*; *Jewish Law from Jesus to the Mishnah*; and *Judaism: Practice and Belief 63 B.C.E.-66 C.E.*; and Dunn, *Jesus, Paul and the Law*; *Jews and Christians*; and *Paul and the Mosaic Law*, especially interesting is Wright's chapter "The Law in Romans 2," 131-150. Furthermore, Biblical texts like James, Matthew and Acts indicate that Jews and Jewish Christians were zealous for the Law. However, especially at focus is Matt 5:17-48 and 19:16-22; Saldarini *Matthew's Christian-Jewish Community* and Kennard, "The Way to Kingdom Salvation: Synoptics and the Law" a paper presented at ETS Mid-West regional meeting in March, 1992; "The Law in James" a paper presented at ETS Mid-West regional meeting in March, 1993; "Paul and the Law" a paper presented at ETS Mid-West regional meeting in March, 1996; *Biblical Covenantalism*, 3:15-161; Klijn, "The Study of Jewish Christianity," *NTS* 20 (1973-74): 419-31; Taylor, "The Phenomenon of Early Jewish Christianity: Reality or Scholarly Invention," *VC* 44 (1990): 313-34; Velasco and Sabourin, "Jewish Christianity of the First Centuries," *BTB* 6 (1976): 5-26; Klijn and Reinink, *Patristic Evidence for Jewish-Christian Sects*; Strecker, "Appendix 1: On the Problem of Jewish Christianity," In *Orthodoxy and Heresy in Earliest Christianity.* ed. Bauer, Kraft and Krodel, 257; Strecker, "The Kerygmata Petrou" in *The New Testament Apocrypha*. ed. Hennecke and Schneemelcher, 2:102-27, esp. 210-22 and 270-71; Strecker, *Das Judenchristentum in den Pseudoklementinen*; Schoeps, *Theologie und Geschichte des Judenchristentums* and his later abbreviated synthesis *Jewish Christianity*; van Voorst, *The Ascents of James*.

sus lips that keeping the Law is the way to everlasting life (Mark 10:17–19; Luke 10:25, 28; 18:18–20). Or as N. T. Wright describes it, the kingdom is obtained by following "Jesus in finding a new and radicalized version of Torah-observance."[153] Jesus further clarifies that the commandments He has in mind are those like the fifth, sixth, seventh, eighth, and ninth of the Ten Commandments, and Leviticus 19:18, all of which have financial overtones.[154] Jesus recognizes that the Law has as its primary focus on the loyalty relationship to the Lord (Matt 22:37–38) however, Jesus focuses on the human side of the Law here emphasizing the love relationship to others which shows whether one truly loves the Lord (Matt 22:39). Jesus has in mind here particularly those commandments that others can see and benefit from or at least not suffer under their violation. The last one, which is of course beyond the Ten Commandments, sums up all the minutia of relationships one to another in the Law (Matt 19:19; 22:39–40). The young man affirmed that under a legally tight reading of the Law, he had kept all these commands. However, he senses that in some way, he is still failing through a lack in his life. Whereas, in the Mark and Luke account, Jesus is the One who declares that the rich young ruler still lacks (Mark 10:21; Luke 18:22). Jesus offers him completion (which He has commanded in Matt 5:48) and obtaining his goal of the kingdom by means of a radical extrapolation of Leviticus 19:18; to really love your neighbor as yourself means sharing the proceeds of the sale of your possessions with those in need, the poor. Jesus does not develop the attitude of being willing to give to the poor; His emphasis is on doing: keeping the commandments, selling and giving (Matt 19:16, 17, 21). Giving up these possessions would enable the young man to follow Jesus in His itinerant ministry as Peter and the disciples had done (Matt 19:21, 27). Perhaps Matthew includes Jesus' statements of giving to the poor for purposes of the itinerant ministry, to address issues in his readers' lives such as: the poor from famine, or the itinerant dispersion of the Jewish Christians outside their homeland due to persecutions. If the young man had complied, he would have had kingdom treasure as the disciples were to receive (Matt 19:21, 29). Unfortunately, the young man was unwilling to pay the price of Jesus' radical Law demands. His departure provided an opportunity to instruct the disciples in the near impossibility of a rich person pursuing the kingdom. The primary focus of the Law is evident as serving God, rather

---

153. Wright, *Jesus and the Victory of God*, 307.

154. These commandments are from the broadly Protestant numbering of the Decalogue. The entire synoptic gospels list the fifth command last after the others, however, Luke 18:20 reverses the first two (giving the order as: seventh, sixth, eighth, ninth and fifth, and Mark inserts "do not defraud" after the ninth and before the fifth command. Neither Mark nor Luke has Lev 19:18 as does Matt.

than money (Matt 6:24). If a person does not generously provide for the needy around him, when he has excess means to provide for himself, then he does not love his neighbor as himself and is at risk of damnation. The fact that the young man went away with his riches shows that ultimately he was unwilling to serve God. In this case the kingdom is missed for failure to keep the Law.

At this point Peter chimes in and says "Behold, we have left everything and followed you; what gain will there be for us?" (Matt 19:27). Jesus reassures the disciples that they have complied with this radical paying the cost of the Law, and that they will have a unique role of judging Israel (Matt 19:28). In fact, everyone who has left house and family members for Christ's sake shall receive many times as much and will inherit everlasting life (Matt 19:29).[155]

Matthew 5–7; Jesus' Teaching of the Law

Interpretation of the Law is a political act of control in society. Small changes in behavior signify major changes in outlook, and mark one group off from another. The early Jewish- Christian community saw Jesus' kingdom teaching in a new flexible enough arrangement that appreciated their Jewish heritage (like new wine skins; Matt 9:16–17).[156] The agenda of this section is set primarily by what Jesus identified to be significant for kingdom and secondarily by how Jesus responded to questions and issues asked of Him. These questions asked expose rigidity of those around Jesus' context that will try to tear the garment or burst in rejection.

Jesus' emphasis is on the practice of keeping the Law for the way to the kingdom. Jesus is the supreme example of the fact that the one who keeps and teaches the Law shall be called great in the kingdom (Matt 5:19). Given ample opportunities, none of His opponents accused Him of violating the Law (Matt 26:59–60; Mark 14:55–56; John 8:46; 18:23). The Orthodox Jewish scholar Pinchas Lapide described Jesus as a traditional observant Jew.

> Jesus never and nowhere broke the law of Moses, nor did he in any way provoke its infringement-it is entirely false to say that he did...In this respect you must believe me, for I know my Talmud...This Jesus was as faithful to the law as I would hope to be. But I suspect that Jesus was more faithful to the law than I am-and I am an Orthodox Jew.[157]

155. Actually, the text sandwiches family members between houses and lands.

156. This text should not be seen as a cause to reject the Mosaic Law emphasis of Jesus teaching; Davies and Allison, *Matthew*, 2:112–117.

157. Lapide and Kung, "Jesus in Conflict," In *Signposts for the Future*. ed. Kung,

The second main portion of the Sermon on the Mount, the six "antithesis," contains the major section where Jesus teaches the Law. However, the pattern of "*and* (δὲ) I say unto you" is quite consistent with the structure of oral *torah* and the rabbinic form for teaching the Law.[158] John Fisher summarizes the rabbinical pattern as evident from Rabbi Ishmael (one of the foremost scholars cited in the *Talmud* and alive in Jesus day), "One might hear so and so. . .but there is a teaching to say that the words should be taken in *this* sense."[159] Then John Fisher concludes, "the point being made by the formula is that to some people Scripture appears to have a certain meaning, but that apparent meaning is an incomplete, or inaccurate understanding."[160] Thus, these statements are Jesus' authoritative rabbinical corrections as new covenant extensions of the Law. Normally, what followed was some form of the verb "to say" such as "there is a teaching to say," which leaves the oral tradition as the authority in the logic of the argument. *However, Jesus' authoritative, "I say," with the "I" emphatic in all the "I say" statements, utilizes the rabbinical pattern to present Jesus as the final or supreme scribal authority.*[161] In the rabbinic literature God is the one who occasionally undertakes these corrections.[162] So that Jesus is utilizing a prerogative normally associated with God. This approach goes beyond the above rabbinical pattern and the prophet pattern "Thus says the Lord," to highlight that Jesus is the authority. Therefore, the authority of Jesus in this teaching role is being emphasized throughout this section. It is quite clear that Jesus' teaching does not annul or loosen (λύσῃ) any teaching of the Law (Matt 5:19). As in Jesus' dealings with the rich young man, mandating that the young man radically keep the Law, so Jesus' authoritative teaching should be considered to be consistent enough with the Law to be teaching the Law (Matt 5:19). Since Jesus' teaching is calling the disciple to internalize the Law, it is helpful to remind oneself that the Law always has had a central concern for the Law being

---

74–75.

158. Bozker, *Judaism and the Christian Predicament*, 194; Fisher, "Jesus Through Jewish Eyes," a paper presented at the Evangelical Theological Society, Nov. 2003.

159. *Mekita* 3a, 6a; Fisher, "Jesus Through Jewish Eyes"; Schechter, "Rabbinic Parallels to the New Testament," In *Studies in Pharisaism and the Gospels*, ed. Abrahams, 1:16.

160. Fisher, "Jesus Through Jewish Eyes;" an early example of this practice is in: *Mekhilta* on Exod 19:20.

161. Dodd, *According to the Scriptures*, 109–10; France, *Jesus and the Old Testament*, 226; Craig Evans, "'Have You Not Read. . .?' Jesus' Subversive Interpretation of Scripture" in *Jesus Research*. ed. Charlesworth with Pokorny, 183, 189.

162. *Midrash Tanhuma*, Jer 4:2 on goodness; Daube, *The New Testament and Rabbinic Judaism*, 55–62.

internalized and not merely externally done (Deut 6:5–6; 10:16). These *halakah* join with the beatitudes as a virtue ethic and epistemology.[163]

Love

One of the last points of this section but the priority and summary of the Law is love (on the basis of the question in Matthew 22:36–40). Jesus identifies the greatest commandment in the Law as "You shall love the Lord your God with all your heart, and with all your soul, and with all your mind." Such a love for God should captivate one's whole being. Such a focus on love resonates with the Jewish traditional understanding that the Love of God is the greatest commandment (Deut 6:4–5; Luke 10:26–27).[164] The second command is like it in loving your neighbor as yourself (Matt 22:39; Luke 10:27).[165] This love emphasis is so critical that the whole Law and the prophets depend upon (or are suspended from) this backbone of love (Matt 22:40). Paul Moser considers that these love commitments warrant and focus all philosophical tasks.[166] *As an epistemic virtue, such love commitment transforms a person's inclination to accept and include those loved and the perspectives held by God and them.* This whole section of Jesus as Law teacher should then be seen as explaining aspects of this love relationship. The affirmation of love as the core does not deny any of the specifics of the Law for Jesus is recognized as teaching the Law correctly and thus not annulling any (Mark 12:32–34). In fact, it is the very same answer a lawyer had earlier given to him when Jesus asked him to summarize the Law (Luke 10:26–27). An affirmation that this so identifies one as not far from the Kingdom (Mark 12:34). A practicing of this radical love commitment obtains the inheritance of everlasting life as sons of the divine Father (Matt 5:45; Luke 10:25, 28). It is a common occurrence to love those who love you back, for even tax-gatherers and Gentiles do this. Such a mutually beneficial love has a way of funding the tradition of love within the community and hate beyond the community (Matt 5:44).[167] The Law was clearly more radical

---

163. Adams, "The Problem of Total Devotion," in *Rationality, Religious Belief, and Moral Commitment.* ed. Audi and Wainwright, 94; Nygren, *Agape and Eros*, 216; Wainwright, "Obedience and Responsibility" in *The Wisdom of the Christian Faith.* ed. Moser and McFall, 68.

164. *Jub.* 20.7–9; *T. Iss.* 5.2; *B. Šabb.* 31a; *b. Ber.* 63a; Josephus, *Contra Apionem* 2.206.

165. Rabbi Akiba considered love of neighbor in Lev 19:18 to be the great commandment (*Sifra Qed.* 4.200.3.7; *Gen. Rab.* 24.7); *T. Iss.* 5.2; *T. Benj.* 3.1–5.

166. Moser, *Jesus and Philosophy*, 14.

167. For example, Qumran, the Essenes and other Jews maintained a love within the

than that, in its command to love sojourners (Lev 19:19, 33–34; 22:39).[168] Jesus radically extends the concept of neighbor, in the parable of the Good Samaritan, to any who show mercy (Luke 10:29–37). Even a despised individual such as a Samaritan[169] who inadvertently happens upon someone in his travels is a neighbor. The issue of compassion takes precedence over issues of ritual cleanliness.[170] The compassion shown costs: time, effort, and money, but it was right to recover the man from his plight. Jesus commands the resistant lawyer to follow the same pattern and to show mercy to others who can never repay his service. However, among Jesus' disciples He commands an even more radical extension of love to include even personal enemies who persecute you (Matt 5:44).[171] This love of one's enemies should include doing good deeds to them and praying for your persecutors (Matt 5:44; Luke 6:27–28). Jesus showed a prime example of loving and praying for the welfare of His persecutors during His crucifixion (Luke 23:34). To evidence such broad love to one's enemies is to evidence a quality of sonship to the Father, for the Father provides sun and rain for both righteous and unrighteous alike (Matt 5:45).[172] The disciple is not to settle on common mutuality but is to seek perfect righteousness in evidencing love as the Father is perfect (Matt 5:48). Such perfection would be maturity, following Jesus and full obedience to the Father's will (Matt 5:48 in its context; 19:21).

---

community and a hate to outsiders (1QS 1.4, 10–11; 2.4–9; 9:21–23; 1QM 4.1–2; 15.6; 1QH 5.4; *b. Ber.* 33a; *b. Sanh.* 92a; Josephus, *J. W.* 2.139). The commitment is present in rabbinic Judaism (*Sipra* on Lev. 19:18 and *Mek.* on Exod 21:35) and outside Jewish tradition (Polybius 18.37.7; Hesiod, *Op.* 342–3, Solon, frag. 1.3–5; Plato, *Tim.* 17d–18a; *Rep.* 375c; *Meno* 71e; Tacitus, *Hist.* 5.5–6; Davies and Allison, *Matthew*, 1:549–552.

168. Other O.T. and Second Temple texts which anticipate Jesus expansive love include also: Exod 23:4–5; 1 Sam 24:17–19; 2 Sam 19:6 LXX; 1 Kgs 3:11; Job 31:29 (Eusebius, *Dem. ev.* 1.6); Ps 7:3–5; Prov 24:17–18 (*m. 'Abot* 4.19); 24:29; 25:21–22; Jer 29:7; Jon 4:10–11; *Test. Iss.* 7.6; *Jub.* 7.20; 20.2; 36.4; Philo, *Decal.* 108–10.

169. There is antipathy between Jew and Samaritans in this second temple Judaism (John 8:48; Sir 50:25–26; Josephus, *Ant.* 18.2.2; *B.T. San.* 57a, where a Samaritan is not worthy of receiving aid from a Jew).

170. There is no evidence in Jesus' parable that the Jew is dead (as is developed in *Mish Berak.* 7.7), but these religious leaders do not even want to check his condition, but rather avoid the injured.

171. Jewish parallels include: *Ep. Arist.* 207, 227, 232; Philo, *De. virt.* 116–18; *T. Gad.* 6.1–7; *T. Zeb.* 7.2–4; *T. Iss.* 7.6; *T. Benj.* 4.2–3; 2 *Bar.* 52.6; 2 *En.* 50.4; *b. Ketub.* 68a; *m. 'Abot* 1.12; 2.11; 4.3; 5.16. Early Christian literature echoes this love of enemies: Acts 7:60; Rom 12:14, 17–20; 1 Cor 4:12–13; 1 Thess 5:15; 1 Pet 3:9; Polycarp, *Ep.* 12.3; Irenaeus, *Adv. haer.* 3.18.5; *Ps.—Clem. Hom.* 3.19; *Ep. Apost.* 18; 2 *Clem.* 13.4; Justin, 1 *Apol.* 14.3; Athenagoras, *Supp.* 12.3.

172. Several rabbinic texts affirm that God is good to the just and the unjust (*b. Ta'an.* 7a; *Mek.* on Exod 18.12; *Pesiq. R.* 48.4; *b. Sanh.* 111a; 2 *Bar.* 12.1–4).

The specific issues that make up the rest of this sermon flow out from this commitment to love.

Murder and Reconciliation

Jesus begins His legal teaching with the sixth law of the Ten Commandments, "You shall not commit murder" (Exod 20:13; Deut 5:17) and the consequences of murder being judgment before the court (Matt 5:21). Internalization of the Law would certainly exclude angry plots and attempts to defraud another. Jesus' authoritative teaching extends the Law by going to the source and rooting out all anger, consistent with Jewish tradition[173] and commanding a zeal for reconciliation (Matt 5:22-26). Jesus forbids anger (ὀργιζόμενος) and any verbal expression which begins to show itself like calling a brother a fool.[174] In this context a brother could be a family member or a fellow traveler heading toward the kingdom (Matt 4:18, 21; 5:9). The Aramaic word רכע transliterated as *raca* means "fool, imbecile, or blockhead." The Greek word Μωρέ (*mōre*) would also mean "fool," but for the Hebrew speaker it might also have had overtones of "apostasy, rebellion and wickedness," through the Hebrew word מרה (*mrh*).[175] Since both words mean fool, the judgment should be seen as the same: eschatological condemnation, which excludes one from the kingdom. Within this framework, where one's legal religious duty included offering sacrifices at the altar (for recovering from sin as well as for gratitude), the more important duty is to live peacefully with all. Such peacemaking as to be reconciled with a brother takes precedence over one's sacrificial duty (Matt 5:24-25).[176] However,

---

173. *T. Gad.* 4.1-7; *Tg. Ps.-J.* and *Tg. Onq.* on Gen 9.6; *Tg. Ps.-J.* on Deut 5.21; *Der. Er. Rab.* 11.13; *m 'Ahot* 4.21; *b. Qidd.* 39b; *b. Ned.* 22b; *b. Pesah.* 66a-b; 1QS 6.26; 7.2-4; *Sifre Deut.* to Deut 19:10-11 and 22:13; *T. Soṭah* 5.11; *b. Kidd* 41a; *Tosefta Dereth Eretz* vol. 2 quoted from Flusser, *Judaism and the Origins of Christianity*, 117; Vermes, *The Religion of Jesus the Jew*, 31.

174. Similar to Sir 28.3-4.

175. Carson, "Matthew," In *The Expositor's Bible Commentary*, 8:149.

176. The Jewish practice would have sacrifice complete the reconciliation process (Lev 1-7; *Ep. Aristeas* 170-1; *Sir.* 34.18-19; 35.12; Philo, *Special Laws* 1.236f.). Continuing this practice, Matthew 5:23-24 and Acts 18:18; 21:23-27 supports Jewish Christian participation in Jewish sacrifices. In contrast, *The Gospel of the Ebionites* 7 as recorded by Epiphanius, *Panarion* 30.16.4-5 has Jesus condemn such practice of Jewish sacrifices. Of course, the Law prescribes the Levitical sacrifices for Israel (Lev 1-7, 16-17:9). Additionally, the O.T. describes the kingdom era under the Messiah as continuing to practice these sacrifices that atone (Jer 33:18; Ezek 43:18-46:24), though the Heb 10:1-8 ceases the sacrifices for now for any new covenant people who would be disturbed by their reminder, and *Lev. Rab.* 9.7, written four centuries after the destruction of the Temple (5th cent. A.D.), ceases the ritual sacrifices in the Messianic kingdom.

when reconciliation is complete then the kingdom bound Jew should bring his sacrifice to the altar for covenantal purposes like atonement, forgiveness, and peace (Lev 1–7). This complies with Judaism's valued piety and ethical behavior as more significant than issues of formal observance of religion.[177] *As an epistemic virtue, reconciliation hears the other without excluding them and then tries to work for a community agreement in which both sides recognize their inclusion together.* Elsewhere, Jesus underscores the need to reconcile to maintain a community heading toward the kingdom (Matt 6:14–15; 18:21–35). To emphasize the urgency of reconciliation, Jesus uses a standardized story (elsewhere used in Luke 12:58 to warn Israel of its eschatological judgment) to emphasize that judgment will be meted out to the fullest extent. In this context at least debtors' prison is intended with its bondage until the full debt was paid but there may be a parallel with verse 22 which would mean that fullest judgment might entail eschatological condemnation, which excludes one from the kingdom. Jesus has taken the Law (which forbids angry plots and attempts to defraud another) and radically extended it under His own authority (consistent with Jewish tradition) to forbid anger and to mandate a zeal for reconciling with others. Jesus' teaching is a consistent Jewish extension of the Law.

Adultery and Lust

The second point of the Law that Jesus takes up is the seventh law of the Ten Commandments, "You shall not commit adultery" (Matt 5:27; Exod 20:14; Deut 5:18). In the Law, the Hebrew word נאף (*n'p*) and the Greek word μοιχεύσεις mean "an illicit sexual relationship." Internalization of the Law would exclude any mental plots of illicit sexual relationships. Such an exclusion of adulterous eye and heart is common in the Jewish traditions.[178] Jesus' authoritative teaching extends the Law's idea of adultery in one's heart (consistent with Jewish tradition) to *looking* upon a woman to *desire* her. The word βλέπων constitutes a simple *look*. The word ἐπιθυμῆσαι means to *desire* even in a positive manner (Matt 13:17) but here it means *lust*. The simple act of empirically looking upon, to lust seems to carry simplicity of

---

177. 1 Sam 15:22; Hos. 6:6; *T. Isaac* 4.18–22, 39; *m. B. Qam.* 9.12; *b. Yoma* 87a.

178. Tob 4.12–13; *Jub.* 20.4–6; 1QpHab 5.7; 1QS 1.6; CD 2.16; 11QTS 59.14; Josephus, *Contra Ap.* 2.183, 217; *Yoma* 29a; *T. Jud.* 14.1–4; *T. Iss.* 7.2; *T. Reub.* 4.8; *b. Nid.* 13b, bar.; *Šabb.* 64ab; *Lev. Rab.* 23.12; *Mek.* of R. Simeon 111; *Jub.* 20.4; *T. Isaac* 4.53; *Sifre* on Num. 15:39; Sextus, *Sent.* 233; *Pesiq. R.* 24.2; Davies and Allison, *Matthew,* 1:522; Montefiore *Rabbinic Literature and Gospel Teachings,* 41 for quote of these texts; Vermes, *The Religion of Jesus the Jew,* 32–33; "A Summary of the Law by Flavius Josephus," *NT* 24(1982): 303.

internalization that extends beyond the Law but is consistent with it. Such a view censors internalization of lust, such as occurs even when there may not be a woman present, like internet porn or fantasization. Then Jesus makes his new covenant extension of the Law; if a body part such as an eye or a hand causes you to stumble, excise it[179] so that you do not end up perishing in hell. The concept of hell (γέενναν) is the eschatological place of judgment modeled after the valley of *Hinnem*, once associated with pagan rites of Molech, but in Jesus' day it was used as a rubbish pit with smoldering fires. Stumbling (σκανδαλίζει) is the sin of falling away in Lawlessness and unbelief (Matt 13:21, 41–42, 57–58; 18:6–9). Those who stumble over Jesus are condemned in judgment. Persecution or affliction or perhaps restricting access to Jesus can set up the possibility of stumbling. Jesus' disciples experienced a temporary betrayal (σκανδαλισθήσεσθε) when Jesus was taken and they all fled (Matt 26:31, 33). Usually such stumbling was not temporary, for those who fell were damned like: Satan, Pharisees, Nazareth occupants, and eschatological traitors (Matt 13:57–58; 15:12; 16:23; 24:10). The strong language presents an extreme insistence upon abstaining from any form of mental adultery. *As an epistemic virtue, Jesus insists upon full integrity of thought, affection, and action.* The repetition of "stumbling" and "hell" shows that compliance with Jesus' radical extension of the Law is imperative. If one permits unbelief or lawlessness in his life (permitting: desiring lust concerning a woman), then that person is in serious threat of damnation.

---

179. The removal of body parts for convicted criminals was sometimes done (Deut 25:11–12; Judg 16:21; Josephus, *Vita* 171–173, 177; *J. W.* 2.642–644; *b. Pes.* 57b) but it is probably not encouraging maiming but rather the seriousness to make sure that you miss hell (cf. Ps.-Clem. *Rec.* 7.37; Origen, *Comm. on Matt.* 15:1). Amputated body parts were thought to be restored to the righteous in the resurrection (2 Macc 7.11). The point here is that Jesus' appeal, which identifies adultery with heading for damnation, underscores the graver seriousness of adultery over the Law's capital punishment practice. Some may appeal to Jesus activity in John 8 or 4 to soften the judgment on an adulteress. However, John 7:53–8:11 is not in the earliest or best manuscripts and if one includes it here its presence distracts from the continuing argument of John. The same could be said for the other placement in the text (after John 7:36 or 7:44 or 21:24 or Luke 21:38), so I do not consider that this pericope is Scripture. There is also something awkward and perhaps a frame-up for only one participant to be accused. In the other situation with the woman at the well, though Jesus knows her through prophecy to be a serial divorcee and an adulteress (John 4:18), Jesus uses the opportunity to bring this non-Jew and her village into the Kingdom way. To bring her to trial would require witnesses catching her in the act; instead, Jesus has her convert to the kingdom.

Divorce

The next point of Law that Jesus considers is the permission and process of divorce (Deut 24:1–4; Matt 5:31). Deuteronomy permits the husband to divorce his wife if he has found some indecency (עֶרְוַת/'rwt) in his wife. This indecency (עֶרְוַת) is best taken as *indecent exposure* or public nakedness (Gen 9:22–23; 42:9, 12; Exod 20:26; 28:42) following the near context parallel that excrement needs to be buried and not left *exposed*, Deut 23:13–14; עֶרְוַת). In this Deuteronomy instance, עֶרְוַת/'rwt cannot mean sexual immorality, for the punishment of sexual immorality is not being sent away in divorce but rather capital punishment (Lev 18:6–19; 20:11–21). In this Deuteronomy instance, legal dissolution of marriage is permitted for indecency. This legal framework was taken in divergent views in Jesus' day. Qumran judged that divorce and remarriage was illicit in all circumstances because God *made* the "male and female" and "they *became* one flesh."[180] In mainstream Judaisms, opinion was divided among the school of Shammai, which permitted divorce with the possibility of remarriage to another for gross indecency,[181] and Hillel, who permitted divorce for real or imagined offenses, including an improperly cooked meal. For example, the Hillelite rabbi Aiba permitted divorce and remarriage to another even for a case of a roving eye for pretty women, the sin Jesus has just condemned in Matthew 5:28–29.[182] Josephus even permitted divorce "for any causes whatsoever."[183] Others tried to diminish divorce as a practice because they saw its abuse to be so devastating.[184] These views show a permissive oral tradition in Judaism.

The discussion of divorce was conducted concerning a male perspective in all the Biblical texts except perhaps Mark 10:12 where there is some concession to non-Palestinian circumstances where a woman could more easily divorce her husband.[185] Divorce was envisioned as a possibility for Jewish

---

180. CD 4:21 justifies no divorce on the basis of original design, the pattern in the ark during the flood, and the command for the king not to multiply wives in Deut 17:17 which is interpreted as no second marriage while wife is still alive; because the ensuing defilement of another in intimate sexual union would separate the previous marriage partner (1QApGen. 20.15 Abrahams prayer against loosing Sarah to Pharaoh), thus an argument against polygamy in 11QTemple 57:17–19; Tosato, "The Law of Leviticus 18:18: A Reexamination," *CBQ* 46(1984): 199–214.

181. These followed this interpretation: Philo, *Spec. leg.* 3.30; Josephus, *Ant.* 4.253; *Sipre* on Deut 24:1.

182. M. Gittin 9:10 or 90b.

183. Josephus, *Ant.* 8.23.

184. B. Gittim 90b; m. Gittim 9.10; Sifre Deut. 269.

185. *Elephantine* papyri in Bammel, "Markus 10:11f und das jüdische Eherecht," *ZNW* 61(1970): 95–101; and Philo, *Spec. Laws* 3.30 in Treggiari, *Roman Marriage,*

women living at the colony at Elephantine in Egypt in the fifth century B.C., because a number of Aramaic marriage contracts mention it explicitly,[186] but the evidence for such a practice in Israel itself is almost nonexistent.[187]

Jesus stands out starkly condemning most of these views as He through a new covenant manner extends the Law to the original design. Matthew 5:31 begins with δέ, implying that the preceding argument continues; divorce is the moral equivalent to adultery. For Jesus, God's design sets the priority: therefore do not divorce or try any other form of separation because God has joined the two together (Gen 2:24; Matt 19:3–6; Mark 10:5–9).[188] Such an argument follows Hillel logical rule seven; the total context of Gen 2:24 must be considered for exegesis.[189] Jesus admits that the Mosaic process of divorce was permitted for those who have hardness of heart. Jesus was not annulling the Law as some of the divergent views in the first century context evidence that they annulled the Law. That is, Jesus permits those who are willfully rebellious from God's design to have a legal loophole which permits divorce, but such an option is precarious at best. However, Jesus transcends the issue of the legal and permissible, to a higher order of what is right by God's design. *As an epistemic virtue, Jesus orients his disciples to the fact that God's design and the best option should direct thought, commitments, and lifestyle, not what is permitted.*

The remainder of Jesus' teaching on divorce reflects a moral problem which is comparable to adultery. The statements in Matthew 19 and Mark 10 are roughly equivalent in emphasizing design priority over legal permission. The statements in Matthew 5:32 and Luke 16:18 come in contexts that emphasize the binding nature of the Law. Three passages make it clear that the husband commits adultery (μοιχεύσεις) if he remarries after divorce (Matt 19:9; Mark 10:11). Mark 10:12 clarifies that the wife also commits adultery (μοιχεύσεις) if she remarries after divorce. Furthermore, if anyone would happen to marry a divorced woman, then even this previously

---

441–46.

186. Cowley, *Aramaic Papyri of the Fifth Century B.C.*, 45; Fitzmyer, "The Matthean Divorce Texts and Some New Palestinian Evidence," TS 37(1976): 205; "A Re-Study of an Elephantine Aramaic Marriage Contract (AP 15)," In *Near Eastern Studies in Honor of William Foxwell Albright*. ed. Goedicke, 137–68; Kraeling, *The Brooklyn Museum Aramaic Papyri*, 142–43 (BMAP 2:9), 206–207 (BMAP 7:25); compare AP 9:8.

187. There is only one instance, Josephus, *Ant.* 15.7.10.

188. Some claim that Jesus' absolute prohibition echoes the view of Tob 6:18 "she was destined for you [to be with in marriage] from eternity," however, Jesus' rationale merely goes back to the design of creation (Gen 1:27; 2:24); Fitzmyer, "The Matthean Divorce Texts and Some New Palestinian Evidence," TS 37(1976): 203.

189. *Sipra* intr 13; *'Abot R. Nat.* 37; *Sukkah* 32a; Ellis, *The Old Testament in Early Christianity*, 130–2.

unmarried individual would commit adultery (μοιχεύσεις) in marrying a divorcee (Matt 5:32; Luke 16:18). Unlike the Mark and Luke passages which have no exception clauses, the two Matthew passages do have exception clauses to the effect of "except for the cause of unchastity" (πορνείας). For example, Matthew 5:32 says that a husband who divorces his wife except for the cause of unchastity (πορνείας) makes her commit adultery (μοιχεύσεις).

The word πορνείας includes every kind of unlawful sexual intercourse including the complete semantic field of μοιχεύσεις.[190] For anyone who is married, the two words are synonymous; a married person who does πορνείας does μοιχεύσεις and a person who does μοιχεύσεις does πορνείας. The illicit sexual act speaks of a deed, not a characteristic of life (such as being a perpetual adulterer or prostitute). However, acts described by these words are sexual immorality in which the Law required the participants to be executed under capital punishment (Lev 18:6–19; 20:11–21). That is, the sin in the Law's exception clause (indecency or public nakedness) is not as grave a sin as sexual immorality (πορνείας), since divorce is permitted.

The exception clauses in Matthew do not render divorce acceptable. Remember that the whole discussion of divorce and remarriage has been rendered equal to adultery (by the δέ; Matt 5:31), and rebellious by the disregard for God's design and involvement in making the couple one flesh (Matt 19:3–6; Mark 10:5–9). There is no substantial reason for Matthew's exception clause to be read into Mark or Luke, since they are themselves inspired Scripture. Mark and Luke have not included an exception clause, and their texts are understandable without any exception clause. Therefore, any remarriage of a divorced person is an act of adultery for both persons being married (Mark 10:10–12; Luke 16:18). Thus, the exception clause in Matthew 5:32 and 19:9 does not prevent adultery in a remarriage situation if the divorce was motivated by immorality. Remember Jesus' ethic on this point of the Law is more restrictive than the Law in its appeal.[191] Therefore, Jesus' exception clause cannot be softening and expanding the Law's exception clause. If Jesus is saying that it is acceptable to divorce a wife for her sexual immorality, then He is denying several commands of the Law that required capital punishment (Lev 18:6–19; 20:11–21) and rendering Himself under His own declaration to be least in the kingdom and therefore self-contradictory (Matt 5:18–19; Mark 10:11–12; Luke 16:18). Not only does the prior context call for a higher ethic but the subsequent context shows that the disciples got the point that a higher ethical order was demanded, as evidenced by their statement, "if the

---

190. In Matt 15:19 and Mark 7:21 these words are synonyms; cf. *BDB*, 528 and 699.

191. Jesus appeals to: God's design, God's involvement in making the couple one flesh, and Moses' permission to accommodate moral hardness of heart (Matt 19:4–8).

relationship of the man with his wife is like this, it is better not to marry" (Matt 19:10). Furthermore, Jesus affirms the disciples in their conclusion, that some for various reasons will prefer celibacy. Those who prefer celibacy have it as a gift (Matt 19:11) even though it might have been a condition from birth or a condition of employment or a condition for kingdom service (Matt 19:12). Jesus concludes His discussion of celibacy by urging those able to accept the preference of a celibate life to accept such a life. So that, this higher ethic is not encouraging divorce, but rather warning that a person does an adultery deed if they divorce and remarry (Matt 5:32; 19:9). That is, one who remarries after divorce does the deed of sexual immorality (πορνείας). Therefore, the exception clause describes that a divorcee commits sexual immorality (μοιχεύσεις) in the act of remarriage, except in the case that they have done so previously, in which case an additional act of sexual immorality does not render them immoral for they are already in an immoral condition. This interpretation permits the inspired passages without the exception clause to declare that remarriage is sexual immorality (μοιχεύσεις; Mark 10:11–12; Luke 16:18), and the whole travesty of divorce and remarriage to be a violation of sexual immorality (μοιχεύσεις), unless they have already violated sexual immorality (πορνείας; Matt 5:32; 19:9). In English the phrase is: "Anyone who divorces his wife makes her commit adultery (μοιχεύσεις) provided she has not already committed adultery (πορνείας)." The verbal construction of the consequences of the divorce force the divorced wife into the act of adultery (μοιχεύσεις). This does not mean that a divorced wife becomes a prostitute and starts taking in clients. The grammatical description of the consequences are an act of adultery and not necessarily a characteristic lifestyle of being an adulteress. In this first century context, for the average divorced woman to make her way virtually requires her to remarry (unless she has significant wealth) in order to deal with her vulnerability and come within the oversight of a man in a male dominated society (Ruth 1:20–21; Isa 1:23; 10:2; 54:4; Jas 1:27). The act of remarriage would be an act of adultery (Mark 10:12). Or perhaps this making her commit adultery (μοιχεύσεις) builds off the preceding verses which discuss the committing of adultery (μοιχεύσεις) through the process of internalized lust (Matt 5:28). That is, in the same way that a man may lust after a woman, prompted by the visual stimulation, so a divorced woman may lust after a man, prompted by the experience of the sexual intimacy which marriage brought and divorce removed. The exception clause fits, in that if she has already done the deed of adultery (πορνείας) in mind or body then she is not somehow in her divorce being forced to do adultery (μοιχεύσεις) by the divorce; she already did adultery (πορνείας) by her own choice.

Oaths

The next point which Jesus takes up is vows, insisting that *Jesus' followers should be outstandingly honest, and thus need no oaths.* Jesus summarized the ancient teaching on vows to be "you shall not make false vows, but shall fulfill your vows to the Lord" (Lev 19:12; Num 30:2; Deut 23:21; Matt 5:33). Likewise, oaths taken in the name of the Lord were binding and perjury was strongly condemned in the Law (Exod 20:7; Lev 19:12; Deut 19:16–19). Every oath contained an affirmation or promise and an expressed or implied appeal to God as the guarantor, which made the oath binding. Once Yahweh's name was invoked the vow was a debt that had to be paid. To protect from taking the Lord's name in vain, oaths began to refer to other things than God Himself. By Jesus' time, a sophisticated casuistry had developed in order to assess which oaths were binding and which were not. This casuistry appears to have been the result of rabbis' fighting abuses of vows among the masses.[192] Their way of fighting abuses was to develop ways of differentiating between the binding and non-binding oaths. Under their casuistry, non-binding oaths included swearing by heaven, by earth, by Jerusalem, by the temple, by the altar, and by one's own head (Matt 5:34–35; 23:16–22).[193] On the other hand, binding oaths included swearing by Yahweh, toward Jerusalem, by the gold of the temple, and the offering on the altar. Such techniques encouraged evasive oaths, and therefore deception. If oaths, designed to encourage truthfulness and greater certainty (as when God swears by an oath; Gen 15), became occasions for clever lies and causistical deceit, then Jesus abolishes oaths consistent with early Jewish integrity (Matt 5:34–37).[194]

---

192. Lieberman, *Greek in Jewish Palestine*, 115–143.

193. CD Geniza A 15.1–5; 11Q19 53.11–54.7; *m. Šebu.* 4.13; *m. Ned.* 1.3; *m. Sanh.* 3.2.

194. Jas 5:12. This stand is similar to the rabbinic teaching in: Eccl 5.4; Sir 23.9; and *Baba Metzia* 49a. It is also similar to that of the Essenes, except for only their entrance oath; cf. Josephus, *Ant.* 15.370-71; *J. W.* 2.134-5, 139; Philo, *Omn. prob. lib.* 84; Stoaeus, *Eclogae* 1.41.44. However, the Dead Sea scrolls are ambiguous on the issue (11QTemple 53–54; CD 7.8; 9.9–12; 15–16; 1QS 5.8; 6.27). Certain Jewish texts identify doubling, as it appears here in Matthew 5:37 "yes, yes" and "no, no" as a legitimate oath (*b. Šebu.* 36a; *2 En.* 49.1–2), but that clearly is opposed to the sense of Jesus' command here. Deliberate abstaining from oaths (like Jesus advocates) is part of integrity within Judaism, wherever possible (Philo, *Omnis probus* 84; *Spec. Leg.* 2.2; *Decal.* 84; Josephus, *J. W.* 2.135). There is also some aversion to oaths in the Non-Jewish world (Sophocles, *OC* 650; Cicero, *Pro Balbo* 5, Plutarch, *Quaest. Rom.* 2.127d; *Mor.* 46A; Epictetus, *Ench.* 33.5; Marcus Aurelius, *Antonius* 3.5; Diogenes Laertius 8.22; Iamblichus, *Vit. Pyth.* 47). The early church followed this no oath policy but said it as: "let your yes be yes and your no no" (Justin, *1 Apol.* 16.5; Clement of Alexandria, *Strom.* 5.99.1; 7.67.5; *Const. Apost.* 5.12.6; *Ps.-Clem. Hom.* 3.55; 19.2; Eusebius, *Dem. ev.* 3.3; Epiphanius, *Haer.* 19.6.2; *2 Jehu* 43).

When Jesus is charged to speak under oath, He refuses and simply replies "You have said so" (Matt 26:63-64).

Jesus recognizes that oaths are used and does not condemn them or contradict his higher ethic (Matt 23:20-22). The use of oaths indicates that all oaths are related to God and therefore binding through a logical analogy like Hillel's seventh logical rule.[195] Swearing by heaven is swearing by the throne of God and by Him who sits upon it (Matt 5:34; 23:22). Swearing by earth is swearing by the footstool of God's feet and thus by God (Matt 5:35). Swearing by or toward Jerusalem is swearing by God since it is the city of the Great King (Matt 5:35). Swearing by the Temple is swearing by the God who dwells within the Temple (Matt 23:21). Furthermore, God and the Temple are more important than the gold of the Temple, which the Pharisees and scribes saw as binding, because God and the Temple sanctify the Temple gold (Matt 23:16-17). The altar is more important than the offering on the altar, because God and the altar sanctify the offering (Matt 23:18-19). So the supposedly non-binding oath of swearing by the altar actually includes the binding oath of swearing by the offering within it (Matt 23:20). All these casuistic oaths are actually binding and obligate the one who swears them because they are actually swearing by Yahweh.

The issue in Matthew 5:34-37 is forbidding oaths where there is abuse; He is not annulling the Law. God binds Himself by an oath when He established covenant grants (Gen 9:9-11; 15:17-18). The Law even requires Israel to vow to obey Yahweh in suzerainty treaty (Deut 27). Jesus is not absolutely excluding all oaths; He even testifies under oath (Matt 26:63-64).[196] What the Law permits as a way to evidence the truth, Jesus forbids, calling His disciples to a higher standard than the Law (Matt 5:34, 37). So, like the previous issue on divorce, the divine priority of simple honesty transcends oaths in the disciples' lives.

Jesus calls his disciples to say that which is within their own control. Therefore, you should not make an oath by your head for you cannot even change the color of your hair (Matt 5:36). Rather a simple statement of yes or no is the best way to reflect honesty (Matt 5:37). Any further complexity that might confuse a simple honest answer is from the evil one,[197] and thus identified with the way to hell in contrast to the kingdom.

---

195. *Sipra* intr 13; *'Abot R. Nat.* 37; *Sukkah* 32a; Pool, *The Traditional Prayer Book for Sabbath and Festivals*, 128-30.

196. Paul also testifies under oath (Acts 26:63-64).

197. The article (τοῦ) before evil (πονηροῦ) indicates a person (Matt 4:1; 5:39; 6:13; 13:38).

Insisting on Legal Rights or Generosity

The next point of the Law which Jesus takes up is the issue of insisting on legal rights, which He replaces with generosity, even if it dishonors the giver. He quotes the *lex talionis* passage of "an eye for an eye, and a tooth for a tooth" (Matt 5:38). The *lex talionis* context provides the legal framework to guide the judges for any crime to an appropriate punishment, excluding excessive abuse or leniency (Exod 21:22–24; Lev 24:20; Deut 19:21).[198] Jesus calls his disciples to transcend the Law by not insisting on their legal rights by not resisting the evil one (Matt 5:39a). *As an epistemic virtue, especially in contexts of threat from power, the disciple should be generous to diffuse risk.* Out from this general teaching Jesus applies illustrations that explain it.[199] For example, if you as an individual are slapped[200] by someone who is evil, you are to turn the other cheek, thus permitting a continuation of the violation of your own rights (Matt 5:39). In the second Temple culture, such abuse or being taken advantage of would mean dishonor. However, Jesus' disciples were to allow themselves to be dishonored if it provided an opportunity to be generous instead. Jeremias identified that such a blow to the right cheek would likely be given to Jesus' disciples as they follow Him and are considered heretics by the Jewish leadership.[201] Furthermore, if anyone attempts to press a legal claim against you (as in a suit for your shirt or the Roman impressments commanding civilians to carry luggage of military personnel a Roman mile), then be doubly generous and give more than is asked (Matt 5:40–41). So the disciple is to give up his outer cloak as well instead of fighting the legal action, even though this cloak is a possession (Exod 22:26; Deut 24:13).[202] Likewise, Jesus' disciple should carry the Roman soldier's baggage twice the legal requirement.[203] A person who owns possessions can insist on his legal rights in keeping them to himself. However, Jesus' disciple is commanded to be generous like the Jewish traditional emphasis on mercy (Matt 5:42).[204] If someone asks for a posses-

---

198. 11QTemple 61.10–12; *Jub.* 4:31–32.

199. Davies and Allison, *Matthew*, 1:538–540 analyze the similarity of Matt and *Did.* 1:4–5, in contrast to Luke 6:27–36.

200. Slapping on the right cheek probably means to strike the cheek with the back of the hand as in an insult (Job 16:10; Ps 3:7; Lam 3:30; *1 Esdr.* 4:30; Arisophanes, *Ra.* 149–150; *m. B. Qam.* 8.6).

201. Jeremias, *The Sermon on the Mount*, 29.

202. B. Mes. 78b; 113b.

203. This would normally mean carrying the pack for two miles, though the Western text says two more miles, for a total of three.

204. *B. Bava; Metzia* 24b, 30b; *b. Avodah Zera* 4b.

sion the disciple is to give it to that person as his own. If someone wishes to borrow something, the disciple is to loan it to the person.[205] Jesus is not annulling the Law but calling His disciples to a higher ethic of generosity in not insisting on their legal rights. Part of this generosity is to forgive those who make these demands upon you.[206] Such generosity reflects the love that summarizes the whole Law.

Notice that this does not mean that Jesus permits the vulnerable to be taken advantage of by those in power for He points out the damnable way that the scribes and Pharisees burden the vulnerable with excess restrictions (Matt 23:4; Luke 11:46) and especially their devouring of widow's households (Mark 12:40; Luke 20:47).[207] So while Jesus encourages disciples to not insist on their own rights, He does defend the vulnerable from abuse by the powerful.

Charitable Giving (Matt 6:1-4)

Jesus supports the Jewish tradition of giving alms or charitable giving (Deut 15:11),[208] but attacks the misuse of such giving of alms for self-aggrandizement (Luke 6:24). *The primary issue is that the disciple should continue to develop the internal purity of the new covenant approach* begun in the beatitudes and continued in Jesus' teaching of the Law. Jewish tradition would label this principled approach a *kĕlāl*, which would then be further developed by a variety of examples.[209] Which means that this section of the sermon is particularly taking issue with a hypocrisy that plays to externals for the purpose so that others would notice (Matt 6:1-6, 16-18). Therefore, personal righteousness is true internal piety. The internal emphasis of right intention rather than right deed alone is very Jewish (Ps 51:16-17).[210] Because

205. Matt 5:42; Luke 6:30; cf. Exod 22:25; Lev 25:36-37; Deut 15:7-11; Prov 28:27; Eccl 4.1-10; 29.1-2; Tob 4.7; *Jub.* 9.1-12.4; *T. Zeb.* 7.2; Heb 10:34. There are also rabbinic texts in which the sages are encouraged to give even to deceivers (*b. Ketub.* 68a).

206. The rabbis likewise urge a person not to seek redress or retaliation but pray for and forgive the offending party even if he does not ask for forgiveness (*T. Jos.* 18:2; *Tosefta Baba Kamma* 9:29-30; *Yoma* 23a).

207. The same point is made by later interpolation into Matt 23:14.

208. LXX of Ps 102.6; Sir 7.10; 29.8; Tob 1.3, 16; 4.7, 16; 12.1-3, 8; 29.8; *T. Job.* 9.8; *m. 'Abot* 5.13; *m. B. Qam.* 10.1; *Tg. Yer.* II for Deut 7:10; *Ps.-Phoc.* 23; *Sib. Or.* 2.78-80; *y. Pe'ah* 15b, bottom 1 *Halakhah* 1; *t. Pe'ah* 4.18; which charitable giving continues in the early church: e.g. Acts 3:2-3; 4:32-37; 9:36; *Did.* 1.6.

209. Examples of Jewish *kĕlāl* teaching include: *m. B. Qam.* 8.1; *m. 'Ed.* 3.1; *b. Hag.* 6a-b; Eccl 3.1-9; 1QS 3.13-4.26; Matt 5:17-48; and perhaps: Gen 5:1-32; Lev 18:1-23; and *Barn.* 18-20.

210. This is exemplified by the rabbinic *kawwānă*, as in *b. Meg.* 20a.

in such a Jewish context, it is believed that God sees what goes on in the dark and in human hearts, and that is what matters (1 Sam 16:7).[211] Matthew 6:2 "therefore" identifies that this example depends upon the general principle of verse one. The sounding of the trumpet is probably a picturesque way to indicate the announcing of one's gift, because trumpets were blown on fast days and when alms were requested (Joel 2:15).[212] Or perhaps, this could also refer to the alms giving process in the temple. In the temple, there was also a trumpet shaped mouth to the treasury box which would resonate like a cymbal if the coins were dumped onto it. Jesus later sat in the treasury area of the Temple and noticed many rich people putting large sums into this trumpet (Mark 12:41-44; Luke 21:1-4; John 8:20). However, Jesus did not call attention to these, except to say that their reward of being honored by man was the full reward that they would receive. In Jewish tradition, even the poor were allowed to give alms.[213] Jesus called attention to a poor woman who gave all that she had, two small copper coins (Mark 12:42-44; Luke 21:2-4). She gave everything, which is a significantly greater gift than the rich, who only gave out of their excess. Jesus identifies that the issue here is secrecy so that others do not know. In this way the only reward is what comes from the Father in His association with the Kingdom (Matt 6:3-4).

Prayer (Matt 6:5-15; 7:7-11)

With regard to prayer, Jewish tradition included at least morning, afternoon (around 3 p.m.) and evening prayers (Dan 6:10; Acts 3:1; 10:3, 30).[214] The foundational prayer for these three daily Jewish prayer times developed into the *Tefillah*, also known as the *Eighteen Benedictions*. So Jesus first calls His disciples' attention to a very Jewish theme of sincerity in prayer (Matt 6:6-7).[215] To aid in this sincerity, Jesus prefers His disciples to pray in secret.

---

211. Sir 17.15; 23.19; 39.19. No Jewish tradition develops what Christians added in a theology of merit (e.g., Boethius, *de Consolatione* 1.4).

212. M. *Ta'an.* 2.5; b. *Ber.* 6b; b. *Sanh.* 35a; Josephus, *Ant.* 3.294.

213. B. *Git.* 7b.

214. T. *Ber.* 3.6; *Did.* 8.3. At the time of the afternoon sacrifice occurred a trumpet was blown and everyone was to put down what they were doing and pray (Eccl 50.16; m. *Sukk.* 5.5; m. *Tamid.* 7.5. Jewish prayer posture was normally standing (1 Sam 1:26; Neh 9:4; Jer 18:20; Mark 11:25; Josephus, *Ant.* 10.255), but on solemn occasions or during times of distress Jews might bend their knee or prostrate themselves (1 Kgs 8:54; Ezra 9:5; Mark 14:32-35; Acts 20:36; 21:5).

215. *Sipre* on Deut 11:13; m. *Ber.* 5.1; b. *Ta'an.* 8a; b. *Ber.* 30b; t. *Ber.* 3.18; *Midr. Ps.* on Ps 108:1.

Jewish tradition supported such private prayer (2 Kgs 4:33–34).[216] Likewise, Jesus prayed in solitude (Mark 1:35; 6:46; 14:32–42: Luke 5:16; 6:12; 9:18, 28–29). Now this emphasis does not ban public prayer (Matt 11:25; Mark 6:41; Luke 11:1; John 11:41–42; 17:1–26), but does put the priority on private prayer, and it does ban ostentatious and repetitive public prayers. Paul Moser utilizes "Gethsemane" as an epistemic metaphor for suffering within unanswered prayer,[217] but this actually symbolizes a historical event in which Hebrews celebrates Jesus' effectiveness in obtaining answered prayer because of His piety (Heb 5:7).[218] In line with this, some Jewish tradition prefers short simple prayers.[219] It was a Pharisee who in Luke 18:9–14 stood alone in the temple and prayed aloud an ostentatious prayer, "I thank God that I am not like other people, swindlers, unjust, adulterers, or even like this tax-gatherer. I fast twice a week; I pay tithes of all that I get." Such a public attempt to show himself superior over others held in contempt was despicable. In contrast to this, the tax-gatherer beat himself and prayed a simple prayer, "be merciful to me a sinner" (Luke 18:13–14). Prayer is performative speech so that in the asking our requests, they are made known to God.[220] God responded by justifying the tax-gatherer with his simple sincere prayer, but God humbled this Pharisee for his self-exaltation in prayer.

The Lord's Prayer is a pattern prayer that Jesus teaches His disciples to pray, giving them performative speech to pray in a kingdom focused manner. Jesus presents it on His initiative and He also responds with this same pattern when the disciples ask for guidance on how to pray (Matt 6:8–13; Luke 11:1–4). Joseph Jacobs points out that the Lord's Prayer is particularly Jewish in that, "His special prayer is merely a shortened form of the third, fifth, sixth, ninth and fifteenth of the *Eighteen Benedictions*."[221] While this

---

216. *B. Ta'an.* 23b; *T. Jos.* 3.3; *T. Jacob* 1.9; Philo, *Vit. cont.* 25.

217. Moser, "Gethsemane Epistemology Volitional and Evidential," *Philosophia Christi* 14(2012): 266.

218. Blaising, "Gethsemane a Prayer of Faith," *JETS* 22(1979): 333–43; Kennard, *Messiah Jesus*, 277.

219. *2 Bar.* 48.26; Eccl 5.2; 7.14; *b. Ber.* 32b–33b; 61a; *m. Ber.* 3.5; 4.4; *Mek.* on Exod 15:25; some see a contrasting voice in *y. Ber.* 4.7b, but I think that this text is not expanding a prayer but arguing for multiplying repeated asking, as in persistence in prayer, which would also resonate with Jesus teaching (Matt 7:7–11; Luke 11:5–13; 18:1–8).

220. Grice, "Meaning," *Philosophical Review* 66(1957): 377–88; "Utterer's Meaning and Intentions," *Phil. Review* 78(1969): 147–77; "Utterer's Meaning, Sentence-Meaning, Word-Meaning," In *The Philosophy of Language.* ed. Searle, 54–70; Austin, *How to Do Things with Words*; Ricoeur, *Oneself as Another*, 44; Kennard, *The Relationship Between Epistemology*, 56, 62–65; *A Critical Realist's*, 232.

221. Jacobs, "Jesus of Nazareth in History," *Jewish Encyclopedia*, 7:102; Jeremias, "Abba as an Address to God," In *New Testament Theology*, 62–63; Davies and Allison,

particular form of the *Eighteen Benedictions* was reformulated at the Jewish council of Jamnia at the end of the first century, there were some shortened forms of the *Benedictions* that existed in Jesus' day.[222] So Jesus' "Lord's prayer" is right in line with developing Judaism of His day. Additionally, the first few lines of the prayer are also a shortened form of the traditional prayer, the *Kaddish*, which was prayed in second Temple synagogues after the sermon.[223] The particular form of the Lord's Prayer is especially an eschatological prayer, which also has some precedence in early Judaism.[224] Israel had entered the land but the full benefits of kingdom had never been realized, so this Lord's Prayer can be seen making requests concerning this full realization of kingdom. N. T. Wright overplays the Exodus theme in this prayer,[225] for there is no near context development of Exodus and as a theme the Exodus could only fit in two ways: 1) as a prophetic theme about the regathering into kingdom like Isaiah 40 develops, or 2) as Jesus' community of disciples follow the narrow way unto kingdom. However, the kingdom theme is clear in the prayer and among similar synagogue prayers where there may be some cross pollination.

The prayer is a corporate prayer and begins with the unusual relational, "Our Father" but it is not unheard of in Jewish references (Deut 32:6; Ps 103:13; Isa 63:16; Mal 2:10).[226] Matthew's account adds, "who art in heaven," which would tend to fit with the Jewish emphasis in prayer of God's transcendence. God is holy, so the petition in the prayer reflects the Isaianic emphasis of God's name standing in as a symbol for God and asks that it be treated by us as holy (Exod 20:8; Lev 19:2, 32; Isa 4:1; 26:8; 52:6; Ezek 36:23). The request for God's kingdom to come longs and asks for the era of beatitude blessing to be realized to end the present difficulties (Matt 5:3–11;

Matthew, 595–6.

222. *Shemoneh 'Esreh*; *m. Ber.* 4.1, 3–4; *m. 'Abot* 2.13; *b. Ber.* 16b–17a; 29a, 34a; *t. Ber.* 3.5; *Sipre* on Num 12.13; *Mek.* on Exod 15.25 probably copying Matt and Luke: *Did.* 8.2; Davies and Allison, *Matthew*, 1:595–600.

223. The Kaddish prayer is cited in Davies and Allison, *Matthew*, 1:595; also similar to *t. Ber.* 3.7; *b. Ber.* 16b.

224. *2 Bar.* 21.19–25.

225. Wright, "The Lord's Prayer as a Paradigm of Christian Prayer," In *Into God's Presence*. ed. Longenecker, 132–3, 138–54.

226. Sir 23.1, 4; 51.1, 10; Wis 2.16; 14:3; Tob 13.4; 3 Macc 5.7; 6.3, 8; *Jub.* 1.24; 4Q372; 1QH 9.34–35; Josephus, *Ant.* 5.93; *T. Job* 33.3, 9; 40.2; *Mekh* on Exod 20.6; *m. Ber* 5.1; *b. Ta'an.* 23b; *Sifra* on Lev. (as cited by Heinemann, *Prayer in the Talmud*, 189–90); Aramaic *Qaddish* (as cited by Vermes, *The Religion of Jesus the Jew*, 178, but 179–183) are relevant as an analysis of Joachim Jeremias' argument for Jesus' uniqueness; in contrast see: Jeremias, "Abba as an Address to God," In *New Testament Theology*, 62–68).

6:10). *As an epistemic virtue, corporate prayer develops corporate reconciliation, dependence upon God, community building, and longing for kingdom.* Matthew's account adds further explanation and an additional petition with "Thy will be done on earth as it is in heaven," which is reminiscent of an Aramaic version of the *Kaddish*, present before the first century A.D.

> Exalted and holy be His great name in the world which He created according to His will, May He let His kingdom rule in your lifetime and in your days, and in the lifetime of the whole house of Israel, speedily and soon. Praised be His great name from everlasting to everlasting. And to this, say amen.[227]

At this point the Lord's Prayer includes personal petitions to spell out particulars of what God's will on earth is desired to be, which fit into the Jewish pattern of adding personal petitions following the *Eighteen Benedictions*.[228] The repeated "and" links the last three requests together as outworking expressions of God's will on earth. For example, in the first century day laborers were paid one day at a time. So the request is "give us our bread for the coming day" or in light of Luke's "each day," the request would then be give us the food we need. Perhaps, it is a hope that the manna of the Exodus would return, because this is a second Temple Jewish expectation for Israel's regathering into the kingdom.[229] If this was the case, then the request would be for a Sabbaths provision of manna, since it is providing for the next day, which might symbolize the provision moving into the kingdom as the age of Sabbath rest (Exod 16:22–30; Heb 4:1–10).[230] Jesus' petition certainly means at least a request for the food we need.

The request to "forgive our debts" is reminiscent of the Jubilee or Sabbatical year which Jesus announced as at the center of His freeing ministry and thus to be expected in Jesus' disciples prayer (Luke 4:18–19). The word "debts" (ὀφειλήματα) is a rare word which is present in the LXX Jubilee account, but Jesus also extends it to refer to sins as well (Deut 24:10; Luke 11:4).[231] The prayerful response is not to justify oneself in prayer before God and others, for such speech is essentially only to oneself, but the sinner left the pattern to humbly ask for forgiveness from God (Luke 18:9–14). *Christ calls disciples to epistemic virtues of not justifying self, generosity to forgive sin*

---

227. Davies and Allison, *Matthew*, 595.

228. B. *'Abod. Zar.* 7b; also claimed by Tertullian, *De orat.* 10; Finkel, *The Pharisees and the Teacher of Nazareth*, 115.

229. *2 Bar.* 29.8; *Sib. Or.* frag. 3, 49; 3.746 (with Exod 16:31); 7.149; *Mek.* on Exod 16:25.

230. *Barn.* 15.

231. *1 Esd.* 3.20; 1 Macc 15.8.

and debt, and humbly depending upon God for inclusion. Such humility in requesting forgiveness will be exalted by God.

However, the shocking thing for evangelicals about the extent of the forgiveness requested of God is that it is *in the same pattern and to the same extent* that (ὡς) "as we also have forgiven our debtors" (Matt 6:12). Thus, *the request for divine forgiveness is made in a context in which human forgiveness is already accomplished toward one's debtors,* as evident by the aorist tense, within this prayer so dominated by eschatological requests. To make sure that His disciples understood this point Jesus emphasizes this point further through His teaching after the prayer, "For if you forgive men for their transgressions, your heavenly Father will also forgive you; but if you do not forgive men, then your Father will not forgive your transgressions" (Matt 6:14-15).[232] Additionally, Mark 11:25 identifies that disciples forgiving others in prayer is imperative "so that" (ἵνα) your Father in heaven may forgive your transgressions. Such prayers for forgiveness reflect the Jewish pattern,[233] from at least the second century B.C. as ben Siraḥ 28.2-5 enumerates,

> Forgive your neighbor the wrong he has done, and then your sins will be pardoned when you pray. Does a man harbor anger against another, and yet seek healing from the Lord? Does he have no mercy toward a man like himself, and yet pray for his own sins? If he himself, being flesh, maintains wrath, who will make expiation for his sins?

Jesus prayer ends[234] with, "And do not lead us into temptation, but deliver us from the evil one[235]" (Matt 6:13; Luke 11:4).[236] When the Holy Spirit came upon Jesus at His baptism, anointing Him for kingdom, the Spirit lead Jesus out into the wilderness to be tempted by the devil (Matt 4:1; Luke 4:1-2). For the disciples contemplating and praying for the coming kingdom, such temptations would become particularly acute in the Messianic woes, which are encroaching into this life in persecutions for Christ's sake (Matt 5:10-12; 24:5-31).[237] Even a moment before, Jesus had urged His

---

232. The same point is made by Byzantine addition of Mark 11:26.

233. Other parallels include: *b. Šabb.* 151b; *T. Zeb.* 5.3; 8.1-2; *T. Jos.* 18.2; *m. Yoma* 8.9; *t. B. Qam.* 9.29; *b. Meg.* 28a; *Polyc.* 6.2; *Mekhilta deRabbi Ishmael* on Exod 15:2; In contrast, the prayer for forgiveness in the *Eighteen Benedictions* does not have a condition.

234. The longer endings of the prayer are not supported by the earliest and best manuscripts.

235. The addition of the article before "evil" normally indicates a person.

236. 11QPs 24.10; *b. Ber.* 60b.

237. *Berk.*60b; Pate and Kennard, *Deliverance Now and Not Yet*, 302-325, 401-469; Davies and Allison, *Matthew*, 1:594.

disciples to pray for their persecutors, which is a pattern that Jesus Himself emulates as He forgives His crucifiers (Matt 5:44; Luke 23:34).

Persistence is an epistemic virtue. Persistence in prayer is a repeated point of Jesus' teaching (Matt 7:7-11; Luke 11:5-13; 18:1-8). For example, Jesus repeatedly states His thesis for His disciples, "ask and it will be given to you; seek and you shall find; knock and it shall be opened to you" (Matt 7:7; Luke 11:9).[238] Jesus develops the basis for this persistence by underscoring that the ones who ask receive (Matt 7:8; Luke 11:10). Jesus goes on to illustrate the point twice in the pattern: if a son asks for a good thing, his father will not give him something that frustrates or harms (Matt 7:9-10; Luke 11:11-12). Luke emphasizes the issue of persistence more fully by further illustrations such as a man's persistence in knocking at a friend's house so that bread might be given to meet a need and a widows persistence in requesting an unjust judge to give her legal protection (Luke 11:5-8). These illustrations of persistence show that at all times we ought to pray and not lose heart (Luke 18:1). The discussion concludes with an inference that because God is better than we evil men, so much more will He give what is good to those who ask Him! (Matt 7:11). Luke especially turns this prayer to the generosity of the heavenly Father to give the Holy Spirit to those who ask Him (Luke 11:13).

John develops Jesus' theme of asking in Jesus' name or authority (John 14:13; 15:7; 16:23). *Dependence upon Jesus is an epistemic virtue.* That is, in a context of obedience to Messiah and love of the brethren (such as faithfulness to Christ in the narrow way) there is a demonstrated connectedness to the root of the vine, Jesus as Messiah that God will grant these requests which we ask in His name.

Fasting (Matt 6:16-18)

Fasting was commanded for the Day of Atonement (Lev 16:24-31) and in the exile fasts were a regular occurrence (Zech 7:3-5; 8:19). Fasting was also used on a personal voluntary level for self-humiliation, confession of sins, for prayer, and for longing for the kingdom (Neh 1:4; Esth 4:3; Dan 9:3; Mark 2:18; Luke 5:33).[239] The Pharisees fasted twice a week (presumably on Monday and Thursday; Luke 18.12).[240] These same Pharisees had a prob-

---

238. This persistence in seeking is echoed in *Gos. Thom.* 2 and *P. Oxy.* 654.1.

239. Fasting was often coupled with prayer: Matt 6:7-18; 1 Sam 7:5-6; Neh 1:4; Acts 13:3; Tob 12.8; Philo, *Spec. leg.* 2.203; Polycarp, *Ep. 7*; *Apoc. Zeph.* 7.6; *T. Jac.* 7.17.

240. *M. Taanith* 1.4-7; 2.9 cf. *Did.* 8.1; Suetonius, *Aug.* 76 and Chrysostom, *Hom. adv. Jud.* 1.1.

lem with Jesus and His disciples because they did not fast (Matt 9:14–15; Mark 2:18–20; Luke 5:33–35). However, Jesus explained that they did not fast because they had the bridegroom, Himself, with them. This bridegroom reference is enigmatic, maybe hinting of kingdom (Joel 2:16; Rev 19:7, 9), but certainly indicating that Jesus presence is to be celebrated, not fasted. However, there will be a time when He will be taken from them, then they will fast. The Byzantine manuscripts have more references to fasting than this but they are not the earliest and best manuscripts. So fasting is assumed in the Sermon on the Mount, to occur for the disciples (Matt 6:16–18), especially when Jesus will be taken away from them (Matt 9:15; Mark 2:20; Luke 5:35). It should be evident that the general point being worked is a genuine sincerity in religious duty, which is also consistent with second Temple Jewish fasting.[241] When a disciple fasts, he should make sure that such fasting is done for internally pure reasons, rather than for show (Matt 6:16–18). For if one neglects his appearance then he is doing it for human reward, and God considers such things to be a waste.[242] Whereas, if one's head is anointed and face washed, that is, the normal steps of hygiene are practiced, no–one can tell if you are fasting, then your Father will take notice and repay you.

The Kingdom as your Treasure (Matt 6:19–24)

The allegiance to God excludes one's allegiance to money and vice versa. "No one can serve two masters; for either he will hate the one and love the other, or he will hold to one and despise the other. You cannot serve God and the love of money" (Matt 6:24; Luke 16:13).[243] *The epistemic virtue of complete loyalty to God controls all thought and life.* That is, behind appearances and possessions is the issue of serving a master. The essence of slavery is that there was a single ownership and full time service. Either God is served devotedly or not at all. This does not demonize commerce, as does the *Gos. Thom.* 64, but raises the issue of loyalty. That is, divided loyalty reveals a deep seated idolatry, not just partial commitment to discipleship. It is like the parable of the steward squandering his master's possessions (Luke 16:1–13).[244] The steward is commended for his shrewd use of money

241. Sir 34.26; *T. Asher* 2.8; *Apoc. Elijah* 1.18–19; *m. Taʿan.* 2.1; *t. Taʿan.* 1.8; *b. Taʿan.* 16a.

242. I suspect that this is not addressing fasting in significant times of mourning, which is often accompanied with sackcloth and ashes (Dan 9:3; Jon 3:5; Jdt 8.5; 1 Macc 3.47; Josephus, *J. W.* 20.89).

243. *Gos. Thom.* 47.

244. A similar parable of Rabbi Jose the Priest occurs in *B.T. Rosh Hashanah* 17b–18a.

to work gain for his allegiance, his own gain. The parable is then applied to the disciples, "No servant can serve two masters; for either he will hate the one and love the other, or he will hold to one and despise the other. You cannot serve God and the love of money" (Luke 16:13; Matt 6:24). That is, the cares of this world distract one from a loyalty to God (Matt 6:24-25; Luke 16:9-13).[245] The disciples are to use their wealth for kingdom purposes and everlasting gain of those who enter into kingdom (Luke 16:8-9). In light of this, "do not lay up for yourselves treasures on earth," or since it is a present tense it could be translated as "stop laying up for yourselves treasures on earth" (Matt 6:19; Luke 12:33-34).[246] As a Jewish sentiment, this reminds us that such treasures do not last, they are destroyed, devoured, or stolen (Matt 6:19-20; Jas 5:2-3).[247] Instead, we should lay up treasure in heaven, because where a person's personal treasure is, there resides that same person's heart focus (Matt 7:21; Luke 12:34).[248]

Likewise, where your treasure is indicates your destiny (Luke 16:19-31). Jesus told the parable of the rich man and Lazarus (whose name means "God helps") to indicate that the way you use wealth indicates your destiny in the afterlife. This parable is similar to the Jewish parable of a rich tax collector named Bar Majan and a poor teacher of the Law who reversed fortunes in the afterlife.[249] The rich man had opportunity but no concern for a poor man Lazarus who laid immediately outside his gate. Even dogs (an unclean animal) licked the poor man's sores. In life, wealth was kept away from the poor man but his longing was for basic sustenance. When poor Lazarus died, he was carried by angels to the blessing of Abraham's lap, having received bad things in life the afterlife provided comfort (Luke 16:25). However, the rich man in death was buried and found himself in torment in Hades, and the torment was made more acute in that he could see Lazarus in blessing at a distance. Such judgment agony was just in that the rich man had squandered the good things of this life on himself and not met the needs in his context (Luke 16:25). Such a miser condition is that of

---

245. Also, *Gos. Thom.* 36.

246. Likewise, *Gos. Thom.* 110 urges those who have riches to "renounce the world" to find the truly valuable riches of God.

247. Sir 29.10-11; cf. 19.3; 42.13; and Job 4:19; 13:28; Isa 33:1 LXX; 50:9; 51:8; Hos 5:12; *Ps.—Phoc.* 27; and echoed in early Christian writing: Justin, *1 Apol.* 15.

248. *T. Job* 33.4-5; Tob 4.8-9; Sir 29.10-13; *Ps. Sol.* 9.5, 9; *2 Bar.* 14.12; 24.1; 44.8; *T. Levi* 13.5; Philo, *Praem.* 104; *4 Ezra* 7.77; *m. Pe'a* 1.1; *b. B. Bat.* 11a; *Tosefta Peah* 4.18; *Gos. Thom.* 76; Young, *Meet the Rabbis*, 72.

249. A similar parable particularly about the rich man's afterlife conversation is present in *Ruth Rab.* 3.3 and *Eccl. Rab.* 1.15.1. There is also an Egyptian story of a man with royal linen and a poor man on a mat who reversed fortunes in the afterlife, Creed, *Luke*, 209-210; Bock, *Luke*, 2:1362.

Jewish "evil eye," signifying intent and leaving one in the dark of judgment (Deut 15:9; Prov 23:6; 28:22).[250] In spite of the fire, Hell is a dark place, and is the outcome of such darkened lives (Matt 8:12; 22:13; 25:30).[251] Such agony is not released in the afterlife, since the blessed are not permitted to travel to aid the damned (Luke 16:26). Likewise, neither the blessed nor the damned of the afterlife can appear to rescue from damnation loved ones who have not died, as Jacob Marley did for Scrooge in Charles Dickens' novel *A Christmas Carol*.[252] The Mosaic Law and the prophets are sufficient to warn an individual to have their loyalty completely with God instead of money. Luke ends the parable with a hint that Jesus' (or Lazarus') resurrection would be ineffective in persuading those who serve money, from the error of their way (Luke 16:31).

The kingdom is itself a treasure (Matt 6:33; 13:44).[253] Luke has Jesus explain that this is accomplished by selling one's possessions and giving to charity to meet real needs of people for the kingdom (Luke 12:33). This is in contrast to the greedy attitude that someone from the crowd had in wanting Jesus to arbitrate an inheritance settlement (Luke 12:13–15). Jesus told a parable of a wealthy farmer who horded his riches and planned to tear down his barns to build bigger ones to continue the hording (Luke 12:16–21).[254] Such a miser presumed that he would keep living, which identifies him to be a fool who was not rich toward God.[255] That is, epistemically *whatever captivates your thought life, your emotions and your choices, controls you and thus the use of wealth is reflective of the core commitments of your very being.*

When this exclusive servanthood of God is pressed against the Pharisees, Luke calls them "lovers of money" (Luke 16:14). Jesus reminds them that God knows their hearts and has other values than men have, namely the kingdom. People are forcing their way into the kingdom but it is governed by a Law that cannot fail, which will exclude them as violators (Luke 16:16–18).

Let the Pursuit of Kingdom Dispel Worry (Matt 6:25–34)

Because a person cannot serve two masters, and thus must serve God, one should not be anxious (Matt 6:25, 31, 34). Again because this command is in

---

250. Tob 4.7; Sir 14.8; 26.11; *m. 'Abot* 2.9, 11; 5.19; 1QS 4.9–11.

251. 1QS 2.8; *1 En.* 103.7.

252. Dickens, *A Christmas Carol and Other Stories*, 14–22.

253. *T. Job.* 26.3; *Gos. Thom.* 109.

254. Some similarities are in the scrooge of *Pesikta de Rab Kahana* 10.3 who continued to horde treasure without paying the tithe.

255. Similar to: Isa 22:13–14 or Sir 11:18–19.

the present tense it could be saying "stop being anxious." Using the deliberative subjunctive, Jesus asks about the absurdity of being anxious about: life, food, drink, body shape, and clothes (Matt 6:25; Luke 12:22). In Matthew, Jesus addresses worry outright as an important kingdom theme. In Luke, the discussion is in response to a request for Jesus to arbitrate a family will (Luke 12:13). Jesus approaches the discussion from the vantage point of a sage giving wise counsel and providing reasons to help motivate our action.

The Lukan account begins with a parable which warns of greed, for life does not consist of possessions (Luke 12:15). This context ties the issue of worry together with the previous concern that the kingdom should be our treasure. The parable is of the rich farmer who decides to tear down his barns in order to build larger ones (Luke 12:16–21). God's evaluation of such a miser is "You fool! This night your life is required of you; and now who will own what you have prepared? So is the man who lays up treasure for himself, and is not rich toward God." So domination by a concern for riches is the other side of anxiety. To be anxious about life or body shape or other trivialities is to call God's generous gift into question, for we owe all this to Him.

Such Jewish wisdom argues for contentment and the confidence that God will provide. Since God has given us the more important things like life and body therefore He will give us the things we need that are also important (Ps 127:2; Isa 32:17; Matt 6:25; Luke 12:23). Such an argument follows Hillel logical rule one; what applies in a minor case like God feeding birds applies in the major case such as God will care for you.[256] Rabbi Simeon ben Yohai also affirmed the sentiment that God looks after those who serve Him and not mammon, so that they need have no anxiety about life's basic needs.[257] Jesus' wisdom strategy resonates with this form of Judaism; don't worry, for the Father is more committed to Jesus' disciples whom He values than the birds (even the ritually unclean raven) who He feeds generously (Matt 6:26; Luke 12:24).[258] Jesus emphasizes the "you" as He asks the question, "are YOU not worth much more than they?" Furthermore anxiety

---

256. Sipra intr 1; 'Abot R. Nat. 37; Gen. Rab. 92.7; Pesaḥ. 18b; Yoma 43a; Ellis, *The Old Testament in Early Christianity*, 130–2.

257. Mek. on Exod 16:4; While the O.T. has scant evidence for Jews depending upon God through the Sabbath year rest, second Temple Judaism has widespread evidence for the return of this practice (1 Macc 6.49, 53–54; 1QS 10.7–8; 1QM 2.6; Josephus, Ant. 11.338–343; 14.202–210; m. Šebu'ot; Safrai, "The Rechov Inscription," *Immanuel* 8[1978]: 48–57; Wacholder, "The Calendar of Sabbatical Cycles during the Second Temple and Early Rabbinic Period," HUCA 44[1973]: 98–116). Hillel is purported to have quoted Psalm 68:19 "blessed is the Lord day by day" to support his conviction that God would provide sufficiently for sabbatical year (b. Besa 16a).

258. "Will not God who created humans, create for him his food?" *Pesiq. R. Kah.* 91a.

does not add to height, or body shape, or prolong life span (Matt 6:27; Luke 12:25-26). Additionally, don't be anxious about clothing but trust God, who values you over time more than the simple flowers of the field which He arrays with Solomon[259] surpassing glory only to be destroyed the next day (Matt 6:28-30; Luke 12:27-28).[260] They grow without toil (the man's work) or spinning (the woman's labor).

Do not take on the common Gentile worry about all these things, rather seek first God's kingdom and all these things will be added to you (Matt 6:31-33; Luke 12:30-31). That is, seeking the kingdom and God's righteousness becomes a condition which enables us to find the kingdom life as well as these inconsequential things we worry about as well (Matt 5:6; 6:33; 7:8; Luke 10:28; 12:31). This fits the rabbinical pattern of doing the will of God unto kingdom.[261] One example of this kingdom seeking is shown in the Lord's prayer that places kingdom concerns first but also prays for daily food (Matt 6:9-11, 33; 7:7-8).

Furthermore, Jesus reminds us, "do not be afraid, little flock, for your Father has chosen gladly to give you the kingdom" (Luke 12:32). Therefore, do not be anxious because: 1) tomorrow will take care of itself, and 2) each day has sufficient misfortune, persecutions and troubles to render foolish an approach which borrows future concerns for today (Matt 6:34).[262] Luke records Jesus' ending to this discussion in a way that reminds us that anxiety is the other side of the issue of wealth and allegiance (the previous section); that is don't be anxious, "for where your treasure is, there will your heart be also" (Luke 12:34).

Don't Condemn Others; Generosity in Speech Identifies With Kingdom (Matt 7:1-6, 12)

Jesus as sage, calls His disciples to not judge lest you be judged in return (Matt 7:1-2; Luke 6:37-38). Perhaps, this implicates Pharisees as wrongly passing judgment on others (Matt 9:10-13; 12:1-8; Luke 7:39; 15:1-2; 18:9-14). However, Jewish rabbinical instruction reminds us that, we should "not assume the place of God by deciding you have the right to stand in judgment over all, do not do it, I say in order to avoid being called to

---

259. Solomon's splendor is an obvious Jewish metaphor for elaborate beauty (1 Kgs 9:26-10:29; 2 Chr 9:13-28; Sir 2:1-11; 1 Esd 1.5; Josephus, *Ant.* 8.39-41; Clement of Alexandria, *Paed.* 2.10.102).

260. Echoed in *Gos. Thom.* 36.

261. Davies and Allison, *Matthew*, 1:660.

262. B. *Sanh.* 100b; b. *Yeb.* 63b; b. *Soṭah* 48b.

account by the God whose place you usurp."[263] The Jewish wisdom theme of reaping what you sow, the retribution principle, is here applied by Jesus, to remind His disciples that they will be judged after the same measure that they do to others (Job 4:8; 5:1–16; Prov 11:18; 22:8; Matt 7:1; Luke 6:37).[264] According to the rabbis, God judged the world by two measures: mercy and justice.[265] The merciful will receive mercy and those concerned about righteousness will receive satisfaction (Matt 5:6–7).[266] Luke more strongly warns "do not condemn or you shall be condemned." However, Luke then encourages generosity in the forms of pardoning and giving, "for whatever measure you deal out, it shall be dealt to you in return." Mark uses this retribution principle in a novel way, to underscore the parable of the soils, "be careful what you listen to and apply...for whoever has, to him more will be given" (Mark 4:24–25).[267] That is, those applying the kingdom message will have further kingdom blessings. However, Jesus, in Matthew and Luke, then applies this issue with colorful imagery much like the rabbis did, "why do you get fixated on the speck[268] in your brother's eye and do not notice the log in your own eye?" (Matt 7:3–4; Luke 6:41–42).[269] The issue is hypocrisy, which is a greater "log" in one's own eye (Matt 5:5; Luke 6:42). However, when a brother in a meek and self-judging spirit, removes the log from his own eye, he has the responsibility for helping his brother remove his speck (Matt 5:5; Luke 6:42).

Imbedded within teaching on the retribution principle in Luke is a warning that a blind man cannot guide a blind man, for both will fall into a pit (Luke 6:39).[270] Likewise, a student "is not above his teacher; but after he has been fully trained he can be like his teacher" (Luke 6:40). This reminds us that Jesus' is calling His disciples to the very practice of non-judging mercy which He emulates.

---

263. *B. Šabb.* 127b; 151b; *m. Soṭah* 1.7; *b. Baba Metzia* 59b; *b. Roš. Haš.* 16b.

264. *Sir* 16.14; *2 En.* 44.5; *Mek.* on Exod 13:19, 21; 14:25; 15:3, 5, 8; 17:14; *m. Soṭa* 1.7; *t. Soṭa* 3.1; *Tg. Ps.–J.* on Gen 38:26; *b. Šabb.* 105b; *b. Sanh.* 100a; *b. Soṭa* 8b; *T. Zeb.* 5.3; *Tg. Isa.* on 27.8.

265. *Lev. Rab.* 29.3.

266. *T. B. Qam.* 9.30; *y. B. Qam.* 8.10.6c.

267. *M. Soṭah* 1.7 is even more different.

268. κάρφος means a small piece of foreign matter, Gen 8:11 LXX; similar speck and log language is used in *b. Baba Bathra* 15b; *b. Arakh.* 16b.

269. Similar to Rom. 2:1; *b. Arakh.* 16b; *b. Baba Bathra* 15b; Sextus, *Sent.* 90; *b. Qidd.* 70a; *b. B. Meṣ.* 107b; *b. Sanh.* 18a, 19b; *Gos. Thom.* 26b.

270. Matthew 15:14 takes this saying to be one of judgment on the Pharisees who resist Jesus' kingdom ministry.

Jesus reminds His disciples that they should only help those who they think will be receptive to their instruction (Matt 7:6).[271] This is reflective of Proverbs 9:8 "Do not reprove a scoffer, lest he hate you, reprove a wise man, and he will love you."[272] Matthew 7:6 continues in this Jewish proverbial tradition; "do not give what is holy to dogs, and do not throw your pearls before swine, lest they trample them under their feet, and turn and tear you to pieces." The "holy" and "pearls" are the valuable and sacred in contrast to the "dogs" and "swine," which are wild unclean animals capable of savage actions (1 Sam 17:43; 2 Kgs 8:13; Job 30:1). If you try to correct the foolish or the scoffer, they may become violent and try to harm you (Matt 7:6, "tear you to pieces"). Likewise, the Jewish tradition urged, "Let not sacred words enter a place of uncleanness."[273] Therefore, be wise about whom you instruct and try to correct. That is, receptivity to correction would indicate that they would likely be heading towards the kingdom.

The section concludes with the golden rule (Matt 7:12).[274] There are many statements of a negative form of the golden rule in early Judaism.[275] For example, about 20 A.D. rabbi Hillel was challenged to summarize the Law in the time it would take a Gentile to stand on one leg. Hillel responded, "What is hateful to you, do not do to anyone else. This is the whole Law; all the rest is commentary. Go and learn it."[276] Jesus shows His continuity with this point of view, but goes further by putting the golden rule into the positive. "Therefore, however you want people to treat you so treat them, for this is the Law and the Prophets" (Matt 7:12).

Jewish Legal Controversies with Jesus

Jewish leadership challenged Jesus' compliance with the Law by raising concerns of Sabbath keeping and purity. These two areas are not primarily epistemic except that they challenge Jesus on the level at which the Law is an authority.

---

271. *Gos. Thom.* 93.

272. Also said in: Prov 23:9; *b. Sanh.* 90b; *m. Tem.* 6.5; *b. Bek.* 15a; *b. Pesah.* 29a; *b. Šebu.* 11b; *b. Tem.* 117a, 130b.

273. This is a quote of *b. Šabb.* 127b; which might raise the impropriety of such critique being said to a Gentile who does not know the Law, cf. *b. Hag.* 13a; *b. Ketub.* 111a.

274. *Gos. Thom.* 6.

275. Tob 4.15; *B. Šabb.* 31a; *Avot R. Nat.* vers. B.26; *Sifre* on Lev 19:18; *T. Naph* 1.6; *2 En.* 61.1–2; *Tg. Yer.* 1 to Lev 19:18; *ARN* 15; *Sent. Syr. Men.* 250–251; Sextus, *Sent.* 89; *Did.* 1.2; Eusebius, *Praep. ev.* 8.7.6 (358d).

276. *B. Šabb.* 31a.

Sabbath

The Jewish commitment to Sabbath meant that some Jews waited until Sabbath was over to carry the sick to Jesus (Mark 1:29–32; Luke 4:38–40). However, Jesus healed on the Sabbath without disputes arising, sometimes because He was among friends (Mark 1:29–31; Luke 4:38–39). At other times Sabbath synagogue healings would take place without dispute because those present were simply amazed at the healing (Mark 1:21–28). Sabbath compliance was deep within Jesus' own followers for the believing Jewish women waited until Sabbath was past to attend to Jesus' body after His death (Matt 28:1; Mark 16:1; Luke 23:56–24:1).

In the gospels, the most repeated issue on which the religious leadership question Jesus is the violation of Sabbath. This issue rises especially during Jesus' healing ministry. This issue is important to the Law, since: 1) the Sabbath Law is in the Decalogue, 2) the severity of the command to "rest from your work" places the violator under sentence of capital punishment, and 3) keeping Sabbath is the everlasting sign of the everlasting Mosaic covenant (Exod 20:8–11; 31:12–17; 34:21; 35:2; Num 15:32–36; Deut 5:12–15).[277] Those who failed to see beyond the pursuit of their business found the Sabbath an irritation to disobey (Amos 8:5; Jer 17:19–27; Neh 13:15–22). However, faithful Jews saw its observance was a delight (Isa 58:13–14). Furthermore, Sabbath keeping was well known as a characteristic which marked off Jewish communal life.[278] As we evaluate this issue, it is important that we do not read Jesus activity as severely unraveling the Law.

Deuteronomy's development of Sabbath idea emphasizes generosity, within its' rest (Deut 5:12–15; Exod 23:12). For example, the sabbatical moratorium extends the seventh day to include a seventh year release of debt and obligation of servitude (Deut 14:28–16:17). Between the seventh year releases (both temporally and structurally within the section) is the charge to be generous in lending to a brother Israelite and the needy (Deut 15:7–11). Even Jewish Christianity later conceived of the kingdom as through the lens of the remaining future Sabbath rest for the people of God (Heb 4:9). This blessing in Sabbath indicates that at the heart of the sabbatical release is *generosity* meeting needs in a manner that does not make oppressive obligations on the debtor. This Deuteronomic ideal predisposes Jesus to view the Sabbath as a time of release and freeing the oppressed. This is most apparent in His healing ministry. For example, when a woman bent

---

277. *Jub.* 2.29–30; 50.6–13; *CD* 10.14–11.18; *m. Šabb.* 7.2; *t. Šabb.* 1.21b; *Sipre* on Num 15:33; Instone-Brewer, *Feasts and Sabbaths*, 15–16.

278. Horace, *Sat.* 1.9.69–70; Philo, *Som.* 2.123–24; *Leg. Gai.* 158; *Vit. Mos.* 2.21; Josephus, *Ant.* 13.252; 14.10.12; 14.237. 16.2.3; 16.6.2–4; *Ag. Ap.* 2.39.

over for eighteen years was healed, the Synagogue official became indignant at Jesus healing on the Sabbath. Jesus responded, "You hypocrites, does not each of you on the Sabbath untie his ox or his donkey from the stall, and lead him away to water? And this woman, a daughter of Abraham as she is whom Satan has bound for eighteen years, should she not have been released from this bond on the Sabbath day?" (Luke 13:14–16). Such an argument follows Hillel logical rule one; *what applies in a minor case* like releasing livestock so they might drink *applies in the major case* such as God will care for you.[279] In the wake of this healing and explanation, the people joined the woman in praising God (Luke 13:13, 17).

In response to some Jewish strictures Jesus identified that "the Sabbath was made for man and not man for the Sabbath" (Mark 2:27). Jesus' approach is instanced also in second Temple Judaism.[280] This approach sees Sabbath as an aid to humans in providing rest, God's generosity, and a time to focus on God, and not a time to be restrictive about the benefits God would have available for those who are His.

In early Judaism, there was considerable debate over what sort of concessions were permitted within the generosity of the Sabbath. A number of texts show considerable restrictiveness but some permit healing on the Sabbath.[281] Other texts show concessions of leniency that were broadly recognized including: saving of a life, alleviating acute pain, curing snake bite and cooking for the sick.[282] Quoting Isaiah 58:13 the rabbis also allowed acts of service to others as in deciding on grants of charity, watering your animals, or making arrangements on a child's education (Luke 13:15).[283] As Jesus summarized, "it is Lawful to do good on the Sabbath" (Matt 12:12; Mark

279. *Sipra* intr 1; *'Abot R. Nat.* 37; *Gen. Rab.* 92.7; *Pesaḥ.* 18b; *Yoma* 43a; Ellis, *The Old Testament in Early Christianity*, 130–2.

280. *Mek. Abbeta* on Exod 31:13; extended discussion of Sabbath issues in Oliver. *Torah Praxis after 70 CE*, 45–240.

281. CD 10.14–11.18; 4Q265 frag. 6; 4Q218 frag. 1; 4Q251 frag. 1–2; *m. Šabb.* 22.5–6; 14.3–4; 18.3–19.2; *m. 'Eduy* 2.5; *m. Yom.* 8.6; *t. Šabb.* 15.16; 16.22; Instone-Brewer, *Feasts and Sabbaths*, 43–46, 55–62, 75.

282. 1 Macc 2.29–41; *Šabb.* 18.3; *T. Šabb.* 15.14; *Šabb. M. Eduyoth* 2.5; *M. Šabb.* 6.3; *Yoma* 8.6; 84b; *b. Yoma* 85b; *M. Yoma* 8.6; *T. Yoma* 84.15; *Mek.* on Exod 22:2 and 23:13; Such an approach is consistent with Hillel logical rule two; an analogy made between two texts on the basis of phrase or word (*Sipra* intr 2; *'Abot R. Nat.* 37; *Šabb.* 64a ; Ellis, *The Old Testament in Early Christianity*, 130–2). Back, *Jesus of Nazareth and the Sabbath Commandment*, 137; Mayer-Haas, "Geschenk aus Gottes Schatzkammer (bSchab 10b)," 321; Evans, "'Have You Not Read...?,'" In *Jesus Research.* ed. Charlesworth with Pokorny, 185.

283. Fisher, "Jesus Through Jewish Eyes," A paper presented at ETS, Nov. 2003; countering this the more rigid sectarian Jewish community at Qumran prohibited helping an animal give birth or out of a pit on Sabbath (CD 11.13–14; *t. Šabb.* 14.3).

3:4), and Hillel agrees with Jesus against Shammai.[284] Such an argument is consistent with Hillel logical rule one; what applies in a minor case like God feeding birds applies in the major case such as God will care for you.[285] So Jesus healed on the Sabbath (Matt 12:13; Mark 3:5; Luke 13:10–13; John 5:8; 7:23). Which healing some rabbis say is a permitted good to occur on the Sabbath, in contrast to Jesus' opponents.[286] Also, the rabbis frequently used the quotation from Hosea 6:6, as Jesus did in Matthew 12:7, to argue that helping others was of greater importance than observing the rituals and customs.[287] Since good deeds were God's business, they were allowed.[288] Additionally, Jesus justified his healing the paralytic because God continued to work on the Sabbath so Jesus saw no problem with continuing to do the work of God in healing on Sabbath (John 5:17).[289] The basic rabbinic principle was as Jesus said, "The Sabbath was made for man, and not man for the Sabbath" (Mark 2:27).[290]

The most obvious example of potentially violating the command to not work on the Sabbath is the instance in which Jesus said to the paralytic "Pick up your mat and walk" (John 5:8). On this point, rabbi John Fisher says, "Upon examining early Jewish sources, we find that what constitutes work was yet to be fully defined. So for example, carrying things within a walled city (Jerusalem) was not always considered work."[291] Carrying a paralytic on the Sabbath was not work but carrying burdens (such as an empty stretcher) was considered to be work and thus not to be carried (Jer 17:21–22).[292] When Jesus caught up with the healed paralytic, Jesus told him to not sin anymore (John 5:14). Perhaps, if a paralytic carried his mat it was a demonstration of praise, but if he kept it up, he would have harm come to him because he was being viewed as sinning and the Jews were

---

284. *t. Šabb.* 16.25.

285. *Sipra* intr 1; *'Abot R. Nat.* 37; *Gen. Rab.* 92.7; *Pesaḥ.* 18b; *Yoma* 43a; Ellis, *The Old Testament in Early Christianity*, 130–2.

286. *M. Šabb.* 22.6; *M. Yoma* 8.6; *Mek.* on Exod 22:2 and 23:13; whereas other Pharisees oppose treating minor medical cases on the Sabbath (*m. Yoma* 8.6; *t. Šabb.* 12.12–13; 17.14; *p. 'Erub.* 10.11; *Ma'aś. Š.* 2.1.4).

287. *Suk.* 49b; *Rab.* on Deut 16:18.

288. *Šabb.* 150a.

289. Some rabbis considered that God continued to work on Sabbath (*Exod. Rab.* 30.9) but Philo disagreed, considering that God also stops work on Sabbath (*Chem.* 86–90); Instone-Brewer, *Feasts and Sabbaths*, 71.

290. *Mek. Sabta* 1; *Mek.* on Exod 31:14, 104a; *Yoma* 85b.

291. Fisher, "Jesus Through Jewish Eyes," A paper presented at ETS, Nov. 2003; additionally, *Eccles Rab.* 9.7 and *m. Šabb.* 7.2 permitted carrying the sick on Sabbath.

292. CD 11.8–9; 4Q251 frag. 1–2; *m. Šabb.* 10.5b; Instone-Brewer, *Feasts and Sabbaths*, 41–42.

seeking Jesus' life (John 5:10-14). In this early Jewish context, Josephus describes that many of the traditional Sabbath regulations were not in force in Jesus' time.²⁹³ The Pharisees in the gospel accounts insist upon the strictures of Sabbath-keeping so tightly as to annul other features of the Law. As we have seen on questions that are not fully settled, Jesus took clear positions, usually opposed the extreme views of Shammai, sometimes in favor of those of Hillel, as on Sabbath.²⁹⁴ As Safri concludes "Jesus' Sabbath healings which angered the head of the synagogue were permitted by *tannaitic* [early rabbinic] law."²⁹⁵ In fact, as Samuel Cohon develops, "What is puzzling to Jewish students is that the attitude about the Sabbath as reflected in rabbinic Judaism is near to that ascribed to Jesus and remote from that ascribed to his opponents."²⁹⁶ While this is true, there are traditional texts to which the Pharisees of the gospels could appeal, but Jesus answered their argument with a wisdom appeal.²⁹⁷ The Pharisees counseled together to destroy Jesus when He violated their view (Matt 12:13-14; Mark 3:5-6; Luke 6:10-11). However, John Fisher shows an example of this resonance of Jesus and the rabbis in the event of eating heads of grain on the Sabbath, in light of sowing and reaping being forbidden (Exod 16:25-30; 34:21; Lev 19:9-10; 23:22; Deut 23:24-25; Matt 12:1-5; Mark 2:23-28).²⁹⁸

> In the first century, it was also apparently the general opinion, at least in Galilee, that it was acceptable not only to pick up fallen ears of grain but also to rub them in one's hand to get to the grain. Some Pharisees objected to this practice, but according to others it was perfectly permissible. The Talmud itself says: "Bundles which can be taken up with one hand may be handled on the Sabbath...and he may break it with his hand and eat thereof"

---

293. Fisher, "Jesus Through Jewish Eyes," A paper presented at ETS, Nov. 2003.

294. *T. Šabb.* 16.21-22; *b. Šabb.* 5b, bar., 18b; *Gen. Rab.* 7.2; Josephus, *J. W.* 2.147; CD 10.9; 11.4-5; Strabo 16.2.40; Mart. *Epig.* 4.43; Suet. *Aug* 76; Lee, *The Galilean Jewishness of Jesus.*

295. Safri, "Religion in Everyday Life," In *The Jewish People in the First Century.* ed. Safri and Stern, 2:805.

296. Cohon, "The Place of Jesus in the Religious Life of His Day," *JBL* 48(1929): 97.

297. CD 10.15-11.18 and especially 11.13-14 argue that one should not lift an animal out of a pit on the Sabbath; cf. 4Q265; *Miscellaneous Roles* fragment 7, 1.6-9; *m. Besa* 3.4. However, Jesus obviously takes issue with this view when He asks the question, "What man shall there be among you, who shall have one sheep, and it falls into a pit on the Sabbath, will not take hold of it, and lift it out? Of how much more value then is a man than a sheep! So then it is lawful to do good on the Sabbath." (Matt 12:11-12; Luke 14:5).

298. 4Q159; Josephus, *Ant.* 4.231-9; *m. pe'a passim; b. B. Mes.* 92a.

(*Shabbat* 128a). This certainly allows for what the disciples did; their actions fall well within the bounds of acceptable practice.[299]

When questioned on the Sabbath healings, Jesus gave a standard Jewish response. As John Fisher continues to explain Jesus' Jewish response to such queries.

> He made these replies in typical rabbinic fashion and form as well, frequently using a specific kind of homily called *yelammedenu*. This involves a question addressed to the teacher, followed by his answer based on a *midrash* (interpretation) or *halakah* authorized opinion). The Sabbath passages (Matt 12:1-13; Mark 2:23-28; 3:1-6; Luke 13:10-17; 14:1-6; John 5:1-16; 7:22-23) record Yeshua's response in this form, in which he cited an interpretation of Scripture or an accepted rabbinic opinion, e.g., "Is it lawful to save life or let it die on the Sabbath?" (*Yoma* 35b). In fact, his argument closely parallel that of the somewhat later Rabbi Ishmael (*Yoma* 85a), particularly in Mark 3. In typical rabbinic fashion he also frequently cited both the principle and an example which helped clarify it. In making his case in situations such as this, he used a variety of familiar Jewish concepts, *halakic* conclusions and rabbinic methods.[300]

Part of the regular rabbinic argument about the needs of life overriding the Sabbath restrictions, include David's taking the tabernacle bread (1 Sam 21:6; like Jesus mentioned in Matt 12:3-4; Mark 2:25-26),[301] and the Temple offerings and circumcisions made on the Sabbath (as Lev 24:5-8 and Num 28:9-10 require these sacrifices, they were offered on Sabbath [1 Chr 23:31] and Jesus pointed to in Matt 12:5; Luke 7:22-23).[302] So the Pharisees are hypocrites in fault-finding when Jesus, the disciples, and priests transcend the Sabbath by the Law.

---

299. Fisher, "Jesus Through Jewish Eyes," A paper presented at ETS, Nov. 2003. Gleaning from another's field was permitted (Deut 23:25; Ruth 2:2) but Essenes would not even permit scooping up water on Sabbath (CD 11.1-2) and the extremists excluded gleaning on Sabbath (*p. Ma'aś* 2.6; CD 10.14-11.18; *Jub.* 50 ; *m. Šabb.* 7.2); *b. Šabb.* 127a; Pines, "The Jewish Christians of the Early Centuries of Christianities According to a New Source," *The Israeli Academy of Sciences and Humanities Proceedings* [Jerusalem], 2(1966): 266.

300. Fisher, "Jesus Through Jewish Eyes" A paper presented at ETS, Nov. 2003; Cohon, "The Place of Jesus in the Religious Life of His Day," *JBL* 48(1929): 98; Finkel, *The Pharisees & the Teacher of Nazareth*, 163-172.

301. The availability of the bread implies that the bread had just been changed.

302. 11QTemple 13.17; *Y'lomm'denu, Yalkut* 2, par. 130; *T. Šabb.* 15b.

It is important to notice that Jesus entered into discussions with others concerning the prohibitions about Sabbath, He did not just suspend Sabbath and its traditions. The *Gos. Thom.* 27.2 presents Jesus affirming Sabbath keeping as including the blessing of seeing the Father in Kingdom. In Matthew, Jesus implied the continuance of Sabbath Laws when He urged the disciples to "pray that your flight is not in winter or on the Sabbath" (Matt 24:20; Exod 16:29; Isa 58:13).[303] Furthermore, if He had broken Sabbath, then evidence of this would have been used against Him at His trial, but there is no trace of that.

Matthew goes beyond these common Jewish appeals in having Jesus claim that something[304] is present, namely the kingdom of love, that is greater than the Temple (Matt 12:6). In this context, where something transcends legal features like the Temple, the Son of Man transcends the Sabbath in any way He wills (Matt 12:8; Mark 2:28; Luke 6:5). However, Jesus transcends Sabbath consistent with the Law and Prophets. Namely, legal strictures transcended by: design, kingdom, and especially compassion.

Touched by the Unclean

That which is clean is a measure of what is appropriate for Israel in light of their relationship with Yahweh.[305] Uncleanness is then a measure of what is inappropriate within this relationship. Cleanness and uncleanness are metaphysical concepts and not merely ethical ones. Therefore, a leper, or a person who has a hemorrhage, or the dead are all unclean (Lev 12–14; 15:4–27; Num 19:11–12). Such uncleanness is transferred by touch as a communicable disease (Lev 5:2–3; 7:19–21; 11:4–47; 12:2; 15:2–33; 17:15; 18:19; 20:25; 22:4–8; Num 19:11–22; Deut 23:10; Ezek 22:10; Hag 2:12–13).[306] In this process, derived uncleanness is usually not as potently unclean as the source, in that the remedy requires less (Lev 15:4–27). The recovery process or atonement is costly with time and sometimes monetarily because of the cost of a sacrifice. However, there are forms of uncleanness that are more virulent and lasting. For these, Priestly inspections and more elaborate sacrifices may need to be provided for atonement to recover one into a clean condition. Ultimately the

---

303. For example, Qumran prohibited walking more than 1000 cubits on the Sabbath (CD 10.21).

304. "Something" is neuter, therefore not just a person but also a quality like kingdom of love.

305. For a more complete discussion of this issue: Kennard, *Biblical Covenantalism*, 1:244–314.

306. *M. 'Ohalot* 18.7 even considers Gentiles and their dwellings unclean.

atonement process included the Israelite's compliance with the Mosaic covenant. The famous first century rabbi, Yohanan ben Zakkai stated, "In life it is not the dead who make you unclean; nor is it the water, but the ordinances of the king of kings that purifies."[307] Yohanan ben Zakkai was once asked does a corpse become purified by the water from red heifer, to which he responded publicly, that to take it as such was no different than paganism. However, privately to His disciples he responded "Neither was uncleanness caused by the corpse nor cleanness by the 'water of separation,' but the statute of the red heifer was one of those which had to be accepted as the will of God though no rational basis for it could be discerned."[308]

From within this framework it is amazing that Jesus actively touches the unclean in healing and allows Himself to be touched by them for healing to occur.[309] It is as though the presence of the King did not become unclean by their communicable uncleanness. Rather, the presence of the King rendered the unclean to be clean in the Jubilee healing process occurring in the surrounding kingdom expression of Jesus' healings.[310] Jesus takes the infirmities on Himself in such an atonement manner as to render the infirmed clean and healed (Isa 53:4; Matt 8:17). For example, a leper is touched by Jesus and the leper is healed (Matt 8:3; Mark 1:41; Luke 5:13). Jesus then instructs the healed leper that he needs to present himself to the priest and make the appropriate offering that Moses had commanded (Matt 8:4; Mark 1:44; Luke 5:14). Likewise, a woman with a hemorrhage was both cleansed and healed by her touch of one of Jesus' tassels (Matt 9:20–22; Mark 5:27–31; Luke 8:44–47). Likewise, Jesus takes a dead girl by the hand to bring her back to life (Matt 9:25; Mark 5:41; Luke 8:54).

The Pharisees criticize Jesus in that He allows the unclean to touch Him (Luke 7:39). The particular criticism was in the house of a Pharisee, when a sinful woman broke an alabaster vial and began to anoint Jesus feet with the perfume and wipe it with her hair (Luke 7:37–38). The Pharisee who had invited Jesus said to himself, "If this man were a prophet He would know what sort of person this woman is who is touching Him, that she is a sinner." The Pharisees were overly restrictive to not be touched by sinners, so that they

---

307. Fisher, "Jesus Through Jewish Eyes," A paper presented at ETS, Nov. 2003.

308. Daube, *The New Testament and Rabbinic Judaism*, 141–142.

309. Jesus actively touches the unclean in healing (Matt 8:3, 15; 9:25, 29; 20:34; Mark 1:41; 5:41; 7:33; 8:22; Luke 5:13; 7:14; 8:54; 22:51). Jesus also allows Himself to be touched by the unclean for healing (Matt 9:20–21; 14:36; Mark 3:10; 5:27–31; 6:56: Luke 6:19; 8:44–47).

310. Kennard, *Messiah Jesus*, 132–33; Holmén, "A Contagious Purity: Jesus' Inverse Strategy for Eschatological Cleanness," In *Jesus Research*. ed. Charlesworth with Pokorny, 199–229.

would not defile themselves. For example, the *Assumption of Moses* 7.9–10 describes these Jews as "their hands and hearts are all corrupt, and their mouths are full of boasting-and yet they complain: Do not touch me lest you make me unclean." Jesus responded to this Pharisee with a parable about a certain moneylender who forgave a debtor who owed five hundred denarii, and another who owed fifty denarii (Luke 7:41–42). Simon, the Pharisee recognized that the one forgiven more would love more (Luke 7:43). Jesus applied the parable by reminding the Pharisee of the lack of his hospitality (no foot washing, no kiss, no anointing) were all made up by the woman who had washed Jesus' feet with her tears and hair, and provided the rest as well. "For this reason I say to you, her sins, which are many have been forgiven, for she loved much; but he who is forgiven little, loves little" (Luke 7:47).[311]

Matthew 21–23;[312] Jesus as the Superior Jewish Scribe of *Hallakah*

In this section we shift from the epistemology and content of Jesus' message to Jesus' ultimate *authority* to teach this content. Here we explore *the epistemic authority of Jesus as Messiah, who judges the leadership of Israel and their Temple* (the symbol of their authority). As Jesus challenges the religious leader's authority through His own teaching on the Law, the religious leaders respond back with a challenge of their own: namely, what authority does Jesus have to make these challenges? This operates on two levels. One level of challenge is what sort of scribal authority Jesus has to present Himself as an authoritative scribe. The professional scribes would usually grant unusually able scribes a level of authority on the basis of tests and demonstrated competency. This level of challenge we will investigate here. The other level of challenge goes further into the content of Jesus' challenge to that of His Messianic authority to judge them. However, if Jesus is stumped, shamed and ridiculed as an inferior scribe it would indicate that He could not be a suitable candidate for Messiah. So the issue of scribal authority is quite significant to this topic. The authority of Jesus as a superior

---

311. Kennard, *Messiah Jesus*, 34, 119.

312. Most Matthew specialists see chapter 21 beginning a new section (Davies and Allison, *Matthew*, 3:111–112) leaving the Galilean ministry for the rejection of Jewish temple and leadership, which sets the tone for: 1) Jesus' rejection and death, 2) the destruction of the temple and Israel, and 3) eschatological Kingdom. The unit also begins with a phrase that returns at the end as an *inclusio*, namely, "Blessed is He Who comes in the name of the Lord" (Matt 21:9; 23:39). Much of the unit explores Jesus as Messianic scribe and judge.

scribe fits in this chapter since it is the contextual warrant for the authority of Jesus' teaching of the Law.

Jesus bests the best that the establishment has to offer. This presentation is heavily dependent upon Jewish rhetorical criticism, for understanding the kind of questions being asked in what turns out to be a very public discourse. This discourse especially presents Jesus as a superior scribe, and who bests the best that the establishment has to offer. For example, the Talmud describes standard forensic interrogation of a rabbi's acumen by means of rhetorical questions in four distinct styles: 1) *halachic* or scientific questions about the application of Torah to specific situations, 2) nonsense questions designed to rattle and ridicule a scholar and his interpretations of Scripture, 3) conduct questions larger than any one text, and 4) *haggadic* or contrary questions.[313] The Jewish leadership broadly wished to use these rabbinical techniques to trap Jesus and show Him deficient and overreaching (Matt 22:15-46; Mark 12:13-37; Luke 20:19-44). Instead, the approach backfired on them, showing Jesus superior ability as a scribe and the religious leadership's deficiency. This issue warrants Jesus as a superior scribe.

The Jewish authority structure during early Judaism meant that the Herodians held high posts aligning with Herodian political authority and with Rome. The Herodians were partisans of the Herodian dynasty including those religious leaders perhaps of the Boethusians and their scribes that accepted Roman dominance and tried to please Herod, so that they could maintain themselves in their political power as religious leaders (compare Luke 20:19 with Matt 22:16 and Mark 3:6; 12:13).[314] The Sadducees were pro-Hasmonean conservative Jews disenfranchised from kingship by Herod the Great yet purchasing their way into high priesthood with Rome and thus closely associated with this power block of religious leaders who controlled the Temple and the High Priesthood (such as: Annas [6-15 A.D.] and Caiaphus [18-37 A.D.], Matt 26:57-65; Luke 3:2; John 18:13; Acts 4:6). The Sadducees were content with the power structure that allowed them decades of control of the Temple and the High Priesthood. These Sadducees only accepted Pentateuch as Scripture and thus did not embrace a resurrection view (Acts 23:6-10).[315] The Pharisees were progressive Jews, tending to accept the prophets and writings, and thus embraced a hopeful resurrection

---

313. Daube, *The New Testament and Rabbinic Judaism*, 158-69 and "Rabbinic Methods of Interpretation and Hellenistic Rhetoric," *HUCA* 22(1949):239-264; Molina and Neyrey, *Calling Jesus Names*, 73-74.

314. M. Menaḥ. 10.3; m. 'Abot 1.3; Harold Hoener, "5. The Herodians," In *Dictionary of New Testament Background*. ed. Evans and Porter, 493.

315. Josephus, *Ant.* 13.297-98; 18.1.4, 18.16-17; *J. W.* 2.8.14, 2.164-66; *Nahum Commentary* on 3.8 (col. 3.8-9), 3.9b-11 (col. 3.12-4.8); m. 'Abot 1.3.

view for the afterlife (Acts 23:6–10; Dan 12:2).[316] The Pharisees' power block was especially in the village synagogues but they had considerable adherents at the Temple as well. In general these Pharisees were hoping for a Messiah to free them from the Romans and to bring in the kingdom.

The first challenge comes from the Herodians and Pharisees in the form of a *halachic* or scientific question, identified by "Is it lawful to. . .?" (Matt 22:15–22; Mark 12:13–17; Luke 20:19–26). Notice that the Herodians (who had accepted Roman dominance) and the Pharisees (who usually opposed Roman domination), cooperated to try to trap Jesus between their concerns. Flattery begins the trap, "Teacher, we know that You are truthful and teach the way of God in truth." Then the critical issue of Jesus' authority is raised, since He defers to no one and is not partial. Now the *halachic* question tried to tighten the noose around Jesus' neck; "is it lawful to give poll-tax to Caesar, or not?" The poll-tax was the most obvious sign in Jewish life of submission to Rome. For example, in A.D. 6 Judas of Galilee led a revolt against the procurator because the procurator took a census for the purpose of collecting poll-tax.[317] If Jesus said that the poll-tax was unlawful, or was against the Jewish Law, then the Herodians would have Him trapped in advocating seditious activity as a zealot, a capital offense under Rome. If Jesus said that the tax was lawful, then the Pharisees and Herodians would have Jesus buckling to the Roman dominance in a manner that would alienate the Jewish populous and deflate their hopes for a removal of the Roman oppressors. Many Jews resented the poll-tax, repeatedly finding that the poll-tax was an oppressive burden and had petitioned for its reduction but to little avail.[318]

Jesus perceived their malice in this dilemma and called them down for their hypocrisy. His response was to empirically see a denarius, the coin used to pay the poll-tax each year.[319] Jesus lays His trap by asking His accusers whose face and inscription is on the coin. The coin identified Tiberius Caesar by head and with its inscription (and several of these coins have been

---

316. Josephus, *Ant.* 13.297–98; 18.1.4; *J. W.* 2.8.14, 2.164–66; *Nahum Commentary* on 2.12 (col. 1.4–8); 3.1–4 (col. 2.1–10), 3.6–7 (col. 3.1–8), 3.9b–11 (col. 3.12–4.8); *m. 'Abot* 1.3.

317. Josephus, *Ant.* 17. 204; 18.3.i.1; *J. W.* 2.8.1 paragraph 118.

318. Tacitus, *Ann.* 2.42 referring especially to A.D. 17.

319. Palmyra inscription in Dittenberger, *OGIS* 629.153–6; This is a superior presentation than the account transpiring in *Gos. Thom.* 100 and Justin Martyr, *1 Apol.* 17.2, because it used audiovisuals that were accurate to the context (e.g. a denarius was a silver coin, not a gold one like the one Thomas claims) and verbally sliced through the issue instead of a blunt response. Additionally, Matthew has increased the parallelism over Mark and Luke.

EPISTEMOLOGY AND LOGIC OF JESUS AS PRESENTED IN MATTHEW   79

found by archeologists in the Jewish Temple ruins near the southern wall).[320] The people responded that it was Caesar's coin. Jesus responded, "render to Caesar the things that are Caesar's and to God the things that are God's." The religious leaders and the people[321] were amazed at His answer. Jesus had removed Himself from the trap and reaffirmed the obligation they had to their authorities, while neither aligning Himself with Caesar nor being a seditious zealot.[322] The people as well as the religious leaders were amazed at the skill at which He had answered them.

The second challenge comes from the Sadducees in the form of a nonsense question (Matt 22:23-33; Mark 12:18-27; Luke 20:27-40). They begin by flattery of calling Him teacher, even though they do not seek to be instructed. The Sadducees instead built a theological riddle on the law for Levirate marriage, which identified that to provide for keeping an inheritance within the family that if a husband died without a child that his brother was to sire a child in his brother's name so that his brother would have an heir (Deut 25:5).[323] The Sadducees (who do not believe in a resurrection)[324] weave a nonsensical question about marriage continuing in the afterlife, and wonder if a wife had seven husbands whose wife would she be in the resurrection.[325] The absurdity is made particularly acute by: 1) their conjectures of marriage in resurrection, which is foreign to the Law[326] and 2) polyandry, which is foreign to Judaism.

---

320. Most of the coinage in Israel from this era are Tyrean shekels but there is evidence of Roman denarii in Jerusalem Temple ruins at this time, especially to pay this tax; J. Kennard, *Render to God*, viii, 51-55; Ariel, "Survey of Coin Finds in Jerusalem (until the End of the Byzantine Period)," *Liber Annus* 32(1982): 284, 312 #22 in table 3, 313 #31 and #54, 314 #60; Burnett, *Roman Provincial Coinage*, 12, 26, 29, 31, 587, 590; Matthews, "The Tax Law of Palmyria," *JRS* 74(1984): 157-80; Collins, *Mark*, 552-55; Davies and Allison, *Matthew*, 3:216, 218.

321. Luke 20:26; *Gos. Thom.* 100; thus Jesus is not a social rebel of Hellenistic Cynic similar to Diogenes of Sinope as proposed by Crossan, *The Historical Jesus*.

322. Contrary to Aslan, *Zealot*.

323. Josephus, *Ant.* 4.8.23; *m. Yebamot*.

324. Josephus, *Ant.* 18.1.4; *J. W.* 2.8.14.

325. "The resurrection" is a Jewish way of referring to the afterlife, especially from a Pharisaic point of view (Wis 2.1-5; *1 En.* 102.6-11; *m. Sanh.* 10.1; *b. Sanh.* 90b).

326. There is no clear development of resurrection in the Pentateuch. Furthermore, there is only a brief mention of procreation and fertility within marriage in the kingdom (Isa 54:1-2; *1 En.* 10.17-19; *B. Šabb.* 30b; *Pirqe Mashiah, BhM* 3.77-78.), but it does not raise the issue of how this works out in the resurrection. However, fertility of the barren in these contexts fits within the broader theme of the fruitfulness of the kingdom (Isa 54:1-3; 55:1-13; 56:9-12; *1 En.* 10.17-19; *2 Bar.* 29; *M. Middot* 2.6; *T. Suk.* 3.3, 10; *B. Yoma* 77b-78a; *Y. Sheqalim* 50a mid.; *B. Šabb.* 30b; *B. Ket.* 111b; *Pirqe Mashiah, BhM* 3.74, 77-78).

Jesus response first deals with the Saducees ignorance about the resurrection, which He takes is evident from the Scriptures, more broadly, as in a Pharisaic orientation, and that the power of God is very able to accomplish these promises. So Jesus' charge back to them is that they are playing with only a half deck of Scriptures and too small a God concept. Jesus then returns to the resurrection and instructs them. The resurrection is an arena that the initiating of marriages to have kids does not apply, because those in the resurrection are like angels in heaven, living forever, so that there is no need to procreate to raise up an inheritor.[327] So these Saducees through their misapplication further show that they are out of touch with the purposes of the Law. Then Jesus passes from the *manner* of the resurrection to its *fact* of continuing existence, populated by at least some of the patriarchs of the faith, like Abraham, Isaac, and Jacob.[328] To demonstrate this, Jesus cites Pentateuch texts which the Sadducees would recognize as Scripture, what God said to Moses in Exodus 3:6, "I am the God of Abraham, and the God of Isaac, and the God of Jacob," and then affirmed that God is not the God of the dead but of the living. Consistent with some Pharisaic Jewish tradition, Jesus claims that the resurrection already occurs for the dead (Luke 16:19–31) and that in this resurrection, Abraham, Isaac and Jacob are already alive and not merely historical figures of the past.[329] Such an

---

327. Jesus does not develop the similarity to angels for those in resurrection beyond the lack of marrying, so to extend this text to similarities like being spirit beings without bodies (*T. Abr.* A 4.9; Philo, *QG* 1.92; maybe LXX of Ps 103:4) or undergoing angelification, would be conjecture, though Jewish tradition does comment upon such a process (Wis 5.5; 4QSb 4.25; 4Q511 fr. 35; 4QM; *1 En.* 70–71; 104.1–6; *2 En.* 22.4–112 *Bar.* 51.5, 10; *T. Isaac* 4.43–48; Philo, *Sacr CA* 1.5; Acts 12:15 may also apply). Jewish afterlife developed to include an astral immortality (Dan 12:2–3; *1 En.* 15.6–7; 104.2–7; 4 Macc 17.5; *2 Bar.* 51.10; *LAB* 33.5; *As. Mos.* 10.9; *CU* 2.43–44, no. 788). For example, Jesus does not develop the Jewish view that as Adam became heavenly he became genderless (Philo, *Opf.* 151–2; *Mek.* on Exod 12:40; *b. Ber.* 61a; *b. Meg.* 9a; *b. 'Erub.* 18a; *Gen. Rab.* on Gen 1:26). Remember that the Jewish tradition understood Genesis 6:2 to mean that at least some angels engaged in sexual intercourse with human women (*1 En.* 6–7; 19.1; 86.1–3; 106.13–17; *Jub.* 4.15, 22; 5.1–11; 1QapGen. 2.1, 16; *2 Bar.* 56.12; *T. Reub.* 5.6; *T. Naph.* 3.4–5; 2 Pet 2:4; Jude 6–7; Justin, *2 Apol.* 5; Tertullian, *De virg. vel.* 7; *Tg. Ps.-Jn.* on Gen 6:1–4. Unfortunately, Christianity accelerated toward asceticism because of this text, as Christians tried to become like angels in Neo-Platonic ways.

328. Vermes argues that Pharisaic rabbis of the third century supplied similar arguments (*The Religion of Jesus the Jew*, 69). For example, Rabbi Simai argues for historical past resurrection of Abraham, Isaac and Jacob for God to be in covenant relationship with them, likewise, Rabbi Yohanan argues for the continued life of Aaron for tithes to be paid to him (*b. Sanh.* 90b).

329. Jesus view (Luke 16:19–31) is consistent with Jewish tradition (*Abr.* 50–55; 4 Macc 7:18–19; 13.17; 16:25; Philo, *Sacr. CA* 1.5; *T. Abr.* 20.8–14; *Qoh. Rab.* 9.5.1; *b. Sanh* 90b; *Ex. Rab.* 1.8; *Deut. Rab.* 3.15; *LAB* 4.11; *T. Isaac* 2.1–5; *T. Benj.* 10.6; *Apoc. Sed.* 14.3; *3 En.* 44.7). The sages could also read "living God" as "God of the living" (*Pesiq. R.* 1.2).

argument is also consistent with Hillel logical rule two; *an analogy made between two texts on the basis of phrase or word* for "life."[330] Mark's account has Jesus returning to emphasize that the Sadducees are greatly mistaken (Mark 12:27). Luke's account has some of the scribes affirming that Jesus as a teacher had spoken very well (Luke 20:39). Matthew indicated that the multitude was astonished at His teaching and the Sadducees were silenced (Matt 22:33-34).

The third challenge comes from a Pharisee legal expert in the form of a conduct question (Matt 22:34-40). The lawyer asked Jesus about prioritizing the Law into the greatest commandment. In response, Jesus provides the correct answer of the *shema* as the greatest commandment, "You shall love the Lord your God with all your heart, and with all your soul, and with all your mind." He quickly followed this with a second command of "You shall love your neighbor as yourself." These two commands are alike in that the whole Law and prophets depend or hang upon these two for their unifying framework. This is not a novel perspective, for it is the very answer given to Jesus by a lawyer earlier in his ministry and elsewhere in Jewish tradition (Luke 10:25-28).[331] At that earlier time Jesus had said that such a Law oriented way of living was salvific. However, in this inquisition, none were seeking such a salvation; they were frustrated at not being able to trap Jesus.

Each of these three questions demonstrated a superiority of Jesus' scribal ability. So Jesus turned the tables on the Pharisees gathered there and asked a *haggadic*[332] or contrary question, which is what would be expected if these questions were being presented as the test of scribal warrant (Matt 22:41-46; Mark 12:35-37; Luke 20:41-44). He did not wait for them to approve Him as in an ordination exam; He had demonstrated His authority, so that He used their own tools to further question their authority and show His scribal proficiency by asking them the final kind of rabbinic question. His question raised the real issue, the authority of the Messiah. "Whose son is the Christ?" The religious leaders answered "The son of David."[333] While not denying their answer, Jesus then asked the contrary question, "Then

---

330. *Sipra* intr 2; *'Abot R. Nat.* 37; *Šabb.* 64a ; Ellis, *The Old Testament in Early Christianity*, 130-2.

331. Akiba, *Sipre* on Lev 19:18; *T. Iss.* 5.2; 7.6; *T. Dan.* 5.3; Aristeas, *Ep.* 229; Philo, *De virt.* 51; 95; *Spec. leg.* 2.63; *De Abr.* 208; *T. Naph.* 8.9-10; *Jub.* 7.20; 20.2; 36.7-8; Josephus, *J. W.* 2.139. The early church was quite committed to following the same perspective (1 Jn. 4:21; *Did.* 1.2; Polycarp, *Ep.* 3.3; Justin, *Dial.* 93; Sextus, *Sent.* 106a-b; Tertullian, *Adv. Marc.* 5.8).

332. Owen-Ball, "Rabbinic Rhetoric and the Tribute Passage (Matt 22:15-22; Mark 12:13-17; Luke 20:20-26)," *Nov. Test.* 35(1993): 4; Keener, *Matthew*, 532.

333. *Ps. Sol.* 17.21-25; 4QFlor. 1.11-13; Justin Martyr, *First Apology* 45.

how does David in the Spirit call him 'Lord,' saying, 'The Lord said to my Lord, Sit at My right hand, until I put Your enemies beneath Your feet?' If David calls Him 'Lord,' how is He his son?" This contrary question pressed the authority of Christ consistent with rabbinical reasoning[334] beyond the Davidic king idea to a One, Who was more. No one was able to answer Him. Furthermore, Jesus had demonstrated His superior scribal ability, so from that day on no one asked any more entrapment questions.

Narrative Story *Haggadah*

Narrative in any form performs the function of re-telling a story.[335] The gospels develop Jesus in a narrative context that communicates character and displays His epistemology is consistent with the previous teachings.[336] As such, Jesus becomes a moral exemplar for disciples to imitate consistent with His teachings.[337] However, Jesus does not present this narrative, the gospel authors do, so this issue will be developed when Luke's historiography and biography is discussed in the next chapter.

In the biblical presentation of narrative *haggadah* Jesus contributes in at least two ways. First, Jesus re-envisions the Passover enactment of God's redemption of Israel into the meal which initiates the new covenant with His disciples so that they will continue to re-enact the new covenant in *Eucharist*. The performance is part of its meaning in the context in which such practice has meaning. As such, *Eucharist becomes performative language and practice in initiating and renewing the disciples place within the new covenant.*[338] Jesus

---

334. None of the following sources is pre-Christian but they show Jesus to be probably unoriginal about the application of Psalm 110 to Messiah (Akiba, *b. Sanh.* 38b; *Gen. Rab.* 85.9; *Num. Rab.* 18.23; *Tg.* on Ps 110; Davies and Allison, *Matthew*, 3:253–4).

335. Grice, "Meaning," *Philosophical Review* 66(1957): 377–88; "Utterer's Meaning and Intentions," *Philosophical Review* 78(1969): 147–77; "Utterer's Meaning, Sentence-Meaning, Word-Meaning," In *The Philosophy of Language*. ed. Searle, 54–70; Austin, *How to Do Things with Words*; Ricoeur, *Oneself as Another*, 44; Kennard, *The Relationship Between Epistemology*, 56, 62–65; *A Critical Realist's*, 232.

336. Ricoeur, *Oneself as Another*, 113, 119, 140; Johnson, "The Jesus of the Gospels and Philosophy," In *Jesus and Philosophy*. ed. Moser, 70–1; a similar role is urged upon any teacher by Seneca, *Moral Epistles* 20.1.

337. Johnson, "The Jesus of the Gospels and Philosophy," In *Jesus and Philosophy*. ed. Moser, 68–9; a similar role is provided by the father in Pseudo-Isocrates, *Demonicus* and the teacher in Lucian of Samosata, *Demonax* and *Nigrinus*.

338. Barton, "Memory and Remembrance in Paul," In *Memory in the Bible and Antiquity*. ed. Barton, Stuckenbruck and Wold, 333–4; Foley, "Indigenous Poems, Colonialist Texts," In *Orality, Literacy, and Colonialism in Antiquity*. ed. Draper, 28–31; Austin, *How to do Things with Words*.

final Passover and upper room discourse provides a level of relationship between Jesus and the disciples that indicates the Master is allowing His disciples to be intimately included (Matt 26:20-29; Mark 14:17-31; Luke 22:14-34; John 13:1-16:33; 1 Cor 11:23-26). Jesus told His disciples that He earnestly desired to eat this Passover with His disciples. While they were eating,[339] Jesus took some bread, blessed it, broke it, and gave it to His disciples saying "Take, eat this is My body."[340] Jesus then took the fourth cup (or a second third cup) of the Passover.[341] Jesus gave thanks and gave it to His disciples to drink saying, "This cup is the new covenant in My blood, shed on behalf of many for forgiveness of sins." Each gospel is enigmatic but when these statements are combined they add to this covenantal atonement model: Luke adds "the new covenant," Mark adds "for the many," and Matthew "for the forgiveness of sins." The statement of "covenant in blood" is reminiscent of Exod 24:8 (especially in Matt and Mark, commemorated in discussions from especially the second until the third cup). Luke provides the lens of the new covenant of Jer 31:31 (Luke 22:20), with its forgiveness (themes common to the fourth cup, which sometimes looks toward the kingdom), and perhaps a hint of Isaiah 53:12 death "for many." Jesus then identified that He would not drink wine again until He did so in the kingdom of God, which would likely be the final (or fourth) cup of the Passover, unless He left Passover unfinished. The subsequent repetition of the meal performs the function of retelling the story which defines the new community.

Second, Jesus tells parables as meaningful stories to flesh out and concretize His teachings, similar to how they were used among the rabbinics. This development could be considered as an ancient Jewish sage.[342] As

---

339. Passover had four cups (*m. Pesaḥ.* 10; Marshall, *Luke*, 797-98; Bahr, "The Seder of Passover and the Eucharistic Words." *NovT* 12 [1970]: 181-202). The third cup would be preceded by the paschal lamb and discussion of the exodus events recounted, then after the third cup, there would be dessert of bread and sometimes-salty items, which was open to tailor the conversation to particulars like this novel appropriation by Jesus.

340. Most accounts have bread first then cup, but Luke 22:17-20 has the meal begin with a cup, bread then cup again, which 1 Cor 10:16 and *Did.* 9:1-4 takes as the order of cup then bread. Historically, the likely order is the bread then cup, which is a second third cup, or a fourth cup (Luke 22:20 "after dining") with the kind of blessings of the third cup.

341. After this cup He does not drink again, so likely the fourth cup (Luke 22:19 mentions "after eating") or a second third cup, based on the blessing (Luke 22:18) and the parallel of vows in Luke 22:15 and 17; Plummer, *Luke*, 495; Bock, *Luke*, 2:1722. The use of a common cup is unusual for Passover but not unprecedented (*t. Ber.* 5.9; *m. Ber.* 8.8; Jeremias, *The Eucharistic Words of Jesus*, 69; SB 4:58-59, 62).

342. Johnson, "The Jesus of the Gospels and Philosophy," In *Jesus and Philosophy*. ed. Moser, 63; Kennard, *Messiah Jesus*, 211-42 I argue for parable contextual meaning

parables their meaning is polyvalent until the context roots its meaning and the *nimshal* (after statement) directs the meaning to address specific issues in a specific manner, thus focusing a particular meaning.[343] For example, the parable of the lost sheep was told six times in three centuries with a different meaning in each context. In Matthew 18:12-13, Jesus urges his disciples as shepherds to humbly look out for the everlasting welfare of all the church, especially any who are vulnerable. This meaning is especially confirmed by the discussion of church discipline and recovery that immediately follows. In Luke 15:2-7 the parable addresses grumbling Pharisees and scribes to urge them to rejoice when sinners are found by Jesus as the shepherd. This meaning is evident by the shepherd's statement in the parable, "Rejoice with me for I have found my sheep which was lost!" (Luke 15:6). This meaning is further confirmed by Jesus' *nimshal* (after statement), "I tell you in the same way that there will be more joy in heaven over one sinner who repents, than the ninety-nine righteous persons who need no repentance" (Luke 15:7). This message for grumblers to get to joy is further echoed through the passage with the subsequent parables (Luke 15:7, 9-10, 24, 29, 32). The *Gospel of Thomas* 107 records that Jesus will rescue the largest and most loved sheep who strayed, which seems odd when compared to Jesus' character as portrayed by the synoptics. *The Gospel of Truth* presents Jesus as the shepherd seeking a lost sheep to be found and when it is found the Father provides interior gnostic knowledge fostering perpetual light.[344] *Genesis Rabbah* 86.4 encourages rabbinic Jews to rescue fellow Jews who stray into Gentile areas and practices. *Exodus Rabbah* 2.2 identifies that Moses is the appropriate leader of Israel because he went after straying sheep. The point is that Jesus and the rabbinics are utilizing a similar method, which cross fertilized each. As Jesus and the rabbinics addressed similar Jewish communities, one can recognize the application of this method. Thus, *the context of the ones addressed, and the after statement identify the meaning of a parable in a specific context*. The epistemic value of

---

and connect them with similar rabbinic parables; McArthur and Johnston, *They also Taught in Parables* nicely collects many of the rabbinic parables; so there is no need to position parables into Aristotelian rhetoric such as Anderson does (*Glossary of Greek Rhetorical Terms Connected to Methods of Argumentation*, 86-87; Aristotle, *Rhet.* 2.20).

343. Meier, *A Marginal Jew*, 5:193-94; Levine, *Short Stories by Jesus*, for this parable especially 29, 42-45; Gregerman, "Critique of *Short Stories by Jesus*" a paper presented at the Society for Biblical Literature, Nov. 22, 2015; Johnson, "Critique of *Short Stories by Jesus*," a paper presented at the Society for Biblical Literature, Nov. 22, 2015; Sandmel, "Critique of *Short Stories by Jesus*" a paper presented at the Society for Biblical Literature, Nov. 22, 2015; Snodgrass, "From Allegorizing to Allegorizing: A History of the Interpretation of the Parables of Jesus," In *The Historical Jesus in Recent Research*. ed. Dunn and McKnight, 248-68.

344. Ehrman, *Lost Scriptures*, 50.

each parable is to evoke the meaning which the after statement declares in ways that first provoke alienation and then provide a clear route of decision to resolve this alienation for kingdom purposes.[345] Since I have already discussed this at length and connected the biblical parables with similar ones among the rabbinics[346] I will not repeat that here.

---

345. Boomershine, "Jesus of Nazareth and the Watershed of Ancient Orality and Literacy," In *Orality and Textuality in Early Christian Literature*. ed. Dewey, 24–29.

346. Kennard, *Messiah Jesus*, 211–42.

3

Lukan Historiography and the Epistemology of Gospel Proclamation

THESIS: THE CALL OF Christ to the disciples provides an expectation for an oral phase of gospel testimony similar to rabbinic oral tradition. A shift to a written phase of testimony referencing their empirical experience with Christ, for Peter, Paul, and Luke occurs as original disciples begin to die and as authoritative legal witnesses, like Cicero, begin to produce substantial written documents of witness outside of a courtroom. Luke writes accurate history, within the established Hellenistic Greco-Roman patterns, which present salvation history and a repeated gospel message grounded in *midrash* of O.T. prophecy, direct communication from God's representative, confirming miracle, authoritative testimony, and empirical evidence. Luke utilized established rhetoric for Greco-Roman historians and framed condensed speeches utilizing appropriate authorial character and rhetoric to engage their audience. Such speeches and narrative of Luke-Acts consistently present epistemic virtues to imitate, such that the readers should follow the disciples in imitating Christ.

Historical studies frame an account drawing on eyewitness testimony and the weaving together of credible testimony from sources. The gospel writers attempted to recover and communicate what can be historically known of Jesus, which is especially appropriate in light of the biblical claims for historicity (Luke 1:1–4; Acts 1:1; 2 Pet 1:16–17; 1 John 1:1). They show awareness of specific events that further evidence a commitment to historical precision.

Modern historical Jesus studies had three quests which reflect the character of critical analysis embedded within them. Having written elsewhere at greater depth, I will briefly summarize certain aspects of historical Jesus studies here.[1] The first quest (1778–1906 A.D.) assumed that the Jesus

---

1. Pate and Kennard addressed these concerns of the historical Jesus at greater depth in *Deliverance Now and Not Yet*, chapter sixteen, "The Historical Jesus and the

of history was not the same as the gospel's portraits of Christ. For example, the first quest was initiated by H. Samuel Reimarus, who considered that Jesus was an apocalyptic preacher whose expectation of the impending arrival of the kingdom of God met stunning disappointment.[2] William Wrede especially showed that identifying Jesus out of the earliest written sources was no longer sufficient for it was necessary to uncover earlier traditions upon which these sources rested.[3] A variety of responses emerged to answer this felt need. This first quest was populated by: 1) traditional conservative responses (J. J. Hess, Adolf Schlatter),[4] 2) the life of Jesus from an antisupernatural perspective (Schleiermacher, Strauss, and Renan),[5] 3) a liberal Jesus as an ethical teacher, dominated by the Sermon on the Mount (Ritschl and Harnack),[6] and 4) Albert Schweitzer's work, *The Quest of the Historical Jesus*[7] which brought the quest to a close. Schweitzer identified three crises of the first quest: 1) bi-furcation of historicity and supernaturalism, 2) which meant that the interpreter landed in either synoptic gospels or John, and 3) either an eschatological Jesus or a non-eschatological Jesus. This quest came to a close with Schweitzer's criticism that the questers looked down the well of time to report on a Jesus, but the Jesus they described was their own

---

Great Tribulation," 519–551. There, we discuss 27 criteria for recognizing historical Jesus statements (culled from Polkow-8, Walke-10, McElenry-11, Stein-11, Breech-10, Borin-10, Evans-3, Meier-10) and evaluate many of them for their usability. For general discussion of the historical Jesus issue see: Brown, "Historical Jesus, Quest of," In *Dictionary of Jesus and the Gospels*. ed. Green, McKnight and Marshall, 326–41; Charlesworth, "Jesus Research Expands with Chaotic Creativity," In *Images of Jesus Today*. ed. Charlesworth and Weaver, 1–41; Meier, "Reflections on Jesus-of-History Research Today," In *Jesus' Jewishness*. ed. Charlesworth, 84–107, Borg, *Jesus in Contemporary Scholarship*; Witherington, *The Jesus Quest*; *Jesus Under Fire*. ed. Wilkinson and Moreland, especially McKnight's article, "Who Is Jesus?," 51–72; Johnson, *The Real Jesus*; Wright, *Jesus and the Victory of God*, 1–224; and especially Evans, *Life of Jesus Research*.

2. Reimarus anonymously wrote and Lessing published, "Von dem Zwecke Jesu" translated as *Reimarus: Fragments*.

3. Wrede, *The Messianic Secret*.

4. Hess, *Geschichte der drey letzten Lebensjahre Jesu*; Schlatter, "Der Zweifel an der Messianität Jesu," In *Zur Theologie des Neuen Testaments and zur Dogmatik*, 151–202; *Die Geschichte des Christus* translated as *The History of the Christ*.

5. Schleiermacher, *The Life of Jesus*; Strauss, *The Life of Jesus Critically Examined*; Renan. *The Life of Jesus*.

6. Ritschl, provides the classic liberal view of Jesus; see his *The Christian Doctrine of Justification and Reconciliation*, along with Harnack, *The Mission and Expansion of Christianity*. The latter prompted the famous quip by Alfred Loisy, "The Christ that Harnack sees, looking back through nineteen centuries of Catholic darkness, is only the reflection of a liberal Protestant face, seen at the bottom of a deep well" quoted by Brown, *Quests for the Historical Jesus*, 331.

7. Schweitzer, *The Quest of the Historical Jesus*.

image looking back at themselves from the bottom of the well. By putting these facets together (rather than bi-furcated) we can let the light that is Jesus Himself glint His image rather than our own. Therefore, Schweitzer concludes that the liberal "lives" of Jesus "never had any existence."[8]

There is general agreement that the second quest (1953–late 1960's) began with the celebrated paper by Ernst Käsemann, "The Problem with the Historical Jesus," which tried to bridge the radical divide of Rudolf Bultmann's frail human Jesus and a docetic Christ of faith.[9] Bultmann's form critical tools were conjectured to be able to bridge this chasm. This phase was followed by scholars like Fuchs, Bornkamm, Robinson and Perrin. Colin Brown criticized this quest as "unhistorical and short-sighted" on several counts, especially: 1) "it remained curiously indifferent to the world of first century Judaism as known from Josephus, the Dead Sea Scrolls, and rabbinic literature,"[10] and 2) for second questers, proclamation of the cross was a central event but they really gave no reason for it.

The third quest (mid 1970's–present) is a composite of conservative, radicals, and the new Jewish perspective. 1) The conservatives continued to heal the rift from Bultmann's radical divide. For example, C. F. D. Moule's *Origin of Christology* rejected the History of Religion's premise that the Jesus of history was transformed into the Christ of Faith under the influence of Savior cults.[11] Martin Hengel provided the groundwork demonstrating remarkable overlap of the two spheres within his work *Judaism and Hellenism*.[12] Building upon this foundation, I. H. Marshall demonstrated the gospels, especially Luke were credibly reliable historical documents, each with their unique theological voice.[13] James Dunn also championed a confidence in oral tradition upon the foundation of Birger Gerhardsson and Kenneth Bailey's investigation of the transmission of tradition within Middle Eastern oral village culture.[14] 2) The radical perspective, continuing

---

8. Schweitzer, *The Quest of the Historical Jesus*, 398.

9. Käsemann, "The Problem of the Historical Jesus," original title, "Das Problem des historischen Jesus," *ZTK* 51 (1954): 125–53.

10. Brown, *Quests for the Historical Jesus*, 337.

11. Moule, *The Origin of Christology*.

12. Hengel, *Judaism and Hellenism; The Hellenization of Judaea in the First Century after Christ*.

13. Marshall, *Luke; The Gospel of Luke; I Believe in the Historical Jesus*; "The Synoptic Son of Man Sayings in Recent Discussion," *NTS* 12(1965–66): 327–51; "The Divine Sonship of Jesus," *Int* 21(1967): 87–103.

14. Dunn, *Jesus Remembered*, 197–254; Gerhardsson, *The Gospel Tradition; Memory and Manuscript*; Bailey, "Informal Controlled Oral Tradition and the Synoptic Gospels," *AJT* 5 (1991): 34–54; "Middle Eastern Oral Tradition and the Synoptic Gospels," *ExpTim* 106(1995): 363–67; Bauckham, *Jesus and the Eyewitnesses*; Walton and Sandy,

Bultmann's heritage has most notably been dominate in the Jesus Seminar, where only eighteen percent of Jesus' gospel sayings are voted to be authentic. Instead the main players, Burton Mack and John Crossan, envision Jesus as a cynic sage thoroughly immersed in Hellenistic philosophy.[15] This radical form has not emerged beyond the criticism of the second quest, in fact the conservative wing of the third quest has strongly answered this form. 3) In 1979 a new Jewish perspective emerged with Ben Meyer's study, *The Aims of Jesus*, rooting Jesus in the Judaism of His day.[16] Meyer was followed by Christian scholars (E. P. Sanders, James Charlesworth, N. T. Wright, John P. Meier, and Craig Evans) and Jewish scholars (Geza Vermes) who argue that there is substantial continuity between Judaism, Jesus' teaching and that of the early church.[17] In fact, the possibilities raised by similar Jewish teachings in the context serves as a strong guide to help prevent reading onto Jesus, interpretations floated by traditions removed from this Jewish context. The Jewish material before and concurrent with Jesus and the composition of the gospels is given more weight than Jewish rabbinic writings of the second and third century A.D., which still may provide a window into possibilities of early Jewish thinking by noticing where such ideas go. However, early Jewish material before and during Jesus' ministry provides continuity contributing toward a greater confidence that the historical Jesus being expounded is the factual Jesus of His time. Adding to this contextual sensitivity is the inclusion of Jewish sensitive rhetorical criticism which recognizes when Jesus' context echoes that of common or sectarian Judaism beyond it. In the mid-nineteen nineties, this perspective began to develop enough nuance and sensitivity to recognize that there were varied voices, some of which were sectarian, and thus we could not read this material as a pan-Judaism.[18] I am indebted to this nuanced perspective by discussing the text and the Jewish possibilities which provide context for making sense of the teaching and life of Jesus, as chapter two developed. As an evangelical, I appreciate a wide array of historical documents but I will also consider

---

The Lost World of Scripture, 97–101, 105–8, 110, 152–66.

15. Mack, *A Myth of Innocence*; Crossan, *The Historical Jesus*; *Jesus*; Kennard, *Messiah Jesus*, 211–42.

16. Meyer, *The Aims of Jesus*; Dever argues for a Lockean inference and externalism to confirm history writing through archeology ("Archeology, Texts, and History-Writing," In *Uncovering Ancient Stones*. ed. Lewis Hopfe, 107, 115).

17. Sanders, *Jesus and Judaism*; *The Historical Figure of Jesus*; Charlesworth, *Jesus Within Judaism*; Wright, *The New Testament and the People of God*; *Jesus and the Victory of God*; Meier, *A Marginal Jew*, vols. 1–5; Vermes, *Jesus the Jew*; *Jesus and the World of Judaism*.

18. Sectarian Judaism is highlighted in studying the sectarian documents themselves but is aided by secondary sources as well, Elliott, *The Survivors of Israel*.

that the canonical Scriptures are privileged as divinely authoritative sources. Thus, Biblical references will often be imbedded within the text as authoritative, whereas extra-biblical manuscripts will be highlighted especially in the notes as less authoritative, yet valuable as a historical source.

I summarize my criteria for evaluating the historical Jesus and apostles to be: 1) multiple attestation, 2) continuity, 3) discontinuity, 4) embarrassment, and 5) memorable form. The *multiple attestation* of the Biblical gospels, and extra-biblical material contribute to the historical confidence of the events described. The *continuity* of Jesus' teachings with the previous revelation and early Judaism context (as in the previous chapter) shows the possibility of contextually sensitive interpretations. Another form of continuity moves the interpreter into biblical theology and the continuity within an authorial approach to the material (e.g., Matthew's perspective). When this is connected with particular *discontinuity*, showing Jesus' teachings also are unique though similar to early Jewish teaching, the combination of continuity and discontinuity further confirms historical reliability of the accounts. These are especially compelling when they couple with *embarrassment* of a main character (like in Peter's denials) or *memorable form* as in the use of parables and maxims.

A biblical theology perspective takes the issue of continuity and discontinuity further, because through this orientation I will also develop the unique voices of those biblical authors who comment upon Jesus. The biblical theology movement rose from Johann Philip Gabler's lecture at the University of Altdorf in 1787.[19] Gabler's approach offered an optimistic empirical spirit that the meaning of the text was accessible to individuals from the straightforward study of the biblical text's details in an attempt to be sensitive to the distinctive voice of each author. This movement builds on the historical Jesus and reflects the particular sensitivity to the biblical authors' voices, without losing the contributions of extra-biblical corroboration of the historical facts, as is evident by the biblical theology Christology volumes of Rudolf Bultmann, N. T. Wright and James Dunn.[20] That is, early Jewish sources provide possibilities but the biblical text is the forum where interpretations must be demonstrated if it is to be exegesis. In this, the voices most emphasized by this movement are those of the inspired biblical authors.

---

19. Gabler's lecture "On the proper distinction between Biblical and dogmatic theology and specific objectives of each," is translated and commented on in Sandys-Wunsch and Eldredge, "J. P. Gabler and the Distinction Between Biblical and Dogmatic Theology," *SJT* 33(1980): 133–58 and In *The Flowering of O. T. Theology*. eds. Ollenburger, Martens, Hasel, 492–502.

20. Bultmann, *Theology of the New Testament*, vol. 1; Wright, *Jesus and the Victory of God*; Dunn, *Jesus Remembered*.

There was an oral phase which was seen as more authoritative than written texts. Perhaps recognizing that the disciples were called to be witnesses (Luke 24:48; Acts 1:8, μάρτυρες). Such a role of a witness is one of memory and testimony from personal experience. As such, the subject matter to which a witness testifies is not likely to be submitted to empirical investigation because the events and statement of views occurred previously to the testimony (Matt 8:4; 18:16).[21] In a Hebrew trial setting multiple witnesses were involved to strengthen credibility (Deut 17:6; 19:15). If the witnesses prove to be contradicted credibly then they were considered a false witness and could suffer the same judgment that they were trying to obtain for the one he accused (Deut 5:20; 19:16-18). In Jewish, Greek, and Roman legal systems, a witness needed to be an adult free male Roman citizen with honorable reputation and not operating for personal gain.[22] Such a witness would make appropriate comments in court as eyewitness testimony he had actually experienced.[23] With legal imagery encouraging the credibility of the role of a witness, Papias found the collective memory of Christian eyewitness testimony to be more valuable than the written texts being produced for as long as available eyewitnesses testified about Jesus' ministry and the early church.

> I shall not hesitate also to put into properly ordered form for you everything I learned carefully in the past from the elders and noted down well, for the truth of which I vouch. For unlike most people I did not enjoy those who have a great deal to say, but those who teach the truth. Nor did I enjoy those who recall someone else's commandments, but those who remember the commandments given by the Lord to the faith and proceeding from the truth itself. And if by chance anyone who had been in attendance on the elders should come my way, I inquired about the words of the elders-[that is] what [according to the elders] Andrew or Peter said, or Philip, or Thomas or James, or John or Matthew or any other of the Lord's disciples, and whatever Ariston and the elder John, the Lord's disciples were saying. For I did not think that information from books would profit me as much as information from a living and surviving voice.[24]

21. Aristotle, *Rhet.* 1.15; Plato, *Leg.* 12; Josephus, *Ant.* 6.66; 1QS 5.24-6.1; Philo, *Spec. Leg.* 4.30, 41-44, 59-61; *Jos.* 242; *m. Mak.* 1.6; *m. Rosh Hash.* 1.8; *Sifre* on Deut 19:19; *Sheb.* 30a; *Gem. Mak.* 5B; Trites, *The New Testament Concept of Witness.*

22. Pind. *Olymp.* 1.54; Plato, *Ap.* 31c; Gorgias, 27-31, 41E-5E; Demosthenes 58.4; Plutarch, *de Amicorum Multitudine* 2.2.93e; *TDNT* 4:479.

23. Plato, *Symp.* 179b; Heracl. 34; Sophocles *Ant.* 515.

24. Eusebius, *Hist. eccl.* 3.39.3-4; Dewey develops an argument from Rom 10 that the written *torah* supported the authoritative and transformative oral gospel testimony

In the second century both Irenaeus and Papias recount that their early memories of the eyewitness testimony took great prominence and were in full accord with the written texts of Scripture.[25] Similar claims for accurate vivid early memories framing later perception were made by Seneca.[26] When such testimony occurred in Christian contexts a corporate memory of tradition could be specifically identified and others of the group would provide a resilience to reinforce the accuracy of their corporate memory.[27] For example, Paul Ricoeur identified that testimony is valid if 1) it agrees with other testimonies about the same event, 2) if it is obtained by means other than violence or corruption, 3) there is no reason to suppose that the witness produced the information for her own agenda, and 4) the testimony fits with the other verifiable information that we possess about the event.[28] Such a pattern mirrors the corporate memory of rabbinic Judaism that began to establish written accounts of their oral discussions beginning around 200 A.D. with the *Mishnah* and then the two corroborating written accounts of the *Talmud* later around 450 and 600 A.D. Such Jewish oral tradition and written oral tradition shows very little shift of account except the addition of

---

("A Re-Hearing of Romans 10:1–15" in *Orality and Textuality in Early Christian Literature*, 109–27; Bauckham, *Jesus and the Eyewitnesses*, 293–4; Kelber, "The Generative Force of Memory," BTB 36(2006): 15–22.

25. Papias recounted in Eusebius, *Hist. eccl.* 5.20.4–7; Irenaeus, *Letter to Florinus*; Bauckham, *Jesus and the Eyewitnesses*, 295.

26. Seneca, *Controversiae*, preface 3–4; Bauckham, *Jesus and the Eyewitnesses*, 295–6; Mackay, *Signs of Orality*; Horsley, Draper, and Foley, *Performing the Gospel*; Cooper, *Politics of Orality*; Horsley, *Oral Performance, Popular Tradition, and Hidden Transcript in Q*.

27. Examples of such claims include: Clement of Alexandria, *Strom.* 7.106.4; Eusebius, *Hist. eccl.* 2.1.4; similar claims were made at Qumran (1QS 6.6–8) and by gnostic 2 *Apoc. of James* 36.15–25; Halbwachs, *Les cadres sociaux de la mémoire* translated as *On Collective Memory*; Assmann, *Das kulturelle Gedächtnis*; Kelber, "The Case of the Gospels," *Oral Tradition* 17(2002): 65; "The Generative Force of Memory," BTB 36(2006): 15–22; Dunn, *Jesus Remembered*, 239–243; "Q as oral tradition," In *The Written Gospel*. ed. Bockmuehl and Hagner, 45–69; *The Written Gospel*. ed. Bockmuehl and Hagner, 45–69; Hengel, "Eye-witness memory and the writing of the Gospels," In *The Written Gospel*. ed. Bockmuehl and Hagner, 70–96, especially 78 and 80; Ricoeur, *Memory, History, Forgetting*; "Toward a Hermeneutics of the Idea of Revelation," In *Essays on Biblical Interpretation*, 73–118; Bauckham, *Jesus and the Eyewitnesses*, 296, 310–57; "The Gospel of John and the Synoptic Problem," In *New Studies in the Synoptic Problem*. ed. Foster, Gregory, Kloppenborg, and Verheyden, 659; Silberman, *Orality, Aurality and Biblical Narrative*; Dewey, *Orality and Textuality in Early Christian Literature*; Draper, *Orality, Literacy, and Colonialism in Antiquity*; Kirk, "Social and Cultural Memory" and Thatcher, "Why John Wrote a Gospel: Memory and History in an Early Christian Community," In *Memory, Tradition, and Text*. ed. Kirk and Thatcher, 14–15, 82–85; Thatcher, *Jesus, The Voice, and the Text*; Kelber and Byrsog, *Jesus in Memory*.

28. Ricoeur, "Toward a Hermeneutics of the Idea of Revelation," In *Essays on Biblical Interpretation*, 101–107; Pokorny, *From the Gospel to the Gospels*, 38.

more recent rabbinic voices.[29] Also in Judaism there was liturgical retelling of narrative in *rabbah* texts composed during the second to fourth centuries, which resiliently re-tell the biblical narratives for liturgical purposes. The resilience and consistency in the agreement of these written accounts of oral *Torah* or narrative re-telling provide a pattern for how local Jewish-Christian corporate eyewitness memory could be corporately preserved into written texts as well.

The inclusion of female witnesses contributes to the Gospels by providing an additional grounding for historicity, since their inclusion would not in that day carry the same weight in courts of law.[30] So when Elizabeth and Mary contribute to Jesus' birth account (Luke 1:39–66) and the women contribute to the resurrection and empty tomb account (Luke 23:55–24:11) there is increased historical credibility that these are the record of real events because their inclusion would not bring greater persuasiveness in ancient Jewish or Roman contexts. In fact, a number of disciples did not believe the women's account of the resurrection until they saw for themselves (Luke 24:11, 22–24).

Written Historical Narrative

As the eyewitnesses began to die off in the second half of the first century, the written testimony took a more prominent role. The eyewitnesses had lived consistently recounting the specifics that they had included in their written gospels so that their written gospels gained in prominence as the living eyewitnesses were no longer accessible in the second century. The pattern of authority is somewhat reminiscent of the prosecutions of corrupt politicians by Marcus Cicero. The repeated court speeches Cicero laid down a noble consistency as a witness and a prosecutor, such that when these trial speeches were written into book length critiques of corrupt politicians, his written testimony took on the same weight even out of court. Corrupt

---

29. Gerhardsson, *The Gospel Tradition*; *Memory and Manuscript*; Bailey, "Informal Controlled Oral Tradition and the Synoptic Gospels," *AJT* 5 (1991): 34–54; "Middle Eastern Oral Tradition and the Synoptic Gospels," *ExpTim* 106(1995): 363–67; Boomershine, "Jesus of Nazareth and the Watershed of Ancient Orality and Literacy," In *Orality and Textuality in Early Christian Literature*. ed. Dewey, 7–11, 16–17; Jaffee, "The Oral-Cultural Context of the Talmud Yerushalmi," In *Transmitting Jewish Traditions*. ed. Elman and Gershoni, 27–73; Dunn, *Jesus Remembered*, 197–254; Bauckham, *Jesus and the Eyewitnesses*; Walton and Sandy, *The Lost World of Scripture*, 97–101, 105–8, 110, 152–66; Bird, *The Gospel of the Lord*, 91–111.

30. Pind. *Olymp.* 1.54; Plato, *Ap.* 31c; Gorgias, 27–31, 41E–5E; Demosthenes 58.4; Plutarch, *de Amicorum Multitudine* 2.2.93e; *TDNT* 4:479; Dewey, "From Storytelling to Written Text: The Loss of Early Christian Women's Voices," *BTB* 26(1996): 71–78.

politicians such as Sicily's governor Gaius Verres fled into exile when the literate population recognized from Cicero's written text the authority of Cicero's charges against Verres' corruption.[31]

The biblical gospels were known products which the early patristics recognized were from specific people. Justin identified the gospels as "memoirs of the apostles."[32] For example, Luke was understood to write to a patron who knew who he was even though we must reconstruct that Luke is the author by noticing the book of Acts, written by the same individual, has "we" sections when Luke is with Paul (Acts 16:10–17; 20:5–21:18; 27:1–28:16; Col 4:14 "beloved physician"; Philemon 24; 2 Tim 4:11) and abundant medical terms (Acts 1:3; 3:7; 9:18, 33; 13:11; 28:1–10). In fact, the normal patron arrangement would probably have had Theophilus providing the materials for Luke to compose the accounts for his patron. Additionally, John's gospel is designated to be from the "beloved disciple" John, one of the inner three disciples (John 21:23–24; also 1 John 1:1–2). However, a more extensive record of the gospel authors is provided by the patristic testimony which recognized who wrote which witness and gave them credit for this writing in their own letters. This patristic witness agrees who wrote which gospel, so the gospels are not anonymous but the patristics identified that the gospels were composed by known authors Matthew, John Mark, Luke, and John.[33]

The patristics recognize that each presentation of Jesus shows unique authorial coloring and strategic vision of what the narrative author tried to portray. For example, in broad brush strokes the gospel produced by Matthew is written by the early sixties A.D. for a Jewish audience, strongly affirming the Messiah as a faithful teacher of the Mosaic Law through a new covenant perspective, and for at least some time limiting the disciple's ministry to that of Israel.[34] Matthew as an eyewitness tells of Jesus calling him to conversion and discipleship (Matt 9:9–10; 10:3). The gospels produced by Luke and Mark are patristically identified as written by the mid-sixties A.D. for a Gentile audience.[35] Tradition has it that Mark reflects Peter's gospel to Italy, and Luke reflects Paul's gospel to Achaia, and that John wrote last of all

---

31. Cicero, *Verr.*

32. Justin, *1 Apol.* 66.3; 67.3.

33. Bauckham, *Jesus and the Eyewitnesses*, 300–5.

34. Irenaeus, *Adv. Haer.* 3.1.1–2; Ignatius, *Smyrn* 1.1.1–2; John Chrysostom, *Hom. Matt.* 1.7.

35. Mark: Justin, *Dial.* 106; Eusebius, *Anti-Marcionite Prologue*; *Hist. eccl.* 2.15.1–2; 3.39.14–15; 6.14.5–7; John Chrysostom, *Hom. Matt.* 1.7; Luke: Justin, *Dial.* 103.19; Tertullian, *Adv. Haer.* 4.2.2; 4.5.3; Acts 28:30–31 with 24:27 occurring in 59 or 60 A.D.; 1 Tim 5:17 quoting Luke 10:7.

from Ephesus.[36] By minimizing the sermons, Mark records an authoritative Christ Who heals all in need. Even though Mark reflects Peter's testimony, it may also reflect a unique eyewitness account of naked Mark fleeing into the night when Jesus is captured (Mark 14:51–52). Luke-Acts show the extension of Christianity to Gentiles and the Law-free resolution for Gentiles at the Jerusalem council. Such an approach of transitioning from Jesus' Jewish ministry to Peter pioneering Gentile ministry and then Paul regularly proclaiming gospel to Gentiles has been termed a salvation history approach.[37] Luke also especially encourages the poor and women as having significant inclusion as a part of the audience to which their voice is especially sensitive. All the Gospels contain ample miracles. However, Mark's primary focus on Jesus' miracles meeting real needs presents an authoritative Jesus in all contexts. While, the other gospels include many of the same miracles, their inclusion of sermonic material adds distinctive character to their voice. For example, Matthew includes a series of long sermons which lay out Jesus' kingdom agenda for His disciples. Luke contains much of the same sermonic material presented on alternative occasions and often in Jesus' response to questions. As such, Luke presents a more interactive and responsive Jesus when compared to that of the other synoptics. The gospel produced by John retains similar eyewitness interactivity in those conversations which Jesus has with individuals and groups. Additionally, John is focused on Jesus' Judean ministry in contrast to the synoptics focus on the Galilean ministry, thus reserving Jerusalem to set up His martyrdom. Furthermore, John has a realized eschatology (of present everlasting life) in a mystical manner very different from the synoptic presentation (of the eschatological kingdom as coming in the context of the Messiah).

Classical historical writing often includes the author in third or first person as the author claims to be eyewitness to part of the story (Luke 1:2; Mark 1:21; 2 Pet 1:16; "we" Acts 16:10–17; 20:5–21:18; 27:1–28:16; claims to be with Jesus from the beginning of Jesus' ministry [John 15:26–27; Acts 1:21–22]).[38] Such a context of eyewitness is dependent upon the memory

36. Eusebius, *Hist. eccl.* 6.14.6–7; Irenaeus, *Adv. Haer.* 3.1.1; Origen, *Frag. En com. in Mt.* 1.1–20; Gregory of Nazianzus, *Carmida dogmatica* 1.12.6–9.

37. Keener, *Acts*, 1:437–41; Conzelmann, *The Theology of St. Luke*, 137–206; Noland, "Salvation-History and Eschatology," In *Witness to the Gospel*. ed. Marshall and Peterson, 63–82; Stegman, "'The Spirit of Wisdom and Understanding,'" In *The Bible and Epistemology*. ed. Healy and Parry, 90–91, 94.

38. Support the claim for eyewitness account: Eusebius, *Hist. eccl.* 3.39.3–4; 5.20.6; Irenaeus, *Haer.* 3.1.2; Byrskog, *Story as History-History as Story*; Bauckham, *Jesus and the Eyewitnesses*; Standard "eyewitness from the beginning" phrase for eyewitness: Josephus, *C. Ap.* 1.55; *Vita* 366; Polybius 3.4.3; Standard third person pattern: Thucydides, 1.1.1; 2.70.4; 4.104.4; Xenophon, *Anab.* 1.8.15; *Cyrop.* 2.2, 10; 3.3.59; 4.5; 6.16, 17; 7.1;

of those who give testimony to these events (1 Cor 11:25).[39] Herodotus and Thucydides function as standards of historiography in their day so they and others will be compared to authenticate high historiography and style of the Lukan material.[40] In each, the author selects historical source material and writes with historical sensitivity[41] (Luke 1:1–2; Acts 16:10) for particular purposes to tell the biography emphasizing outstanding character features of the hero in view. Luke's approach gathers empirical observations from a communal application of Thomas Reid's empiricism rather than Reid's individual common sense realism,[42] Luke presents his perspective to be accurate chronological historical writing so that his readership would have the exact truth of Jesus' and the apostles' deeds and teaching.

> Inasmuch as many have undertaken to compile an account of the things accomplished among us, just as they were handed down to us by those who from the beginning were eyewitnesses and servants of the word, it seemed fitting for me as well, having investigated everything carefully from the beginning, to write *it* out for you in consecutive order, most excellent[43] Theophilus; so that you may know the exact truth about the things you have been taught (Luke 1:1–4).

> The first account I composed, Theophilus, about all that Jesus began to do and teach, until the day when He was taken up

---

8.1.40; 8.2; 8.8.2, 27; *Symp.* 1.1; Plutarch, *Aem.* 1.5–8; *Alex.* 4.3–4; 69.8; *Cim.* 1.8; *Them.* 32.6; *Sull.* 34.4; Lucian, *Hist. Conscr.* 47; 1 and 2 Macc; Philo, *Moses; Abraham; Flaccus;* Josephus, *Ant.; J. W.; Ag. Ap.* 1.45–47 Ps-Philo.

39. Eusebius, *Hist. eccl.* 3.39.14–15 consistent to Socrates comment *Memorabilia* 1.3.1.

40. Theon, *Prog.* 66 cites Herodotus, 1.31; 5.71 and Thucydides, 1.126; 2.68 as best examples of "factual" narratives. They are also often quoted in *progymnasmata* and rhetorical handbooks (Theon, *Prog.* 84–85; 91–92; 118–19; Ps.-Herm., *Prog.* 4, 22; John of Sardis, *Prog.* 17; Quintilian, *Inst.* 10.1.31–34; Lucian, *How to Write History* 5, 15, 18–19, 26, 38–39, 42, 54, 57; Craig Gibson, "Learning Greek History in the Ancient Classroom: The Evidence from the Treatises on Progymnasmata," *CP* 99[2004]:103–29, esp. 117; Alicia Myers, *Characterizing Jesus: A Rhetorical Analysis on the Fourth Gospel's Use of Scripture in its Presentation of Jesus* [London: T & T Clark, 2012], 31).

41. Josephus, *Ant.* 20.156–7; *C. Ap.* 1.49–50; Aristotle, *Poetics* 9.2–3, 1451b; Tacitus, *Ann.* 4.53; 5.9; Silius Italicus, *Punica* 9.66–177; Diod. Sic. 21.17.1; Dionysius of Halicarnassus, *De Veterum Censura* 1.1.2–4; 1.2.1; 1.4.2; 5.

42. Reid, *Thomas Reid*; Kirk and Thatcher, "Jesus Tradition as Social Memory" in *Memory, Tradition, and Text.* ed. Kirk and Thatcher, 28; Abraham, "The Epistemology of Jesus" in *Jesus and Philosophy.* ed. Moser, 158–9; Brueggeman, *A Pathway of Interpretation*, 115.

43. Aristotle argues for the necessity of praising one's audience in writing biographic material to them (*Inst.* 3.7.23–24).

to heaven, after He had by the Holy Spirit given orders to the apostles whom He had chosen (Acts 1:1–2).

Such introductions to the two Lukan volumes fit within the patterns of introductions to Hellenistic technical and historical volumes.[44] Notice that Luke appeals to things known by a group broader than him, presumably much already known by Theophilus himself. Such an approach appealing to facts already known by others is a standard rhetorical technique to lend credibility for text claims.[45] John also identifies that his testimony is dependent upon corporate empirical eyewitness experience.

> What was from the beginning, what we have heard, what we have seen with our eyes, what we have looked at and touched with our hands, concerning the Word of Life and the life was manifested, and we have seen and testify and proclaim to you everlasting life (1 John 1:1–2).

Historical narrative was to be truthful in accurately reflecting the events of such recent history[46] (Luke 1:1–4; Acts 1:1–2). Craig Keener and many others conclude that Matthew and Luke rank high with regard to accuracy among ancient historical works.[47] Such multiple attestation of events

---

44. Josephus, *Ant.* 1.8–10; Cicero, *De Natura Dearum* 1.1; Vitruvius, 1.1; Augustus, *De Architectura* 1.1; Pliny the Elder, *Nat. Hist.* 1.1; Quintillian, *Inst.* 1.6; Dionysius of Halicarnassus, *On Thucydides* 55; Maier, "Luke as a Hellenistic Historian," In *Christian Origins and Greco-Roman Culture.* ed. Porter and Pitts, 416–17; Moessner, "Triadic Synergy of Hellenistic Poetics in the Narrative Epistemology of Dionysius of Halicarnassus and the Authorial Intent of the Evangelist Luke (Luke 1:1–4; Acts 1:1–8)," *Neot* 42:2(2008): 289–303; Alexander, "Paul and the Hellenistic Schools," In *Paul in his Hellenistic Context.* ed. Pedersen, 60–83; Downing, "Writers' Use or Abuse of Written Sources," In *New Studies in the Synoptic Problem.* ed. Foster et al., 536.

45. Dionysius of Halicarnassus, *Ant. Rom.* 1.6.1; 7.43.2; Arrian, *Alex.* 6.2.4; Plutarch, *Alex.* 30.7; 31.2–3; Josephus, *Ag. Ap.* 1.50–52; 2.107.

46. Josephus, *Ag. Ap.* 1.18, 26; Dionysius, *Thucydides* 8; Diod. Sic. 4.8.3; Livy 6.1.3.

47. Keener, *Matthew*, 21; Marshall, *Luke*; Talbert, *Literary Pattern, Theological Themes, and the Genre of Luke-Acts*, and Maier, "Luke as a Hellenistic Historian," In *Christian Origins and Greco-Roman Culture.* ed. Porter and Pitts, 413–34 conclude Luke to be both a precise historian and adept theologian; on the issue of historicity, there many to support this point as are especially developed in articles that either reflect Luke 1:1–4, or specific passages connection with the place and culture described, e.g., Hemer, "The Speeches in Acts II: The Areopagus Address," *TynB* 40(1989): 239–59; as to Luke being a theologian, cf. Cadbury, "The Speeches in Acts," In *Acts.* ed. Jackson and Lake, 5:402, 410–422, defends the continuity of Luke's language in these speeches that further support that Luke is a deft theologian, like other N. T. writers (or as Dibelius ["The Speeches in Acts and Ancient Historiography," In *Studies in the Acts of the Apostles.* ed. Dibelius, Greenan, and Ling, 138–85] proposed even if Luke invented them they are Luke's writings with clear Lukan literary evidence); then there are several theologies of Luke which

helps to strengthen the historical claims of the texts. The substantial overlap between the synoptic gospels (roughly seventy percent)[48] would argue against the claim that Matthew *midrashically* expanded elements of his account by adding stories.[49] Such corroboration also extends into the book of Acts. For example, Stephen's illegal stoning is also discussed by Josephus with some of the ramifications for Roman authorities removing Ananus from the high priesthood (Acts 7:54–60).[50]

There are also two forms of the book of Acts: the Western[51] and the Alexandrian[52] (which contains ninety percent of the Western text). The two texts of Acts corroborate the historical events through textual criticism as substantially providing multiple attestation. Most textual critics follow Jean Leclerc and John Lightfoot in conjecturing that Luke supplied two editions of his work, the shorter with a bit less development of the narrative accounts and the longer with more fullness to fill out areas of interest to the extent of a full portable scroll.[53] With the synoptic gospels corroborating each other and the two versions of Acts corroborating each other and extra-biblical accounts corroborating the biblical accounts, the biblical accounts should be seen as accurate corroborated historical accounts.

Such corroborated historical writing also stands against the Bultmannian hermeneutic that considers that those accounts were substantially

---

are worth consulting and confirm Luke as a able theologian with his distinctive agenda, for example: Conzelmann, *The Theology of St. Luke*; Green, *The Theology of the Gospel of Luke*; Harrington, *Luke*; Jervell, *The Theology of the Acts of the Apostles*; Karis, *Luke*; Kee, *Good News to the Ends of the Earth*; O'Toole, *The Unity Luke's Theology*.

48. Mark shows the highest percentage of overlap of around eighty percent, then Matthew around seventy percent, and Luke with about fifty percent.

49. Payne, "Midrash and History in the Gospel," In *Studies in Midrash and Historiography*. ed. France and Wenham, 3:177–215; Cunningham and Bock, "Is Matthew Midrash?," *BSac* 144(1987): 157–80; Blomberg, *The Historical Reliability of the Gospels*; Keener, *Matthew*, 22; contrary to Gundry, *Matthew*, 37 "embellishments" and 40–41 midrash following Bourke "The Literary Genus of Matthew 1–2," *CBQ* 22(1960): 160–75.

50. Josephus, *Ant.* 20.9.1.

51. Represented by P^{45}, P^{74}, ℵ, A, B, C, , 33 81, 104, 326 and 1175.

52. Represented by D, P^{29}, P^{38}, P^{48}, Syriac, African Old Latin, citations by Cyprian and Augustine.

53. Discussion of these versions and approaches is in Metzger, *A Textual Commentary on the Greek New Testament*, 222–36. Other ancient historians released their material in stages to provide corporate oral memory to fill out areas of interest in the document (Suetonius, *Vergil.* 33; Pliny, *Ep.* 5.12.1–2; instead of providing helpful comments such practice at times simply produced flattery [Horace, *Ars.* 428–31]; Shiell, *Reading Acts*, 115; Keener, *Acts*, 1:47).

constructed from Hellenistic mythology.[54] Greco-Roman historical narrative did not permit the use of mythology.[55] Furthermore, the biblical authors specifically rejected the use of mythology in narrative accounts (1 Tim 1:4; 2 Pet 1:16). With both Christian and Greco-Roman canons of historical writing rejecting a place for mythology, it is better to see Luke's accounts as historically accurate accounts.

Narrative asides and summaries were utilized to provide interpretive guidance among the narrator's account (Acts 2:47; 6:7; 9:31; 12:24; 16:5; 19:20; 28:31).[56] Such material helps to organize the thrust of the narrative and to show important overarching concerns. These Lukan summaries emphasize salvation history and the continued development of the Church into new regions. Additionally, repeated aspects bring a certain degree of emphasis by the author to show virtues like unity and the voluntary socialism that generously met all needs within the community (Acts 2:42–47; 4:32–37; 5:42–6:7). Furthermore, divine providence was often important in developing the narrative direction of historical texts[57] (Acts 2:23; 4:24–30; 6:7). One expression of divine involvement was a supernatural element of miracle in the account that would also play a corroborative role for the message especially while eyewitnesses remained alive[58] (Luke 8:49–9:9; John 11:43–47; 1 Cor 15:5–7). As such, Greco-Roman historical accounts utilized supernatural miracles as an apologetic role demonstrating the hero's superiority[59] (Luke 20:9–47).

The title "Acts" has been noticed on Acts manuscripts at least by 150 A.D.[60] The title reflects continuity with his description of the gospel of

54. Bultmann, *Jesus Christ and Mythology*, 18, 36, 39; Bultmann, Bartsch, Fuller, *Kerygma and Myth*; Miegge, *Gospel and Myth in the Thought of Rudolf Bultmann*, 8, 91; MacDonald, "The Synoptic Problem and Literary Mimesis: The Case of the Frothing Demoniac," (which is too slight a parallel to Euripides' *Hercules Furens*) In *New Studies in the Synoptic Problem*. ed. Foster, et.al., 509–21.

55. Dionysius, *Thucydides*, 45–47.

56. Irenaeus, *Haer.* 3.1.1; 3.14.1; Eusebius, *Hist. eccl.*3.4.7; Rood, "Thucydides" in *Narrators, Narratees, and Narratives in Ancient Greek Literature*. ed. de Jonge, Nünlist, and Bowie, 123; Sheeley, *Narrative Asides in Luke-Acts*, 40–96.

57. Diod. Sic. 1.1.3.

58. Josephus, *Life* 359–66; *Ag. Ap.* 1.50.

59. Josephus, *Ant.*; Aristotle, *Rhet.* 1.9.39; Theon, *Prog.* 108–9; Ps. Herm., *Prog.* 12; Aphth. *Prog.* 17R; Nic., *Prog.* 42–47; Quintilian, *Inst.* 5.10.72–73; 11.22–26; *Rhet. Her.* 2.14.21–22; 2.30.49; Cicero, *Top.* 23.68–71; *Part. Or.* 55; Aristotle, *Rhet.* 1.9.38–41.

60. Irenaeus, *Her.* 3.12.11; 3.13.3; Clement of Alexandria, *Strom.* 5.82.4; Tertullian, *Bapt.* 10.4; *Anti-Marcionite Prologue to Luke*; *Muratorian Canon*; Eusebius, *Hist. eccl.* 3.4.6; texts א, B and D; Harnack, *Acts*, xvii; Jackson and Lake, *Acts*, 4:1; Pesch, *Die Apostelgeschichte*, 1:22–23; Jervell, *Die Apostelgeschichte*, 56; Pervo, *Acts*, 29; Keener, *Acts*, 1:88, 645.

Luke being a statement about all Jesus began to do (Acts 1:1 ποιεῖν). Such a second volume of historical work was common in Judaism to develop the legitimacy of kingship, the failure of Israel to obey the Law and salvation history (1 and 2 Sam; 1 and 2 Kgs; 1 and 2 Chr; 1–4 Macc).[61] This title indicates a narrative account of heroic deeds and by itself identifies the writing to be a historical work[62] (Acts 1:1).

At times biographic works were also referred to as "good news" or "gospel." For example, the *Priene Inscription* 2.81–82 used the word "good news" (εὐαγγελίου) twice identifying a narrative describing Augustus life up until the time when he began to rule as Caesar. The Gospel of Mark utilized the term in the same biographical manner (Mark 1:1), which in the context identifies the good news of the narrative of Jesus Christ and His kingdom message (Mark 1:14–15; 8:35; 13:10; 14:9; 16:15; Matt 4:23; 9:35) which is repeatedly proclaimed by the apostles (Matt 24:14; 26:13; Mark 16:15).

Often biography intentionally has virtues for the reader to imitate[63] (Luke 6:20–23; Acts 4:32–37). For example, Quintilian folds qualities of the person in the narrative to be illustrated by the person's works[64] (Luke 1:1; Acts 1:1). Often the ancestry and origins indicate who the person will be like.[65] For example, Jesus is predicted to be the Messiah to bring in the Abrahamic and Davidic covenants elevating the poor in eschatological reversal of His reign and destroying the opposition (Luke 1; 3:23–34). Jesus exemplifies the beatitude virtues of the narrow way unto kingdom that His sermons call His disciples to embrace.

---

61. Uytanlet presents Luke used first rate Jewish historiography in *Luke-Acts and Jewish Historiography*.

62. Diod. Sic. *Libr. Of Hist.* 3.1.1; 16.1.1; Josephus, *Ant.* 14.68; Valerius Maximus, *Memorable Deeds and Sayings*; Pophyry, *Ar. Cat.* 57.15–19; Keener, *Acts*, 1:88, 645.

63. Philo, *Moses* 1.158; Josephus, *J. W.* 1.4–8, 13–16; *Ant.* 1.1–2; Plutarch, *Aem.* 1.1, 5; Tacitus, *Agr.* 1; Dionysius, *Ant. Rom.* 8.56.1; Kurz, "Narrative Models for Imitation in Luke-Acts," in *Greeks, Romans, and Christians.* ed. Balch, 171–189; Fiore, *The Function of Personal Example in the Socratic and Pastoral Epistles*, especially chapter 3, "Example in Rhetorical Theory, Education, and Literature," 26–44; de Boer, *The Imitation of Paul*; Crouzel, "L'imitation et la 'suite' de Dieu et du Christ," *JAC* 21(1978): 7–41 especially 7–30; Cothenet, et al., "Imitation du Christ," *Dictionnaire de Spiritualité* 7(1971): 1536–1601; Gutierrez, *La Paternité spirituelle selon S. Paul*; Pate and Kennard, *Deliverance Now and Not Yet*, 369–372; Trompf, *The Idea of Historical Recurrence in Western Thought*, 97–101; Talbert makes from "Biographies of Philosophers and Rulers as Instruments of Religious Propaganda in Mediterranean Antiquity," *ANRW* 2.16.2 (1978): 1643; Fornara, *The Nature of History in Ancient Greece and Rome*, 104–120.

64. Quintilian, *Inst.* 3.7.10–22; 5.10.24–31.

65. Quintilian, *Inst.* 3.7.12; Ps. Hermogenes, *Prog.* 15–17.

The birth narrative and perhaps one childhood account illustrate the qualities for which the person becomes known (Luke 1–2)[66] or at times ancient biography simply begins with adulthood (e.g., Mark).[67] So classic historical writing will not provide a detailed account of childhood, as say the creative writing of *The Infancy Gospel of Thomas* invents.

At times the biography would end with praising the hero for the many more things that could be said about the person but that no account can include everything within it[68] (John 20:30–31).

Gospel Proclamation

Jesus' statements in the gospels and the sermons in the book of Acts are all summaries. Each sermon can be read in three to fifteen minutes, and likely the speaker talked longer than that. So the important feature of classical historical accounts recording speeches was to provide teaching consistent with the narrative hero's character and speech patterns.[69] Partly this is because Aristotle argues that ancient witnesses are known broadly by many humans, so that uncharacteristic speech would render accounts less credible.[70] Such speeches are quite significant within the gospels because Jesus occupies a rabbinic role for developing a tradition for Christians, as was developed in the chapter on Matthew's Jesus.

Any good itinerant speaker will say the same content in different locations. Thus the similarity of Jesus' Sermon on the Mount (Matt 5–7) with His Sermon on the Plain (Luke 6) is easily understandable without forcing them onto the same location. So likely the author will include that sermonic material only once in a representative form to cover for the repetitive sermons, as Luke and Matthew treat this material but often from different locations. Whereas, the book of Acts has the stated purpose of recording salvation history and thus repeated telling of the gospel message. If the same speaker is recorded to be speaking the same gospel at different locations in the same written account, then those similar sermons subsequently are shortened as Luke does for subsequent sermons from Peter and Paul. However, the contextual engagement and the characteristic language are retained throughout the sermons.

66. Quintilian, *Inst.* 3.7.12; Plutarch, *Lives*; Ps. Hermogenes, *Prog.* 15–17.

67. *Life of Aesop*

68. Thucydides, *Prog.* 38.

69. *Rhetorica ad Herennium* 4.52.65; Quintilian, *Inst.* 3.8.51; Thucydides, 1.22.1; Dionysius of Halicarnassus, *Rom. ant.* 7.66.2–3; 11.1.3–4.

70. Aristotle, *Rhet.* 1.15.13, 15.

The Lukan material in Acts shows some of the consistent language of Peter's and Paul's writing[71] even though the gospel speeches in Acts accomplish a different purpose than their written epistles attempt. For example, Kistermaker finds convoluted Greek in Peter's sermons (Acts 3:16; 10:36–37) similar to 1 Peter 4:11 and 2 Peter 3:5–6.[72] Additionally, characteristic phrases are utilized by Peter, such as "God's foreknowledge" (Acts 2:23; 1 Pet 1:2, 20) and "judge of the living and the dead" (Acts 10:42; 1 Pet 4:5). Likewise, Stanley Porter provides verbal parallels within Paul, including "Jews and Greeks" (Acts 20:21; Rom 3:9; 1 Cor 1:22, 24; 10:32; 12:13), "build up" (Acts 20:32; Rom 15:20; 1 Cor 8:1, 10; 10:23; 14:4, 17; Gal 2:18; 1 Thess 5:11), and many more.[73] So the consistency of the record of the speakers is confirmed by their writings.

The gospel as contemporary evangelicalism would say it would be something like: the divine and human Jesus has died as a substitute for your sins, so that in your trust of this efficacious death and resurrection, you can be saved from damnation to eternal life in heaven with God. Luke's gospel message from his gospel and the book of Acts is rather different than this. Dibelius describes these sermons as follows: "An introduction suggested by the actual situation is normally followed by the kerygma of Jesus' life, passion and resurrection, usually with the disciples' witness; to this is subjoined a scriptural proof and an exhortation of repentance."[74] Luke does not deny the evangelical gospel, he merely says it differently. This is *not* placing us into inclusivism, for Luke clearly remains within an exclusivist strategy for salvation (Acts 4:12). Luke merely says the gospel unto the kingdom differently than evangelicalism usually does. N. T. Wright captures the essence of this gospel as: "*Jesus the crucified and risen Messiah, is Lord.*"[75] The fact that the *vicarious atonement* is not developed in Luke's statement of gospel is disturbing to me because it shows that evangelicalism is prone to latch onto certain traditional or biblical thought forms and ignore other legitimate biblical concepts. Perhaps evangelicalism is too Reformationally-Pauline to the neglect of other biblical authors. However, even Luther is closer to this biblical pattern in Luke than contemporary evangelicalism for he describes "the gospel is a story about Christ, God's and David's Son, who died and was raised and is established as

---

71. Peter's consistency: Selwyn, *The First Epistle of St. Peter*, 33–36; Williams, *Acts*, 11.

72. Kistemacher, *Acts*, 9–11.

73. Porter, *Paul in Acts*, 117; Keener, *Acts*, 1:313–15.

74. Dibelius, "The Speeches in Acts and Ancient Historiography," In *Studies in the Acts of the Apostles.* ed. Greeven, 165.

75. Wright, *What Saint Paul Really Said*, 46.

Lord. This is the gospel in a nutshell."[76] It is reassuring to see the Reformation begin with the biblicism that I am calling us to here. Lukan gospel and conversion reorders reality in a collectivistic experience of the community with God and Christ.[77] The Lukan emphasis of gospel may be summarized as follows:[78]

1. The focus of Gospel messages is that Jesus is the Davidic King (i.e. Lordship), Who you will have to deal with in the end times judgment.

2. The core salvation benefits have to do with the kingdom being realized now in: forgiveness, and the Spirit being poured forth. However, additional kingdom benefit also ensues like: healing, Jubilee, eschatological reversal, special Spirit manifestations and freedom from one's previous entanglements of the Law or idolatry.

3. The Gentile gospel message may have a preliminary focus emphasizing the creator God as well.

4. Jesus' death provides an example for Jesus disciples to imitate and it shows the responsibility of rebellion, it is never referred to by Luke as a vicarious atonement.

5. The awareness of Jesus' resurrection (grounded in prophecy, personal empirical experience and testimony) shows God's vindication identifying that Jesus is the Davidic King.

---

76. Luther, "A brief instruction on what to look for and expect in the Gospels," In *Luther's Works*, 35:118.

77. Green, *Conversion in Luke-Acts*, 10–16; Crook, *Reconceptualizing Conversion*, 253; Gaventa, *From Darkness to Light*, 11–15; utilizing perspectives of Berger and Luckmann, *The Social Construction of Reality*.

78. Some of this material has been reworked from Kennard, *Messiah Jesus*, 439–40 used by permission from Peter Lang; Conzelmann, *Acts*, xliv and Schweizer "Concerning the Speeches in Acts" in *Studies in Luke-Acts*. ed. Keck and Martyn, 208–16 but especially 210 have similar lists affirming my numbers: 1, 6, and 7 (e.g., Conzelmann's "Christological kerygma." Their lists make more of stylistic rhetorical devices like connecting the speech with the situation and the role for O.T. quotes as beginning and demonstrating the message (e.g., Conzelmann's call for a hearing from miracle or prophecy, connection with the situation, use of O.T. quotation, *kerygma* attempted to be scripturally proven), supporting my #6. Conzelmann's response is more strongly slated toward "repentance the condition for salvation (where appropriate)." Instead, see my more balanced assessment in my #7.

6. Every Gospel sermon appeals to evidence to confirm the message, such as a *pesher* interpretation of prophecy[79] and the immediate empirical experience of miracles.[80]

7. For Peter in Acts, repentance is what Jews in rebellion need to do, while Gentiles need to come to faith. Whereas, Paul and Luke use the terms interchangeably (Acts 20:21).

8. Baptism is tightly connected to this initial salvation response as the external evidence *performing the function of aligning with Christ*[81] (Acts 2:38, 41; 8:12, 36–8; 9:18 10:47–8; 11:16; 16:15, 33; 18:8; 19:3–5; 22:16).

9. This salvation message brings the converts into the Way of salvation extending Jesus' way unto kingdom (Acts 9:2; 13:10; 16:17; 18:25–6; 19:9; 22:4; 24:14, 22).

This topic is usually studied in more microscopic detail.[82] As such, it is rather rare for works to explore and compare the gospel speeches as a group,

---

79. Bock, *Proclamation from Prophecy and Pattern*; Bovon, "The Role of the Scriptures in the Composition of the Gospel Accounts," In *Luke and Acts*. ed. O'Collins and Marconi, 27–28; Evans and Sanders, "The Gospels and Midrash" In *Luke and Scripture*. ed. Evans and Sanders, 1–13; Evans, "Luke and the Rewritten Bible" In *The Pseudepigrapha and Early Biblical Interpretation*. ed. Charlesworth and Evans, 170–201; Lim, *Pesharim*, 44–53; Johnson, *Luke*, 15–21; Hays, "The Persecuted Prophet and Judgment on Jerusalem," *BBR* 25:4(2015): 462; Stegman, "'The Spirit of Wisdom and Understanding,'" In *The Bible and Epistemology*. Healy and Parry, 92; Josephus, *Ant*. 13. 171–3, 297; 18.12–15; *J. W.* 2.119, 162–3; 4 Macc 5:16–27; Philo, *Dreams* 1.124–5; *m. Yad*. 4.6–8; *B. Qidd*. 66a; Resurrection: 2 Macc 7.9–14, 22–23; 14.43–46; *1 En*. 22; 58.3; 62.14–16; 91.10; 92.2; 104; 108.11–14; *Jub*. 5.10; 10.17; 22.22; *L.A.B.*; CD 3.11–16, 20–21; 7.5, 9; 13.11; 20.17–20, 25–27; 1QH 11.19–23 [3.18–22]; 19.10–14 [11.7–11]; 1QS 3.7–12; 4.7; 4Q228 frag. 1 1.9; 4Q266, frag. 11; 4Q385 2; 4Q386 1–2; 4QMMT C; 4Q521 2.2.12; 5.2.5–6; *2 Bar.*[Syriac] 30.1–5; 49–51; 4 Macc 7.19; 16.25; *4 Ezra* 7.26–44; *Sib. Or*. 4.180; *T. Benj*. 10.6–8; *T. Levi* 18; *T. Jud*. 24.

80. Locke, *Concerning Human Understanding* 1.1.15; 2.11.8–9; 2.32.6; 3.3.6–8; "A Discourse of Miracles," In *Works*, 9:256–65; "The Reasonableness of Christianity," In *Works*. Vol. 6; pre-modern empiricism is apparent in Lactanius, *Workmanship of God* 9–10; Keener, *Miracles*, 1:35–208; "Miracle Reports and the Argument from Analogy," *BBR* 25:4(2015): 475–95.

81. Performance act (namely, Church ordinance or sacrament [Acts 2:38–41; 8:38; 10:28; 19:4–5; John 18:28] following the conversion pattern of Jewish proselyte baptism [1QS 3.3–9; 4QTLevi ar; Josephus, *J. W.* 2.150; *Ant*. 14.285; 18.93–94, 117; *T. Levi* 2.3.1–2; *Sib. Or*. 4.162–70; Epictetus, *Dissertiones* 2.9.19–20; *Apoc. Moses* 29.6–13; *m. Tohar* 7.6; *Midrash Sifre Num*. 15.14; *b. Yebam*. 46a–48b; *t. Yoma* 4.20; *t. Pesaḥ* 7.13]) rather than performance language of Austin, *How to do Things with Words*.

82. Usually each feature of the respective sermons is mentioned verse by verse in a commentary but occasionally closer looks of a particular sermon are undertaken such as: Balch "The Areoagus Speech," In *Greeks, Romans, and Christians*. ed. Balch, 52–79; Barrett, "Paul's Speech on the Areopagus," In *New Testament Christianity for Africa and*

but this has been done before by a few.[83] Marion Soads has done the best summary as follows:

> When one views the speeches together, one observes a remarkable coherence. The consistency occurs in terms of the forms and the contents of the speeches. There are 1) regularly repeated elements–for example, the manner of address, the tendency to speak beyond the immediate situation, the declaration of truth claims, the use of the past in explanation or support of the claims made, and the act of offering God's now-available salvation to the hearers for acceptance or rejection; 2) regularly repeated motifs–for example, divine necessity, a Christological

---

the World. ed. Glasswell and Fashole-Luke, 69–77; Gärtner, *The Areopagus Speech and Natural Revelation*; Dibelius, "Paul on Areopagus" and "The Speeches in Acts and Ancient Historiography" In *Studies in the Acts of the Apostles.* ed. Greeven, 26–77, 138–85; Hemer, "The Speeches in Acts II: The Areopagus Address," *TynB* 40(1989): 239–59; Kilgallen, "Acts 13, 38–39: Culmination of Paul's Speech in Psidia" *Bib* 69(1988): 480–506; Montague, "Paul and Athens," *TBT* 49(1970): 14–23; Neyrey, "Acts 17, Epicureans, and Theodicy" in *Greeks, Romans, and Christians,* ed. Balch, 118–134; Porter, "Thucydides 1.22.1 and Speeches in Acts" *NovT* 2(1990): 121–42 re-evaluated the issue in favor of Bruce's previous works; Schubert, "The Final Cycle of Speeches in the Book of Acts," *JBL* 87(1968): 1–16; "The Place of the Areopagus Speech in the Composition of Acts" in *Transitions in Biblical Scholarship.* ed. Rylaarsdam, 235–61; Shields, "The Areopagus Sermon and Romans 1.18ff," *ResQ* 20(1977): 23–40; Zehnle, *Peter's Pentecost Discourse*; Karl Kuhn, "The Kingdom Story through Speech and Theme in Luke 24 and the Acts of the Apostles," In *The Kingdom according to Luke and Acts,* 147–178.

83. Soards, *The Speeches in Acts* is the most profitable here in analyzing content with a special sensitivity to rhetorical device but he does not correlate the speeches together like I am doing in this paper; Ridderbos, *The Speeches of Peter in the Acts of the Apostles* nicely summarizes the content in each speech, especially with a focus on: eschatology apostolicity, Christology (especially my point #1), and paraenesis; Schweizer, "Concerning the Speeches in Acts," in *Studies in Luke-Acts,* 208–16 appraised the contents of the sermons, cf. note #2; Dodd, *The Apostolic Preaching and Its Developments* mostly develops a continuity of the gospel through the whole N.T., with a few pages on the Spirit, Messianism and eschatological nature of the gospel *kerygma,* and a nice overview chart covering the whole N.T. gospel statements; which gems are foreshadowed in "The Framework of the Gospel Narrative," *ExpTim* 43(1931–32): 396–400 which primarily examines the gospel of Mark; Cadbury, "The Speeches in Acts" in *Acts.* ed. Jackson and Lake, 1:402–426; Bruce, *The Speeches in the Book of Acts the Apostles* and "The Speeches in Acts-Thirty Years After," In *Reconciliation and Hope,* 53–68 are rapid surveys of the speeches in Acts with an emphasis on showing that Luke has responsibly handled them after the pattern of the historian Thucydides; Hemer (*The Book of Acts in the Setting of Hellenistic History,* 75–79, 415–27) defends the historicity of the speeches by comparing them to other Greek historians and the surrounding Acts context; Horsley ("Speeches and Dialogue in Acts," *NTS* 32[1986]: 609–14) primarily shows that Acts is consistent and more generous with the placement of speeches in Greek classical narrative; Kennedy (*New Testament Interpretation through Rhetorical Criticism,* 114–140) surveys the speeches in Acts for some of the gems through rhetorical criticism. Kennard, *Messiah Jesus,* 439–65.

contrast scheme, the Holy Spirit, the early Christian witness, and salvation; and 3) regularly repeated basic vocabulary... What is "the meaning to be attributed to the speeches in the work as a whole"? One finds that the speeches unify the Acts account, and through them Luke advances his theme of divinely commissioned unified witness to the ends of the earth.[84]

In the spirit of this synthetic approach, I delineated, in my book *Messiah Jesus*[85], the basic content that Luke (and perhaps his speakers) thought constituted the gospel message as expressed in Acts.

It is widely recognized that Greco-Roman rhetoric in the speeches emphasize paradigms for imitation by the readers.[86] Henry Cadbury especially points out that it is the speeches in Acts that bring vibrant interpretation with prescription as of a theologian to the book of Acts.[87] The narrative sets up and accentuates the content of statements and especially intentional speeches as prescriptive, provided the speaker is speaking commands or warning to his audience and is seen as an authority for the community (as Jesus, Peter, and Paul are clear authorities for the church). Additionally, those speakers who associate positively with such an authority also tend to have their message elevated to the level of authority as well in those contexts where they are making such a positive identification with an authority (such as John the Baptist and those of Luke 1–3 in their affirmation of Jesus). In contrast, the things that opponents (like the Sanhedrin) say are not taken as authoritative for Christians. Secondly, the gospel speeches take on an authoritative role to the readership of the document, if the speeches repeatedly say the same thing. Such repetition accentuates that the content of the sermon is what the textual author (Luke) wishes to communicate and prescribe for his audience, and not merely a coincidence of the agreement among his characters (Peter and Paul) for their respective audiences. Likewise, the content comes to the audience with prescriptive emphasis if those sermons repeatedly *warn their audiences with consequences that the*

---

84. Soads, *Speeches*, 14–14.

85. Kennard, *Messiah Jesus*, 439–65.

86. Kurz, "Narrative Models for Imitation in Luke-Acts" in *Greeks, Romans, and Christians*. ed. Balch, 171–189; Fiore, *The Function of Personal Example in the Socratic and Pastoral Epistles*, especially chapter 3, "Example in Rhetorical Theory, Education, and Literature," 26–44; de Boer, *The Imitation of Paul*; Crouzel, "L'imitation et la 'suite' de Dieu et du Christ dans les premiers siècles chrétiens," *JAC* 21(1978): 7–41 especially 7–30; Cothenet et al., "Imitation du Christ," *Dictionnaire de Spiritualité* 7(1971): 1536–1601; Gutierrez, *La Paternité spirituelle selon S. Paul*; Pate and Kennard, *Deliverance Now and Not Yet*, 369–372; Trompf, *The Idea of Historical Recurrence in Western Thought*.

87. Cadbury, "The Speeches in Acts," In *Acts*. ed. Jackson and Lake, 1:402.

narrative develop. So the reader should become identified within the Spirit benefits of salvation by heeding the exhortations of these sermons. That is, the narrative development that realizes the consequences shows that this gospel is an intentional issue that Luke prescribes. So the study that follows is not merely a descriptive one exploring the Lukan gospel, but by Luke's emphasis, Luke's statement of the gospel is a legitimate statement we could repeat as the gospel in our day as well.

Luke uses "gospel proclamation" (εὐαγγελίου) only twice, both in the book of Acts. In Acts 15:7 it refers to the gospel message to be believed for salvation. In this context, the issue is the content that is to be included within this gospel, so the idea of evaluating the content of the gospel is within Luke's thought forms. The Judaizing sect wished for Gentiles to have the Law of Moses included among the gospel, but the Jerusalem council declared that God had accepted the Gentiles by the Holy Spirit, without this Law being included, so that the Law should not be considered as part of the gospel. This appeal was empirically grounded by the miraculous Spirit manifestation of tongues among the Gentiles in the same manner as had occurred among the Jewish Christians at Pentecost (Acts 10:47-48; 11:15-17; 15:8-9).[88]

The other instance is in Acts 20:21-24 where Paul summarizes his gospel as the good news of God's grace for Jews and Gentiles (εὐαγγέλιον τῆς χάριτος τοῦ θεοῦ). The repetition of his phrase "solemn testimony" (διαμαρτυρόμενος v. 21, διαμαρτύρασθαι v. 24) identifies that the statements in verse 21 and 24 are both referring to the concept of communally trusted gospel message. Paul envisions the testimony to prompt response to this gospel to be repentance to God and faith to our Lord Jesus Christ.[89]

The parallel εἰς clauses in Acts 20:21 (εἰς θεὸν μετάνοιαν καὶ πίστιν εἰς τὸν κύριον ἡμῶν Ἰησοῦν) draw repentance and faith together as largely underscoring a synonymous response in aligning the believer with God. That is, Peter in the Acts gospel proclamations, maintains repentance (μετάνοιαν) as the turning from rebellion that Jews must do as they respond to the gospel (Acts 2:38; 3:19; 5:31) and faith (πίστις) as the response for a Gentile who is already predisposed to the gospel (Acts 10:43), but Paul sees these terms as interchangeable in this context where both Jews and Gentiles are described by both of them (Acts 19:2, 4; 20:21; 26:20). Luke also uses

---

88. Locke, *Concerning Human Understanding*, 1.1.15; 2.11.8-9; 2.32.6; 3.3.6-8; "A Discourse of Miracles," In *Works*, 9:256-65; "The Reasonableness of Christianity," In *Works*, vol. 6; pre-modern empiricism is apparent in Lactanius, *Workmanship of God* 9-10; Keener, *Miracles*, 1:35-208; "Miracle Reports and the Argument from Analogy," *BBR* 25:4(2015): 475-95.

89. Ricoeur, "The Hermeneutics of Testimony" cited in Ford, "Paul Ricoeur: A Biblical Philosopher on Jesus," In *Jesus and Philosophy*. ed. Moser, 190.

these terms interchangeably (μετάνοιαν [Luke 13:1–5; 24:47; Acts 11:18], πίστις [Acts 15:9; 20:21; 24:24; 26:18] and πιστεύω [Acts 2:44; 4:4, 32; 5:14; 8:12–13, 37; 9:42 etc.]). This is parallel to Josephus' use when he confronted Jesus the Galilean brigand leader "to repent and believe in me."[90] In other words, this person must give up his agenda of trying to throw the Romans out of Israel and become a loyal follower of Josephus' agenda instead.[91] John the Baptist, Jesus, and Peter used the term *repentance* only for the Jews in signifying *what Israel must do if Yahweh is to restore her fortunes at last*.[92] Peter sees that Israel must especially repent from their culpability in killing Christ. Whereas, Paul (as recorded by Luke) also uses the term "repentance" of Gentiles to communicate their need to depart from their idolatry and entrapment to Satan (Acts 26:18). Paul and Luke prefer to use the term "faith" sometimes without the mention of repentance (Acts 13:48; 16:31; 17:34; 18:8). N. T. Wright reminds us that both repentance and faith (in Acts) appear in contexts linking them inescapably with eschatology and the narrow way to Kingdom.[93]

Preparation Frameworks for Gospel

The expectation of salvation informs Luke's concept of gospel to be a Spirit produced kingdom in which Davidic King Jesus reigns. For example, the angel Gabriel's empirical presence and announcement to Mary that Jesus will be born from the Spirit through her to be the Son of the Most High, that is the Davidic King (Luke 1:32–35). Such an angelic announcement carried authoritative weight within a Pharisaic epistemology.[94] The announcement clarifies that Jesus' kingdom is to have no end. Likewise, in response to Elizabeth's empowerment filling by the Spirit, Mary praised God for the eschatological reversal in the kingdom, which as performative language fulfills the promises made to Abraham and the fathers (Luke 1:50–55).[95] This

---

90. Josephus, *Life* 110.

91. Josephus, *Life* 110 in the LCL edition by Thackery where he translates this text (1.43) as "if he would. . .prove his loyalty to me."

92. Wright, *Jesus and the Victory of God*, 249.

93. Wright, *Jesus*, 249–251.

94. *Jub.* 1.27–29; 10.10–14; *1 En.* 4.19, 21–26; 7; 8; 17–36; 89.61–77; 90.14–20; *T. Levi* 9.6; *T. Reub.* 5.3; *T. Jos.* 6.6; Such angel communication provided by God could be identified within Moser's attunement to filial knowledge of God and thus provides authoritative evidence for the message communicated (*The Elusive God*, 46–7, 98, 113–123).

95. Grice, "Meaning," *Philosophical Review* 66(1957): 377–88; "Utterer's Meaning and Intentions," *Philosophical Review* 78(1969): 147–77; "Utterer's Meaning,

eschatological reversal benefits: the poor, humble, and those who fear God. It includes an everlasting defense of Israel from their enemies. Additionally, the Spirit prompts Zacharias to praise God for the eschatological redemption of Israel, in which the Davidic King is raised up to provide salvation from Israel's enemies (Luke 1:61-79). This kingdom is seen as fulfilling the Abrahamic covenant. This kingdom realization should bring about the desired effect of serving God without fear and with holiness and righteousness. Zacharias announces that John's role will be to give knowledge of salvation by the forgiveness of sins. Next in the narrative, the angel empirically announced to the shepherds that the Savior King was born (Luke 2:11). As in other authoritative angel announcements the natural response is toward fear but these angels reassure the shepherds (Luke 1:12-13, 29; 2:10). The shepherds are provided with an odd evidential sign to recognize the baby King Jesus as the babe in a feeding trough of a stable (Luke 2:12). All these events Luke is told likely by Mary testifying to her treasuring them in her heart (Luke 1:28-29-56; 2:19, 51).[96]

John the Baptist's gospel message (Luke 3:18, εὐηγγελίζετο) calls Jews to be baptized as an expression of repentance for sins and alignment with the coming kingdom of God. Baptism becomes a *performance action* that aligns Jews with John's kingdom oriented Judaism. As such this performance act is a way of bodily knowing and expressing one's new allegiance in the narrow kingdom way. This distinctive way of generosity and justice aligned with the coming King avoids God's eschatological wrath fire (Luke 3:3, 7, 9, 11, 13-18). The coming King will baptize with a single baptism, which will immerse in two groups in two different directions reflective of the distinctive way people live. Those kingdom bound will experience baptism in the Spirit while the damned will experience baptism into eschatological wrath fire. The fire (πῦρ) of Jesus baptism is to be understood how fire (πῦρ) is used in the immediate context, that of unquenchable destruction fire (πῦρ, Luke 3:9, 16-17).[97] The Holy Spirit's empirical presence upon Jesus indicates divine empowerment of Jesus in His ministry. The divine audible voice or *bath qol* (granted authoritative status among Pharisees)[98] announces that Jesus is

---

Sentence-Meaning, Word-Meaning," In *The Philosophy of Language*. ed. Searle, 54-70; Austin, *How to Do Things with Words*; Ricoeur, *Oneself as Another*, 44; Kennard, *The Relationship Between Epistemology*, 56, 62-65; *A Critical Realist's*, 232.

96. Ricoeur, "The Hermeneutics of Testimony" cited in David Ford, "Paul Ricoeur: A Biblical Philosopher on Jesus," In *Jesus and Philosophy*. ed. Moser, 190.

97. Therefore, this fire imagery is no allusion to the Pentecost tongues of fire for that is foreign to this context.

98. B. 'Abot 6.2; B. Bat. 73b, 85b; Mak. 23b; 'Erub. 54b; Shab. 33b; 88a; Soṭa 33a; p. Soṭa 7.5, sect. 5; Pesiq. Rab Kah. 15.5; Lev. Rab. 19.5-6; Deut. Rab. 11.10; Lam. Rab.

God's Son, anointed to be King to reign, and thus those who experience this empirical voice or any testimony concerning Jesus' authority should heed it.

Jesus shows Himself to be this King, aligned with God. The kingship is clearly announced by Luke in identifying Jesus as the Son of God, coming through the context of extending John's ministry and dogged by the grand conflict with Satan (Luke 3:38; 4:3, 9). Jesus aligns Himself with God and His Word rather than Satan's quick counterfeit solutions. Jesus then embodies in His incarnation the noble way to kingdom.

Jesus' Gospel in Luke

Jesus announces His ministry purpose by quoting Isaiah 61:1-2 (Luke 4:17-21). These quotes are utilized in a *pesher* thematic arrangement in order to direct proclamation and authority to Jesus as Lord.[99] So these quotes are not claims that this O.T. text only has the set meaning developed, but rather the O.T. quotes bring authority and direction for what the speaker and Luke develop. So the O.T. quotes become an authoritative testimony in this new context, contributing credibility to the speaker's message. Jesus' ministry purpose for the Isaiah quote is that: the Spirit has empowered Him to proclaim the Gospel, with a jubilee of eschatological reversal result attesting to it. So the miracles further pragmatically demonstrate that Jesus is the divine Spirit empowered King initiating kingdom as it surrounds Him.[100]

> The Spirit of the Lord is upon Me, because He anointed Me to preach the gospel to the poor. He has sent Me to proclaim release to the captives and recovery of sight to the blind, to set free those who are downtrodden, to proclaim the favorable year of the Lord (Isa 61:1-2; Luke 4:17-21).

Proem 2, 23; *Lam. Rab.* 1.16 sect. 50; *Ruth Rab.* 6.4; *Qoh. Rab.* 7.12, sect. 1; *Pesq. Rab Kah.* 11.16.

99. Lim, *Pesharim*, 44–53; Bock, *Proclamation from Prophecy and Pattern*; Hays, "The Persecuted Prophet and Judgment on Jerusalem," *BBR* 25:4(2015): 462.

100. The use of Isaiah 61 is similar to Jewish use of the time (11Q13; 4Q521; Brooke, *Exegesis at Qumran*, 319–23; Puech, "Une Apocalypse messianique (4Q521)," *RevQ* 15[1992]: 475–519; Collins, "The Works of the Messiah," *DSD* 1[1994]: 98–112) utilizing pragmatic verification later developed by Peirce, *Collected Papers*. ed. Hartshorne and Weiss, vol. 5 paragraph 9; "The Fixation of Belief," *Popular Science Monthly* 12(Nov., 1877): 1–15; "How to Make Our Ideas Clear," *Popular Science Monthly* 12(Jan., 1878): 286–302; Locke, *Concerning Human Understanding* 1.1.15; 2.11.8–9; 2.32.6; 3.3.6–8; "A Discourse of Miracles," In *Works*, 9:256–65; "The Reasonableness of Christianity," In *Works*, vol. 6; Keener, *Miracles*, 1:35–208; "Miracle Reports and the Argument from Analogy," *BBR* 25:4(2015): 475–95.

The issue is the public acknowledgement of the Son of Man for who He is as the Spirit endowed King. The one who publically acknowledges Jesus before men, Jesus will acknowledge before the angels of God (Luke 12:8-9). Likewise, the one who denies Jesus before men, Jesus will deny before the angels of God. This has ramifications to the acceptance or denial of the Spirit's empowerment of the Son's miracles. Those who blaspheme the Spirit will be damned without forgiveness in this life and in the afterlife as well (Luke 12:10-12). Unfortunately, the people responded to His amazing announcement with rage and rejection; they tried to kill Jesus (Luke 4: 28-30). Furthermore, the religious leaders rejected Jesus for his persistent healing and doing good on the Sabbath (Luke 6:1-5, 11; 13:10-17; 14:1-6).[101] However, the more basic rejected issue that Jesus proposed is that Jesus is King. The right response is to align with Jesus as the King (Luke 19:37-38; 20:17-18). The people are warned to repent or perish, for exclusion will bring destruction for Israel and hell for the individuals (Luke 13:3, 5, 23-30). Unfortunately, the religious leaders reject Jesus and head for their destruction (Luke 19:27, 39; 20; 22:47-23:49).

Luke reiterates that Jesus primary purpose was to preach the gospel of the kingdom of God (Luke 4:43-44; 8:1; 9:11). This is reflected in the mimetic role in which the twelve are sent out to also preach the kingdom of God (Luke 9:1-6). They carry Jesus' message and extend His ministry.

Therefore, the gospel gets framed by Jesus' preached content as He directs His disciples toward the kingdom. Luke frames Jesus' message to kingdom in a classic two ways strategy. The salvific way is a narrow way to life, while the broad way ends in damnation. Luke identifies that these two ways are grounded upon wisdom (wise or fool, Luke 7:35 with 8:4-15) and the Law (blessed or cursed, Luke 10:25-28). This is both a cognitive and a moral commitment to Jesus and His kingdom way of life.[102] The way toward kingdom is to identify with Jesus and His way of life. This way holds out kingdom blessing for the poor, weeping, and ostracized who identify with Jesus (Luke 6:20-27). One's commitment to Jesus is shown by loving one's enemies and doing good as they try to abuse you (Luke 6:27, 35, 45). The defining issue is do you hear the Word of Jesus to do it (Luke 8:15, 21; 10:42; 11:28). It is in this way that Jesus kingdom teaching extends the Law's blessing strategy for His Jewish disciples; the kingdom is the era of Deuternomic blessing (Luke 10:25-28). Those who internalize the Law, love others as they

---

101. Also, the religious leaders raised difficulties with Jesus over fasting (Luke 5:33-39) and the lack of ceremonial washing before meals (Luke 11:30-52).

102. Talbert, "Conversion in the Acts of the Apostles," In *Literary Studies in Luke-Acts*. ed. Thompson and Phillips, 135-36 dependent upon Shumate, *Crises and Conversion in Apuleius' Metamorphoses*.

love themselves. Such an approach is also a wisdom strategy because by following Jesus' teaching "wisdom is vindicated by all her children" (Luke 7:35). One such child is the sinful woman who expressed her great love for Jesus by washing, kissing and anointing Jesus feet with her tears (Luke 7:36–50). Furthermore, the wisdom strategy of parables shows that in the parable of the soils, it is the honest and good application of the Word which will bear fruit with perseverance unto kingdom (Luke 8:4–15). That which is hidden, like who are the kingdom oriented ones, will be revealed by deeds (Luke 8:16–17). However, this is not a works salvation; it has to do with aligning with Christ. Even a criminal on a cross may align with Christ and enter into paradise with Jesus on that very day (Luke 23:40–43).

The other side of this two ways gospel is that if Israel does not identify with Jesus as the Christ, they will be destroyed.[103] Jesus cursing of the fig tree in Luke 13:1–9 argues for the Deuteronomistic curses to be implemented upon unrepentant Israel. However, this is the bad news, not the gospel, and Marv Pate and I developed this extensively in our book *Deliverance Now and Not Yet* so there is no need to do so again.[104]

The kingdom way has the kingdom encroach into the present time as well. The most obvious way to see the present encroachment of kingdom is in the miracles that surround the King. The jubilee of eschatological reversal, as seen in Jesus miracles, is provided as attesting evidence to identify Jesus as this King. For example, in the midst of Luke's emphasis on miracles, John's disciples come to Jesus to ask Him if He is the King, He quotes Isaiah 61:1–2 and then turns their focus to the empirical evidence of His miracles (Luke 7:21–22). Jesus demonstrated through His miracles that He had divine authority as King, the Holy Son of God sent from God. The variety of miracles[105] show His dominant authority as an expression of kingdom wherever the King is present. Immediately following Luke's emphasis on the miracles, Jesus asked the disciples whom they considered Him to be. They identified that the people at that time understand Him to be a prophet, but Peter at least recognized Jesus to be the King (Luke 9:19–20). At the

---

103. Sanders, *The Jews in Luke-Acts*, 189–190.

104. Pate and Kennard, *Deliverance Now and Not Yet*, 304–309, 312–319, 402–420, 433–461.

105. Jesus' authority is demonstrated by: 1. He cast out demons (Luke 4:33–36; 6:18, 33; 9:42–43; 11:14), 2. He healed the sick (Luke 4:40–41; 5:24; 6:8–10, 18–19; 7:8–10; 8:43–48; 13:13; 18:41–43), 3. He cleansed lepers (that is, going beyond healing to cleansing them from their uncleanness as well, Luke 5:12–13; 17:11–14), 4. Jesus accomplished nature miracles like a catch of fish, calming a storm and feeding the multitude (Luke 5:6–9; 8:24; 9:13–17), and 5. Jesus resurrected others (Luke 7:16; 8:52–56). A good discussion of these issues from the view of the historical Jesus is presented in Meier, *A Marginal Jew*, 2:509–970.

triumphal entry the people also recognize Him to be the King, because of the miracles (Luke 19:37).

A further expression of the eschatological reversal encroaching into time is that the status of intimate family with Jesus is taken from Jesus' mother and brothers and given to those who hear and apply the Word of God to do it (Luke 8:18–21).

The two ways strategy shows itself most blatantly in the mimetic atonement of *imitation Christi*.[106] The first mention of Jesus death in the gospel of Luke is quickly followed by the charge to the disciples that they cannot try to save their lives, for authentic discipleship puts them at risk for daily martyrdom, even by a scandalous cross (Luke 9:22–26). The cost of discipleship under Jesus became severe with: itinerancy, endurance of tribulation, daily heading for martyrdom and un-swayed by one's family (Luke 14:25–35; 21:19). If a disciple is ashamed of Jesus and His Words, then Jesus will be ashamed of him, when the Son of Man comes in His glory as the King to reign (Luke 12:8–9). Instead, the disciple should seek the kingdom and strive to enter by the narrow door; this way brings intimacy of being known by the Lord (Luke 12:31–34; 13:23–35).

Within this two ways, authentic conversion is apparent by identifying whole heartedly with Christ.[107] For example, when Jesus called Matthew to follow Him, Matthew hosted a great feast for a great number of tax-collectors (Matt 9:9–13; Luke 5:27–32). Jesus explains to the Pharisees why He joined such festivities with tax-collectors and sinners, as He is calling those who understand that they need Jesus as a physician for their condition. In contrast, one Pharisee hosted Jesus for a meal but he provided no foot washing, greeting, nor kiss (Luke 7:36, 44–45). However, a sinful woman[108] crashed the meal to weep and anoint Jesus' feet with her tears, expensive dowry oil, and kisses, wiping Jesus' feet with her hair. Jesus identified that she loves Jesus much with the result that her many sins are forgiven (Luke 7:47, 50). Likewise, Zacchaeus, the short chief tax-collector of the Jericho region wished to see Jesus so he climbed a tree on Jesus' route (Luke 19:1–10). Jesus noticed him there and announced that He must stay at his house. When the crowd complained that Jesus had chosen to stay with a

---

106. Pate and Kennard, *Deliverance Now and Not Yet*, 461–467 continuing the dominant Jewish tradition of mimetic atonement during second temple Judaism (pp. 29–57).

107. Adams, "The Problem of Total Devotion," In *Rationality, Religious Belief, and Moral Commitment*. ed. Audi and Wainwright, 94; Nygren, *Agape and Eros*, 216; Wainwright, "Obedience and Responsibility," In *The Wisdom of the Christian Faith*. ed. Moser and McFall, 68.

108. Mary Magdala is introduced in Luke 8:2 (she is not the un-named forgiven woman of Luke 7:36–50 as Gregory the Great first proposed in 591 A.D).

sinner, Zacchaeus spoke up, "Lord I give half of my goods to the poor; and if I have taken wrongly from anyone, I restore fourfold." Jesus responded to the empirical evidence of the testimony and changed life, "Today salvation has come to this house, because he also is a son of Abraham; for the Son of Man has come to seek and save that which was lost."

The two ways are also shown by how one identifies with the disciples' ministry. Only those who follow Jesus and identify with those following Jesus are fit for the kingdom (Luke 9:10, 57–62; 11:23). The acceptance of the disciples' ministry is an acceptance of Jesus and God (Luke 10:9–16). So Luke's Gospel ends with a great commission for disciples to proclaim in Jesus name repentance for the forgiveness of sins (Luke 24:47). This very message sets up the second volume, the book of Acts which continues the saga.

Peter's Gospel Sermons in Acts

Luke recorded four of Peter's gospel presentations in Acts, and I have correlated these to surface the Petrine pattern of the gospel (Acts 2:14–39; 3:12–26; 4:8–12; 10:34–43). The pattern is similar even though these messages emerge from very different situations and audiences. This either shows that Peter was consistent with his presentation of gospel or it shows Luke's selectivity, only recorded that portion of what Peter said. Either way these sermons become authoritative gospel statements (on Peter and Luke's authority or merely on Luke's authority).

The gospel begins with an introduction transitioning from the circumstances at hand to the person of Jesus. These introductions begin where the listeners are and encourage them to follow the speaker to focus on Jesus is Lord.[109] These circumstances are as varied as the Spirit poured out, or a man healed or a trial or the fact of Jewish exclusivity, when a Gentile requests Peter's salvation message. Those accounts which begin with miracles continue to evidence authority in the context based upon this expression of kingdom (Acts 10:44–47; 11:15; 15:8 with 2:4, 17–21; and 3:11 and 4:8–10 with 3:7–9).[110] This introduction bridges to the person of Jesus.

---

109. A rhetorical introduction interposes a topic (Aristotle, *Rhet.* 3.14.6) and predisposes toward good will (Pseudo-Cicero, *Rhet. Ad Her.* 1.3.6; 1.11.18; Aristotle, *Rhet.* 3.14.6–7; 3.17.1), which Peter and Paul accomplish in his introductions in Acts 2:15–21; 3:11–12; 4:8–9; 10:34–37; 17:23; 23:1; 24:10–11; 26:2–3.

110. Locke, *Concerning Human Understanding* 1.1.15; 2.11.8–9; 2.32.6; 3.3.6–8; "A Discourse of Miracles," In *Works*, 9:256–65; "The Reasonableness of Christianity," In *Works*, vol. 6; Keener, *Miracles*, 1:35–208; "Miracle Reports and the Argument from Analogy," *BBR* 25:4(2015): 475–95.

The focus of the gospel message is that the person of Jesus is the One Who you will have to deal with in kingdom salvation. Each sermon develops this theme a little differently but the commonality places the focus on Jesus and whether the audience aligns with Him. To facilitate this end, Peter utilized *midrash*-like concatenation combining O.T. quotes for his Christological ends.[111] For example, Acts 2 develops that Jesus is the Davidic King promised (Acts 2:30 quoting 2 Sam 7:12–13) announced as the anointed One to be King by God (Acts 2:36), and functioning in this exalted Christ role as receiving and giving the Holy Spirit (Acts 2:33). While in this context "Lord" (κύριος) stands for Davidic King and Deity, as a term it was also appropriated by the Caesars (Augustus, Tiberius, Caligua, Nero and Domitian) and the Jewish rulers (Herod the Great, Agrippa I and Agrippa II).[112] Contrary to these others, Acts 2 demonstrates Jesus is the Lord (Davidic King and God). The Lord concept of this Acts 2:36 reference is elevated by the *midrash* use of the quote from Psalm 110:1 in Acts 2:34 which takes the אֲדֹנִי /*Adonai* as Lord (κύριος) in referring to Christ. However, since in Acts 2:34 the κύριος also translates Psalm 110:1 יְהוָה /*Yahweh*, this draws Jesus' divinity within a Jewish monotheism as an essential part of the gospel as well.

In Acts 3 Jesus serves many roles including healer, forgiver, ἀρχηγὸν (the prince or leader of life), the prophet after Moses pattern, and the One Who will bring in the Kingdom. For a more hostile audience, on trial Jesus is presented as the only savior of physical and spiritual healing (use of σῴζω in Acts 4:9 and 12). For a receptive Gentile audience, Jesus is presented as the Lord and Judge of all, who also heals (Acts 10:38, 42). So the focus of Peter's gospel statement is the person of Jesus Christ (as the One that they have to deal with in their salvation), rather than an event that this person does. Reception of the gospel entails aligning oneself with this Jesus as King and Savior.

One of the repeated supports for Jesus as Lord is that Peter and others saw and testify that God raised Jesus from the dead (Acts 2:31–32; 3:15; 10:41–42). Peter's testimony, grounded upon his empirical experience being with the resurrected Christ, helps to support[113] that Jesus is the Lord that his audience will need to respond when Christ comes in His Kingdom.

Repentance and baptism are the combined performative expression indicating that those who align with Jesus as Lord are forgiven and receive the Holy Spirit (Acts 2:38 μετανοήσατε καὶ βαπτισθήτω..εἰς ἄφεσιν τῶν

---

111. Stuhlmacher, "The Pauline Gospel," In *The Gospel and the Gospels*, 172.

112. Bietenhard, "Lord, Master," In *DNTT*, 2:511; Cullmann, *The Christology of the New Testament*, 197–99; Suetonius, *De Vita Caesarum* 13.2; the title was also used to describe gods (e.g., 1 Cor. 8:5); Deismann, *Light from the Ancient East*, 352–3.

113. Ricoeur, "The Hermeneutics of Testimony" cited in Ford, "Paul Ricoeur: A Biblical Philosopher on Jesus," In *Jesus and Philosophy*. ed. Moser, 190.

ἁμαρτιῶν ὑμῶν). Baptism becomes a *performance action* that aligns with Jesus as Lord. As such, this performance act is a way of bodily knowing and expressing one's new allegiance in the narrow kingdom way much like baptism functioned for Gentiles proselyting into Judaism. The Church recognized the practice as part of disciple-making practice even to the end of the age (Matt 28:19–20; Acts 8:12, 38; 10:46).

Philip's Evangelism

The gospel that Philip communicates is summarized as "proclaiming Christ" and "the good news about the kingdom of God and the name of Jesus Christ" (Acts 8:5, 12, 35). Notice again the kingdom emphasis of the gospel here. Such a gospel came with miracles to corroborate it (Acts 8:12).[114] However, Philip could not provide the Holy Spirit like the apostles did when they came to see his newly baptized converts. Thus with the giving of the Spirit, Philip's gospel completes the Lukan pattern.

When Philip was sent to the Gaza road, the Ethiopian eunuch was reading from Isaiah 53, so Philip preached Jesus to him (Acts 8:26–36). The interchange with the Ethiopian eunuch engaged the question who Isaiah 53:7–8 describes (Acts 8:32–33). This provided Philip with the opportunity to testify as a witness.[115] The Ethiopian eunuch expressed his allegiance with Christ through his baptism (Acts 8:38).

This whole servant song wonderfully unpacks the meaning of Christ's vicarious atonement probably more fully than any other biblical passage. However, Luke did not quote or develop any vicarious atonement portions of the servant song. Luke cited a section immediately after and stopping immediately before the vicarious atonement Isaianic statements, so he avoided raising the issue. Luke quotes instead a section on the silent martyrdom of Jesus in his death. In this context, Philip preaches Christ as the One who is empirically recognizable by silence in His death. This gospel expression merely connects Jesus with a martyrdom death. The dominant Jewish interpretation available at this time was the view of mimetic atonement.[116]

---

114. Locke, *Concerning Human Understanding* 1.1.15; 2.11.8–9; 2.32.6; 3.3.6–8; "A Discourse of Miracles," In *Works*, 9:256–65; "The Reasonableness of Christianity," In *Works*, vol. 6; pre-modern empiricism is apparent in Lactanius, *Workmanship of God* 9–10; Keener, *Miracles*, 1:35–208; "Miracle Reports and the Argument from Analogy," *BBR* 25:4(2015): 475–95.

115. Ricoeur, "The Hermeneutics of Testimony" cited in Ford, "Paul Ricoeur: A Biblical Philosopher on Jesus," In *Jesus and Philosophy*. ed. Moser, 190.

116. Kennard, *Messiah Jesus*, 269–90; Pate and Kennard, *Deliverance Now and Not Yet*, 29–58, 433–468.

However, if we let the few strands that we have of Philip's gospel fill in the message, it does so by focusing on kingdom (Acts 8:12). Additionally, if we let Luke's emphasis fill in the gospel message, the vicarious atonement is not emphasized but rather a martyrdom that demonstrates Jesus the servant was killed by rebellious Jews but God vindicated Him by raising Him to be the King. Either way, we are left with Luke intentionally not developing the vicarious atonement that is present in the Isaiah text. That is, Luke goes out of his way to avoid developing vicarious atonement here.

Paul's Gospel Sermons in Acts

Luke developed Paul's gospel seven times in the book of Acts (Acts 13:16-48; 14:15-17; 16:31; 17:22-32; 18:3-6; 19:1-7; 20:21). Two of these statements are merely summaries. For example, in Acts 16:31 Paul's gospel is summarized as "Believe in the Lord Jesus and you shall be saved." Likewise, in Acts 20:21 Luke records that Paul solemnly testifies to "repentance toward God and faith in our Lord Jesus Christ." Both these summaries join with the sermons in emphasizing the focus of Paul's gospel is to believe in Jesus as the Christ.

Each gospel presentation begins with a transition to move Paul's audience to consider the gospel.[117] To Jews in a synagogue, this entailed a brief history of Israel from exodus to the Davidic king, to the One proclaimed by John the Baptist (Acts 13:16-25). To Jewish followers of John the Baptist the transition was more direct, finding out whether they had received the gift of the Holy Spirit (Acts 19:2-3). To Gentile audiences, the transition connected with their ignorant practice of idolatry and tried to move them first to a worship of the monotheist God Who created everything (Acts 14:15; 17:22-24).

To a Gentile audience the gospel partakes of two foci: 1) God is the creator of everything and 2) Jesus is the One with Whom you will have to deal for salvation. For example, at Lystra Paul healed a man lame from birth and the people wished to offer sacrifices presuming Paul to be Hermes and Barnabus to be Zeus (Acts 14:8-18). Trying to restrain them from this pagan practice they admitted that they were mere men and preach the gospel that they might turn from these vain things to the One who created everything and sustains everything by His providence. That is as far as they could get at this time.

---

117. A rhetorical introduction interposes a topic (Aristotle, *Rhet.* 3.14.6) and predisposes toward good will (Pseudo-Cicero, *Rhet. Ad Her.* 1.3.6; 1.11.18; Aristotle, *Rhet.* 3.14.6-7; 3.17.1), which Peter and Paul accomplish in their introductions in Acts 2:15-21; 3:11-12; 4:8-9; 10:34-37; 17:23; 23:1; 24:10-11; 26:2-3.

In a later more fruitful occasion at Athens, the whole gospel was heard (Acts 17:16–34).[118] The Athens context transitions from reasoning in the market place to that of the Agorapagus. The epistemic issues present in this speech are explored in the chapter on Paul's epistemology.

To an audience of Jewish and God fearers in a synagogue, the focus of the gospel is directly on Jesus as the Davidic King and Savior (Acts 13:27–39; 18:5). There is no need to develop a monotheistic Creator that sustains everything, since that is already part of the audience's world view. The Davidic King emphasis is especially built off the fact that God raised Jesus as a vindication, indicating that Jesus is that Davidic King (Acts 13:30–37).[119] When Paul's ministry is summed up at the end of Acts it especially underscores this Christological kingdom emphasis as "preaching the kingdom of God, and teaching concerning the Lord Jesus Christ" (Acts 28:31).[120]

Prophecy permeated the gospel to Jews and God-fearers for they had the worldview to make sense of it. Paul utilizes the O.T. quotes as a *pesher* foundation to proclaim Christ without unpacking all aspects that the quote might contain in the O.T. context.[121] For example, Paul acknowledges that Jesus was predicted to suffer by Moses and the prophets (Acts 26:22–23).

---

118. Balch ("The Areopagus Speech," In *Greeks, Romans, and Christians*, 52–79) confirms Luke as using credible historical practices of his day by comparing it with Poisdonius and these later historians; Barrett ("Paul's Speech on the Areopagus," In *New Testament Christianity for Africa and the World*, 69–77) primarily appreciates the role of Hellenism as he compares Paul's and the Epicurean appreciation for popular religion; Gärtner, *The Areopagus Speech and Natural Revelation*; Dibelius ("Paul on Areopagus," In *Studies in the Acts of the Apostles*, 26–77) analyzes the speech for a common ground in creation and providence with Hellenistic religious and philosophical views; Hemer ("The Speeches in Acts II: The Areopagus Address," *TynB* 40[1989]: 239–59) primarily tries to show that this sermon is Pauline by connecting it with Athenian culture; Montague, "Paul and Athens," *TBT* 49(1970): 14–23; Neyrey ("Acts 17, Epicureans, and Theodicy" in *Greeks, Romans, and Christians*, 118–134) compares Paul with Epicurean theodicy and has a particularly good section on Providence in Paul's sermons; Porter, "Thucydides 1.22.1 and Speeches in Acts" *NovT* 2(1990): 121–42 re-evaluated the issue in favor of Bruce's previous works; Schubert ("The Place of the Areopagus Speech in the Composition of Acts," In *Transitions in Biblical Scholarship*, 235–61) helps to confirm the legitimacy of the gospel going to the Gentiles; Shields ("The Areopagus Sermon and Romans 1.18ff," *ResQ* 20[1977]: 23–40) explores creation based theology from the positive and the negative trajectory of these texts.

119. This point is especially strong in Kilgallen, "Acts 13, 38–39: Culmination of Paul's Speech in Psidia," *Bib* 69(1988): 480–506.

120. Cf. the conclusion of Schubert, "The Final Cycle of Speeches in the Book of Acts," *JBL* 87(1968): 16.

121. Bock, *Proclamation from Prophecy and Pattern*; Lim, *Pesharim*, 44–53; Johnson, *Luke*, 15–21; Hays, "The Persecuted Prophet and Judgment on Jerusalem," *BBR* 25:4(2015): 462; Stegman, "The Spirit of Wisdom and Understanding," In *The Bible and Epistemology*. Healy and Parry, 92.

However, Jesus' resurrection is especially the divine fulfillment of prophecy as well (Acts 13:27, 32–37). Likewise, the offer of forgiveness, everlasting life, and freedom beyond which the Law could provide is an extension of this prophetic gospel word (Acts 13:38–39, 46, 48). Furthermore, Paul appealed to prophecy to warn them not to fulfill the prophetic word as a scoffer, for such live in a precarious condition (Acts 13:40–41). Unfortunately, a major group of Jews did return the next Sabbath as scoffers and blasphemers, prompting Paul to again respond with prophecy indicating the gospel will now be directed to a Gentile audience (Acts 13:47–49). The rebellious culpability of the Jews indicated it was time to go to the Gentiles (Acts 13:46–47; 18:6–7). Paul and Luke cite the servant song of Isaiah 49:6[122] and extend it from the singular (σε) to the plural (ἡμῖν) as a command from the Lord Jesus Christ in grounding Paul's and Barnabus' Gentile ministry. The last line of the quote is reminiscent of Acts 1:8, "to the end of the earth." From this focus of the gospel going to Gentiles, many Gentiles responded with joy and worship, believing as God had appointed them.

The most important thing included in authentic Lukan-Pauline salvation is that the believer identifies with Jesus, Who is the Messiah and Judge (Acts 9:5; 13:33–34; 16:31; 17:31; 19:4; 20:21; 22:8; 26:15). This has implications for seeing Jesus as Lord and permitting Jesus Lordship to be the core of the gospel. The gospel issue becomes then: *Will you submit to Jesus and His way*. Authentic salvation also entails: 1) forgiveness of sins, 2) freedom from the things that the Law could not free you from, 3) freedom from the domain of darkness and Satan, and 4) everlasting life (Acts 13:38–39[123], 46, 48; 26:18). However, most of Paul's gospel statements in Acts do not develop these additional benefits. It is as though promising them is not as critical as identifying with Jesus.

Baptism is still a performative practice that aligns one with Jesus and forgiveness (Acts 19:6; 22:16) but it recedes among Paul's statements, such that aligning with Jesus can occur in other ways of reconciliation and allegiance.

This salvation message brings the converts into the Way of salvation extending Jesus way unto kingdom from Luke's Gospel (Acts 9:2; 13:10; 16:17; 18:25–6; 19:9; 22:4; 24:14, 22). That is, in this metaphor the focus is not on a past-accomplished salvation but rather on continuing toward the goal of kingdom. This fits within the two ways salvation previously developed in Luke. The most critical aspect that identifies one on this kingdom way is one's identification with Jesus as the King.

---

122. The quote comes from Isaiah 49:6 rather than similar 42:6, because Τέθεικά is used.

123. Kilgallen, "Acts 13,38–39: Culmination of Paul's Speech in Psidia." *Bib* 69(1988): 480–506.

Paul's trials provide him with the opportunity to give his testimony to his being confronted on the Damascus road by Christ (Acts 9:1–22; 22:3–21; 26:2–23).[124] Christ confronted Paul on the Damascus road, providing Paul authoritative warrant within his Pharisaic epistemology for a radically altered worldview, existentially extending Paul's total commitment to Christ and the Trinity (Acts 9:1–22; 22:3–21; 26:2–23; Rom 6:6; Gal 2:20).[125] Christ asked Saul why he was persecuting Christ. The voice and bright light were empirically verifiable to those who traveled with Saul but they did not understand the message. This empirical Christophany provided Paul and Luke with the authority for Paul's ministry and gospel.

Conclusion

The call of Christ to the disciples provides the expectation for an oral phase of gospel testimony similar to the rabbinic oral tradition. A shift to a written phase of testimony of the empirical experience with Christ, Peter and Paul occurred as original disciples begin to die and as authoritative legal witnesses, like Cicero, begin to produce substantial written documents outside of a courtroom. Luke wrote accurate history, within the established Greco-Roman patterns, which present salvation history and a repeated gospel message grounded in O.T. prophecy, direct communication from God's representative, confirming miracle, authoritative testimony, and empirical evidence. Luke utilized established rhetoric for Greco-Roman historians while the speakers utilize appropriate rhetoric to engage their audience. Such speeches and the narrative of Luke-Acts consistently present virtues to imitate, such that the readers should follow the disciples in imitating Christ.

---

124. Ricoeur, "The Hermeneutics of Testimony" cited by Ford, "Paul Ricoeur: A Biblical Philosopher on Jesus," In *Jesus and Philosophy*. ed. Moser, 190.

125. Exod 3; Isa 6; *Jub.* 1.27–29; 10.10–14; *1 En.* 4.19, 21–26; 7; 8; 17–36; 89.61–77; 90.14–20; *T. Levi* 9.6; *T. Reub.* 5.3; *T. Jos.* 6.6; Such communication provided by God's representative is authoritative within a Pharisaic worldview and could be identified within Moser's attunement to filial knowledge of God and thus provides authoritative evidence for the message communicated (*The Elusive God*, 46–7, 98, 113–123); Kim, *The Origin of Paul's Gospel*; Gooch calls Jesus resurrection as foundational for Paul ("Paul, the Mind of Christ, and Philosophy," In *Jesus and Philosophy*. ed. Moser, 86); Kierkegaard, *Fear and Trembling*, 40–41 discussion on "infinite resignation" as total commitment; which means when Paul defends himself he makes a rhetorical appeal that the alternatives would have been more harmful (Acts 24:14–21; 26:19–23; Pseudo-Cicero, *Rhet. Ad Her.* 1.14.24; 1.15.25).

4

Petrine Epistemology of Testimony, Prophecy as Proclamation and Evidentialism

THESIS: PETER USES A divinely given faith and knowledge to epistemically inform and confirm a Pharisaic supernatural realism grounded in his eyewitness experience with Christ. Such an epistemic commitment fosters the believer in a growing total commitment evident through virtues which foster doing good deeds. Such a virtue epistemology and revelational eyewitness testimony further pragmatically confirm that the believer will be saved in kingdom.

Peter is one of the most significant speakers of the first century Christian Church.[1] Canonically, apart from Acts, Peter has two small epistles where in mid-century he wrote from Rome to the northern two thirds of Turkey concerning salvation and to encourage the churches in their suffering (1 Pet 1:1; 2 Pet 1:1).[2] Perhaps Silvanus carried the letter since the use of the διὰ in 1 Peter 5:12 indicated a letter carrier rather than amanuensis.[3] 2 Peter is

1. Peter is principal speaker in first half of Acts; 1 and 2 Pet; *Gos. Pet.*; *Acts Pet.*; *Acts of Pet. and Twelve Apos.*; *Pseudo-Clem.*; *Apoc. Pet.*; *Coptic Apoc. Pet.*; Lapham, *Peter*.

2. First and Second Peter are cited by *1 Clement* around 96 A.D. (*1 Clem.* 1.1–2; 4.8; 5.4; 7.1–6; 9.4; 16.3–4, 17; 31.2; 22.1–7; 23.3; 30.2; 36.2; 37.3; 38.1; 49.5; 57.1; 59.2; 61.1–3; 64; 65; *2 Clem.* 11.2; 16.3; also *Barn.* 1.5; 4.12, 19; 5.1, 6; 6.2; 7.2; 14.6; 16.8–10; *Herm. Vis.* 3.5, 11; 4.2.4–5; 4.3.4; *Herm. Sim.* 9.16.5, 28; *Did.*; Pol., *Phil.*; *Mart. Poly.*; Justin Martyr, *1 Apol.*; *Dial.*; Melito, *Peri Pascha*). Other patristics cite Peter by name (Irenaeus, *Haer.* 4.9.2; 4.16.5; 4.34.2; 5.7.2; Eusebius, *Hist. eccl.* 2.3.2; 3.3.4; 3.4.2; 3.25.2; 3.39.17 [Papias]; 6.25.8; 13.13.84 [Origen]; Tertullian, *Scorp.* 12; *Mart.* 4.13; *Or.* 15). Pliny (*Ep.* 10.96) identifies an apostasy in Pontus around 92 A.D that Peter does not mention, so Peter writes before this. Rome began to be called "Babylon" around the Jewish war (66–73 A.D.; 1 Pet 5:13; 2 *Bar.* 11.1; 67.7; *Sib. Or.* 5.143, 159; 4 *Ezra* 3.1, 28, 31). Elliott, *1 Peter*, 134–48.

3. Berkowitz, Squiter, Johnson, *Thesaurus Linguae Graecae Canon of Greek Authors and Works*; Richards, "Silvanus Was Not Peter's Secretary," *JETS* 43(2000): 417–32;

presented as Peter's farewell letter shortly before he is crucified (2 Pet 1:1, 12–14).[4]

Peter uses a multitude of words to communicate the idea of knowing (γινῶσις, words intensified by ἐπι-, and οἶδά). All these words include the field of *know, understand, perceive, acknowledge and recognize*.[5]

Peter uses οἶδά more broadly than any other word for knowledge. It is used for the recall of facts and events like the ministry and signs of Jesus (Acts 2:22; 3:17; 10:37). This approach is an externalism of a practical realistic non-foundational empiricism similar to Thomas Reid's common sense realism.[6] When miracles are involved, such knowledge evidences authority in the context as Lockean supernatural evidence of kingdom (Acts 10:44–47; 11:15; 15:8 with 2:4, 17–21; and 3:11 and 4:8–10 with 3:7–9).[7] Within this framework, believers can provide testimony that they know they were not redeemed with perishable things (1 Pet 1:18).[8] *Such knowledge extends beyond the cognitive to that of filial knowledge of God and the life change wherein God transforms the believer's experience.*[9] Peter reminds and commands believers to fully know what they already have (2 Pet 1:1–6, 12). Such knowledge is both a blessing that they have already begun to experience and an obligation which they can continue to grow within for the rest of the believer's life.

Peter used the word γινωσκω to indicate knowledge that extends beyond facts to include an assertion of faith. Initiating this knowledge, Peter's statement of the gospel message calls a person to align with Jesus

---

Peter Davids, *A Theology of James, Peter, and Jude*, 108.

4. Similar written farewell statements include: Acts 20:17–34; 2 Tim; *T. Mos.*; *T. 12 Patr.*; *T. Job*; 1 *En.* 91–104; Tob 14.3–11; 4 *Ezra* 14.28–36; 2 *Apoc. Bar.* 57–86; *Jub.* 21–22; 35; 36.1–18; *Bib. Ant.* 19.1–5; 24.1–5; 28.3–10; 33; *Adam and Eve* 25–29; Josephus, *Ant.* 4.309–19; *Acts Pet.* 36–39; *Acts John* 106–7; *Acts Thom.* 159–60; Bauckham, *Jude, 2 Peter*, 131–5.

5. *BAG*, 159–62, 290–1, 558–59.

6. Reid, *Thomas Reid*; Abraham, "The Epistemology of Jesus," In *Jesus and Philosophy.* ed. Moser, 158–9; Brueggemann, *A Pathway of Interpretation*, 115.

7. Locke, *Concerning Human Understanding* 1.1.15; 2.11.8–9; 2.32.6; 3.3.6–8; "A Discourse of Miracles," In *Works*, 9:256–65; "The Reasonableness of Christianity," In *Works*, Vol. 6; pre-modern empiricism is apparent in Lactanius, *Workmanship of God* 9–10; Keener, *Miracles*, 1:35–208; "Miracle Reports and the Argument from Analogy," *BBR* 25:4(2015): 475–95.

8. Ricoeur, "The Hermeneutics of Testimony" cited in David Ford, "Paul Ricoeur," In *Jesus and Philosophy.* ed. Moser, 190.

9. Moser, *The Elusive God*, 46–7, 98, 113–123; Locke, *Concerning Human Understanding* 1.1.15; 2.11.8–9; 2.32.6; 3.3.6–8; "A Discourse of Miracles," In *Works*, 9:256–65; "The Reasonableness of Christianity," In *Works*, Vol. 6; Keener, *Miracles*, 1:35–208; "Miracle Reports and the Argument from Analogy," *BBR* 25:4(2015): 475–95.

as Lord and Christ (Acts 2:36). Through a *pesher* rabbinic approach, Acts 2 develops that Jesus is the Davidic King promised (Acts 2:30 quoting 2 Sam 7:12-13) announced as the anointed One to be King by God (Acts 2:36), and functioning in this exalted Messianic role as illustrated by Christ receiving and giving the Holy Spirit (Acts 2:33).[10] While in this context "Lord" (κύριος) stands for Davidic King and Deity, as a term it was also appropriated by the Caesars (Augustus, Tiberius, Caligula, Nero and Domitian) and the Jewish rulers (Herod the Great, Agrippa I and Agrippa II).[11] Contrary to these others, Acts 2 demonstrates Jesus is the Lord (Davidic King and God). The concept of "Lord" in Acts 2:36 reference is elevated by the quote from Psalm 110:1 in Acts 2:34 which replace the אדֹנָי /*Adonai* as Lord (κύριος) in referring to Christ. However, since in Acts 2:34 κύριος also translates יְהוָה /*Yahweh* in Psalm 110:1, this repetition of κύριος draws Jesus' divinity within a Jewish monotheism as an essential part of the gospel as well. Such knowledge of God and Christ express allegiance to Them (2 Pet 2:20; 3:18). The one who has the knowledge identifies himself within the bounds of present salvation benefits.

Much of this knowledge is revealed knowledge through prophecy and promises, expressed by Peter in a *pesher* application to the new context's agenda.[12] God made known to the psalmist the revelational ways of life (Acts 2:28). Prophets (sensitive to the inspiration of the Holy Spirit and themselves investigating thoroughly) sought to know this Christ and the events which they were predicting (1 Pet 1:11).[13] Peter's quoting these statements of

---

10. Lim, *Pesharim*, 44-53; Bock, *Proclamation from Prophecy and Pattern*; Josephus, *Ant.* 13. 171-3, 297; 18.12-15; *J. W.* 2.119, 162-3; 4 Macc 5:16-27; Philo, *Dreams* 1.124-5; *m. Yad.* 4.6-8; *B. Qidd.* 66a; Resurrection: 2 Macc 7.9-14, 22-23; 14.43-46; *1 En.* 22; 58.3; 62.14-16; 91.10; 92.2; 104; 108.11-14; *Jub.* 5.10; 10.17; 22.22; L.A.B.; CD 3.11-16, 20-21; 7.5, 9; 13.11; 20.17-20, 25-27; 1QH 11.19-23 [3.18-22]; 19.10-14 [11.7-11]; 1QS 3.7-12; 4.7; 4Q228 frag. 1 1.9; 4Q266, frag. 11; 4Q385 2; 4Q386 1-2; 4QMMT C; 4Q521 2.2.12; 5.2.5-6; 2 *Bar*.[Syriac] 30.1-5; 49-51; 4 Macc 7.19; 16.25; 4 Ezra 7.26-44; *Sib. Or.* 4.180; *T. Benj.* 10.6-8; *T. Levi* 18; *T. Jud.* 24.

11. Bietenhard, "Lord, Master," In *DNTT*, 2:511; Cullmann, *The Christology of the New Testament*, 197-99; Suetonius, *De Vita Caesarum* 13.2; the title was also used to describe gods (e.g., 1 Cor. 8:5); Deismann, *Light from the Ancient East*, 352-3.

12. Schutter, "1 Peter 4.17, Ezekiel 9.6, and Apocalyptic Hermeneutics," In *SBL Seminar Papers*. SBLSP 26, 276-84; *Hermeneutical Composition in First Peter*, 100-10, 122; Ps 2 is utilized by Peter in Acts 4 similar to *Ps. Sol.* 17.21-46; Marcus, *The Way of the Lord*, 59-61 and in 120-22 Marcus develops *pesher* of Ps 118:22 in 1 Pet 2:7 similar to 1QS 8.4; 1QH 6.25-29; 7.8-9.

13. These patristics also support the same epistemic concern of the prophets for their era of concern (Ignatius, *Magn.* 8.2; *Barn.* 5.6; *Herm. Sim.* 9.12.1-2; *2 Clem.* 17.4; Justin Martyr, *1 Apol.* 31-53; 62.4; *Dial.* 56-7; Irenaeus, *Haer.* 4.20.4).

revelation fit them into his agenda for knowing Christ.[14] However, there are limited options to properly interpret the meaning of such statements since the revelation process expresses itself in performative statements of promise (2 Pet 1:20).[15] Peter urges his readership to know God through the promises that God has made available (2 Pet 1:2, 4). In such situations, any interpreter, such as Peter must embrace the performative meaning that the Spirit revealed if they wish to understand God's revelational communication. Unfortunately, false teachers, untaught, and unstable twist such knowledge of these statements to their own destruction by interpreting them in ways that do not fit the textually clear performative meaning (2 Pet 3:16–17).

Peter even claimed to be more sure of the coming reality of the kingdom than the prophecies provide because he experienced a moment of the kingdom through the experience of Jesus' transfiguration (2 Pet 1:16–19). This experience serves as *a Peircean pragmatic verification of the future coming reality of the kingdom* (2 Pet 1:19).[16] Such an approach couples with a Pharisaic authoritative voice (*bath qol*) as well (2 Pet 1:17).[17] These epistemic verifications reassure Peter that he was not simply following myth (μύθοις) as Bultmann claimed.[18] Rather Peter claims to be giving eyewitness testimony: seeing and hearing the evidence directly (2 Pet 1:16, 18).[19] Similar eyewitness claims provided greater credibility in Greco-Roman writings.[20] Not just in Peter's writing but also in Peter's statement of the gospel orally communicated eyewitness claims strongly testify to historical events (Acts 2:14–39; 3:12–26; 4:8–12; 10:34–43).

---

14. Bock, *Proclamation from Prophecy and Pattern*; Elliott, *1 Peter*, 407.

15. Austin, *How to Do Things with Words*.

16. Alston, *Perceiving God*, 14–35; Peirce, *Collected Papers*. Hartshorne and Weiss, vol. 5 paragraph 9; "The Fixation of Belief," *Popular Science Monthly* 12(Nov., 1877): 1–15; "How to Make Our Ideas Clear," *Popular Science Monthly* 12(Jan., 1878): 286–302.

17. B. 'Abot 6.2; B. Bat. 73b, 85b; Mak. 23b; 'Erub. 54b; Shab. 33b; 88a; Soṭa 33a; p. Soṭa 7.5, sect. 5; Pesiq. Rab Kah. 15.5; Lev. Rab. 19.5–6; Deut. Rab. 11.10; Lam. Rab. Proem 2, 23; Lam. Rab. 1.16 sect. 50; Ruth Rab. 6.4; Qoh. Rab. 7.12, sect. 1; Pesq. Rab Kah. 11.16.

18. Bultmann, *Jesus Christ and Mythology*, 18, 36, 39; Bultmann, Bartsch, Fuller, *Kerygma and Myth*; Miegge, *Gospel and Myth*, 8, 91.

19. Papias recounted in Eusebius, *Hist. eccl.* 5.20.4–7; Irenaeus, *Letter to Florinus*; Bauckham, *Jesus and the Eyewitnesses*, 295; Elliott, *1 Peter*, 309–10.

20. Seneca, *Controversiae*, preface 3–4; Clement of Alexandria, *Strom.* 7.106.4; Eusebius, *Hist. eccl.* 2.1.4; Halbwachs, *Les cadres sociaux de la mémoire*; Kelber, "The Case of the Gospels: Memory's Desire and the Limits of Historical Criticism," *Oral Tradition* 17(2002): 65; Dunn, *Jesus Remembered*, 239–243; Ricoeur, *Memory, History, Forgetting*; Bauckham, *Jesus and the Eyewitnesses*, 295–296, 310–57.

One repeated Lockean evidential support for Jesus as Lord is that Peter and others saw that God raised Jesus from the dead (Acts 2:31–32; 3:15; 10:41–42; 1 Pet 1:3–4, 3:18).[21] In such miraculous accounts an epistemic dualism is implied by having communal and eyewitness experience confirm Peter's perception. Furthermore, Peter's testimony helps to support[22] that Jesus is the Lord that his audience will need to respond to when Christ comes in His kingdom.

With the emphasis of *the one who knows being identified as the one who has faith within salvation* (2 Pet 1:1–3, 5–6), Peter develops that *the one without knowledge is the one who does not have faith and salvation*. The person who has not initially come to salvifically experience Christ is one who is ignorant (1 Pet 1:14, ἀγνοίᾳ). For example, the killing of Christ by the Jewish leaders was a sin of ignorance (Acts 3:17). Further, the governmental leaders who persecuted believers demonstrate that they were ignorant foolish men (1 Pet 2:15). They are culpable in their ignorance and destined for condemnation by God.

However, there is another form of ignorant life which has come to know (ἐπεγνωκέναι) the way of righteousness and after experiencing (ἐπιγνοῦσιν) this way with Christ, he it rejects it and departs to apostasy (2 Pet 2:21). This rejection of knowledge has plunged these apostates into a situation where they act without knowledge (2 Pet 2:12, ἀγνοοῦσιν). These ignorant apostates stand justly condemned by God in their rejection of Him. This spotlights the deadly ramifications of denying Christ that Peter had briefly experienced (2 Pet 2:2; Matt 26:69–75). That is, when Peter claimed to not know Jesus, he was actually apostatizing and departing from the sphere of knowledge which surround salvation (Matt 26:70, 72, 74; Mark 14: 68, 71; Luke 22:34, 57, 60). However, Peter returned to openly proclaim Christ. Those who do not return continue in their denial and ignorance. God causes these deniers of Christ to be forgetful concerning these things (2 Pet 1:9, λήθην λαβών where λαβών means received from another in Peter's use 1 Pet 4:10; 2 Pet 1:17; Acts 1:20, 25; 2:33, 38; 10:43, 47). These deficient ones receive forgetfulness from God which renders them doubly blind (2 Pet 1:9). Such individuals are bound to remain in their divinely imposed ignorance. God then condemns them in their ignorance (2 Pet 2:1, 4–9).

---

21. Locke, *Concerning Human Understanding* 1.1.15; 2.11.8–9; 2.32.6; 3.3.6–8; "A Discourse of Miracles," In *Works*, 9:256–65; "The Reasonableness of Christianity," In *Works*, Vol. 6; cf. Keener, *Miracles*, 1:35–208; "Miracle Reports and the Argument from Analogy," *BBR* 25:4(2015): 475–95.

22. Ricoeur, "The Hermeneutics of Testimony" cited in Ford, "Paul Ricoeur," In *Jesus and Philosophy*. ed. Moser, 190.

Peter and his readers know that their redemption by Christ was through Jesus' valued life to bring about a life transformation from a life of futility to that of a meaningful life of resurrection hope (1 Pet 1:3–4, 18). As such Christ's atonement grounds a kingdom virtue ethic that surrounds the process of knowing.[23] This virtue ethic incorporates faith given (λαχοῦσιν) by God and Christ (2 Pet 1:1)[24] which supplies a *divinely fostered basic belief of filial loyalty to God and Christ*.[25] This epistemic faith is supplemented with knowledge grounded by God's promises (2 Pet 1:2–4). Together these virtues join other kingdom virtues, such as diligence, moral excellence, self-control, perseverance, godliness, brotherly kindness, and love choosing to benefit others (2 Pet 1:5–7). So *if a believer wishes to pragmatically reassure herself that God has elected her unto kingdom then she needs to cultivate these virtues in Christ* (2 Pet 1:10–11).[26] Such an individual with a passionate commitment in a virtue epistemology and narrow way salvation is reassured that it will never stumble but will be abundantly supplied in kingdom.

Cultivating these virtues in the midst of the crucible of suffering and difficulty provides common sense evidence of God's authentic election of these believers as possessing authentic faith within the true knowledge of Christ (1 Pet 1:7; 2 Pet 1:8, 10).[27] It is as though gold is being refined in a crucible over a hot fire, and the refiner scrapes the dross away leaving a purer "tested faith" coming through the heat of suffering and persecution. Such a refining process fosters an ever greater total commitment and love for Christ (1 Pet 1:7–8).[28] Such a matrix and growth of these virtues demonstrates that the believer will be eschatologically saved into kingdom (1 Pet

---

23. Other virtue lists with faith, knowledge and virtue: Gal 5:22; Phil 4:8; 1 Cor 8:7; 2 Cor 6:6; 8:7; 1 Tim 4:12; 6:11; 2 Tim 2:22; 3:10; Titus 2:2; Rev 2:19; *1 Clem.* 1.2; 62.2; 64.1; *2 Clem.* 10.1; *Herm. Vis.* 3.8.7; *Herm. Mand.* 1.2; 6.1.1; 6.2.3; 8.9; 12.3.1; *Herm. Sim.* 6.1.4; 6.2.3; 8.10.3; 9.15.2; *Act. Ver.* 2; *Barn.* 2.2–3; *Acts John* 29; *Acts Paul and Thecla* 17; Wood, *Epistemology*; Roberts and Wood, *Intellectual Virtues*.

24. After the pattern Peter uses in Acts 1:17; *BAG*, 463.

25. Plantinga, *Knowledge and Christian Belief*, 57–79; Moser, *The Elusive God*, 46–7, 98, 113–123.

26. Peirce, *Collected Papers*. Hartshorne and Weiss, vol. 5 paragraph 9; "The Fixation of Belief," *Popular Science Monthly* 12(Nov., 1877): 1–15; "How to Make Our Ideas Clear," *Popular Science Monthly* 12(Jan., 1878): 286–302.

27. Wis 3.4–6; Sir 2.1–9; Seneca, *Prov.* 5.10; Elliott, *1 Peter*, 340–1; Reid, *Thomas Reid*. ed. Brookes; Abraham, "The Epistemology of Jesus," In *Jesus and Philosophy*. ed. Moser, 158–9; Brueggeman, *A Pathway of Interpretation*, 115.

28. Kierkegaard, *Fear and Trembling*, 40–41; Adams, "The Problem of Total Devotion," In *Rationality, Religious Belief, and Moral Commitment*. ed. Audi and Wainwright, 94; Nygren, *Agape and Eros*, 216; Wainwright, "Obedience and Responsibility," In *The Wisdom of the Christian Faith*. ed. Moser and McFall, 68.

1:7; 2 Pet 1:11).[29] Likewise, vices demonstrate that the rebellious denier is damned (2 Pet 1:9; 2:1–17).[30]

Consistency of life reflecting a commitment to Christ as Lord provides the best apologetic to others of the authentic knowledge and faith in Christ (1 Pet 3:15–16). *Maintaining a consistent good conscience of life is the best positioning for one's life to convince others that one's faith and knowledge of Christ is authentic.* Though the conscience is a person's fallible personal assessment of herself, in a new covenant relationship the conscience can be good affirming the believer in proper helpful choices and acts. This good conscience is maintained by doing practical good deeds (1 Pet 2:12, 15, 18, 21–22; 3:1, 4, 13, 16). With some others wooed and won by good deeds (1 Pet 2:12, 15; 3:1), an apologetic door is open to explain the Christian hope with gentleness and reverence (1 Pet 3:15).

Peter used a divinely given faith and knowledge epistemically to inform and confirm a Pharisaic supernatural realism grounded in his eyewitness experience with Christ. Such an epistemic commitment fosters the believer in a growing total commitment evident through virtues which foster good deeds. Such a virtue epistemology and revelational eyewitness testimony further pragmatically confirm the believer will be saved in kingdom.

---

29. Virtues identify authentic belonging: Wood, *Epistemology*; Roberts and Wood, *Intellectual Virtues*; Westphal, "Taking St. Paul Seriously," In *Christian Philosophy*. ed. Flint, 201), similar to Judaism (Deut 6:4–9; Wis 12–15; 1QS 3–4) and Stoicism (Seneca, *Ep.* 20.1).

30. Virtue lists provide vice lists as contrast heading to the opposite outcome, similar to Judaism (Deut 6:4–9; Wis 12–15; 1QS 3–4) and Stoicism (Seneca, *Ep.* 20.1).

5

Epistemology and Logic of the Apostle Paul

THESIS: PAUL'S RABBINICAL JEWISH and diaspora education crafted an epistemology and logic that permits the Damascus road encounter with Christ to present a basic belief of Trinitarian election concerning Jews and Gentiles within mystically empowered Christianity, funded through filial epistemology, directed by 1) mystical perception in an existential total commitment to the Trinitarian God, and 2) the LXX *torah* through Hillel rabbinic analogical patterns of logic, with 3) sensitivity to rhetorically engage contemporary philosophies of his day. Paul's basic belief is also warranted through non-foundational empiricism including Lockean senses and an Edwardsian sixth sense, Spirit produced virtue epistemology, imitating example, testimony, rabbinic logic, analogy, performative speech, and abductive pragmatic inference.

Paul was born and raised in Tarsus, capital of Cilicia (Acts 9:11, 30; 11:25; 21:39; 22:3). Strabo writes that a well-rounded philosophical education was available in Tarsus, "The people at Tarsus have devoted themselves so eagerly, not only to philosophy, but also the whole round of education in general, that they have surpassed Athens, Alexandria, or any other place that can be named where there have been schools and lectures of philosophers."[1] In such a context, Paul would have been exposed to Epicurean, Stoic, and other philosophies, for he utilizes understanding of them later (Acts 17:18). Epicurus of Samos emphasized sensation to build up a mental reserve of pleasure from past conversations with friends so that a person can rise through present distress and be encouraged as the circle of life comes to an end.[2] Whereas, Zeno of Citium, founding Stocism, emphasized a de-

---

1. Strabo, Geogr. 14.5.13. Athens also was excellent in philosophical training (Cicero, *Off.* 1.1.1; *Tusc.* 2.11.26).

2. Epicurus, frag 374; *Letter to Herodotus*, 37, 50; Hicks, *Epicurus Principle Doctrines*,

terministic temporal circle of fire empowering the continuum of matter to fund an impassioned ethic upon natural law, the acceptance of one's fate, and self-sufficiency.³ At the Agora in Athens, Paul begins by introducing the gospel in a manner which predisposes his audience to good will (Acts 17:23).⁴ Paul shows himself to be well versed in these rival philosophies, even quoting the Stoic poet Aratus of Soli (Acts 17:28) and the Epicurean doctrine that God needs nothing from humans (Acts 17:25).⁵ Paul called attention to their common ground including monuments to an unknown god which were set up following Epimenides' counsel in averting plague. Paul expanded upon this God concept (using terminology τὸν θεόν for "God" to which stoicism can relate), where God stretches beyond both philosophies as creator and sustainer of all (Acts 17:23-28).⁶ Paul treats the concept of God to entail part of the design plan recognized from empirical knowledge of the creation, so humans are culpable if they do not honor Him as God, and that this very condition of dark futile thinking by those who deny God is in fact part of the present experience of the wrath of God upon then (Rom 1:19-21, 24, 26).⁷ Paul's Jewish-Christian concept of God is personal and

---

23 accessed April 16, 2014, http://Classics.mit.edu/Epicurus/princdoc.html; Diogenes Laertius, *Lives of Eminent Philosophers*, 10.33.

3. Diogenes Laertius, *Vit.* 7.87-89; Marcus Aurelius Antoninus, *Med.* 3.11; 4.4, 40; 7.55; 11.1; Chrysippus in Cicero, *De Natura Deorum*, 1; Graver, *Stoicism and Emotion*; Allen, *Philosophy for Understanding Theology*, 66-69; Kennard, *A Critical Realist's*, 10-11; "πῦρ," In *TDNT* 6:928-45.

4. A rhetorical introduction interposes a topic (Aristotle, *Rhet.* 3.14.6) and predisposes toward good will (Pseudo-Cicero, *Rhet. Ad Her.* 1.3.6; 1.11.18; Aristotle, *Rhet.* 3.14.6-7; 3.17.1), which Paul accomplishes in his introductions in Acts 17:23; 23:1; 24:10-11; 26:2-3. This author's approach to Paul's rhetoric is appreciative of the common sense early Jewish approach that Tobin proposed in *Paul's Rhetoric in its Contexts*.

5. Aratus of Soli, *Phaenomena* 7; Euripides, *Heracles* 1345-6; Plato, *Euthyphr.* 14c; Kennard, *Messiah Jesus*, 460; Hemer, "The Speeches in Acts II," *TynB* 40(1989): 243-4; Bruce, *Acts*, 357.

6. Diogenes Laertius, *Lives of Eminent Philosophers*, 1.110; Epictetus 2.20.22; Neyrey, "Acts 17, Epicureans, and Theodicy," In *Greeks, Romans, and Christians*. ed. Malherbe, et al., 118-34; altars to unknown god: Pausanins, *Description of Greece*, 1.1 and 4; Philosttus, *Appolanius of Tyana*.

7. Most early Judaisms do not maintain natural knowledge of God, so this is a novel Pauline idea in his context (Bietenhard. "Natürliche Goetteserkenntnis der Heiden?," *ThZ* 12(1956): 275-88; Jewett, *Romans*, 154; design plan fits Plantinga, *Warrant and Proper Function*, 6-17; Scott, *Paul's Way of Knowing*, 15-23, especially 18, unfortunately Scott universalizes moral lack of knowing God as a noetic effect of the present human condition, rather than treating it as one of several culpable conditions (such as violating conscience and violating Law in Rom 2-3; Jewett, *Romans*, 148-267; Fitzmyer, *Romans*, 283; Mayordomo, *Argumentiert Paulus logisch?*, 181, 228). Paul reflects Wis 13.1 and 14.11 in recognizing that a person who is ignorant of God is a fool (Rom 1:21-22). In such a condition idolatry fosters immorality both of which God condemns (Rom

cares about humans as His offspring rather than being an unmoved impersonal idol (Acts 17:28–29).[8] Next Paul wooed the cyclical worldviews of Epicureanism and Stoicism toward his testimony[9] for a Judeo-Christian linear history consisting of creation unto kingdom (Acts 17:26, 31). Jesus Christ is the climactic judge to Whom his audience must submit. The evidence for Jesus being the climactic judge of all humans was that Jesus was divinely raised from the dead, which concept of resurrection was foreign or repulsive to many Greek philosophical schools (Acts 17:31–32).[10] Paul later warned his converts not to be taken in by such Greek rejection, deception, or foolishness (1 Cor 1:23; Col 2:8). However, Paul tries to end his appeal with a summary that predisposes his audience favorably (Acts 17:31).[11] In response to this presentation of gospel in Athens, Dionysius, Damaris and others compellingly believed in Christ (Acts 17:34).[12]

Dom Jacques Dupont follows Bultmann in arguing that Paul polemics Jewish means of knowing in order to present a Hellenistic mystery religious epistemology that best positions itself as engaging and providing an

---

1:23–32; Wis 14.12–14, 22–31). A stoic appeal for harmony among rivals based on creation similar to Paul's (Acts 17:26) was also made by Dio Chrysostom (*Or.* 40.35–39), including setting of seasons and boundaries (*Or.* 12.27–30; frag. 368 Th.; Balch, "The Areopagus Speech," In *Greeks, Romans, and Christians.* ed. Balch, Ferguson, Meeks, 56–57).

8. Statement that humans are gods' offspring made by: 1) Epimenides of Crete (Clement of Alex, *Strom.* 1.14.59; 2) Aratus, *Phenomena* 5; 3) Cleanthes, *Hymn to Zeus* 4) after Paul by Dio Chrysostom, *Or.* 12.27, 29, 39, 43, 47, 61, 75, 77. This statement is consistent with Judaism (Wis 11:15–16; 13:121–2, 10–19; 14:8–11, 27) and Christianity (Rom 1:18–25). Thus God is not far from humans (Acts 17:27; Dio Chrysostom, *Or.* 12.28). Such philosophical statements polemic an Epicurean view of gods as having human shape (Lucretius, *De Rerum Natura* 2.16583; 1090–1104; 5.146–234; Plutarch, *Stoic Rep.* 1034B; Cicero, *Nat. D.* 1.15.71; 1.27.75–77). Some stoics also polemicized the futility of idols as empty such as Paul does (Acts 17:29; Plutarch, *Superst.* 167DE; Strabo, *Geog.* 16.2.35–39; frag. 133 Th.; Dio Chrysostom, *Or.* 12.80–81; Lucian, *Iup. Trag.* 7–12; *Gall.* 24; Balch, "The Areopagus Speech," In *Greeks, Romans, and Christians.* ed. Balch, Ferguson, Meeks, 69, 74, 78).

9. Ricoeur, "The Hermeneutics of Testimony" cited in Ford, "Paul Ricoeur," In *Jesus and Philosophy.* ed. Moser, 190.

10. Hemer, "The Speeches in Acts II," *TynB* 40(1989): 244, 246; Aeschylus, *Oresteia and Eumides,* 647–8.

11. Paul also ends his defense hearings with a summary designed to fund good will (Acts 24:21; 26:19–29), which Aristotle suggests for conclusions (*Rhet.* 3.19.1).

12. Eusebius, *Hist. eccl.* 3.4.10; 4.23.3. Moser presents Jesus (Luke 18:8) and Paul (Acts 17) as recognizing that humans have a volitional role in knowing and being sincerely willing to participate in God's powerful life ("Introduction: Jesus and Philosophy," In *Jesus and Philosophy,* 6).

alternative to Gnosticism.[13] Dupont claimed that the same words used to express Christian epistemology emerge from an epistemology for mystery religions,[14] but no examined words or nuances require this perspective, though some are the same words. In fact, he repeatedly develops similarity to Jewish terminology and the use of the O.T. in Hebrew as well as Greek to inform Paul's claims.[15] Dupont attempts to develop his view from the assumption that Jesus transfiguration was best understood through a Hellenistic myth and thus Paul's claim for doxologous language should be understood as myth (such as praise, claims to have seen the risen Christ, his claim to experience the heavenly divine throne room, and eschatological language of Christ seated on a throne in heaven).[16] Paul explicitly rejected the mythological view as distracting from the truth that provokes love and faith (1 Tim 1:4; 4:7; 2 Tim 4:4; Titus 1:14). Dupont claims these experiences are grounded in Paul's illumination, but Dupont means that this is a revelation strategy by the Holy Spirit,[17] which will be developed in a few pages (1 Cor 2:6–16). However, factual claims like Paul and others empirically seeing the risen Christ (1 Cor 15:3–8) do not fit a Bultmannian hermeneutic that considers that such accounts were substantially constructed from Hellenistic mythology.[18] The fact that there are hundreds of living witnesses who could be asked by Paul's readers about Christ's resurrection confirms that this event was empirically viewed[19] rather than constructed myth. Paul joins Peter in specifically rejecting the use of mythology in theological speech and writing (1 Tim 1:4; 2 Pet 1:16 where Peter identifies that the transfiguration is not myth). Furthermore, Greco-Roman historical narrative did not permit the use of such mythology.[20] With both Christian and Greco-Roman canons rejecting a place for Hellenistic mythology, it is better to not position Paul within Hellenistic mythology.

13. Dupont, *Gnosis*, 11–12, 18, 23, 37, 57–58, 66, 149–80, 266–377.

14. Ibid, 37, 91–93, 180–81, 187–90.

15. Ibid, 77–79, 114–19, 214–16.

16. Ibid, 58–69.

17. Ibid, 44–46.

18. Bultmann, *Jesus Christ and Mythology*, 18, 36, 39; Bultmann, Bartsch, Fuller, *Kerygma and Myth*; Miegge, *Gospel and Myth*, 8, 91.

19. Locke, *Concerning Human Understanding* 1.1.15; 2.11.8–9; 2.32.6; 3.3.6–8; "A Discourse of Miracles" In *Works*, 9:256–65; "The Reasonableness of Christianity," In *Works*, vol. 6. Additionally, Locke pioneered a view that saw the resurrection of Christ supernaturally rose in a spiritual existence (Rom 1:4) to parallel Jesus earthly human flesh existence (Rom 1:3; *A Paraphrase and Notes on the Epistles of St. Paul*. ed. Wainwright, 487).

20. Dionysius, *Thucydides*, 45–47.

Moises Mayordomo argued that Paul utilized Aristotelian Hellenistic rhetorical criticism after surveying the inadequacies of F. C. Bauer's Hegelian logic and Barthian dialectical existentialism.[21] I have previously argued the inadequacies of Aristotelian, Hegelian, and dialectical logic and their misappropriation in biblical hermeneutics[22] but we agree that the latter two are foreign to Paul's thought. However, nowhere does Moises show Paul was schooled in Hellenistic rhetoric, it is merely an assumption,[23] as Moises applies Hellenistic logic into three of Paul's passages. One might ask, what is it to which Paul mostly appeals. If most of Paul's appeals are to the biblical text then Paul's rhetorical method is foreign to Hellenistic rhetoric and very common for the rabbinic education that Paul does identify himself as growing through, namely Hillel's rabbinic school in Jerusalem under Hillel's successor Gamaliel (Acts 22:3; 23:6-9; 26:5; Phil 3:5-6). In fact, Duane Litfin and Bruce Winter unpack 1 Corinthians 2:1-5 to explain that Paul claims that he resisted utilizing Aristotelian rhetoric when he was in Corinth.[24] Furthermore, Thomas Tobin's analysis of the logic of the book of Romans argues for a simpler common sense Jewish rhetoric rather than Aristotelian rhetoric because Paul's arguments were salted with authoritative biblical quotations to compel his conclusions.[25] So, I challenge the inadequacies of Aristotelian rhetoric in subsequent passages (especially in the notes). I will also show where such rhetoric might help in a secondary manner but it is not primary in discerning either Paul's epistemology, or his primary logic. The agenda of Paul's thought will not be given over to a framework which is substantially foreign to Paul's thought.

---

21. Mayordomo, *Argumentiert Paulus logisch?*, 38–79 by examining Galatians positions Paul in Aristotelian logic after surveying rejected alternatives 8–20; Tobin, *Paul's Rhetoric in its Contexts*, 229–31 by examining Romans rejects Paul's use of Aristotelian rhetoric for a common sense early Jewish rhetoric. Similarly, Bultmann's view that Paul utilized Stoic rhetoric (*Der Stil der paulischen Predigt*) should be rejected for a more common sense Jewish dialog rhetoric (Malherbe, "MH ΓΕΝΟΙΤΟ in the Diatribe and Paul," *HTR* 73[1980], 239; Stowers, *Diatribe and Paul's Letter to the Romans*, 76–78, 176–79; Longenecker, *Romans*, 244).

22. Kennard, *A Critical Realist's*, 18–122, 175–202, 214–20, 239–42; "Evangelical Views of Illumination of Scripture and Critique," *JETS* 49(Dec. 2006): 797–806.

23. Most consider that *The Correspondence Between Paul and Seneca* 9 claim that Seneca provided Paul with a book of rhetoric is not historically accurate but an attempt to elevate Paul in the Hellenistic context (Ehrman, *Lost Scriptures*, 160, 162).

24. Litfin, *St. Paul's Theology of Proclamation*; Winter agrees (*Philo and Paul among the Sophists*, 147–48) though Winter shows some similarities between 1 Cor 2:1–5 and Dio's apology in *Orations* 47 (Winter, *Philo and Paul*, 152). Philo regularly allegorizes in a Platonic direction and Paul does this rarely (Frag. A 654; *Post.* 48, 167; *Somn.* 123, 149; *Leg.* 3.61, 175; *QE* 2.2; *Opif.* 152; Tobin, *Paul's Rhetoric in Its Contexts*, 116, 170, 176, 179).

25. Tobin, *Paul's Rhetoric in Its Contexts*, 229–31.

Ian Scott and Mary Healy argue that the foremost feature of Paul's epistemology is that the Holy Spirit reveals the mind of God, clarifying what for many is a mystery (1 Cor 2:6–16).[26] So Paul depends upon revelation as contained in the Bible rather than Aristotelian rhetoric. Healy sees this as a downward divine act of revelation, a self-disclosure and a self-gift of the Son.[27] The revelational content is the eternal divine plan accomplished through the death and resurrection of Christ (1 Cor 2:1–2).[28] The *halakhah* citing Isaiah 64:4 further confirms from the context of kingdom that this revelational message is essentially salvific (1 Cor 2:9). This is the message that the Spirit searches through the mind of God and reveals to the Christian so that in the revealed condition this salvation message no longer remains a mystery (1 Cor 2:6–16).[29] The blatancy of Paul's focus on the death and resurrection of Christ challenges a normal unbelieving perspective and is considered foolish by them (1 Cor 1:22–23; 2:2).[30] Not that this message can't be considered by human criteria as Conzelmann claims, nor that it is "ontologically incompatible" with human knowledge as Gärtner claims,[31] for Mayorodomo and Tobin show otherwise in their different rhetorical analyses which show that the Spirit's revelatory content brings about a proper valuing of salvific content (including Christ's death and resurrection). Those to whom this message is revealed welcome Paul's bold claims that Christ is the wisdom and power of God (1 Cor 2:6–16). Those to whom the message is not revealed reject Christ's power and wisdom unto their own damnation (1 Cor 1:18, 25; 2:8).

However, Mary Healy developed that this Holy Spirit sourced knowledge is provided by an intuitional illumination to remove the veil, permitting comprehension.[32] This view of a hermeneutical illumination from the

26. Scott, *Paul's Way of Knowing*, 35; Healy, "Knowledge of the Mystery," In *The Bible and Epistemology*. ed. Healy and Parry, 135–37; Thiselton, *The First Epistle to the Corinthians*, 241–42.

27. Healy, "Knowledge of the Mystery," In *The Bible and Epistemology*. ed. Healy and Parry, 137.

28. Ibid.

29. Thiselton, *The First Epistle to the Corinthians*, 242, 245–50.

30. Thiselton, *The First Epistle to the Corinthians*, 158–59.

31. Conzelmann, *First Epistle to the Corinthians*, 55; Gärtner, "The Pauline and Johannine Idea of 'To Know God' against the Hellenistic Background," *NTS* 14(1968): 217–20; However, Scott (*Paul's Way of Knowing*, 27 and especially 50–68) seems haunted by a deeper irrationality than either of these but is present in Leisengang, *Der Apostel Paulus als Denker*, 9–10.

32. Healy, "Knowledge of the Mystery," In *The Bible and Epistemology*. ed. Healy and Parry, 149; also mentioned by Stegman, "'The Spirit of Wisdom and Understanding," In *The Bible and Epistemology*. ed. Healy and Parry, 95.

Holy Spirit began in 1685 following Lutheran pietism.[33] Evangelicalism has largely owned Spener, Quenstedt, and Hollanz's cognitive illumination view, with others in evangelicalism joining Franke's spirit transformational illumination view.[34] If such a view were supported by the biblical texts, it raises the possibility of an internalist authority on the level of a divine intuition. In this vein, Schleiermacher developed a psychological side of the hermeneutical process, echoing Spener's personal inspirational view, which Cardinal John Henry Newman cultivated into an "illative" (or confident intuitive) sense similar to Michael Polanyi's tacit intuitional way of knowing[35] to provide E. D. Hirsch's validity in interpretation through divine "authorial intent."[36] In conservative circles, this illumination view is often supported through textual appeals to John 14:26; 16:12–15; 1 Cor. 2:6–16; and 1 John 2:27. Elsewhere I argued that these texts do not teach such an illumination view.[37] The scholarly commentaries on these passages agree that these

33. Kennard, "Evangelical Views of Illumination of Scripture and Critique," *JETS* 49(Dec. 2006): 797–806; Spener, *Consilia Et Judicia Theologia*, 3:700; Stein, "Phillip Jakob Spener (1635–1705)" and Matthias, "August Hermann Franke (1663–1727)," In *The Pietist Theologians*. ed. Carter Lindberg, 88 and 105–6; Wallmann, *Philipp Jakob Spener und die Aufänge des Pietismus*, 92–96; Hirsch, *Geschichte der neuen Evangelische Theologie*, 2:114; Jung, *Das Ganze der Heiligen Schrift*, 100–1; Quenstedt, *Theologia Didactico-Polemica*. The relevant portion (chapters 1–3) of this is available in English as: *The Nature and Character of Theology*. ed. Poellot, ch. I "Of Theology in General": question I "Is Theology Given?" paragraph XI, p. 36; ph. XIV, p. 39; ph. XXXI-Observe (1), p. 54; ph. XXXV, p. 57; Section II "Polemic"-"Sources of Rebutals or Dialysis of Objections": q. I "Is Theology Given?," pp. 64–5; q. II "Is Revealed Theology Necessary in the Church?," pp. 71, 72–3; q. III "Is Theology a God-Given Practical Aptitude?," exposition III & IV, pp. 73–4; rebuttal I, p. 80; ch. III "Of the Sources of Theology," porism IV, pp. 199–200; Hollaz, *Examen Theologicum Acroamaticum*. Grenz, in *Beyond Foundationalism*, 99 claims that this illumination view originated earlier by at least the time of John Hus and cites Tavard in *Holy Writ or Holy Church*, 47–66 which discusses John Hus' view of the soteriological transformation in which the Holy Spirit enables the new believer to be responsive to application of the Word of God. From my reading of the Hus material, I agree with Tavard, contrary to Grenz; Hus does *not* teach this view of the illumination through the Holy Spirit aid to cognitively understand the Bible. I have not found the view any earlier than Spener's, Quenstedt's and Hollanz's pietistic Lutheran systematic theologies. Franke, *Praelectiones Hermeneuticae*, 57; Matthias, "August Hermann Franke (1663–1727)," In *The Pietist Theologians*. ed. Lindberg, 106–7.

34. The Chicago Statement on Biblical Hermeneutics as contained in *Hermeneutics, Inerrancy, and the Bible*. ed. Radmacher and Preus, 891.

35. Newman, *An Essay in Aid of A Grammar of Assent*; Polanyi, *The Tacit Dimension*.

36. Hirsch, *Validity in Interpretation*.

37. Kennard, *The Relationship Between Epistemology*, 139–42; *A Critical Realist*, 141–3, 224–31; "Evangelical Views on Illumination of Scripture and Critique," *JETS* 49:4(Dec. 2006): 797–806.

passages do not teach such an illumination view.[38] Therefore, the interpreter is left with the revelational textual trajectory which promises that the Holy Spirit will supernaturally reveal the gospel message.

Speech-acts as commands and promises are clearly indicated in the divinely accommodated biblical text itself without the need of an intuitive work of the Spirit to render the meaning of the text clear. Most speech-act theorists would agree that the meaning of the statement is apparent in the contextualized textual statement, rather than through an evangelical appeal to illumination behind the text.[39]

Additionally, the absence of such an illumination aid makes more sense of two hermeneutical conditions. The first is that rather repeatedly *godly commentators disagree* with features which other godly commentators may say are within the meaning of a text. If godly Christians were given this illumination aid, then it would unify Christian commentaries but we find that they repeatedly disagree. For example, Pauline hermeneutics is spread over a variety of perspectives including: William Whiston (Paul cites accurately but then Jews modified texts)[40], Roepe, Kautzsch, Vollmer and Harris (Paul uses Jewish text lists to prove legitimacy of Christian faith)[41], Dietrich-Alex Koch (witness to the Gospel)[42], Francis Watson (a common Jewish hermeneutic for Christian faith)[43], Richard Hays (story of Jesus, and ecclesiocentric hermeneutics fusing Jewish and Gentile Christians

---

38. For example, the following sample of commentators support my view: Dunn, *The Theology of Paul the Apostle*; Barrett *The First Epistle to the Corinthians*; Bruce, *1 and 2 Corinthians*; Fee, *The First Epistle to the Corinthians*; Grosheide, *First Epistle to the Corinthians*; Leon Morris, *The First Epistle of Paul to the Corinthians*; Orr and Walther, *1 Corinthians*; Robertson and Plummer, *First Epistle of St. Paul to the Corinthians*; Thiselton, *The First Epistle to the Corinthians*; Ciampa and Rosner, *The First Letter to the Corinthians*, 129.

39. Barr, *The Semantics of Biblical Language*.

40. Whiston, *An Essay Towards Restoring the True Text of the Old Testament*.

41. Roepe, *De Veteris Testamenti locrum in apostolorum libris allegation*; Kautzsch, *De Veteris Testamenti Locis Paulo Apostolo Allegatis*; Vollmer, *Die altestamentlichen Citate bei Paulus*, 23–35, 48; Harris, *Testimonies*, esp. 2:12–37; though Dodd unravels the view that there are Jewish short testimonial lists by arguing he uses longer texts in context (*According to the Scriptures*, 126). Koch, *Die Schrift als Zeuge des Evangeliums*, 254 concludes that Paul is using the scriptures proper, mostly from LXX. Lindars, *New Testament Apologetic*, 222, 242, 247 argues that in Rom 9–11 Pauline quotations are original with Paul. Tobin, *Paul's Rhetoric in its Contexts*, 173–5, 179, 229, 231, 259 presented that Paul utilized the quotes in a common sense early Jewish approach similar to 4 Macc 1.15–17 and 2.1–6. Kennard, *Biblical Covenantalism*, 3:144–48 argued that Paul utilized common early Jewish language in this argument.

42. Koch, *Die Schrift als Zeuge*, 216–224.

43. Watson, *Paul and the Hermeneutics of Faith*, 1–6, 516–17.

into a new covenant community)[44], Earle Ellis (hermeneutics of midrash *pesher*)[45], Daniel Boyarin (Paul as a Hellinistic allegorist)[46], Christopher Stanley (standard practice of contemporaneous Greco-Roman and Jewish literature)[47], Thomas Tobin (common sense early Jewish approach extended to Christianity)[48], and Matthew Bates (pre-patristic voice behind the voice).[49] The reason for this disagreement is not that some of these commentators are not listening to the illumination of the Spirit but rather each commentator has his own sensitivities to context, grammar, authorial thought forms and theological construct. Perhaps they are fusing the text to a construc-

---

44. Hays, *The Faith of Jesus Christ*, 132–41; *Echoes of Scripture in the Letters of Paul*, xiii, 122–49, esp. 137, 157, 160–61.

45. Ellis, *Paul's Use of the Old Testament*, 11, 14–15.

46. Boyarin, *A Radical Jew*, 10, 13–38 claimed but did not defend well that Paul follows Philo's pattern in order to present Paul teaching Platonic human duality (which Paul does not teach, Kennard, *A Critical Realist's*, 367–408); Bekken, *The Word is Near You*, 28–55. Philo allegorizes in a Platonic direction and Paul does not (*QE* 2.2; *Opif.* 152; *Frag. A* 654; *Post.* 48, 167; *Somn.* 123, 149; Tobin, *Paul's Rhetoric in Its Contexts*, 116, 170–1, 176, 179). Bekken, 56–59 undermines this connection of Paul with Philo by limiting his consideration to the Deuteronomist concerns which he acknowledges are common among early Judaism arguing that Bar 3:29–30 also is dependent upon LXX as is Paul and Philo. Tobin repeatedly identified that Paul was closer to non-Platonic early Judaism (Tobin, *Paul's Rhetoric in Its Contexts*, 173–5, 179, 229, 231, 259; 2 Bar 54.13–19; 4 Ezra 3.21–27; *Apoc. Mos.* 8.2; 14.2; 30.1; 4 Macc 1.15–17; 2.1–6). Early Jewish texts could be expanded substantially (Kennard, *Biblical Covenantism*, 2:90–128); *Jub.* 1.15–16, 20, 22–25; 5.11, 15; *Sir.* 11.26; 16.12, 14; 17.23; *1 En.* 95.5; 100.7; *Pss. Sol.* 2.7, 16, 25, 34–35; 17.8–9; *Jos. Asen.* 28.3; Philo, *Spec.* 4.164; *L.A.B.* 3.10; 44.10; 64.7; *2 Bar.* 54.21; 1QS 2.7–8, 11–14; 10.11, 17–18; 1QH 4.18–19, 31–32; 5.5–6; 14.24; 1QM 6.6; 11.3–4, 13–14; 18.14; CD 3.4–5; 5.15–16; 7.9; 19.6; 20.24; 1QpHab. 12.2–3; 4QpPs37 4.9; 4Q266 18.6 (=4Q270 11 I 19–20) exclude disobedient from people of God; Josephus, *Ant.* 10.138; *J. W.* 1.378; Gathercole, "Torah, Life, and Salvation: Leviticus 18:5 in Early Judaism and the New Testament," In *From Prophecy to Testament.* ed. Evans, 126–139.

47. Stanley, *Paul and the Language of Scripture*, 267–337, though 83–251 he makes a strong case for Paul largely following a version of LXX, so by putting these sections together, most early Jewish literature is shown to largely follow the LXX, especially from the dispersion.

48. Tobin, (*Paul's Rhetoric in Its Contexts*, 173–5, 179, 229, 231, 259) resists Philo for non-Platonic early Jewish method (of 2 Bar 54.13–19; 4 Ezra 3.21–27; *Apoc. Mos.* 8.2; 14.2; 30.1.); p. 229 Tobin concludes against Epicurean, Stoic, Middle Platonic and Aristotelian methods; p. 231 Tobin concludes that Paul's method is much closer to the simplicity of 4 Macc 1.15–17; 2.1–6 than the more sophisticated philosophical discussion of Philo, *Decal.* 142–53, 173–74 and *Spec.* 4.79–131.

49. Bates, *The Hermeneutics of the Apostolic Proclamation*, 2, 140–41, 183–328; perhaps following Justin Martyr, *Dial.* 7.2–3; 41.1–3; *1 Apol.* 36.1–2; 38.1–3; 44.8–10; 65–66; *Barn.* 12.1; Ignatius, *Smyr.* 1.1; Irenaeus, *Haer.* 2.6; *Epid.* 79, 92; Origen, *Comm. Rom.* 8.6.11; Cyprian, *Test.* 1.21; Ps-Gregory of Nyssa, *Test.* 2.4, 16; Hippolytus, *Noet.* 12; however, these patristics may not set a pattern but likely copy part of Paul's pattern instead.

tive model that allows the secondary authority of tradition to be primarily determinative over the primary authority of the biblical text. They allow an agenda to determine meaning rather than textual meaning challenging and modifying a growing and developing tradition. Here their sensitivity to these textual features identifies why their interpretations differ and there is broad agreement that Paul is a contextual interpreter.[50] The author's preference is a hybrid of Watson, Hays, Ellis, and Tobin.

Secondly, if such an illumination aid occurred for Christians then they would always be able to produce superior commentaries, *but sometimes non-Christians have produced the best commentaries on a book of the Bible.* For example, the best commentary on Leviticus 1–16 is by Jacob Milgrom,[51] who as a Jew is very sensitive to the textual and contextual features within that book. Milgrom accurately and passionately embraces his interpretation; he is not merely working on the level of intellectual assent. Thus, such illumination is an impotent aid or no aid at all if merely attention to text in context produces a superior product of understanding. Anything that God does not promise to give and is not effective in demonstrating its ability to provide superior interpretation, accuracy, and unity should not be depended upon as coming from God. Thus claims from illumination as authority are not properly warranted.

In Paul's day, rulers had rejected the gospel as demonstrated by their killing Christ (1 Cor 2:6–8). However, this simple gospel has extensive kingdom benefits prepared for those who love God (1 Cor 2:9). The Spirit of God knows the mind of God and revealed to Paul and the Corinthians this gospel message which the spirit of the world considers foolishness (1 Cor 2:10–12). Paul expresses this gospel in spiritual thoughts and words, rather than human wisdom (1 Cor 2:1–2, 13). The medium through which this gospel is conveyed is through Paul's testimony to salvation (1 Cor 2:1–5) and appeal to authoritative biblical revelation (1 Cor 2:9).[52] So the Spirit orchestrates the contextual means of gospel information and opens the believer to be receptive to what the gospel message says and implies. A natural (ψυχικὸς) man does not accept this gospel from the Spirit of God (1 Cor 1:23; 2:6–8, 14) because the gospel is appreciated from spiritual appraisal or examina-

---

50. Wilk, *Die Bedeutung des Jesajabuches für Paulus*, 219–65; Wagner, *Heralds of the Good News*, 22, esp. n. 84.

51. Milgrom, *Leviticus 1–16*. Of course with the completion of Milgrom's third volume this case could be expanded for Milgrom has the best commentary on the whole of Leviticus.

52. Aquinas, *Summa Theologica*, 1.1.1; Stegman, "The Spirit of Wisdom and Understanding," In *The Bible and Epistemology*. ed. Healy and Parry, 95, countering Healy's view on page 149.

tion (ἀνακρίνεται, 1 Cor. 2:14). Even broader that this, the Jews who do not accept the gospel remain blinded with veil over their hearts whenever the Law is read to them; such Law condemns them in their unbelief (2 Cor 3:7, 13, 15). The Spirit is about a moral re-orienting of a person so that she reflects the character of the Spirit (Rom 8:1–17; 1 Cor 2:15; 2 Cor 3:16–18; Gal 5:22–23). A person who fleshes out the spiritual gospel message is a spiritual or mature person who appreciates this gospel revealed by the Spirit (1 Cor. 2:6, τελείοις; 1 Cor. 2:15, πνευματικὸς). The Spirit unveils the believer's heart so that in turning to the Lord for salvation, the Spirit produces a new covenant perceptivity to the biblical message. Such a Christian takes on the character of the Lord and reflects the Spirit's revelation (1 Cor 2:16; 2 Cor 3:18). This spiritual person will not be appreciated by natural men because these men do not appreciate the message which the spiritual person fleshes out. However, the spiritual person's gospel perspective enables her to examine or appraise all other things. This gospel perspective is the mind of Christ, which the Spirit revealed (1 Cor. 2:10–13, 16). Exposure to such a new revelational perspective forces a radical re-evaluation to a Christocentric perspective.[53]

Ian Scott, Stanley, and Dupont explain this process of knowing by the Spirit as being an actual revelation through prophecy, rather than illumination, but Stanley focused on the divine authority of the text utilized and Scott focused it through Paul's narration of his empirical experience with the Spirit.[54] However, with regard to epistemology, Scott clarifies that he is not reconstructing Paul's "own process of discovery" which he admits may be different but that he is exploring the epistemology that Paul utilized in providing a logical argument to persuade his audience, especially in the argument of Galatians.[55] I think that Scott's claims are mostly correct for the limited parameters that he sets for his study so that he further shows that Healy and Mayordomo were false starts, especially Mayordomo since Scott and Mayordomo both argue their rival approaches through Galatians. The focus of this chapter is a bit broader than Scott's logic for Pauline audience in that Paul not only provides epistemic comments for his readers but to the extent that Paul is self-revelatory, he also provides comments about his own epistemology and process of discovery. Obviously, if Paul has not left a statement he might also be utilizing other epistemic means than what he

---

53. Becker, *Paul*, 377; Leander Keck, "Paul as Thinker," *Int* 47(1993): 27–33, especially 30.

54. Christopher Stanley, "'Pearls Before Swine?'" *NovT* 41(1999): 124–44; *Arguing with Scripture*; Scott, *Paul's Way of Knowing*, 10, 34–48, 67–68; Dupont, *Gnosis*, 44–47, 77–79, 114–119, 214–16.

55. Scott, *Paul's Way of Knowing*, 11.

informs the reader. However, this chapter focuses on the normal epistemic methods of the statements which Paul leaves available.

This revelation is mostly developed by Paul within the community reception consistent with the emphasis of the N. T., however, there are individual implications of the Spirit and personal response. For example, Paul personally met Christ on the Damascus road and was called to a specific ministry to Gentiles. Furthermore, in the wake of the revelational ministry of the Spirit, "he who is spiritual" is developed by singular nouns and pronouns identifying that each of these matured Christians can think and appraise from her own Spirit transformed mindset to reflect the mind of Christ (1 Cor 2:15-16). A similar expression in singular nouns describes "a mind set upon" the Spirit or flesh reflects the broad domain of Spirit thinking and acting or flesh thinking and acting (Rom 8:6-7). So Paul admits an individual epistemology and logic functions for the people even though his emphasis is on communities. Additionally, Paul writes letters to individuals (Timothy, Titus and Philemon) for them to think through and respond to the implications within their unique relationship with Christ. This individualism is not Paul's emphasis, nor does it go as far as John will develop, but it is a contrast to both Paul's and the whole N. T. emphasis on community edification and development. Thus again most epistemic concepts developed by the philosophers need to be expanded to a community operating in a respective manner, even though Paul also shows that in his thought epistemic and logical methods can also function on an individual level.

Ian Scott identifies the reasoning act to include "understanding" and "judging." Understanding "organizes the desperate phenomena of one's perception, memory, language, and produces a coherent and true model of some part of the world."[56] This complexity of recognizing the difference between objects, ideas as acts of thought corresponding to these objects and the coherent meaning of one's thought forms to represent a part of the world best fits within a Lockean epistemic dualism and method.[57] Scott nicely supports his view of "understanding by appealing to lexicons for the following words: 1) νοούμενα, God "being understood" by what is made to fund a cosmological intuition, perception, and argument.[58] 2) The words "perceived" or "recognized" are translations of κατενόησεν in Rom 4:19, συνιᾶσιν in 2 Cor 10:12 and cognate in Col 1:9, αἰσθήσει in Phil 1:9, and

56. Scott, *Paul's Way of Knowing*, 68–69, 91–94.

57. Scott, *Paul's Way of Knowing*, 71–73; Locke, *Concerning Human Understanding* 1.1.15; 2.11.8–9; 2.32.6; 3.3.6–8; "A Discourse of Miracles," In *Works*, 9:256–65; "The Reasonableness of Christianity," In *Works*, vol. 6.

58. Similar to Augustine, *Lib.* 2.1–15; Anselm, *Mon.* 1–3; Aquinas, *Summa Theologica* 1.2.2–3; Descartes, *Meditations* 3; Kennard, *A Critical Realist's*, 21–25.

ἀσύνετος in Rom 1:21 and 31. 3) Paul often uses empirical metaphors of vision for understanding as in Rom 1:20 καθορᾶται and βλέπω in Rom 7:23; 11:8, 2 Cor 7:8, floating the possibility of Sextus Empiricus that this last word is used intuitionally as "self-evident" and elsewhere as a moral self-evidence.[59] This is the same word that Paul metaphorically used to describe as obscured vision of now seeing through a mirror dimly (1 Cor 13:12; also 2 Cor 3:18 κατοπτριζόμενοι).

Scott also champions that Paul's epistemic terminology is utilized as "judging," which "terms for 'judging' denote the act itself, without implying anything about whether or not the act is successful."[60] Again Scott nicely summarizes lexicon and textual evidence for the meaning of these terms. For example, Paul's opponents' lack of understanding (2 Cor 10:12, συνίημι) "arises from improper exercise of the faculty of judgment"[61] (κρίνω). "Paul denies that he 'classifies' (ἐγκρῖναι) or 'compares' (συγκρῖναι) himself with his opponents,"[62] identifying that he is thinking through a view of Lockean correspondence. These opponents do these kinds of comparison but do not arrive at the understanding (οὐ συνιᾶσιν) to which the sensations should lead. Also, the fallible judgement of conscience (συνείδησις) showcases inner evaluation of morality, which unlike a classical Greek context where one's conscience always condemns, in Paul the new covenant can facilitate a profoundly encouraging conscience evaluation to keep the believer going in the right direction.[63]

Paul also admits to reaching the limits of his knowledge in the extremes of a mystical experience but one of *mirkabah* mysticism accessing the divine throne room, not one of Gnosticism. Paul acknowledges he knows that he was personally present in the heavenly throne room empirically seeing Paradise around him and audibly hearing what was not permitted to be repeated (2 Cor 12:1–4).[64] Such a mystical experience filtered through an empirical lens is

59. Sextus Empiricus, *Math.* 1.184; *P. Oxy* 9.1220.22; *P. Lond.* 964.9; Scott, *Paul's Way of Knowing*, 69.

60. Scott, *Paul's Way of Knowing*, 70.

61. Ibid.

62. Ibid.

63. Kennard, *A Critical Realist's*, 406–7.

64. There is no development of the unutterable description such as is developed by the fourth century *The Apocalypse of Paul* which claims to complete the details of this vision to the third heaven or Dante Alighieri who develops even more in his "Paradise" section of *The Divine Comedy*. Green, *Conversion in Luke-Acts*, 33; Such vision descriptions and denigrating terminology by Paul of himself in the vision does not require Hellenistic rhetoric as was claimed by Schellenberg (*Rethinking Paul's Rhetorical Education*, 7–8, 11), since Ryan claims that it is broadly recognized that Paul did not have such formal Hellenistic rhetorical training (Schellenberg, 7, 23; Norden, *Die antike*

nicely within William Alston's view of perceiving God,⁶⁵ because the empirical evidence is mediated strongly while hinting that God is still more than what is experienced. Though in this case the mystical knowledge and limitation of knowledge is a bit beyond Paul's ability to grasp whether Paul was bodily present in heaven when he was really present in heaven (2 Cor 12:2).

Returning to Paul's testimony of the focus of his education, Paul's education was in *torah* to develop socially and psychologically in belief development as a Pharisee from the rabbinic schools of Tarsus and then in Jerusalem within the school of Hillel, under Hillel's successor and grandson Gamaliel (Acts 22:3; 23:6–9; 26:5; Phil 3:5–6).⁶⁶ Completing one's education elsewhere from Tarsus was common according to Strabo.⁶⁷ Paul and other Pharisees resisted Hellenization as "separate" (from Hebrew *perushim*), extending Judaism into all of daily life (such as vows and sacrifices) and hoping in resurrection afterlife (Luke 18:12; Acts 18:18; 21:23–26; 23:6).⁶⁸ Paul's rabbinic study, especially in synagogue (Acts 13:15), utilized authoritative *mishnahic* method (apodictic laws grouped in lists to aid memorization) and *midrashic* method (focusing on biblical reasons for action heavily funded by written Jewish *torah*, prophets and psalms).⁶⁹ This divides practice into the obligatory *torah*

Kunstprosa, 2:502) and Isaiah provides a Jewish pattern of denigrating (boasting in weakness) language within his vision sighting and call of the Holy God (Isa 6:5 within Isa 6 parallel to 2 Cor 10:8, 11:21, and 12:5 within 2 Cor 10–12, which divine call is not self-boasting; Ambroisiater, *Comm.* 200; Chrysostom, *Laud. Paul* 5.12; *Hom. 2 Cor. 11:1*, 4). Furthermore, tribulation rhetoric better resembles biblical and early Jewish texts than stoic rhetoric (Sir 39.24–30; Wis 8.17–18; 1 *En.* 60.11–13; 2 *En.* 65.9; 2 *Bar.* 59.5–11; *T. Jos.* 1.4–7; *T. Jud.* 23; *T. Iss.* 6; *T. Dan.* 2; *Sib. Or.* 3.601–3; 4.67–69; Schrage, "Leig, Kreuz und Eschaton," In *Kreuzestheologie und Ethik im Neuen Testament*, 23–57; Schellenberg, 130–36).

65. Alston, *Perceiving God*, 14–35.

66. Josephus, *Ant.* 13.289; *m. 'Abot* 1.16, 18; 5.17; *b. Šabb.* 17a; *b. Giṭ.* 60b; *y. Meg.* 4.74a; *b. Yoma* 28ab; *y. Pe'ah* 2.17a; Lundbom, *Deuteronomy*, 486; and Wittgenstein utilizes this game of language acquisition following Augustine to frame a student's worldview thus supporting Wittgensteinian language games as an epistemic lens for a world-view (*Philosophical Investigations*, 11e–12e, 15e–16e, paragraphs 23 and 32; Matthews, "Jesus and Augustine," In *Jesus and Philosophy.* ed. Moser, 109, 111).

67. Strabo, Geogr. 14.5.13.

68. Josephus, *Ant.* 13. 171–3, 297; 18.12–15; *J. W.* 2.119, 162–3; 4 Macc 5:16–27; Philo, *Dreams* 1.124–5; *m. Yad.* 4.6–8; *B. Qidd.* 66a; Resurrection: 2 Macc 7.9–14, 22–23; 14.43–46; 1 *En.* 22; 58.3; 62.14–16; 91.10; 92.2; 104; 108.11–14; *Jub.* 5.10; 10.17; 22.22; *L.A.B.*; CD 3.11–16, 20–21; 7.5, 9; 13.11; 20.17–20, 25–27; 1QH 11.19–23 [3.18–22]; 19.10–14 [11.7–11]; 1QS 3.7–12; 4.7; 4Q228 frag. 1 1.9; 4Q266, frag. 11; 4Q385 2; 4Q386 1–2; 4QMMT C; 4Q521 2.2.12; 5.2.5–6; 2 *Bar.*[Syriac] 30.1–5; 49–51; 4 Macc 7.19; 16.25; 4 *Ezra* 7.26–44; *Sib. Or.* 4.180; *T. Benj.* 10.6–8; *T. Levi* 18; *T. Jud.* 24.

69. Josephus, *Ag. Ap.* 2.175–81; Jerusalem synagogue Theodotus inscription; Philo, *Embassy* 311–3; *Megillat Ta'anit*; *b. Tem.* 14b; *b. B. Meṣ.* 59a–b; *Sifre Deut.* 351; *Iggeret*

(or *halakhah*) and the narrative story or presentation of nonbinding different positions (*haggadah*).[70] Paul continues *halakhah* logical appeals through written and oral *torah* as authority, reflecting warrant and obligation from Law, rather than Aristotelian logic (Rom 4:3; 13:9; 1 Cor 7:12; Gal 6:2; 1 Tim 5:18).[71] Furthermore, Chrysostom argues that Paul being a tent-maker (Acts 18:3) would imply that Paul did not obtain the upper-class Hellenistic rhetorical training when he was rabbinically educated in Tarsus.[72] In fact, Ryan Schellenberg acknowledges that Paul's use of figures do not indicate Hellenistic rhetorical training.[73] Instead, E. Earle Ellis presents Paul as a rabbi authorita-

---

Rav Sherira Gaon 1–2; Farrar, *The Life and Work of St. Paul*, 1:44–45; Chilton, *Rabbi Paul*, 1–27; Teeter, *Scribal Laws*, 28–33, 189; Alexander, "The Rabbinic Hermeneutical Rules and the Definition of Midrash," *PIBA* 8(1984): 96–125; "Quid Athens et Hierosolymis?," In *A Tribute to Geza Vermes*. ed. Davies and White, 153–66; Lieberman, "Rabbinic Interpretation of Scripture," In *Hellenism in Jewish Palestine*, 47–82; Bialoblocki, "Hermeneutik," In *Encyclopaedia Judaica*, 7:1181–94; Jacobs, "Hermeneutics," In *Encyclopedia Judica*, 8:366–72; Maass, "Von den Ursprüngen der rabbinischen Schriftauslegung," *ZThK* 52(1955): 129–61; Zeitlin, "Midrash: A Historical Study" *JQR* 44(1953): 21–36; Wright, *Midrash: The Literary Genre*, 52–59, 64–67; Ellis, "Midrash, Targum and New Testament Quotations," In *Neotestamentica et Semitica*. ed. Ellis and Wilcox, 61–69; le Déaut, "Apropos a Definition of Midrash," *Int* 25(1971): 259–82; Miller, "Targum, Midrash and the Use of the Old Testament in the New Testament," *JSJ* 2(1971): 29–82; Bloch, "Midrash," In *Approaches to Ancient Judaism*. ed. Green, 29–50; Richard Hays utilizes an appeal from authority to explain Paul's argument in "Psalm 143 and the Logic of Romans 3," *JBL* 99:1(1980): 107–15; Porton, "Defining Midrash," In *The Study of Ancient Judaism*. ed. Neusner, 1:55–95; McNamara, "Some Issues and Recent Writings on Judaism and the New Testament," *IBS* 9(1987): 136–49; Tobin, *Paul's Rhetoric in its Contexts*.

70. *Y. Hor.* 3.5 (48c); Meeks provides a Pauline example of rabbinic *midrash* (story and exhortation) following *m. 'Abot* 5.4 sins and plagues of the Exodus in "'And Rose up to Play': Midrash and Paraenesis in 1 Corinthians 10:1–22," *JSNT* 16(1982): 64–78, following the lead of Weiss, *Der erste Korintherbrief*, 250.

71. Ellis, *Paul's Use of the Old Testament*, 11; Gooch, "Paul, the Mind of Christ, and Philosophy," in *Jesus and Philosophy*. ed. Moser, 89; Tobin, *Paul's Rhetoric in its Contexts*, 229–31. This use of authoritative scripture places Paul's logic within rabbinic patterns rather than those of diatribe as Epictetus uses (contra Stowers, *The Diatribe and Paul's Letter to the Romans*; Schmeiler, *Paulus und die "Diatribe"*). In this, Paul argues logically but nothing as philosophically cogent as Aristotle, *An. post.* or *An. pr.* or *Soph. elench*; Tobin, *Paul's Rhetoric in its Contexts*, 229–31. The closest Hellenistic rhetoric comes to these rabbinic biblical appeals is an authoritative divine appeal (Quintilian, *Inst.* 5.11.42; Tobin, *Paul's Rhetoric in its Contexts*, 91–107). Tobin (114–5) identifies this logic with Hellenistic early Judaism such as found in Philo but Philo is much more aligned with Platonic thought (Frag. A 654; *Post.* 48, 167; *Somn.* 123, 149; *QE* 2.2; *Opif.* 152; Tobin, *Paul's Rhetoric in Its Contexts*, 116, 170, 176, 179) and demeans the *logos* (*Leg.* 3.61, 175) than Paul.

72. Chrysostom, *Laud. Paul.* 4.10; *Scand.* 20.10; *Hom. 1 Cor.* 3:4; 15:5 (PG 61.28, 128); Mitchell, *The Heavenly Trumpet*, 240–48, 374–77.

73. Schellenberg, *Rethinking Paul's Rhetorical Education*, 7 even though Ryan argues

tively quoting the Old Testament ninety-three times from memory with many more allusions to populate his arguments.[74] However, since Paul grew up in the dispersion and writes to the dispersion, he primarily uses a version of LXX in these quotes.[75] Earle Ellis, E. P. Sanders, and Koch make the case that these quotes and allusions are substantially of the *pesher* type (or about 71 percent of the time contemporizing of the *torah* to new issues).[76] However, several schol-

---

a formal rhetorical education is not necessary to utilize first rate Hellenistic rhetoric because rhetoric was in the air (Schellenberg, 8; Mitchell, *Paul and the Rhetoric of Reconciliation*, 6) and non-Western trained native American rhetorician Red Jacket parallels Paul in not obtaining Hellenistic rhetorical education and yet both utilized rhetorical tools (such as both softening elevated language in describing himself within a vision with God (Schellenberg, 11, 304-308) even though Judaism has folks like Isaiah expressing similar personal denigration before the Holy God (Isa 6:5). Schellenberg misses the point, both Paul and Red Jacket obtained rhetorical training: Paul through his Pharisaic education and Red Jacket through narrative story telling among the tribe; neither is untrained. Instead, both reflect the education for which there are biographical claims.

74. Ellis, *Paul's Use of the Old Testament*, 11, 14-15, though Ellis wished to distant Paul from rabbinic interpretive conclusions on p. 83; Michael, *Paulus und Seine Bibel*, 80-82; Bonsirven, *Exégèse rabbinique et Exégèse paulinienne*, 337; Neusner, *Judaism When Christianity Began*, 15-27; Wagner, *Heralds of the Good News*, 22, esp. n. 84; O'Dowd, "Memory on the Boundary," In *The Bible and Epistemology*. ed. Healy and Parry, 4.

75. 1 Thess 4:8 combines LXX Ezek 36:27 and 37:14; Phil 2:15 includes "blemish" from Deut 32:5 LXX which is absent in MT; 2 Cor 10:17 taken from LXX 1 Kgdms 2:10 is absent in MT 1 Sam 2:10, but maybe a conflation from Jer 9:22-23 [Eng 23-24]; Hays, *The Faith of Jesus Christ*, 139; *Echoes of Scripture in the Letters of Paul*, 80-81; Stanley, *Paul and the Language of Scripture*, 83-251 provides an extensive comparison of LXX versions and MT to Pauline quotations; Bekken, *The Word is Near You*, 56-59; Sanders, "Paul Between Judaism and Hellenism," In *St Paul Among the Philosophers*. ed. Caputo and Alcoff, 80-81, 89; Philo, *Vita Mos.* 2.7; *Letter of Aristeas* 305-317; Kennard, *A Critical Realist's*, 263; Jobes, "When God Spoke Greek," *BBR* 16(2006): 219-236; Gentry, "The Septuagint and the Text of the Old Testament," *BBR* 16(2006): 193-218; Hengel, *The Septuagint as Christian Scripture*, 22; Haacker agrees with Paul's LXX use except for Paul's use of Psalms is argued to mostly reflect the MT (*The Theology of Paul's Letter to the Romans*, 101-2). For example, Rom 3:10-12 reflects MT and LXX with the addition that the first virtue "goodness" with "righteousness" as in the context of Rom 3:13-17 follows MT (and diverges from LXX) Pss 5:9; 140:3; 10:7; Isa 59:7-8; Rom 3:18 follows LXX dropping an article but also parallels MT.

76. Koch, *Die Schrift als Zeuge*, 11-24 identifies that 56 percent of Paul's quotes are LXX and 71 percent of them are modified to support the argument; Stanley, *Paul and the Language of Scripture*, 260-61 agrees and demonstrates it in each Pauline quote (83-251), proposing that Paul's introduction usually determines any change for the *pesher* use (Stanley, 23); Ellis, "A Note on Pauline Hermeneutics," *NTS* 2(1955-6): 131-2; Hays, *Echoes of Scripture in the Letters of Paul*, 79-81; Wilckens, *Der Brief an die Römer*, 2:225; Sanders, "Habakkuk in Qumran, Paul, and the Old Testament," In *Paul and the Scriptures of Israel*. ed. Evans and Sanders, 107-8; Fitzmyer, *Romans*, 588; Lim, *Pesharim*, 44-53; Longenecker, *Romans*, 852; Josephus, *Ant*. 13. 171-73, 297; 18.12-15; *J. W.* 2.119, 162-3; 4 Macc 5:16-27; Philo, *Dreams* 1.124-5; *m. Yad.* 4.6-8; *B. Qidd.* 66a; Resurrection: 2 Macc 7.9-14, 22-23; 14.43-46; *1 En.* 22; 58.3; 62.14-16;

ars present that Paul's Christian core kerygma also includes knowing Christ and the early Christian's experience with Him (1 Cor 7:10; 9:14).[77] However, Pharisaic-rabbinic logic facilitates Paul's Christian repositioning of himself. For example, Alfred Resch analyzes Paul's letters to surface one hundred and ten parallels to rabbinic *haggadah* method.[78] In one specific instance, Rodolphe Morrissette applies one such rabbinic argument to explain compelling logic for the resurrection of the human body from 1 Corinthians 15:35–49 by comparing Paul to *b. Sanh.* 90b–91 as a pattern Morrissette uses that might be available in first century rabbinic expression. Namely, 1) an *opening question*, then 2) everyday *realities* (bodies of sun, moon, animal, bird and human) to reassure the observer, 3) which are then applied by *analogy* to imply the resurrection.[79] Within such rabbinic argumentation, the fact that Jesus' resur-

---

91.10; 92.2; 104; 108.11–14; *Jub.* 5.10; 10.17; 22.22; *L.A.B.*; CD 3.11–16, 20–21; 7.5, 9; 13.11; 20.17–20, 25–27; 1QH 11.19–23 [3.18–22]; 19.10–14 [11.7–11]; 1QS 3.7–12; 4.7; 4Q228 frag. 1 1.9; 4Q266, frag. 11; 4Q385 2; 4Q386 1–2; 4QMMT C; 4Q521 2.2.12; 5.2.5–6; 2 *Bar.*[Syriac] 30.1–5; 49–51; 4 Macc 7.19; 16.25; 4 Ezra 7.26–44; *Sib. Or.* 4.180; *T. Benj.* 10.6–8; *T. Levi* 18; *T. Jud.* 24.

77. From Matt 5:31–32; 10:10; Luke 10:7; Patte, *Paul's Faith and the Power of the Gospel*, 227; Hays, *Echoes of Scripture in the Letters of Paul*, 83; Davies, "Canon and Christology in Paul," In *Paul and the Scriptures of Israel.* ed. Evans and Sanders, 38; other allusions to Jesus might also be seen (Haacker, *The Theology of Paul's Letter to the Romans*, 146–9).

78. Resch, *Der Paulinismus und die Logia Jesu*; these results are briefly surveyed by Davies, *Paul and Rabbinic Judaism*, 137; Belleville, "Tradition or Creation?," In *Paul and the Scriptures of Israel.* ed. Evans and Sanders, 168; Bultmann, *TDNT*, 2:701, 706. Paul uses rabbinic patterns with Jewish rhetoric, rather than Aristotle (*Rhet.*), show an occasional similarity to the philosophical diatribe to help compel his dispersion audience, namely: 1) short sentences (Rom 3:27; Epictetus, *Diatr.* 1.16.3; 1.18.11; 2.16.11; Bultmann, *Der Stil der paulinischen Predigt*, 55); 2) imperatives (1 Cor 10:31; Phil 4:4; Epictetus, *Diatr.* 4.6.23; Bultmann, *Der Stil der Paulinismus Predigt*, 32–33); 3) exclamations to heighten explosive character (2 Cor 11:16–23; Epictetus, *Diatr.* 2.20.29; Quintilian, *Inst.* 9.2.65; Dionysius of Halicarnassus *Rhet.* 9.323.1; Bonhoffer, *Epiketet und das Neue Testament*, 143; Stowers, "Paul on the Use and Abuse of Reason," In *Greeks, Romans, and Christians.* ed. Balch, Ferguson, Meeks, 257); 4) questions followed by a strong negative (Rom 6:1–2, 15; Dio Chrysostom, *Dial.* 23.6; 26.6; Epictetus, *Diatr.* 1.6.13; 4.8.2; 11.17, 22; 14.14; Maximus of Tyre, *Discourse* 6.1d; Seneca, *Ep.* 36.4; 60.3); 5) hardships expressed (2 Cor 6:3–10; 11:23–28; Epictetus, *Diatr.* 1.24.1; Seneca, *Ep.* 24.20; Athenaeus, *Deipn.* 12.522b; Philo *Against Flaccus* 175; Bultmann, *Der Stil der paulinismus Predigt*, 19–20, 71–72); 6) quotations in an argument (Rom 4:3–17; Stowers, *The Diatribe and Paul's Letter to the Romans*; Malherbe, *Paul and the Popular Philosophers*, 25–33, 80–83). Even Aristotle admits that the rhetorical categories appealed to in N. T. epistles (namely, judicial [in tight arguments], epideictic [in praise sections], and deliberative [in mixed arguments]) are imprecise and overlap (*Rhet.* 1.23) and Longenecker concurs (*The Epistle to the Romans*, 15).

79. Morrissette, "La condition de ressuscité, 1 Cor 15, 35–49," *Bib* 53(1972): 208–28; Bonneau, "The Logic of Paul's Argument on the Resurrection Body in 1 Cor

rection is the basis and the paradigm for the Christian's resurrection makes more sense in a Pharisaic worldview that admits that Paul empirically saw the risen Christ (1 Cor 15:8; Acts 23:6; 24:14, 21; 26:5-8) rather than Aristotelian rhetoric and worldview, which ignores resurrection (Acts 25:26).[80]

For Paul, Jesus' teaching rises to the level of *torah* to warrant authoritative instruction (1 Cor 7:10; Matt 5:32; 19:3-9; Mark 10:2-12), while Paul permits his own opinion and rhetoric to logically compel with less authority (1 Cor 7:6). By extension, imitating one's mentor's example is compelling for practice and an appeal to such consistency funds rhetoric (1 Cor 4:16; 11:1; Gal 4:12; Phil 3:17; 1 Thess 1:6; 2:14).[81]

In such comparisons of biblical texts and analogies, Paul imbibed the seven logical rules which Hillel proposed and Gamilial as his successor taught for Hillel's rabbinic school. After describing the Hillel rule which identifies the logic involved in the instance of *pesher*, I have added a range of Pauline biblical texts (in parenthesis and notes to my exegesis explaining this meaning) which utilized that Hillel rule to rhetorically argue in that context, namely:

15:35-44a," *Science et Esprit* 45:1(1993): 79-92 concurs with this analysis; There are many such analogical arguments in Paul including: Rom 7:2-3; 9:21-23; 11:16-24; 1 Cor 3:5-17; 9:25-27; 12:14-27; 14:7-8; 2 Cor 2:14-17; 3:1-3; 5:1-6; Gal 3:13-18; 4:1-2; 6:7-9; 1 Thess 5:2-8; a common form of argument so one does not need to appeal to Hellenistic logic to make the argument cogent (Lloyd, *Polarity and Analogy*; Dawes, "But if you can Gain your Freedom," *CBQ* 52[1990]: 686 n 20, and Bonneau, 79; Lausberg, *Handbook of Literary Rhetoric*, 354; analogies are common in ancient philosophical argument: Plato, *Tim.* 30b; *Phileb.* 29b; Aristotle, *Mot. an.* 703a; *Pol.* 1295a; *Eth. nic.* 1113a; analogies are also common in rabbinic argument: m. '*Abot* 5.4; y. *Hor.* 3.5 [48c]; Neusner, *Handbook of Rabbinic Theology*, 29, 43-4, 88-103).

80. Aristotle, *Eth. eud.* 3.6.25-30; 3.9.7-15; 10.4.18-22; Contra Mayordomo, *Argumentiert Paulus logisch?*, 97, 107, 115.

81. Similar practice and consistency contributed to rhetoric in public philosophy: Aristotle, *Rhet.* 1.2.4; 2.1.5; Plutarch, *Cat. Maj.* 3.4; Cicero, *Off.* 2.13-46; Pliny, *Ep.* 6.11; 8.14.4-6, 23; Seneca, *Ep.* 6.5; Quintilian, *Inst. Orat.* 3.8.13; Fiore, "Paul, Exemplification, and Imitation," In *Paul in the Greco-Roman World*. ed. Sampley, 228-57.

1. What applies in a minor case also applies to the major case[82] (Rom 5:8–9, 10, 15, 17;[83] 11:12, 24;[84] 1 Cor 6:3; 9:11–12; 12:22; 2 Cor 3:7–9, 11;[85] 8:22; Phil 2:12; 1 Tim 5:18;[86] Phlm 1:16).

2. An analogy is made between two separate texts on the basis of a similar phrase, word or root[87] (Rom 4:3–8;[88] 9:33;[89] 11:8–10; 11:26–27;[90] 12:19–20; 2 Cor 6:16–18; Gal 3:16[91]).

3. A family of texts applies a principle to all of the textual family[92] (Rom 3:10–18;[93] 10:18–21; 15:9–12).

---

82. Sipra intr 1; 'Abot R. Nat. 37; Gen. Rab. 92.7; Pesaḥ. 18b; Yoma 43a; t. Šabb. 7.11; Pool, *The Traditional Prayer Book for Sabbath and Festivals*, 128–30. These seven Hillel hermeneutical rules were expanded into thirteen in the second century by rabbi Ishmael ben Elisha. Occasionally, as with Hays (*The Faith of Jesus Christ*, 190) Ishmael's hermeneutic is appealed to as a Pauline framework but it is not available until the second century, after Paul has made his contribution. It is thus better to position Paul in the wake of Hillel's logical rules of analogy taught by Hillel's successor Gamilial (Acts 22:3; 23:6–9; 26:5; Phil 3:5–6).

83. Kennard, *Biblical Covenantalism*, 3:46–47, 108–18 explain this exegesis.

84. Kennard, *Biblical Covenantalism*, 3:144–48.

85. Kennard, *Biblical Covenantalism*, 3:36–37.

86. Kennard, *Biblical Covenantalism*, 3:155–56.

87. Sipra intr 2; 'Abot R. Nat. 37; Šabb. 64a; t. Šabb. 7.11; Gezerah Shavah; CD 4.20–5.1; Binyan Ab; Pool, *The Traditional Prayer Book for Sabbath and Festivals*, 128–30. There is no need to appeal to Hellenistic rhetoric to make sense of this argument as does Anderson, *Glossary of Greek Rhetorical Terms Connected to Methods of Argumentation*, 50, using repetition of figures (as in Aristotle, *Rhet.* 3.9.7), or when Greek follows a Hebraic figure of assonance (Rom 1:28–31; which Hellenistic rhetoric divides into similar sound [p. 93; anonymous, *Rhet. ad Herennium* 4.29–32] or similar root [p. 69; Alexander, *de Figuris* 2.5], or similar endings [78, 103; anonymous, *Rhet. ad Herennium* 4.18, 28, 31] or p. 53 as in a quote (as does Demetrius, *Eloc.* 280) which is exactly Hillel's point with this rule, or p. 91 as in a proverb (Gal 5:9; as does Demetrius, *Eloc.* 156, since there is a strong rabbinic parable tradition [McArthur & Johnston, *They also Taught in Parables*]).

88. Kennard, *Biblical Covenantalism*, 3:44–49, 90–107.

89. Kennard, *Biblical Covenantalism*, 3:73–74.

90. Kennard, *Biblical Covenantalism*, 3:144–48.

91. Kennard, *Biblical Covenantalism*, 3:133–42.

92. Sipra intr 3; 'Abot R. Nat. 37; t. Šabb. 7.11; Pool, *The Traditional Prayer Book for Sabbath and Festivals*, 128–30.

93. Kennard, *Biblical Covenantalism*, 3:89.

4. An analogy built from two texts can then be applied to another text[94] (Rom 4:3-8 applied to 4:17;[95] 1 Cor 1:19 applied to 1:31; 2 Cor 6:14-18; 1 Tim 5:17-18[96]).

5. A general principle may be restricted by a particularization of it[97] (Rom 4:3 is restricted to Jewish sacrificial construct by the Davidic penitential lament in Rom 4:7-8).[98]

6. An analogy is made from another passage to inform a relationship where there is often an apparent conflict[99] (Rom 1:17 just live by faithfulness but "there is none righteous" in Rom 3:10 or Rom 2:6 God renders according to deeds[100] but "blessed are those whose Lawless deeds will be forgiven" Rom 4:7-8 are tensions that are both resolved by Rom 4:3, 22 "Abraham believed God and it was credited to him as righteousness";[101] Rom 9:19-21; 11:19-24;[102] 2 Cor 3 Mosaic covenant with veil compared to New covenant direct sight in Christ;[103] Gal 4:21-31 Sarah and Hagar set up an allegory to characterize the children of promise as free and the children of the bond-woman as bound[104]).

---

94. Sipra intr 4; 'Abot R. Nat. 37; t. Šabb. 7.11; Pool, *The Traditional Prayer Book for Sabbath and Festivals*, 128-30.

95. Kennard, *Biblical Covenantalism*, 3:44-49, 90-107.

96. Kennard, *Biblical Covenantalism*, 3:155-56.

97. Sipra intr 7-8; 'Abot R. Nat. 37; Šabu. 26a; Sanh. 1c; t. Šabb. 7.11; Pool, *The Traditional Prayer Book for Sabbath and Festivals*, 128-30.

98. Kennard, *Biblical Covenantism*, 3:44-49, 90-107.

99. Sipra intr 9-12; 'Abot R. Nat. 37; t. Šabb. 7.11; Pool, *The Traditional Prayer Book for Sabbath and Festivals*, 128-30. There is no need to appeal to Hellenistic rhetoric to make sense of this logic as does Anderson (*Glossary of Greek Rhetorical Terms*, 104; Anaximenes, *Rhetorica ad Alexandrum* 18) because this is exactly Hillel's point of argument within rabbinic patterns.

100. Mayordomo (*Argumentiert Paulus logisch?*, 194) presents that Paul's argument is aided by Aristotelian logic through a chiasm of positive, negative, negative, concluding with positive. Such an alternation does not require Aristotelian logic to make sense, in fact that such everlasting life of resurrection or damnation under God's wrath makes more sense in a Jewish Pharisaic view and interactive with the Abrahamic narrative similar to how Scott portrays in *Paul's Way of Knowing*, 199-230.

101. Kennard, *Biblical Covenantalism*, 3:90-105.

102. Kennard, *Biblical Covenantalism*, 3:146-148.

103. Kennard, *Biblical Covenantalism*, 3:36-37.

104. Kennard, *Biblical Covenantalism*, 3:133-39.

7. The total context, not an isolated statement must be considered for accurate exegesis[105] (Rom 14:1–15:21 and 1 Cor 8:1–10:33 Paul knows that "nothing is unclean in itself" does not abrogate kosher laws in the Roman or Corinthian church context but the Gentile Christians are free to eat "unclean" food, however, no one should eat in such a manner as to destroy others in the Church; Rom 14:10–11).[106]

This rabbinic method populated a basic belief or language game for Paul's Jewish worldview based in warrant provided primarily by the written and oral *torah* through which it was interpreted.[107] Basic belief is a good operating framework for Paul since both knowledge methods and faith are intertwined as overlapping synonyms to describe the process by which Paul believes and knows. In fact, while "faith" is strongly developed in Romans, "knowledge" is surprisingly absent, and in 1 and 2 Corinthians "knowledge" is strongly developed for the same roles while the term "faith" is surprisingly absent.[108] Fitted into this worldview was an externalism of a practical realistic non-foundational empiricism similar to Thomas Reid's Common Sense Realism and connected to supporting work and relationships.[109] Such a Pharisaic Judaism was also mystically warranted as developed by William Alston providing direct perceptions from God or angels through vision, dreams, or authoritative audible speech (Acts 16:9–10; 23:8–9).[110] Such a

---

105. *Sipra* intr 13; *'Abot R. Nat.* 37; *Sukkah* 32a; Pool, *The Traditional Prayer Book for Sabbath and Festivals*, 128–30. There is no need to appeal to Hellenistic rhetoric to make sense of this logic as does Anderson with regard to a progression (*Glossary of Greek Rhetorical Terms*, 58; Anaximenes, *Rhetorica ad Alexandrum* 18) because this is merely a special case in Hillel's broader rule within rabbinic patterns.

106. Kennard, *Biblical Covenantalism*, 3:148–56.

107. *B. Qidd.* 66a; *2 Bar.* 48.18–24; Plantinga, *Warrant and Proper Function*, 6; Wittgenstein, *Philosophical Investigations*, 11e–12e, 15e–16e, paragraphs 23 and 32; Matthews, "Jesus and Augustine," In *Jesus and Philosophy.* ed. Moser, 109, 111.

108. Healy, "Knowledge of the Mystery," In *The Bible and Epistemology.* ed. Healy and Parry, 153–4.

109. Rabbi Gamaliel advocates work and relations along with *torah* study in *m. 'Abot* 2.2; Reid, *Thomas Reid.* ed. Brookes; Scott, *Paul's Way of Knowing*, 91–4; Abraham also presents Jesus within such an externalism "The Epistemology of Jesus," In *Jesus and Philosophy.* ed. Moser, 158–9.

110. Alston, *Perceiving God*, 14; This could also be identified within Moser's attunement to filial knowledge of God providing authoritative evidence for the message communicated (*The Elusive God*, 46–7, 98, 113–123); Angels as revelatory messengers: *Jub.* 1.27–29; 10.10–14; *1 En.* 4.19, 21–26; 7; 8; 17–36; 89.61–77; 90.14–20; *T. Levi* 9.6; *T. Reub.* 5.3; *T. Jos.* 6.6; Authoritative heavenly voice: b. *'Abot* 6.2; *B. Bat.* 73b, 85b; *Mak.* 23b; *'Erub.* 54b; *Shab.* 33b; 88a; *Soṭa* 33a; *p. Soṭa* 7.5, sect. 5; *Pesiq. Rab Kah.* 15.5; *Lev. Rab.* 19.5–6; *Deut. Rab.* 11.10; *Lam. Rab. Proem* 2, 23; *Lam. Rab.* 1.16 sect. 50; *Ruth Rab.* 6.4; *Qoh. Rab.* 7.12, sect. 1; *Pesq. Rab Kah.* 11.16; Authoritative Dreams: LXX additions

Pharisaic Jewish worldview essentially focused on the monotheistic creator God electing Israel into a covenant relationship and faithfulness unto kingdom blessing (Rom 2:17–20; 3:2; 9:3–5).[111]

As Christianity emerged, Paul's mentor, Gamaliel, argued for the Sanhedrin to allow Christianity to fail if God would not support it (Acts 5:34–39).[112] However, Saul broke from his mentor and persecuted Christians as Jewish heretics, even obtaining authority to extend the persecution to Damascus (Acts 7:58–8:3; 9:1–3).

Christ confronted Paul on the Damascus road, providing Paul with authoritative warrant within his Pharisaic epistemology for a radically altered worldview, existentially extending Paul's total commitment to Christ and the Trinity (Rom 6:6; Acts 9:1–22; 22:3–21).[113] Christ asked Saul why he was persecuting Christ. The voice and bright light were empirically verifiable to those who traveled with Saul but they did not understand the message. Christ's revelatory statement funds Paul's concept of the body of Christ (persecuting Christians means one is persecuting Christ; 1 Cor 12). W. D. Davies developed Paul's profound transformation.

> His experience on the road to Damascus led to a tremendous deliverance and transformation in the life of Saul of Tarsus. On the one hand it meant for him redemption from the power of sin (Rom 8:3), from the bondage of the Law (Rom 10:3; Gal 3:13) and from the dominion of unseen forces of evil, what we

---

to Esther; *1 En.*; *2 En.*; *2 Bar.*; *4 Ezra*; *Apoc. Ab.*; *T. Levi*; *T. Job*; *Bib. Ant.*; *Jub.*; *Life of Adam and Eve* and several at Qumran, Flannery, "Dreams and Vision Reports," In *The Eerdmans Dictionary of Early Judaism*. ed. Collins and Harlow, 550; When Paul defends himself he denies the charges (Acts 24:12–13; Aristotle, *Rhet.* 3.14.6–7) and calls attention to these Pharisaic circumstances of seeing the vision of Christ (Acts 24:14–15, 21; 26:13–18), a reasonable rhetorical appeal to circumstances (Aristotle, *Rhet.* 3.15.3). Also in Acts 23:4–5 Paul rhetorically excludes offence (Aristotle, *Rhet.* 3.15.3).

111. Sir 17.17–18; 47.22; Jdt 7.30; Sus 16.5; 19.29; *Pss. Sol.* 9.17–18; Davies, *Paul and Rabbinic Judaism*, 82; These are very different oriental relational categories of study than Aristotle's *Cat.* and *Top.* which drive Western logical conceptions.

112. Corroborated by the *Epistle of James to Quadratus* 11 as translated by Landau from Syriac and Armenian in "The Epistle of James to Quadrantus," A paper presented at Society for Biblical Literature, Nov. 22, 2015.

113. Kim, *The Origin of Paul's Gospel*; Gooch calls Jesus resurrection as foundational for Paul ("Paul, the Mind of Christ, and Philosophy," In *Jesus and Philosophy*. ed. Moser, 86); Kierkegaard, *Fear and Trembling*, 40–41 discussion on "infinite resignation" as total commitment; Dupont, *Gnosis*, 34–37 considers that Paul's conversion frames Paul's epistemology; However, when Paul defends himself he makes a rhetorical appeal that the alternatives would have been more harmful (Acts 24:14–21; 26:19–23; Pseudo-Cicero, *Rhet. Ad Her.* 1.14.24; 1.15.25).

might call the demonic element in life (Rom 8:15; Col 2:15; Eph 6:10–16).[114]

Davies continues to apply many of Paul's soteriological concepts to this transformative event but more space would be needed to develop them. In the midst of this confrontation Paul was authoritatively called by Christ to proclaim a Christian gospel to Gentiles (Acts 26:15–18).[115] N. T. Wright identifies that in the wake of this event, "Paul's theology consists precisely in the redefinition, by means of Christology and pneumatology, of those two key Jewish doctrines" the monotheistic God electing Israel.[116] Paul's transformation resulted in a Trinitarian mysticism transforming Jews and Gentiles into the new covenant Church already with a grander expression of kingdom transformation in the resurrection (2 Cor 3–4). Under Christ's revelatory command, Paul risks everything to follow Abraham as a "knight of faith" who suspends aspects of exclusive Judaism that do not fit with this Trinitarian elected inclusion and liberation of Gentiles within the body of Christ (Rom 4; 14:1–15:21; 1 Cor 8:1–10:33; Gal 3).[117]

Instead of Jewish believers being in the Law (1 Kgs 2:3; Dan 9:11; Rom 2:12, 20, 23; 3:19; 1 Cor 9:9; 14:21; Gal 3:11[118]; 5:4; Phil 3:6), Christian believers are now in Christ (Eph 1:1–20). Adolf Deismann developed "in Christ" as theo-centric mysticism immersed within communion with God.[119] Such an approach fits within Alston's mystical concept of perceiving God.[120] Wilhelm Bousset developed this relationship to entail one of "intense feeling

---

114. Davies, *Paul and Rabbinic Judaism*, 58.

115. This "sent" role is similar to Arrian, *Discourses of Epictetus* 3.22.23–24, 45–46, however, the sender is different.

116. Wright, "Toward a Synthesis of Pauline Theology (1 and 2 Thessalonians, Philippians, and Philemon)," In *Pauline Theology I.* ed. Bassler, 184.

117. Kierkegaard, *Fear and Trembling*, 9–67; Bruggemann, "Impossibility and Epistemology in the Faith Tradition of Abraham and Sarah (Gen 18:1–15)," *ZAW* 94:4(1982): 633; Henningsson, "Faith, Obedience, Understanding and Liberation," *Swedish Missiological Themes* 88:2(2000): 183.

118. Mayordomo (*Argumentiert Paulus logisch?*, 128–9, 134–139, 162) argues that Paul's argument in Gal 3:6–14 is aided by Aristotelian logic through cryptically condensing the text, utilizing Abraham as exemplar (Mayordomo, 139 following Betz, *Galatians*, 143), and an alternation of positive (Gal 3:6–9) and negative (Gal 3:10–12). None of these features is telling to Aristotelian logic. In fact, there are other saints affirmed in the O.T. than merely Abraham but he is a good paradigm for both Jewish and non-circumcised (thus Gentile). Scott makes sense of this argument without such Aristotelian rhetorical appeals but to a simple building of an argument on premise and corollaries, methodology available within rabbinic rhetoric (*Paul's Way of Knowing*, 199–230).

119. Deismann, *Paul*, 150–1.

120. Alston, *Perceiving God*, 14–35.

of personal belonging and of spiritual relationship with the exalted Lord" parallel to the same relationship which the Christian has with the Spirit.[121] Albert Schweitzer advocated that an apocalyptic covenantal model of "in Christ" was so foundational as to make it the source of everything connected with redemption.[122] Thomas Boomershine argues that this already and not yet quality of Jesus apocalyptic coming identifies that Paul maintains an epistemic dualism to make sense of the continuing "old age" and the emerging "new age," and the Christian's perception of these eras including her.[123] Alfred Wikenhauser rejected the Hellenistic context that Bultmann had advocated (following Platonic absorption), because Wikenhauser developed that a personal relationship was facilitated with the Trinitarian persons.[124] W. D. Davies extended Schweitzer's covenantal and relational participation with Jewish monotheism present within first-century Judaism at Qumran.[125] Both Davies and E. P. Sanders developed the relational participation further including involvement with the Spirit.[126] Michel Bouttier defended that the concept of "in Christ" had primarily communal and eschatological emphasis.[127] This communal aspect through Christ empowered by the Spirit transforms a community cultivating life together, as Bonhoeffer and Vanier develop.[128] Adam Neder accentuated the issue of "participation in Christ" (found within Karl Barth which undergirds this relationally).[129] Incorporation into the mystical Christ provides relational knowledge of God.[130] Richard Gaffin identified that a substantial aspect of this participation in Christ is realized mystically within baptism into Christ's resurrection, while Michael Gorman developed this participation with Christ as being realized

---

121. Bousset, *Kyrios Christos*, 153, 160, 164; Murray, echoed the role of Spirit and expanded it to personal relationship with the persons of the Trinity (*Redemption-Accomplished and Applied*, 201).

122. Schweitzer, *The Mysticism of Paul the Apostle*, 124.

123. Boomershine, "Epistemology at the Turn of the Ages in Paul, Jesus, and Mark," In *Apocalyptic and the New Testament*. ed. Marcus and Soards, 148–9.

124. Wikenhauser, *Pauline Mysticism*, 14, 166–7; contrary to Bultmann, *Theology of the New Testament*, 298.

125. Davies, *Paul and Rabbinic Judaism*, ix–x, 86–7, 91.

126. Davies, *Paul and Rabbinic Judaism*, 86–7; Sanders, *Paul and Palestinian Judaism*, 540–9.

127. Bouttier, *En Christ*, 133.

128. Bonhoeffer, *Life Together*, especially 32–47; Vanier, *Community and Growth*.

129. Neder, *Participation in Christ*, 78; Barth, *Church Dogmatics* IV/3.2, 536–40.

130. Armstrong, "St. Paul's Theory of Knowledge," *The Church Quarterly Review* 154:313(Oct-Dec 1953): 438–52, esp. 439.

in joining Christ in His death.¹³¹ Constantine Campbell celebrated the full range of diverse uses of the prepositions in categorizing the multifaceted aspects of the Christian's participation with Christ.¹³²

In Romans 6, the issue is enslavement and the consequences that follow from being rescued from the realm of sin (or the realm of the Law) as an old human, rescued into the more powerful realm and person of Christ as a new human (Rom 5:13; 6:1, 14; 7:1–4). This exodus from the realm of sin into new covenant transformation within Christ is what Paul means by the present experience of redemption (Rom 3:24; 1 Cor 1:30). To follow these strands, Romans six has two primary points as indicated by the questions in verses 1 and 15. First, in mystically connecting with Christ's death and resurrection we are changed into new humans with a new covenant relationship in Christ and removed from the realm of sin ("old man," ὁ παλαιὸς ἡμῶν ἄνθρωπος) so we should think and live differently reflecting this change (Rom 6:1–14).¹³³ This mystical¹³⁴ beginning is visibly identified as occurring at a Christian's conversion marked by the performative initiation rite of baptism into Christ, after the pattern of second Temple proselyting baptism into Moses (Rom 6:3–4; Gal 3:27)¹³⁵ and John the Baptist's baptism into kingdom oriented Judaism (Matt 3:6, 11; Mark 1:4, 8; Luke 3:3, 6; John 1:26; 3:5; Acts 19:3–5 baptism into [εἰς] John or Christ). Paul describes that the believer is baptized into (εἰς) Christ, that is, mystically baptized into (εἰς)

---

131. Gaffin, *The Centrality of the Resurrection*, 50–1; Gorman, *Inhabiting the Cruciform God*, 1–4, 32.

132. Campbell, *Paul and Union with Christ*, 67–199, 410–3.

133. Kennard, *Messiah Jesus*, 313–21, 342–4; Schweitzer, *The Mysticism of Paul the Apostle*, 101–40; Kim, *The Origin of Paul's Gospel*.

134. Mystical in the relational sense of Alston and Schweitzer, in which a believer retains identity in close relationship with revelation from the Trinitarian God, rather than a Platonic absorption or Eastern loss of identity.

135. Baptism into Moses as a Jewish metaphor is evident on the Dura Europas synagogue west wall with a beehive-shaped rock pouring water like a fountain to satiate Israel when they tested Yahweh (Goodenough, *Jewish Symbols in the Greco-Roman World*, vol. 11, plate 12; Exod 17:6; Num 20:8–11; 1 Cor 10:2; Josephus, *Ant.* 10.7; *Num. Rab.* 1.2; 19.25–26; Targum *Onkelos* on Num 21:17; Etheridge, *The Targums of Onkelos and Jonathan ben Uzziel on the Pentateuch*, 142–3; *Sifre* on Num. 11:21; b. Šabb. 35a; Ap. Eusebius, *Praep. Ev.* 9; 29.16; Ellis, *Paul's Use of the Old Testament*, 66–67; Willis, *Idol Meat in Corinth*, 133). Convert baptism to Qumran (1QS 3.3–9; 4QTLevi ar). Gentile proselyte baptism to Judaism (Josephus, *J. W.* 2.150; *Ant.* 14.285; 18.93–4; 18.117; *T. Levi* 2.3.1–2; *Sib. Or.* 4.162–70; Epictetus, *Diatr.* 2.9.19–20; *Apoc. Moses* 29.6–13; m. Tohar 7.6; b. Yebam. 46a–48b; Midrash Sifre Num. 15.14; t. Yoma 4.20; t. Pesaḥ 7.13). Christian conversion baptism is performative practice (Rom 6:3–4; 1 Cor 1:13–16; John 18:28; Acts 2:38–41; 10:28; Austin, *How to do Things with Words*).

Christ's death (Rom 6:3–4).[136] Such a mystical awareness that we are new humans in Christ is conceived after the pattern in which Paul was rendered new by meeting Christ on the Damascus road (Rom 6:6; Acts 9:1–22; 22:3–21).[137] Kim develops that in the same manner that the murderous sinning Paul died when Christ met him on the Damascus road to become mystically Christ's new human in new covenant, so it is when anyone comes to faith in Christ. So the "old man" (ὁ παλαιὸς ἡμῶν ἄνθρωπος) is all we were prior to coming to Christ (Rom 6:6; Col 3:9).[138] So the death of the non-Christian self is accomplished by Christ as a person becomes in Christ (Rom 6:6 and Eph 4:22 are passive verbs; Col 3:9 middle). Likewise, the "body of sin" (τὸ σῶμα τῆς ἁμαρτίας) is a holistic description of the embodied life prior to Christ because in this context "body" (σῶμα) is used holistically (Rom 6:6, 12–13). Therefore, with the intended outcome of having "the body of sin done away" either means that we lose our flesh body when we resurrect in spiritual body (Rom 6:6; 7:24–25; 8:23; 1 Cor 15:42–44) or that within a person's embodiment she would progressively be utilizing her members as instruments *for worship and allegiance*[139] to God instead of as weapons[140] of idolatrous allegiance to sin (Rom 6:12–13). This new beginning in Christ makes an individual a "new creation" in which these old allegiances have passed away and new empowerment and allegiances have begun (1 Cor 5:17; Gal 5:17 καινὴ κτίσις). This new beginning ushers the Christian into a continuing ministry of peace and reconciliation. A similar idea for this growth is evident in Ephesians 4:22–24, replacing (Eph 4:24 infinitive) the removed (Eph 4:22 passive) old human clothes with the clothes of the new human as we reflect God's qualities of righteousness, holiness, and truth to fund a virtue epistemology.[141] It is possible that this human transformation

---

136. Paul provides no explanation for how the baptism mystically transforms the Christian as is provided in Valentinian Christianity by the Spirit transforming baptismal water to then transform the initiate by removing evil from her (*Exc. Theod.* 81.2; 82.2; also *Gos. Phil.* 59.19; 68.22–69.8; 74.18–21) but Paul ties the mystical transformation to that which is accomplished in Christ's death (similar to Gregory Nazianzen, *In Defense of His Flight to Pontus* 1.3–4 and *Second Oration on Easter* 24).

137. Kim, *The Origin of Paul's Gospel*.

138. Though the Augustinian-Dispensationalist Christian life tradition takes this concept as a sin nature, which is part of a person. No other Christian life tradition joins them in this and the context does not support their view. It is better to see this exchange of the old-self as a re-generational idea like Paul losing his old-self on the Damascus road.

139. The word "present" (παραστῆσαι) indicates loyalty and worship (Rom 6:13, 19; 12:1).

140. The word ὅπλα can mean helpful "instruments" or threatening "weapons" (Rom 6:13; 13:12; 2 Cor 10:4).

141. Wood, *Epistemology*; Roberts and Wood, *Intellectual Virtues*.

includes an already aspect of embodied worship and allegiance to God in a transformed lifestyle while there is a not yet reality of her resurrected spirit body, with previous character traits progressively being removed. So this death with Christ ceases the previous way of life so that the new way of life may be thought through and lived by faith in Christ (2 Cor 5:17; Gal 2:20).[142] Being a new human means thinking through and choosing to not sin and nor to allow death to reign as master in our lives, as we had done before we came to Christ (Rom 6:6, 9–20 contrast with 5:14, 17, 21).

Such a new human (in the new covenant) is Spiritually created with a new mindset[143] to choose to renew one's mind[144] and to live in righteousness (Eph 4:17–24; Rom 6:9–14; 12:2; Col 3:10–11). The choices made as a new human in Christ should be appropriate, that of righteous deeds (Rom 6:13, 16, 18–19). Second, in Romans 6, we should not do acts of sin because such behavior shames us and leads away from the truth to damnation (in a two ways salvation within this context: "the wages of sin is death" Rom 6:23). That is, sin comes to maturity (τέλος) in a person earning her death (Rom 6:21). Or focusing on the narrow way, we are heading for everlasting life, so we should choose consistent righteous behavior that leads and matures (τέλος, Rom 6:22) unto that goal of everlasting life (Rom 6:15–23). This discussion is developed by alluding to slavery terminology that described the old person entangled with impurity and lawlessness (Rom 6:19). However, to be freed from this previous enslavement is redemption from this slavery (Rom 6:18–20).[145] Paul explains the Christian thought and choices through the lens of everyday implications of redemption. In this narrow way, righteousness should grow and deepen, through a habituated commitment developing more consistency (Rom 6:11, 16, 19, 22). The lifestyle impact is that of (Christ mystically [Rom 6:4–8] along with our choices [Rom 6:11–22]) setting a person apart more and more like Christ as we head toward everlasting life, a gift of God (Rom 6:22–23). The fact of Christ mystically transforming us (Rom 6:4–8) serves

---

142. Paul values that faith is demonstrated by consistent deeds (Eph 2:10; Col 3:10–11; Westphal, "Taking St. Paul Seriously," In *Christian Philosophy*. ed. Flint, 201), similar to Judaism (Deut 6:4–9) and Stoicism (Seneca, *Ep.* 20.1).

143. A similar mindset and lifestyle presented in Jewish texts in contrast to that of Gentiles (Wis 12–15; 1QS 3–4). Ricoeur describes how God mystically transforms Christ's mind onto the Pauline concept of conscience so that which is identified with Enlightenment interiority is revelationally from God and thus neither from Plato's unifying forms, nor autonomous (as through Kant or Heidegger; *Figuring the Sacred*, 267–75; Ford, "Paul Ricoeur," In *Jesus and Philosophy*. ed. Moser, 188–9).

144. Bond, "Renewing the Mind," *TynB* 58:2(Jan, 2007): 317–20; Scott, *Paul's Way of Knowing*, 119–41.

145. Morris, "Redemption," In *Dictionary of Paul and His Letters*. ed. Hawthorne, et al., 785.

as the basis upon which the reflective commitment (λογίζεσθε) is made to corral one's life to be dead to sin and alive to God in Christ (Rom 6:11). Such a commitment ushers in the implication of not allowing sin to reign within one's own mortal body (Rom 6:12).

In the midst of the struggle for consistent Christian living, the Spirit becomes the guarantor of growth, indwelling the Christian. This indwelling and empowerment is reminiscent of early Judaism's new covenant transformation as empowered by God's Spirit prompting Israel to obey the Mosaic covenant (Ezek 34:25 with 36:26-27; Joel 2:28-29; Jer 31:33).[146] While the Spirit identifies that the Christian is in the new covenant, such a ministry of the Spirit also fulfills the essential obligation of the Mosaic covenant as well, which retains Paul's Pharisaic concern for authority but not by letter, rather in a new covenant internalism of transformed conscience for the major virtues of *torah* (Rom 8:4; 13:9; Gal 5:22-23).[147]

The non-Christian[148] is recognizable as the person who thinks and acts according to the things of the flesh including prideful hostility to God and

---

146. *1 En.* 61.7; *Jub.* 6.17; *Charter of a Jewish Sectarian Association* (1QS; 4Q255-264a; 5Q11) 3.7, 15-4.1; 4.5, 18-23; 1QpHab col. 11.13; *The War Scroll* (1QM, 4Q491-496) 1.1-20; 16.11; 1QH 4, 5, 18; 4Q548 frag. 1 col. 2 9-16; 11Q13 22-25; VanderKam, "Covenant," *Encyclopedia of the Dead Sea Scrolls.* ed. Schiffman and VanderKam, 1:152; Thomas Blanton, "Spirit and Covenant Renewal," *JBL* 129(2010): 137.

147. *Jos. Asen.* 8.9; 19.11.

148. The contrast of flesh and Spirit in Romans 8 is taken by advocates of Keswick and Augustinian-Dispensational Christian life teachings to be that of the carnal and spiritual Christian. Whereas, the contrast of flesh and Spirit in Romans 8 is taken by advocates of Reformed, Two Ways, and Lutheran Christian life teachings to be that of a non-Christian and vital Christian. A decision between these views is best weighed by considering the descriptions of the affect from the Spirit's enablement. Because Paul provides encouragement of the assurance of salvation in contrast to being a better Christian, it is better to take this text as a contrast between non-Christian and Christian (Rom 8:9-10, 15-17). By listing the flesh and Spirit descriptions one can notice that the flesh has death as the mindset and outcome of flesh existence (Rom 8:6, 13) while life is: the mindset, spiritual condition at present and ultimate resurrection description of life according to the Spirit (Rom 8:6, 10-11, 13). Such a contrast better fits that of non-Christian and Christian. Additionally, Paul is convinced that the Christians to whom he writes are not in the flesh, probably best taken as the realm of the flesh (Rom 8:9). Paul is inclined to grant that his audience has the Spirit indwelling them, which evidences that they belong to Christ (Rom 8:9, 11). This assurance of belonging to Christ better fits an assurance context, contrasting Christian and non-Christian. Additionally, the Spirit's testimony that we are adopted as sons, that we are children of God, that we are fellow heirs with Christ all better describe the assurance a Christian should have in contrast to non-Christians (Rom 8:15-17) rather than spiritual and carnal Christian live styles.

the Mosaic Law (Rom 8:5–8).[149] The Law became "sick" or "weak"[150] because of the non-Christian's flesh (Rom 8:3; 7:5–6, 14–24). The deeds of the flesh are evident as immorality, idolatry and fragmenting of any community (Gal 5: 19–21). All people have spent some time in this non-Christian flesh life, since "all have sinned and fallen short of the glory of God" (Rom 3:23). Any person who habitually practices such deeds will not inherit the kingdom of God, which in Paul's thought identifies such a person as neither belonging to Christ but excluded from God's family and nor inheriting with Christ (Gal 5:16–21; Rom 8:7, 9, 15, 17; 1 Cor 6:9–10). Merold Westphal argues that such deeds of the flesh are epistemic vices, especially prideful hubris, which would have a "distorting role in human belief formation and retention, personal and corporate."[151]

In contrast, the Christian is one who is broadly characterized by the Spirit such that his life and mind reflect the Spirit's concerns. This process is begun by Christ mystically connecting His embodiment (Rom 8:3, "in the likeness[152] of sinful flesh") to our own (Rom 7:25, "sinful flesh"), so that our outcome might have Christ condemning sin in our flesh by Christians living the Law through the Spirit (Rom 8:3–4; 2 Cor 6:11; Gal 5:22–23; Phil 1:11).[153] Such a life lived through the agency of the Spirit bears the fruit of the Spirit permeating the believer's life aligning the believer with kingdom, namely: love, joy, peace, patience, kindness, goodness, faithfulness, gentleness and self-control (Gal 5:22–23; Rom 14:17).[154]

---

149. Gooch identifies that Paul targets such "epistemological hubris" and clarifies Paul is not a fideist in this move ("Paul, the Mind of Christ, and Philosophy," In *Jesus and Philosophy*. ed. Moser, 96–8; contra Tertullian, *Praescr.* 7 and Popkin, "Fideism," In *The Encyclopedia of Philosophy*. ed. Edwards, 3:201).

150. The verb "it became weak or sick" is an expression of someone ill (John 11:1; Xenophon, *Anab.* 1.1.1; 6.2.19).

151. Westphal, "Taking St. Paul Seriously," In *Christian Philosophy*. ed. Flint, 203.

152. Paul uses this term ὁμοιώματι for similarity (Rom 1:23; 5:14; 6:5; 8:3) rather than identity as Barth proposed (*Romans*, 90).

153. Such compliance to the Law is expected from second Temple Spirit empowerment (*Jub.* 6.17; *Charter of a Jewish Sectarian Association* [1QS; 4Q255–264a; 5Q11] 3.15–4.1; 4.5, 18–23; 1QpHab col. 11.13; *The War Scroll* [1QM, 4Q491–496] 1.1–20; 16.11; 1QH 4, 5, 18; 4Q548 frag. 1 col. 2 9–16; 11Q13 22–25; VanderKam, "Covenant," In *Encyclopedia of the Dead Sea Scrolls*. ed. Schiffman and VanderKam,1:151–5; Blanton, "Spirit and Covenant Renewal," *JBL* 129[2010]: 137–8); this position is affirmed by the *Reformed Episcopal Articles of Religion 1875*, Article XII "Of the Justification of Man" in *Creeds of Christendom*. ed. Schaff, 3:818.

154. There is no need to multiply the fruit of the Spirit in this text to that of twelve fruit as is done in the Latin *Vulgate* Gal 5:23 by adding faith and modesty before, and chastity after the fruit of self-control.

This fruit of the Spirit become epistemic virtues which facilitate divine aid in knowing and living rightly. *Love in choosing to benefit another orients the person to a communal knowledge and practice for the common good* (Gal 5:22; 1 Cor 13:1-8). Oriented to the other facilitates the Spirit to prompt an affect change to *rejoice with the truth, the other, and to hope in kingdom* (Gal 5:22; Rom 15:13; 1 Cor 13:6; 2 Cor 1:24; Phil 1:4). The depth of this epistemic virtue in *being other-orientated in a communal manner aids the Spirit to facilitate reconciliation and peace with God and others*, especially the household of faith (Gal 2:22; Rom 5:1-10; 14:17; 2 Cor 5:18-20; 2 Tim 2:22). Such Spirit wrought disciplines facilitate the epistemic virtue of patience (Gal 5:22). Such *patience looks for and waits for character transformation in one's own and others' lives* (Rom 5:4; 1 Cor 13:4; 2 Cor 1:6; Eph 4:2; 1 Thess 5:14). Such *Spirit prompting persevering disciplines facilitate the epistemic virtues of goodness and generosity in working for the benefit of the other* (Gal 5:22; 6:9-10; 1 Cor 10:24; 2 Cor 9:8). As one benefits others, *one should be epistemically sensitively kind and gentle to the other*, not forcing ourselves upon them but allowing the Spirit to facilitate receptivity and growth (Gal 5:22-23; 1 Cor 13:4; Eph 4:32; Phil 4:5; 2 Tim 2:24; Titus 3:2). Such epistemic virtues facilitate *a Spirit fostered epistemic consistency of thought and practice over time which continues faithfully in Christ's narrow way* (Gal 5:22; 1 Cor 4:2, 17). Such epistemic virtues facilitate *a Spirit prompted epistemic commitment to control oneself within these morally appropriate bounds*, further prompting oneself and others to think and live within these epistemic virtues (Gal 5:23; Titus 1:8; 2:2, 5-6, 12). Robert Adams and William Wainwright describe that in this virtue epistemology, God is the ground and basis for these Spirit produced virtues, so that the Christian will love his neighbor as himself.[155]

Notice that such a Spirit fruitful life condemns sin in our flesh by bringing about the outcome of having the requirement of the Law fulfilled *in us* (Rom 8:4 ἵνα τὸ δικαίωμα τοῦ νόμου πληρωθῇ ἐν ἡμῖν; Gal 5:23). For example, Spirit fruited love (for God and one's fellow human) fulfills the Law (Rom 8:4; 13:9; Gal 5:22-23; Deut 6:4-5; Lev 19:18, 34; Matt 22:39-40; Mark 12:32-34; Luke 10:26-27).[156] The result is that the indwelling Spirit

155. Adams, "The Problem of Total Devotion," In *Rationality, Religious Belief, and Moral Commitment.* ed. Audi and Wainright, 94; Nygren, *Agape and Eros*, 216; Wainwright, "Obedience and Responsibility," In *The Wisdom of the Christian Faith.* ed. Moser and McFall, 68.

156. *T. Iss.* 5.2; *T. Dan.* 5.3; *Jub.* 36.3-8; Josephus, *Ag. Ap.* 2.206; Philo, *Spec.* 2.63; *Decal.* 20.154; 108-10; *Abr.* 208; *m. Sanh.* 10.1; Rabbi Akiba in *Sifra Lev.* 19:18; *Sifre* on Deut. 6:4; *b. Šabb.* 31a; *b. Ber.* 63a. Rabbi Akiba considered love of neighbor in Leviticus 19:18 to be also the great commandment (*Sifra Qed.* 4.200.3.7; *Sifra* on Lev. 19:18; *Gen. Rab.* 24.7; *Šabb.* 31A). Such love extends even to personal enemies and persecutors

transforms the thought and life of the Christian to encourage departing from fearful unrighteous condemning ways in death to embrace a mindset of Christ and Spirit with an intimate relationship of prayer reflective of her adoption as a child of God (Rom 8:8, 13–15; Phil 2:5; 3:19).[157] Foundational to this privilege, early Judaism also identified that those who obey the Law are righteous and called Sons of God, and thus heirs (usually of the Abrahamic promise, such as in Rom 4:13–14).[158] In the same manner, the Christian is seen as a new covenant person in the Spirit with a greater reality of new covenant benefits upon inheriting eschatological kingdom. So this Christian vindication by the Spirit fostered life transformation with an ultimate kingdom inheritance role. Such spiritual life accomplishes the same life transformation that a Jewish Law based assessment previously intended in Jewish covenant nomism. The judgment[159] removed in Romans 8:1 is thus likely a servitude to indwelling sin as a master and its fostered condemning fear and death lifestyle, rather than the imposition of forensic condemnation from a distant context. Mystically in the new covenant Christ, the Christian is set free from a condemning lifestyle dominated and characterized by the flesh, redeemed to the joyous privilege of living life in the Spirit by the agency of the indwelling Holy Spirit (Rom 8:1, 6, 15).

There is a difference of opinion on whether Romans 8:4 "requirement of the Law [which] might be fulfilled in us" is *obedience of Christ* resulting in Christian justification,[160] or the *obedience of the Christian* resulting in a lifestyle transformation fulfilling the virtues of the Law like the fruit of

---

(Rom 12:14, 17–20; 1 Cor 4:12–13; 1 Thess 5:15; 1 Pet 3:9; Acts 7:60; *Ep. Arist.* 207, 227, 232; Philo, *Virt.* 116–18; *T. Gad.* 6.1–7; *T. Zeb.* 7.2–4; *T. Iss.* 7.6; *T. Benj.* 4.2–3; *2 Bar.* 52.6; *2 En.* 50.3; *b. Ketub.* 68a; *m. 'Abot* 1.12; 2.11; 4.3; 5.16; Polycarp, *Ep.* 12.3; Irenaeus, *Haer.* 3.18.5; *Ps.-Clem. Hom.* 3.19; *Ep. Apost.* 18; *2 Clem.* 13.4; Justin, *1 Apol.* 14.3; Athenagoras, *Supp.* 12.3.

157. The revelatory contribution to elevate the Christian through partial knowledge is provided by the Holy Spirit (Gooch, *Partial Knowledge*, 29–37, 46–51; "Paul, the Mind of Christ, and Philosophy," In *Jesus and Philosophy*. ed. Moser, 95; Healy, "Knowledge of the Mystery" and Rae, "'Incline Your Ear so that You may Live," In *The Bible and Epistemology*. ed. Healy and Parry,135–49 and 175–7.

158. Sir 4.10; *Ps. Sol.* 17.26–27; *Jub.* 1.24–25; Wis 16.10; *As. Mos.* 10.3.

159. This word κατάκριμα is used of legal servitude as a consequence of conviction of a crime such as non-payment of taxes (Danker, "Under Contract: A Form-Critical Study of Linguistic Adaptation in Romans," in *Festchrift to Honor F. Wilbur Gingrich.* ed. Barth and Concroft, 105; Kruse, "Kantakkrima-Strafzahlung oder Steuer?" *Zeitschrift für Papyrologie und Epigraphik*, 124[1999]: 166–90; Deismann, *Bible Studies*, 164–5; Bruce, *Romans*, 159; Halicarnassus, *Antiq. rom.* 13.5.1 cited by Moulton and Milligan, *The Vocabulary of the Greek Testament*, 327 from *Corpus Papyrorum Raineri* 1.15–16).

160. Calvin, *Romans*, 283; Jacomb, *Sermons on the Eighth Chapter to the Epistle to the Romans (Verses 1–4)*, 347–8; Hodge, *Romans*; Moo, *Romans*, 481–84.

the Spirit,[161] or a hybrid of both.[162] The last two options could be described as a vindicating Spirit transformation or a living justification, a concept that Jonathan Edwards frames as a Lockean empiricism extended into a sixth sense for the spiritual life.[163] The focus of νῦν and νυνὶ in the context is "now" within the Christian's life as opposed to initial salvation, so my preference is for lifestyle transformation which is emphasized in the context (Rom 6:19, 21, 7:6; 17; 8:1, 18). For example, in Paul the term "walking" (περιπατοῦσιν) indicates ethical behavior in the Christian life (Rom 8:4; Gal 5:16).[164] That is, not momentary commitments but long term virtues of being a person reflective of the Spirit's qualities rather than flesh traits. In light of these Pauline virtues, the Law is fulfilled through the fruit of the Spirit, and especially through deeds of love (Rom 13:8, 10; Gal 5:13-14, 23).[165] Jewish fulfillment of the Law did not require perfection but repentance and availing oneself of the means of recovery available within the covenant.[166] The sphere within which fulfillment is obtained is "in us" as we become broadly characterized by the Spirit (Rom 8:4-5). As such, in Romans 8:2, "The Law of the Spirit of life in Christ Jesus" is the Spirit's transformative life empowerment of

---

161. Augustine, *Spir. et litt.*, 26-29 and especially 46; Luther, *Romans*, In *Works*, 25:243-44; *Deuteronomy*, In *Works*, 9:179; Melancthon, *Loci communes von 1521*. *Melancthons Werke 2.1.* ed. Engelland, 123; Oecolampadius, *In Hieremiam prophetam commentariorum libri tres Ioannis Oecolampadii*, 2.162a; *The Thirty Nine Articles of the Church of England (1571)*, article 7; Augustine, Ambroisiater, and Pelagius held this Christian life view (Bray, *Romans*, 205-6); Godet, *Romans*, 302; Murray, *Romans*, 283; Cranfield, *Romans*, 383-4; Keck, "The Law and 'the Law of Sin and Death' (Rom 8:1-4)," In *The Divine Helmsman*. ed. Crenshaw and Sandmel, 52-53; Sanders, *Paul, the Law, and the Jewish People*, 93-4; Räisänen, *Paul and the Law*, 65-67; Hübner, *The Law in Paul's Thought*, 146-7; Schnabel, *Law and Wisdom from Ben Sira to Paul*, 288-90; Dunn, *Romans 1-8*, 423-24; Wright, *The Climax of the Covenant*, 212; Stuhlmacher, *Romans*, 120; Schreiner, *The Law and Its Fulfillment*, 71-73; *Romans*, 404-8; Thielman, *Paul & the Law*, 242-43; Dabney, "'Justified by the Spirit,'" *International Journal of Systematic Theology* 3:1(Mar. 2001): 50; Seifrid, *Christ, Our Righteousness*; Das, *Paul, the Law and the Covenant*, 226; McFadden, "The Fulfillment of the Law's DIKAIŌMA," *JETS* 52(2009): 483-97.

162. Melanchthon, *Romans*, on 8:4a; Henry, *Matthew Henry's Commentary*, 2211; Lloyd-Jones, *Romans*, 337-42.

163. Edwards, *Religious Affections; Freedom of the Will*, 4:1, 337-42; YE6:342-3; *Miscellanies*, number 267; Jenson, *America's Theologian*, 30.

164. Rom 6:4; 13:13; 14:15; 1 Cor 3:3; 2 Cor 4:2; Gal 5:16; Eph 2:2, 10;4:1, 17; 5:2, 8, 15; Phil 3:17-18; Col 1:10; 2:6; 3:7; 1 Thess 2:11; 4:1, 12; 2 Thess 3:6, 11; Schreiner, *The Law & Its Fulfillment*, 151.

165. McFadden, "The Fulfillment of the Law's DIKAIŌMA," *JETS* 52(2009): 489-97; Scott, *Paul's Way of Knowing*, 59.

166. Sanders, *Paul and Palestinian Judaism*, 137, 183; Kennard, "Instances of Covenant Nomism in Second Temple Judaism," In *Biblical Covenantalism*, 2:90-135.

the person in Christ to be characterized by Law virtues, such as love and righteousness (Rom 7:6; 8:2, 4; Gal 5:18, 23).

The Spirit guarantees such intimate growth and virtue epistemology so as to foster thoughts and habits of: life, peace, belonging to Christ, righteousness, resurrection of the body, intimacy in prayer and fellow inheritor with Christ (Rom 8:6, 9–11, 13–17). Such a mindset reflects the revealed mind of God, the character of the Spirit who reveals it, and the mind of Christ, such that one would be called spiritual (1 Cor 2:10–12, 15–16).[167] This mystical relationship continues to reveal, prompt, and transform the believer throughout her life. Such a spiritual mindset provides perspective through which the believer can appraise all things and acknowledge that in everything Jesus is Lord (1 Cor 2:15; 12:3).

This is a lifestyle free from condemnation from the Mosaic Law for in Christ the inner man empowered by the Spirit is free from the peripheralized Mosaic Law related to the flesh (Rom 8:1–2). Therefore, in the way life is lived by the inner-working Spirit, the Mosaic Law-of-the-mind does not condemn. The Mosaic Law was rendered impotent to accomplish its tasks as an external standard in light of the weakness of one's flesh (Rom 7:6; 8:3). However, Jesus' condemning of sin in his human flesh made possible this Spirit transforming of a Christian life so that the righteousness of the Mosaic Law is fulfilled in the Christian Spirit-produced life (Rom 8:2, 4). Instead of using the Jewish metaphor of "walk by God's Law" (Exod 16:4; Lev 18:4; 1 Kgs 6:12; Prov 20:7; Jer 44:23; Ezek 5:6–7),[168] Paul replaces it with "walk by the Spirit" (Rom 8:4; Gal 5:16, 25). Therefore, the Spirit guarantees that the Christian who appropriately has assurance of his belonging to Christ will be living a righteous life as defined by Mosaic Law virtues. This new mind reflects the virtues and fruit of the Spirit to prompt ethical insight and incline one's will to live in a manner that shows the Spirit's character.[169] This life that puts to death the deeds of the body will live (Rom 8:13; similar to Deut 30:15–20). Such a life is the beginning of resurrected life fostered by the Spirit as guarantor of eschatological redemption (Rom 8:6, 11, 23; Eph 1:13–14). So the Spirit is the means by which the righteous may hope in the eschatological justification (Gal 5:5). Such a righteous person as a Christian produces abiding righteousness (namely good deeds) that meets real needs (2 Cor 9:9–10). Such abiding righteousness will still have its affect when it comes to the eschatological judgment.

167. Healy, "Knowledge of the Mystery" and Rae, "'Incline Your Ear so that You may Live,'" In *The Bible and Epistemology*. ed. Healy and Parry,135–49 and 175–7; Scott, *Paul's Way of Knowing*, 256.

168. *T. Ash.* 6.13; 2 Macc 6.23; 1QS 3.18–4.26; *halak* 3.

169. Scroggs, "New Being: Renewed Mind," *The Chicago Theological Seminary Register* 72:1(1982): 1–12.

Coupled with this mysticism with Spirit is also the fact that Christ is mystically present in the believer as well (Rom 8:10; Eph 3:16-17; Col 1:27).[170] Such an internal relationship with Christ is completely transformative. With Christ now living in the believer, the life that the believer lives reflects faith and transformation parallel to that which the Holy Spirit performs, thus provoking the believer to hope and love in Christ (Gal 2:20). Paul's and the Church's purpose is to form Christ within the community of faith, so as to reflect Christ's character through believers (Gal 4:19; Eph 4:15-16; Phil 2:5).

Normand Bonneau argues that rhetoric and logic help but do not provide the empowerment that Jesus' crucifixion and resurrection provide to bring the new community into Christ and the Spirit.[171] He recognizes that James Dunn places the Law's curse within Paul's basic belief of the way the Law binds Deuteronomic curse on any Jewish person disobeying the Law within the Law program.[172] However, Bonneau also sees that the Gentile inclusion creates circumstances from Galatians 2 and the Antioch context that show Paul addressed a new community in Christ and Spirit.[173]

Exploring other epistemic tools available to Paul, Russell Sisson argued that in 1 Cor 9 rhetoric, Paul uses abduction because he infers a conclusion for edification from a related issue of his apostleship.[174] The primary argument is for edifying the other in a context where meat sacrificed to an idol is available. Chapter nine contributes with rhetoric loosely parallel to that of Cicero[175] in which: 1) *Thesis* and a *rationale* are provided by two rhetorical questions each (1 Cor 9:1). 2) An *argument from the contrary* becomes an argument for Paul's apostleship (1 Cor 9:3-18). 3) Paul's self-control within freedom becomes an *argument from example* to imitate (1 Cor 9:19-23).[176]

---

170. Wright, *Paul and the Faithfulness of God*, 858-9.

171. Bonneau, "The Logic of Paul's Argument on the Curse of the Law in Galatians 3:10-14," *Nov Test* 39(1997): 78; Litfin develops Paul's claim in 1 Cor 2:1-5 to not be dependent upon rhetoric (*St. Paul's Theology of Proclamation*) and Winter agrees (*Philo and Paul among the Sophists*, 147-48).

172. Dunn, "Works of the Law and the Curse of the Law (Galatians 3:10-14)," *NTS* 31(1983): 523-42.

173. Bonneau, "The Logic of Paul's Argument on the Curse of the Law in Galatians 3:10-14," *NovT* 39(1997): 80.

174. Sisson, "Abductive Logic and Rhetorical Structure in 1 Corinthians 9," *Proceedings* 26(2006): 93, 97-8; Abduction was floated from C. S. Peirce's concept of "guessing," cf. "On the Logic of Drawing History from Ancient Documents Especially from Testimonials," and "A Letter to F. A. Woods," In *Collected Papers*, v 7, paragraph 219, and v 8, paragraphs 385-8.

175. Cicero, *Rhet. ad Her.* 2.18.18.

176. Similar practice and consistency contributed to rhetoric in public philosophy: Aristotle, *Rhet.* 1.2.4; 2.1.5; Plutarch, *Cat. Maj.* 3.4; Cicero, *Off.* 2.13-46; Pliny, *Ep.* 6.11;

4) This is followed by an *argument from analogy* of athletic self-control available and contextually contributing to edify others (1 Cor 9:24-27).[177]

Additionally, Paul follows the pattern of Passover in maintaining a Eucharistic role for performative speech and practice that simultaneously remembers and proclaims the Lord's death until He comes (1 Cor 11:23-26).[178] Such a performative pattern etches the knowledge of truth of Christ's atonement and second coming into the Christian worldview.

Paul does not consider that he has arrived, since he only knows in part before Christ returns and brings him into the kingdom (1 Cor 8:2; 13:9; Phil 3:13). So on the basis of basic belief in Christ warranted by *torah*, Christ's statements, and the mystical experience with the Trinitarian God, Paul hopes for being like Christ in kingdom, including knowing as he has been known (Rom 5:2-5; 8:20; 12:12; 15:4, 13; 1 Cor 13:11-13; Col 1:5; 1 Thess 1:3; 5:8; Titus 1:2). Through this process there is an exchange of the soulish body for a continuity of a resurrected spiritual immortal body (1 Cor 15:35-50). With this exchange we give up childish partial indirect knowledge for a greater knowledge as Christ has known us intimately (1 Cor 13:9-12).[179] However, this does not elevate humans to omniscience but brings believers into face to face communion with God with no intervening agents, which is partly why such hoped for intimacy with God identifies that the greatest virtue is love (1 Cor 13:12-13).[180]

8.14.4-6, 23; Seneca, *Ep.* 6.5; Quintilian, *Inst. Orat.* 3.8.13; Fiore, "Paul, Exemplification, and Imitation," In *Paul in the Greco-Roman World.* ed. Sampley, 228-57.

177. Morissette, "La condition de ressuscité, 1 Cor 15, 35-49," *Bib* 53(1972): 208-28; Bonneau, "The Logic of Paul's Argument on the Resurrection Body in 1 Cor 15:35-44a," *Science et Esprit* 45:1(1993): 79-92 concurs with this analysis; There are many such analogical arguments in Paul including: Rom 7:2-3; 9:21-23; 11:16-24; 1 Cor 3:5-17; 9:25-27; 12:14-27; 14:7-8; 2 Cor 2:14-17; 3:1-3; 5:1-6; Gal 3:13-18; 4:1-2; 6:7-9; 1 Thess 5:2-8; a common form of argument, Lloyd, *Polarity and Analogy*; Dawes, "But if you can Gain your Freedom," *CBQ* 52(1990): 686 n 20, and Bonneau, 79; e.g., analogies in ancient philosophical argument: Plato, *Tim.* 30b; *Phileb.* 29b; Aristotle, *Mot. an.* 703a; *Pol.* 1295a; *Eth. nic.* 1113a; analogies in rabbinic argument: *m. 'Abot* 5.4; *y. Hor.* 3.5 (48c); Neusner, *Handbook of Rabbinic Theology*, 29, 43-4, 88-103.

178. Barton, "Memory and Remembrance in Paul," In *Memory in the Bible and Antiquity.* ed. Barton, Stuckenbruck and Wold, 333-4; Austin, *How to do Things with Words.*

179. Gooch, *Partial Knowledge*, 146-7; Martley ("The Mirror and 1 Cor 13:12 in the Epistemology of Clement of Alexandria," *VC* 30(1976): 109, 113) proposed that Paul was reflecting Neoplatonism similar to Clement of Alexandria ("seeing in a mirror dimly") and searching for a vision ("face to face") to rectify his lack of knowledge but this is unlikely because Paul celebrates deep knowing through Holy Spirit revelation (1 Cor 2) and the mystical experience in Christ (Rom 6), and admits to limited lack of knowledge through vision (2 Cor 12:2-7).

180. Thiselton, *The First Epistle to the Corinthians*, 1070-1.

6

Johannine Empirical Epistemology with Revelation and Early Jewish Perspectivalism

THESIS: JESUS CHRIST IS the Father's sent agent in His humanity to know, to say and to do what the Father has for Him. The disciples know the Father through the Son. As Jesus ascends, He leaves the Holy Spirit to reveal to the apostles what they need to know including reminders of what Jesus had said and predictions for the future as well. These reminded witnesses also are reassured by empirical evidence and their memory of the empirical evidence that they remember from when they were with Jesus. Much of the perspective that John reflects in this inspired empirical presentation of Jesus reflects a perspectivalism that is also apparent in early Judaism, especially strongly instanced by Qumran documents *Charter of a Jewish Sectarian Association* (1QS, 4Q255–264a, 5Q11).

John's gospel is designated to be from the "beloved disciple," John, one of the inner three disciples (John 21:23–24; also 1 John 1:1–2). A more extensive record of the gospel authors is provided by the patristic testimony which recognized that John wrote his gospel and his letters in the Ephesus region for those to whom he ministered.[1] So as before with the synoptic gospels the author is not anonymous but known by his earliest readers.

Howard Clark Kee identified that in the Gospel of John there are four modes of knowing.

> Recognition of the true identity of a person; 2) knowing God, which includes mystical participation in the divine life; 3) knowing or understanding the truth; 4) making the truth known to those within the community of faith.[2]

---

1. Irenaeus, *Ag. Her.* 3.1.2; Eusebius, *Ecc. Hist.* 5.20.6; Bauckham, *Jesus and the Eyewitnesses*, 300–5.

2. Kee, "Knowing the Truth," In *Neotestamentica et Philonica*. ed. Aune, Seland,

This expression of knowing in the Gospel of John addressed and explained an answer to Pilate's skeptical question, "What is truth?" (John 18:38). The link between truth and knowledge is set out in John 8:32, "You shall know the truth and the truth will make you free." In response to this text, Stanley Porter clarified that "the Jews confine their question regarding their descent and slavery simply to the earthly realm, rather than recognizing that the liberation or freedom that Jesus is speaking of would free them from slavery to sin, so that they too could be in true and free relation with God."[3] The essential truthful revelation is that Jesus is God "I Am" to reveal the Father to His disciples (John 1:1, 18; 8:54-55, 58). The repeated problem that Pilate or Jews present to Jesus' truthful testimony is that they do not believe Him (John 8:59; 18:38). However, Porter identified that beneath this relationship, John presents propositional truths in "incontrovertible assertions."[4] Such propositional statements are grounded in empiricism and expressed through testimony. Propositional divine revelation is coupled with this corporate experience because God's "word is truth" (John 17:17). Porter identified that this revelational statement is grounded in the nature of God as true and committed to communicating His revelatory word.[5] This truth of God's word is the means by which Jesus' disciples are made pure or sanctified. As D. A. Carson said, "No-one can be 'sanctified' or set apart for the Lord's use without learning to think God's thoughts after him, without learning to live in conformity with the 'word' he has graciously given."[6]

Additionally, Porter developed the relational aspect of this knowledge further in categories that would fit Paul Moser's filial relational knowledge, "the notion of truth is not strictly propositional but relational, that is, it is explicated through relational patterns among the Father, Son, and Spirit and by human beings in relation to them, especially Jesus."[7] Such knowledge is provided through the community experience of Jesus and then the Holy Spirit's authentic and life changing revelation of the Father.

While John joins the rest of the N. T. in communicating within community, the Gospel of John stands out in the N. T. as also emphasizing individualism.[8] This individualism is not that of modern Western indi-

---

and Ulrichsen, 255.

3. Porter, *John, His Gospel, and Jesus*, 191; Henningsson, "Faith, Obedience, Understanding and Liberation," *Swedish Missiological Themes* 88:2(2000): 182-83.

4. Porter, *John, His Gospel, and Jesus*, 192.

5. Porter, *John, His Gospel, and Jesus*, 193-94.

6. Carson, *John*, 566.

7. Porter, *John, His Gospel, and Jesus*, 191; Moser, *The Elusive God*, 46-7, 98, 113-123.

8. Moule, "The Individualism of the Fourth Gospel," *NovT* 5(1962): 171-90; *Essays*

vidualism which might float the possibility of autonomy in epistemology and logic but rather that an individual believer is in relationship to Christ among the community of believers. This individualism would mean that the idea of Paul Moser's filial relational knowledge operates both on a community and an individual level. Bauckham developed this individualism in terms of each individual as subjectively aware of himself "as distinct subjects of feeling, thinking, decision, and action."[9] Moule extended this individualism to 1 John and Bauckham to second and third John but to a lesser extent similar to Paul's admission of individualism.[10] The evidence of this individual relationship with Jesus presents itself in individual relationship, coherence, and dialog with individuals. For example, more than any other N. T. author John presents Jesus in extended conversations with individuals (Nathanel [John 1:47-51], Nicodemus [3:1-21], a Samaritan woman [4:7-26], Martha [11:20-27], Mary [11:32-33], Pilate [18:33-38], Mary Magdalene [20:14-17], Peter [21:15-22], and several shorter conversations similar to those in the synoptic gospels around healings). These conversations with individuals do not develop all aspects of the individual but they do accentuate the individual's role in choosing to believe in Jesus' claims and act on them. So John operates within ancient dramatic character development,[11] subsuming the development within the larger purposes of his Gospel presentation of Jesus. More than any other, Bauckham develops sixty seven aphoristic sayings in John about an individual's relationship with Jesus, identified by singular pronouns and participles "the one who," "if anyone," and "whoever."[12] For example, "The one who believes in the Son has everlasting life, but the one who refuses to believe in the Son will not see life, but the wrath of God abides on him" (John 3:36). Likewise, Jesus said "if anyone keeps My word, he will never see death" (John 8:51). These aphorisms emphasize the individual role for faith and cultivating relationship with Jesus. Within these contexts, the individual surfaces as a coherent individual referent throughout the narrative,[13] such as "Each branch in Me

---

in *New Testament Interpretation*, 91-109; "A Neglected Factor in the Interpretation of Johannine Eschatology," In *Studies in John*. ed. Rientsma, 155-60 where he extends the argument to 1 John; O'Grady, "Individualism and the Johannine Ecclesiology," *BTB* 5(1975): 235-45; Bauckham, *Gospel of Glory*, 1-19.

9. Bauckham, *Gospel of Glory*, 3.

10. Moule, "A Neglected Factor in the Interpretation of Johannine Eschatology," In *Studies in John*. ed. Rientsma, 155-60.

11. Bennema, "A Theory of Character in the Fourth Gospel with Reference to Ancient and Modern Literature," *BibInt* 17(2009): 375-421; *Encountering Jesus*.

12. Bauckham, *Gospel of Glory*, 6-7.

13. Bauckham, *Gospel of Glory*, 10-11.

that bears fruit, He prunes it, that it may bear more fruit" (John 15:2). So while community is still emphasized, in John the individual in relationship also has an emphasis, indicating that John's epistemology functions both on an individual and community level.

John appeals to things known by a corporate group broader than himself who were also eyewitnesses. Such an approach is a standard rhetorical technique to lend credibility for text claims.[14] John claims this corporate empirical knowing focuses on Jesus as the incarnating agent who fleshes out God as the embodiment of the truth.[15]

> What was from the beginning, what we have heard, what we have seen with our eyes, what we have looked at and touched with our hands, concerning the Word of Life and the life was manifested, and we have seen and testify and proclaim to you the everlasting life (1 John 1:1–2).

The empirical involvement of John and others with Jesus is strongly claimed for multiple senses of seeing, handling and hearing Jesus in His ministry.[16] This empirical experience with Jesus' life in their midst was the primary forum through which Jesus' revelation was known. The corporate experience these eyewitnesses had with Jesus' person and teaching funds their mutually confirming testimony with many of them still alive (like John) if the readers wished to pursue their credible witness further.[17] Such corporate memory provided the interface of history and theology in John.[18] Craig Keener concluded that John's theology is supported by its historicity.

Most scholars today concur that the Fourth Gospel includes both history and theology. Even many patristic interpreters, who often harmonized

---

14. Dionysius of Halicarnassus, *Ant. Rom.* 1.6.1; 7.43.2; Arrian, *Alex.* 6.2.4; Plutarch, *Alex.* 30.7; 31.2–3; Josephus, *Ag. Ap.* 1.50–52; 2.107.

15. Kee, "Knowing the Truth: Epistemology and Community in the Fourth Gospel," In *Neotestamentica et Philonica.* ed. Aune, Seland, and Ulrichsen, 256; Thatcher develops the most prolonged discussion of the corporate memory present within the Johannine material (*Why John Wrote a Gospel*).

16. Locke, *Concerning Human Understanding* 1.1.15; 2.11.8–9; 2.32.6; 3.3.6–8; "The Reasonableness of Christianity," In *Works*, vol. 6; pre-modern empiricism is apparent in Lactanius, *Workmanship of God* 9–10; Bauckham, "The Gospel of John and the Synoptic Problem," In *New Studies in the Synoptic Problem.* ed. P. Foster, et. al., 658–85.

17. Ricoeur, "The Hermeneutics of Testimony" cited in Ford, "Paul Ricoeur: A Biblical Philosopher on Jesus," In *Jesus and Philosophy*, 190.

18. Painter, "Memory Holds the Key," In *John, Jesus, and History, Volume 1: Critical Appraisal of Critical Views.* ed. Anderson, Just, and Thatcher, 1:229–48.

John with synoptics (hence apparently stressing history), recognized John as a 'spiritual' Gospel, emphasizing its interpretive aspects.[19]

Keener argued for this empirically grounded historical gospel as the Gospel develops its high Christology theologically.

John's stated purpose for writing the gospel is to communicate this empirically grounded testimony to foster faith by considering the miracles as confirmed empirical experience.[20]

> Many other signs therefore Jesus also performed in the presence of the disciples, which are not written in this book but these have been written that you may believe that Jesus is the Christ, the Son of God, and that believing you may have life in His name (John 20:30–31).

> This is the disciple who bears witness of these things, and wrote these things; and we know that his witness is true. And there are also many other things which Jesus did which if they were written in detail I suppose that even the world itself would not contain the books which were written (John 21:24–25).

Keener concludes that as in Judaism so also for John, knowledge of God is especially dependent upon divine self-revelation, especially evident in the miraculous signs (John 2:11).[21] John recognized that his Gospel was a select account but that he as an eyewitness had chosen a truthful account of the events and teaching in detail. The truthfulness of John's testimony depends upon the evidentially grounded revelation that John conveys.[22] The selection reflected John's agenda was communal knowledge of Jesus' miracles to prompt continuing growing faith in his readership. Likewise, in 1 John the corporate empirical experience that many had with Christ is selectively developed for the agenda of providing tests for everlasting life (1 John 1:1–2; 2:1, 12, 29; 5:13).[23] Whereas, the book of Revelation is presented

---

19. Keener, "We Beheld His Glory! (John 1:14)," In *John, Jesus, and History, Volume 2: Aspects of Historicity in the Fourth Gospel*. ed. Anderson, Just, and Thatcher, 2:15 and argued for 2:15–25; Appold, "Jesus' Bethesaida Disciples," In *John, Jesus, and History*, 2:27–34; this argument for historicity of John is also made by Tertulian in *Ag. Praxeas* 26 by comparing John with Matt and Luke.

20. Locke, *Concerning Human Understanding* 1.1.15; 2.11.8–9; 2.32.6; 3.3.6–8; "A Discourse of Miracles," In *Works*, 9:256–65; "The Reasonableness of Christianity," In *Works*, vol. 6; pre-modern empiricism is apparent in Lactanius, *Workmanship of God* 9–10; Keener, *Miracles*, 1:35–208.

21. Keener, *John*, 1:246.

22. Porter, *John, His Gospel, and Jesus*, 195.

23. Law, *The Tests of Life*.

as an individual testimony of what John saw and heard during his mystical travels through the heavens and earth (Rev 1:10, 12, 17, 19; 4:1, 10; 5:1, 5–6, 11–12; 6:1–12; 7:1, 9: 8:2; 9:1, 13; 10:5, 8; 12:1, 10; 13:1, 3, 11; 14:1–2, 6–7, 13–14; 15:1–2; 16:1, 5, 7, 13; 17:1, 6, 15, 18; 18:1; 19:1, 5–6, 9, 11, 17, 19; 20:1, 4, 11–12; 21:1, 3, 6, 15, 22: 22:1, 8). There is even one instance where John adds the sense of taste to the empirical senses as a sweet prophecy turns to a bitter taste of judgment in his mouth (Rev 10:10).

Jesus as the monotheistic God with the Father and Spirit is the true light who enlightens every man to God the Father (John 1:1–2, 9).[24] This enlightening goes beyond revealing the divine ability to create (John 1:3–4) and the divinely given Law, which came through Moses (John 1:17). The enlightening is a revelation of the true God Himself as expressed through the human embodiment that Jesus incarnation brings (John 1:14, 18). So not only is the divinity of the Son communicated in this incarnation but the reality of the divine Father is also communicated in the life and teaching of the Son. In this Jewish manner, Jesus is a revelatory Word message that also is involved in creation and penetrates the darkened sinful condition of humans with truth and generosity (John 1:1–5, 17).[25] However, such a divine

---

24. Kennard, *Messiah Jesus*, 471–83, 500–502.

25. The *personal* nature of John's λόγος actively involved with an *initial Jewish creation* of everything in a *linear history unto kingdom* which *revelationarily explains* God (John 1:3–4 8, 14, 18; 3:3, 5, 19–21; this author agrees with Dunn who rejects all of the subsequent options including limited Hebraic wisdom parallel for revelatory word of God [*Christology in the Making*, 215–30]; Pss 33:6; 107:20; 147:15, 18; Isa 9:8; 55:10–11; 55:10–11; Wisd 18.14–16 incarnated *torah* for exodus; *1 En.* 14.24; 15.1; *Song Rab.* 1.2.2; 5.16.3; *b. Ḥag.* 14a; Justin, *Dial.* 130; Ignatius, *Magn.* 8.2; *Ep. Diogn.* 7.2; Tatian 5; Keener, *John*, 1:354–63 affirms this view as a personification of a new *torah*). Thus this view includes but extends beyond an early Judaism personification of wisdom (John 1:2–3 contrary to a proposed parallel to personified metaphor lady wisdom which passively accompanies God in creation: Prov 1:20–32; 8:27–30; Job 28:25–27; Sir 1.1–19; 24.1–11). Thus, the Johannine *logos* is: neither a Platonic realm of forms (Plato, *Resp.* 6.509–11 cave diagram of forms where elements are explained in *Theaet.* 199–202 with λόγος as absolute existence: *Theaet.* 157, 182; structuring knowledge to make sense of sensation: *Theaet.* 168, 182, 204; Philo, second god: *QG* 2.62; *Her.* 119; *Agr.* 51; *Conf.* 146; *Cher.* 36; in beginning: *Virt.* 62; with god: *Ebr.* 30; *Leg.* 2.49; *Cher.* 48–50; *Fug.* 50; realm of forms: *Opif.* 31; *Post.* 69; *Migr.* 52; intermediary between God and humans: *Her.* 2–5, 119; *QG* 2.13, 94; *Deus* 138; *Sacr.* 119), nor Heraclitus' amorphous determinism driving the ever-changing world (Diels, *Die Fragmente der Vorsokratiker*, 1:67–113; Barnes, *The Presocratic Philosophers*, 57–60 funding stoicism: Diogenes Laertius 9.1.1), nor a stoic synonym for the immanent non-personal divine fire (Cleanthes, *Hymn to Zeus*, line 21; *Orphic Hymns* 64; Sandbach, *The Stoics*, 74; Long, *Hellenistic Philosophy*, 145–46), nor an esoteric knowledge only known through gnostic mysticism (Bultmann, "The History of Religions Background of the Prologue to the Gospel of John," In *The Interpretation of John*. ed. Ashton, 27–46; *John*, 14–18; Robinson, "The Johannine Trajectory," In *Trajectories Through Early Christianity*. ed. Robinson and Koester,

light of Christ penetrating the darkness of human ignorance and sin obtains a mixed response with many not comprehending it (John 1:5, 10). John the Baptist pointed to Who this True Light was so that people might understand (John 1:6-8, 19-37). Any who received Jesus as the True Light generously realized the truth of becoming relationally children of God (John 1:12-13, 17). Therefore, Jesus' truth is intimately intertwined with His person and filial relationship He established with the family related to God.[26]

As author, John retains eyewitness interactivity in conversations through the gospel which Jesus had with individuals and groups (John 3-13; 18; 21). Additionally, John focused on Jesus' Judean ministry in contrast to the synoptic focus on the Galilean ministry. Furthermore, John has a realized eschatology (of present everlasting life) in a mystical relationship with the divine persons very different from the synoptic presentation (of the eschatological Kingdom as coming in the context of the Messiah).

Knowing God and Christ is apparent in a person's life by the moral obedience observed by others empirically as in a Jewish setting.[27] One knows that one knows God and Christ because she keeps the commandments they provide (1 John 2:3; 3:6; 5:2, 18; John 14:15, 22-23; 15:10). Such an obedient life is a life known to love God and one loved by God and Christ (John 14:15, 22-23; 15:10; 1 John 4:7-8). This is actually a life lived within a covenant relationship of love, thus filial knowledge in relationship with God and Christ (John 10:4, 14-15; 14:15, 22-23; 15:10; 1 John 4:7-8; 5:2).[28] Such a life is one known for loving others (1 John 3:14; 4:7-8, 13; 5:2), which love is empowered by the Holy Spirit (1 John 3:24; 4:13).

Inspired Jesus sent *from* God

John the Baptist identified that Jesus to Whom he pointed is *from* (ἐκ) the Father and heaven, and is thus above all (John 3:31). As the authorized revealer sent from God, Jesus knows and bears witness to the Father known by Him.[29] As the apocalyptic Son of Man *from* the Father, Jesus comes to provide in this knowledge of God also that knowledge which establishes

---

232-66, esp. 252-66; view disproved by Evans, *Word and Glory*).

26. Moser, *The Elusive God*, 46-7, 98, 113-123 framed within his empirical commitment (*Empirical Knowledge*).

27. Keener, *John*, 1:246; Manson, *On Paul and John*, 96-97.

28. Keener, *John*, 1:246; Moser, *The Elusive God*, 46-7, 98, 113-123.

29. Neyrey, "John III-A Debate," *NovT* 23:2(1981):119-23.

the penultimate age of kingdom (John 3:13–14; 6:27, 53–62; 8:28; 12:23, 34; 13:31; Dan 7:13–14).[30]

Jesus presented Himself to be *from* God the Father Whom humans have never seen (John 1:18; 3:16, 18; 5:37; 7:16, 28–29; 8:14, 18, 23, 26, 42; 16:28; 17:8, 25; 1 John 4:9). Thus without special revelation, humans will be in the position of lacking knowledge about God the Father. Jesus developed that this very condition of not seeing the Father means that the Father and the scriptures bear witness to the Father sending Jesus through empirically observing Jesus doing the works of the Father (John 5:37, 39, 44). So Jesus claims that He is "the Way, the Truth, and the Life, so no one comes to the Father except through Me" (John 14:6). Jesus is thus the revelatory agent through whom the believer comes to understand God. Those who recognize that Jesus is *from the Father* enter into those who know, whereas those who do not recognize this fact remain among those who are ignorant (John 1:10–13).[31]

The *logos* is a Hebraic revelatory communication personally incarnating God as Jesus Christ (John 1:1–2, 15). The Gospel of John begins with the remnants of a hymn celebrating the divinity of the Word and His revelatory role in revealing the Father.[32] There is no allusion to an impersonal stoic divine metaphor, nor an impersonal realm of the forms in Platonic thought, nor an esoteric knowledge only known through gnostic mysticism.[33] Rather, the *logos* is the revelatory Word as God in a context of O.T. creation, thus reflecting personal divinity Who creates in a Jewish monotheism (John 1:1–2). This same Word is personal Jesus Christ parallel to personal Moses, who previously provided the Law (John 1:16). John utilized the knowledge of God as grounded in O.T. writings as a parallel revelatory concept to the

---

30. Marcus, "Mark 4:10–12 and Marcan Epistemology," *JBL* 103:4(1984): 558, 567.

31. Neyrey, "John III- A Debate," *NovT* 23:2(1981): 116–18.

32. The prologue rhetorically introduces Christ as the subject (similar to: Quintilian 4.1.1; Dionysius of Halicarnassus, *Lysias* 17; *Thucyd.* 10–12). Form-critical hymnic analysis grounds on Norden, *Agnostos Theos*, 144–276 with appendixes 4 (347–54), 5 (355–64), 6 (365–66), and 8 (380–87); *Die Antike Kunstprosa*, 2:810–29; with parallels to the *Odes of Solomon*: Bernard, *John*, 1:cxliv–cxlv; Fortna, *The Gospel of Signs*, 162; re-worked to remove a critical agenda to leave verses 1–4 and 9–11 as remains of a hymn: Porter, *The Criterion for Authenticity in Historical-Jesus Research*, 63–69; *John, His Gospel, and Jesus*, 91–99; Bultmann, *John*, 16–17; Käsemann, "The Structure and Purpose of the Prologue to John's Gospel," In *New Testament Questions of Today*, 138–67 esp. 139–52; Schnackenburg, *John*, 1:224–29; Sanders, *New Testament Christological Hymns*, 21–23 or because the prologue only has elements of a hymn and they are not continuous it is likely that John composed the prologue: Evans, *Word and Glory*, 183 n. 3; Carson, *John*, 111–12; Keener, *John*, 1:333–34.

33. One who tries to fuse these ideas into a Johannine Jesus is Ely, *Knowledge of God in Johannine Thought*, 24, 71–72, 97–98, 149, 150.

Word, which the Word excels.³⁴ Though both Moses and Christ were from the Father to reveal a message, Christ actually comes as the divine presence from the Father (John 1:1-2, 14, 17-18). Additionally, Christ's revelatory role is one of explaining God the Father to believers who have not seen Him (John 1:17).

This coming from heaven means that Jesus is the heavenly food as a replacement *manna* to provide spiritual subsistence and to do the Father's will (John 6:38). Jesus utilized Jewish symbols, not sacramental ones, to reveal powerful transcendent images of God's involvement in Israel's history.³⁵ Extending these Jewish symbols to Christ appropriates *manna's* substance to the Promised Land into a new Exodus framework in which Christ is the sustenance unto kingdom. Internalizing Christ spiritually feeds the believer and repulses those who find this statement to be too hard, akin to cannibalism. There is no mention of Eucharist here, it is Christ Himself Who is the sustenance without any allusion in the context to Jesus' death or second coming being remembered or commemorated. To recognize that Jesus is from God provides the believer with further divine sustenance and the miracle of becoming family with God.³⁶

One expression of coming from the Father is that Jesus is uniquely born from God as the divine-human representative on earth. One expression of this is that biblical theologians develop generation (μονογενὴς) as a *"unique birth" in time to missionally reveal God* rather than a systematic theology of "eternal generation" (John 1:14, 18; 3:16, 18 and 1 John 4:9). This word μονογενὴς elsewhere in the Bible means "only child" as the case of the *only child* of a synagogue official who needs Jesus' healing or Abraham's *only child* of promise, whom God has commanded to be sacrificed (Luke 7:12; 8:42; 9:38; Heb. 11:17). However, in John the word is used exclusively of Jesus Christ with theological reference to His unique historical birth as the revelatory Word, to reveal God through the flesh. For example, John 1:14 describes the unique birthing process as the incarnation of Christ's humanity in flesh so that He as the Word could reveal the divine glory historically through His humanity. The fact that the Word is God (John 1:1) means that the uniquely born God (divine One adding humanity in his birth) is uniquely bodily enabled to explain the Father, which explanation took place in the historical incarnation prior to John's writing his gospel (the aorist ἐξηγήσατο; John 1:18). This *explanation* (ἐξηγήσατο) is a testimony about the divine Father from Jesus. The divine Son Jesus is uniquely qualified to

---

34. Ibid, 53, 139.
35. Painter, "Johannine Symbols," *JTSA* 27(1979): 26–41.
36. Gaffney, "Believing and Knowing in the Fourth Gospel," *TS* 26(1965): 217.

explain what the Father is like to fellow humans around him because Jesus has been with the Father and is God (John 1:1-2, 18). This uniquely born Word (incarnated for the purpose of revealing the Father) has revealed God. After the ascension (as John is writing[37]), the divine Word interpenetrated the anthropomorphic breast (κόλπον) of the Father. The Father gives the *uniquely born* (μονογενὴς) Son of God (in His incarnation coming into the world) for men to believe in Him and thereby obtain everlasting life (John 3:16, 18; 1 John 4:9). Since the biblical texts used to defend the doctrine of generation emphasize μονογενὴς to be *a historical birthing* of Jesus' humanity in incarnation, it is best to consider the ancient tradition, that Jesus Christ was generated before all ages in eternity, as having no biblical evidence. The unanimous voice of scholarly commentators agree,[38] further confirming the exegetical view that the generation of the Son should be biblically understood as a missional initiation of the divine Word incarnating to reveal the Father through His humanity.

---

37. ὢν the present tense of εἰμί, indicates a present relationship, but not a continued enwombment because the incarnation was the μονογενὴς *unique birth*.

38. Moody, "God's only Son," *JBL* 72(1953): 213-19; Brown, *John i-xii*, 13-14, 30-34, 129, 134; *The Epistles of John*, 516-17; Morris *John*, 105-6, 113-14, 230-4; Lindars, *John*, 95-6, 98-99, 159-160; Westcott, *John*, 10-14, 55; Beasley-Murray, *John*, 14-16, 51; Keener, *John*, 1:412-16, 566-68; Smalley, *1, 2, 3 John*, 1 John 4:9. On rare occasions, an individual suggests that, the quotes of Ps 2:7 in the N.T. can be taken in support of eternal generation. Ps 2:7 "Thou art My Son, today I have begotten Thee" fits into the context of the day in which the Davidic king is installed as king in Jerusalem (Ps 2:6). In Heb 1:5 this statement is already said to the Son and connected with the Davidic covenant (2 Sam 7:14 also quoted in Heb 1:5). In Heb 5:5 the *today* is identified with the earthly life of Jesus (Who was perfect and did not need a sacrifice [Heb 5:1-3] and at Gethsemane cried out in effective prayer [Heb 5:7-8]) in contrast with Ps 110:4 quoted in Heb 5:6 perpetuity of Jesus as a Melchizedekian priest, once He began it in His humanity. Such priesthood is not eternal because Jesus had to become incarnated before it could begin. In Acts 13:33 Paul's sermon at Pisidian Antioch quote Ps 2:7 connected with the resurrection of Jesus. Similar affirmations of the beloved Sonship of Jesus are also said in His baptism and transfiguration but none develop eternal generation (Matt 3:17; 17:5; Mark 1:11; Luke 3:22). When Carson was asked about these uses of Ps 2:7 at the Southeast ETS, 2003 meeting, he denied that they had anything to do with eternal generation and denied the concept traditionally attached to μονογενὴς as well. Then he responded with a text in John 6 that he claimed developed aseity, but I think that his text better teaches an economic ministry of sustenance. For example, in John 6:32-33 Jesus (the bread of God) is true bread given by the Father coming out of heaven revelationally for sustenance and thereby life to the world, in a time something like manna had been given out in the wilderness (John 6:31). Notice that this is not aseity for it would only be appropriate after creation had occurred, for He came to give life to the world. Additionally, this comment by Jesus would only be appropriate after Jesus' incarnation, for in John 6:38 Jesus identifies that He had come down from heaven, sent by the Father to do His Father's will. Therefore, these do not teach aseity, and I agree with Carson that they do not teach eternal generation.

The authoritative audible voice (*bath qol*) from the Father empirically corporately mystically confirmed that Jesus was God's man on location sent by Him and that God was pleased with Jesus' ministry such that God was glorifying Jesus as corroboration of the fact that Jesus was sent from the Father (John 12:28).[39]

Jesus Reveals the Father

A primary epistemic quality for John is that Jesus is presented by him to be the authorized heavenly revealer Who reveals the Father.[40] No human has seen the Father (John 1:18; 6:46). So if humans are to understand the Father there is an advantage if someone can explain Him and flesh Him out. Jesus provides that unique explanation of the Father for fellow humans because He is God and has been with God and is now accessible to humans to facilitate this explanation.

Jesus clarified that His testimony was not of human origin but for human salvation (John 5:34). Jesus' teaching was from the Father (John 7:16-17; 8:26-28; 14:31; 17:14). The fact that Jesus did the works that the Father sent Him to do provided corroboration for His testimony and relationship (John 5:36-38; 8:55; 10:25; 15:10, 15; 16:15). John expressed a nonfoundational Lockean empiricism with an induced epistemic dualism interpreting the evidence of Jesus' words and corroborating it through the continued evidence of Jesus' works.[41] Further, if Jesus' audience did the Father's will then they too would know that Jesus' teaching came from the Father (John 7:16-17; 8:55). However, the disciples coming to know that the Father is the source of Jesus' teaching through doing the Father's will is better understood within a Peircean pragmatism which accomplishing the

---

39. B. *'Abot* 6.2; B. *Bat.* 73b, 85b; *Mak.* 23b; *'Erub.* 54b; *Shab.* 33b; 88a; *Soṭa* 33a; p. *Soṭa* 7.5, sect. 5; *Pesiq. Rab Kah.* 15.5; *Lev. Rab.* 19.5-6; *Deut. Rab.* 11.10; *Lam. Rab. Proem* 2, 23; *Lam. Rab.* 1.16 sect. 50; *Ruth Rab.* 6.4; *Qoh. Rab.* 7.12, sect. 1; *Pesq. Rab Kah.* 11.16; such divine speech would be an empirical mystical experience of God as developed by Alston but on a corporate rather than individual level that he argues in *Perceiving God*, 14-35.

40. Neyrey, "John III- A Debate," *NovT* 23:2(1981): 115, 121, 123; Bultmann, *John*, 132-4; Borgen, "God's Agent in the Fourth Gospel," In *Religion in Antiquity*. ed. Neusner, 137-48.

41. Locke, *Concerning Human Understanding* 1.1.15; 2.11.8-9; 2.32.6; 3.3.6-8; "A Discourse of Miracles," In *Works*, 9:256-65; "The Reasonableness of Christianity," In *Works*, vol. 6; pre-modern empiricism is apparent in Lactanius, *Workmanship of God* 9-10; Keener, *Miracles*, 1:35-208.

Father's will frames the disciple within a worldview epistemically sensitive to know the Father.[42]

Jesus incarnates as the divine-human to reveal the Father Who no human has ever seen (John 1:18; 6:46). John identified Jesus' incarnation facilitating Jesus in *explaining* testimony[43] about the divine Father. Jesus the divine Son is uniquely qualified to explain what the Father is like to fellow humans around him because Jesus has been with the Father and is God (John 1:1–2, 18). Thus one purpose of the incarnation is to reveal the Father.

In the John 3 context, Nicodemus realized that God enables Jesus' miracles, so he approaches Jesus with respect attributed toward a rabbi (John 3:1–21). This encounter occurred in the darkness of night probably because of Nicodemus' fear (John 3:2; 7:50–52), but John's gospel plays off this empirical darkness in this account by metaphorically setting Jesus up as the light that shines in darkness (John 3:19–21). Jesus responded to Nicodemus, that only those who are born "again" or "from above"[44] will be able to see the kingdom of God. Jesus was using an empirical concept of entering and experiencing the kingdom of God. Nicodemus was confused about how new birth could take place. Jesus identified that our first birth brought about our human flesh condition, but the new birth to become a spiritual being is created by the Spirit of God, and illustrated by baptism (which is the Church's performative initiation rite unto kingdom).[45] Jesus was surprised

---

42. Peirce, *Collected Papers*. Hartshorne and Weiss, vol. 5 paragraph 9; "The Fixation of Belief," *Popular Science Monthly* 12(Nov., 1877): 1–15; "How to Make Our Ideas Clear," *Popular Science Monthly* 12(Jan., 1878): 286–302.

43. Its meaning is apparent as testimony from its use; Luke 24:35; Acts 10:8; 15:12, 14; 21:19.

44. ἄνωθεν can mean: 1) "from above" as from God or the Spirit, which is an emphasis in the context (John 3:6, 13), or 2) "again" as either: 2a) born unto Kingdom, instead of into this world (John 3:3–5, 16), or 2b) as a Spirit birth in contrast to a human flesh birth (John 3:4–6).

45. "*Born by water* and the Spirit" could have the "water" mean: 1a) Semen (as in born initially). 1b) Water sack (as in born initially). 2) Water as metaphor for the Spirit (Titus 3:5). 3) Born from above, with baptism as the initiation rite unto the kingdom, which baptism in the context is associated with the Spirit (John 1:26–33; proselyte baptism among the Jews: *m. Pesaḥ* 8.8; *t. 'Abod. Zar.* 3.11; 1QS 2.25–3.12; Epictetus *Diatr.* 2.9.20; probably Juvenal *Sat.* 14.104; *Sib. Or.* 4.162–65; *Yeb.* 2.29). 4) Some also claim the water is kingdom purifying immersion (with John 2:6–7, 14–16; 1QS 4.21; *p. Qidd.* 3.12.8 *Num. Rab.* 7.10 reading Ezek. 36). Views 1a and 1b are unlikely since they have occurred and Jesus presents what is necessary to happen to enter kingdom. View 2 is unlikely because there is already a closer metaphor for the Spirit in this context with that of wind (John 3:8). View 3 is the likely way to take this metaphor of water for baptism because of the near context use in John (1:6–8, 19–36, 40) and in the culture, and the early church clearly embraced this view that baptism was the authorized iniation rite performing the function of identifying authentic conversion (Acts 2:38, 41;

that Nicodemus did not understand and believe these earthly things. Jesus clarified that He referred to a spiritual (πνεύματος) birth brought about by the causality of the Spirit (πνεῦμά), like the causality of wind (πνεῦμα) functions; you cannot see the Spirit or wind but you can see their effect.

Jesus responded that He is uniquely qualified to reveal heavenly truth because He is simultaneousness in heaven and on earth, the Chalcedonian Christological position. The majority of Bruce Metzger's United Bible Societies' editorial committee rejected this reading of "in heaven" as too advanced a development of Christology and let John 3:13 be parallel to John 1:18; 3:31; 6:38, 42, which teaches that Jesus "has come from heaven" to reveal God and implement the Son of Man's role into an already established mystical judgment and kingdom. Such a meaning would be profound in its already mystical realization of the Son of Man's judgment and kingdom consequences (Dan 7:13–14). Metzger makes the claim that the "in heaven" reading is "supported almost exclusively by Egyptian witnesses," contrary to the case.[46] Whereas, in the second edition he acknowledged that his own reading was the reading almost exclusively supported by Egyptian sources.[47] A minority on the team argued that "there is no discernable motive that would have prompted copyists to add the words 'who is in heaven,' resulting in a most difficult saying"[48] and thus a likely original textual reading. Additionally, some of the support for the minority reading come from third and fourth century sources, before and not normally identified with Chalcedon (like Origin). I join the minority of the UBS editorial committee which considered Jesus' "present-ness" in heaven as a more difficult textual statement to be preferred as the earlier text and as a reading it does have stronger and broader textual support than the other options. Thus, I conclude in this verse for a two-natures view of Christ that permits a simultaneous Jewish monotheistic divine presence in heaven while His earthly human presence is visually before Nicodemus. Such a meaning would still convey that the Son of Man has come for judgment and kingdom, but simultaneously

---

8:12; Rom 6:3; 1 Cor 12:13; 1 Pet 3:21; Austin, *Doing Things with Words*). View 4 is unlikely because it would occur as the kingdom begins, so it would be redundant to entering kingdom and thus not a requirement to enter kingdom as Jesus presents it to Nicodemus.

46. Byzantine textual support for the "in heaven" reading: A, E. F, G, H, K, M, S, V, Γ, Λ, Π, *Byz. Lect.*, Basil, Chrysostom, Didymus, Nonnus, Theodoret. Western textual support: Old Latin, Syriac (Harclean), Hippolytus, Novation, Hilary. Alexandrian textual support: 892 Coptic (mss. of the Bohairic), Dionysius, Origen. Caesarean textual support: Θ, *f1*, *f13*, 28, 565, Armenian Georgian. This reading "in heaven" is indicated in the margin for the *English Standard Version*.

47. Bruce Metzger, *A Textual Commentary*, 174.

48. Ibid.

this view would also underscore the Chalcedonian position of Jesus as the God-man. With Jesus' presence in heaven simultaneous to being with Nicodemus, Jesus is uniquely able to explain heavenly things to humans with whom He ministers.

Jesus clarified that His simultaneity in heaven (John 3:13)[49] and present before Nicodemus (John 3:3, 5, 10) as the Son of Man enables Him to become the healing object of faith, like the bronze serpent on a pole (Num 21:9). Instead of obtaining healing from snake bite by looking to God through means of the bronze serpent, the follower of Jesus looks to Christ as the God-man Who through the Holy Spirit brings them healing unto kingdom. Jesus Himself is the revelational bridge from heaven to earth because He occupies both. In Jesus' incarnational role Jesus reveals that His followers must see Him as the object of their on-going faith.

Inspired Apostles Sent by God and Christ

On Jesus' last night with the disciples before He dies, Jesus indicated that His ministry with them would be continued by the coming ministry of the Holy Spirit. The texts that many systematic theologians point to indicating eternal procession are better understood as the historic coming of the Holy Spirit's ministry with the apostles (John 14:25–26, 15:26 and 16:5). For example, John 14:17–18 indicates that the disciples with Jesus in the upper room have the Holy Spirit *with* them but there will be a change as Jesus leaves, for then the Holy Spirit will be *in* them. After Jesus leaves the Father *will send* (πέμψει, future) the Holy Spirit to the disciples to remind these disciples about the things Jesus said to them when He was in fact with them (John 14:25–26). The Holy Spirit *will come* (future) after Jesus leaves, *sent by* (πέμψω) Christ and *going out from* (ἐκπορεύεται) the Father (John 15:26). However, the Son must leave first and return to the Father who sent the Son. Thus, the disciples will have an advantage as Christ leaves, for the Son *will send* (πέμψω, future) the Holy Spirit to them so that the Spirit might convict the world concerning sin, righteousness and judgment (John

---

49. The claim to be presently in heaven is a significant textual variant with strong and broad manuscript support (much more than the omission option that has support from ℵ and B), and the simultaneous claim to be present in heaven while He is also present before Nicodemus is clearly the most difficult reading even if it is no shorter. The other options of "coming from heaven" have significantly less textual support and other Johannine texts to explain why they might have been harmonized to soften this option. The omission option would also internally soften this issue. Cf. Bruce Metzger, *A Textual Commentary*, 203–204; Black sides with the minority that prefers the reading of Jesus present-ness in heaven, *New Testament Textual Criticism*, 49–56.

16:5, 7-8). The same economic relationship of being sent that the Son had, the Holy Spirit will have, and thus the Holy Spirit is another comforter like Christ. After Jesus' resurrection, Jesus meets with the disciples in the upper room and breathes on them, promising them that they will receive the Holy Spirit (John 20:22). From John's perspective, the Spirit might come upon the disciples at that time or if this is harmonized with Luke-Acts, then in Acts 1:8 Luke presents that the Holy Spirit had not been received by the disciples, so that they awaited His empowerment in their future. Christ finally ascends in Acts 1:9 leaving His disciples. On the feast of Pentecost the Holy Spirit filled the disciples providing dramatic empowerment to proclaim the gospel (Acts 2:2-4). God declares that in the last days He *will pour forth* (ἐκχεῶ) the Spirit on all humankind (Acts 2:17). Jesus Christ in His exaltation *receives* (λαβὼν) the promise of the Holy Spirit from the Father and so Christ *pours forth* (ἐξέχεεν) this Holy Spirit phenomenon which the Jews available around the apostles can empirically see and hear (Acts 2:33). It is best to see that this procession is economically from the Father and the Son by comparing that the same Greek words describe the Father's *sending* of the Spirit (πέμψει, ἐκχεῶ) also describe the Son's *sending* of the Spirit (πέμψω, ἐξέχεεν). The unanimous voice of scholarly commentators at this point agree further confirming the exegetical view that the sending of the Spirit in these passages is an economic historical coming to perform certain ministries beginning at Pentecost or the upper room.[50]

Among John 14:26 and 16:12-15 are contextually developed promises of inspiration to the disciples, so that as Jesus leaves these disciples (John 14:25, 27-28; 16:4-8, 16-20), they would be reminded of what Jesus had said to them when He was with them (John 14:26), and that the Spirit would also instruct the disciples about future prophetic things (John 16:13) that they could not handle that night. These promises took place for these disciples (and are thus said in second person plural address to the disciples whom Jesus was about to leave) and we have the results of these promises in documents like the biblical gospels and the book of Revelation.

These passages have been taken instead by some as a hermeneutical idea of illumination from the Holy Spirit, a view beginning in 1685 following Lutheran pietism.[51] Evangelicalism has largely owned Spener, Quenst-

---

50. Brown, *John xiii-xxi*, 650-1, 699-700; Lindars, *John*, 484, 496; Morris, *John*, 656-7, 683-4; Westcott, *John*, 208-9, 224-225; Beasley-Murray, *John*, 261, 286-7; Keener, *John*, 2:951-973, 1022-27, 1035-43.

51. Kennard, "Evangelical Views of Illumination of Scripture and Critique," *JETS* 49(Dec. 2006): 797-806; Spener, *Consilia Et Judicia Theologia*, 3:700; Stein, "Phillip Jakob Spener (1635-1705)" and Markus Matthias, "August Hermann Franke (1663-1727)," In *The Pietist Theologians*. ed. Lindberg, 88 and 105-6; Wallmann, *Philipp Jakob*

edt, and Hollanz's cognitive illumination view, with others in evangelicalism joining Franke's spirit transformational illumination view.[52] If such a view were supported by the biblical texts, it raises the possibility of an internalist authority on the level of a divine intuition. However, Schleiermacher developed a psychological side of the hermeneutical process, echoing Spener's personal inspirational view, which Cardinal John Henry Newman cultivated into an "illative" (or confident intuitive) sense similar to Michael Polanyi's tacit intuitional way of knowing[53] to provide E. D. Hirsh's validity in interpretation through divine "authorial intent."[54] In conservative circles this illumination view is often supported through textual appeals to John 14:26; 16:12–15; 1 Cor. 2:6–16; and 1 John 2:27. Elsewhere I argued that these texts do not in fact teach such an illumination view.[55] The scholarly commentaries on these passages agree that these passages do not teach such an illumination view.[56] So the interpreter is left with the revelation promise

---

Spener und die Aufänge des Pietismus, 92–96; Hirsch, *Geschichte der neuen Evangelische Theologie*, 2:114; Jung, *Das Ganze der Heiligen Schrift*, 100–1; Quenstedt, *Theologia Didactico-Polemica*. The relevant portion (chapters 1–3) of this is available in English as: *The Nature and Character of Theology*, ch. I "Of Theology in General": question I "Is Theology Given?" paragraph XI, p. 36; ph. XIV, p. 39; ph. XXXI-Observe (1), p. 54; ph. XXXV, p. 57; Section II "Polemic"-"Sources of Rebutals or Dialysis of Objections": q. I "Is Theology Given?," pp. 64–5; q. II "Is Revealed Theology Necessary in the Church?," pp. 71, 72–3; q. III "Is Theology a God-Given Practical Aptitude?," exposition III & IV, pp. 73–4; rebuttal I, p. 80; ch. III "Of the Sources of Theology," porism IV, pp. 199–200; Hollanz, *Examen Theologicum Acroamaticum* published in 1707 is available as *Acromaticum Universam Theologiam*. Stanley Grenz, in *Beyond Foundationalism*, 99 claims that this illumination view originated earlier by at least the time of John Hus and cites Tavard in *Holy Writ or Holy Church*, 47–66 which discusses John Hus' view of the soteriological transformation in which the Holy Spirit enables the new believer to be responsive to application of the Word of God. From my reading of the Hus material, I agree with Tavard, contrary to Grenz; Hus does *not* teach this view of the illumination through the Holy Spirit aid to cognitively understand the Bible. I have not found the view any earlier than Spener's, Quenstedt's and Hollanz's pietistic Lutheran systematic theologies. Franke, *Praelectiones Hermeneuticae*, 57; Matthias, "August Hermann Franke (1663-1727)," In *The Pietist Theologians*. ed. Carter Lindberg, 106–7.

52. The Chicago Statement on Biblical Hermeneutics as contained in *Hermeneutics, Inerrancy, and the Bible*. ed. Radmacher and Preus, 891.

53. Newman, *An Essay in Aid of A Grammar of Assent*; Polanyi, *The Tacit Dimension*.

54. Hirsch, *Validity in Interpretation*.

55. Kennard, *The Relationship Between Epistemology*, 139–42; *A Critical Realist's*, 141–3, 224–31; "Evangelical Views on Illumination of Scripture and Critique," *JETS* 49:4(Dec. 2006): 797–806.

56. For example, the following sample of commentators support my view: Tasker, *John*; Morris, *John*; Lindars, *John*; Godet, *John*, Brown, *John xiii–xxi*; Westcott, *John*; Keener, *John*; Dunn, *The Theology of Paul the Apostle*; Barrett *The First Epistle to the Corinthians*; Bruce, *1 and 2 Corinthians*; Fee, *The First Epistle to the Corinthians*;

that the Holy Spirit will remind the apostles what Jesus said so that the oral and written testimony would accurately recount the words and thus ground the Church with an accurate recounting of Jesus' words that Jesus had said with the disciples when He had been with them and prophecy that they could not handle on that last night before Jesus died (John 14:26; 16:12–15). This pneumatological empowerment extends the very revelatory ministry that Jesus had done in revealing the Father and the message that the Father had for Jesus to share. Now the Holy Spirit will reveal the Father and Son to continue the comforting and revealing role.

Schnackenburg and Thatcher suggest that this reminder of Jesus' revelation means that the Spirit "'simply continues Jesus' revelation, not by providing new teachings,' but only by enhancing and clarifying his words, thus fulfilling the ministry of 'a commemorative deepening of that revelation.'"[57] This facilitates memory through a pneumatological process rather than a mechanical means, such that memory is a spiritual gift to recreate recollections of the total person of Christ for the apostles to ground the Church.[58] John's text is a continuing revelatory testimony for the Church to be prompted in the agenda that John states, so both John and the Spirit combine to recount Jesus' miracles to prompt growing faith among believers.

This empirically grounded recounting of the words and experience with Christ involves the community in a co-sharing fellowship or a salvific relationship of filial knowledge with the Father and other Christians (1 John 1:1–3).[59] Such a filial knowledge as this relationally identifies the believer with Christ (the anointed One) through an anointing that continues to teach the believers about all things (1 John 2:27) because it is not limited to past Scripture but prompts engagement on all life issues related to abiding in Christ. This anointing is the message from Christ that abides in Christians providing them with everlasting life and anointing them (identifying them with Christ, the anointed One; 1 John 2:24–25). Simply put, Jesus' message within the believer transforms the believer into one who has a salvific family relationship with Father, Son and other Christians. Such intimate knowledge of Jesus' message and relationship continues to provide the believer with a perspective concerning the value of everything in its place.

Grosheide, *First Epistle to the Corinthians*; Morris, *The First Epistle of Paul to the Corinthians*; Orr and Walther, *1 Corinthians*; Robertson and Plummer, *First Epistle of St. Paul to the Corinthians*; Thiselton, *The First Epistle to the Corinthians*; Brown, *The Epistles of John*; Cook, *The Theology of John*; Law, *The Tests of Life*.

57. Thatcher, *Why John Wrote a Gospel*, 32 citing Schnackenburg, *John*, 3.144, 83, 142.

58. Thatcher, *Why John Wrote a Gospel*, 34–35.

59. Moser, *The Elusive God*, 46–7, 98, 113–123 framed within his empirical commitment (*Empirical Knowledge*).

The analysis of these texts through the lens of speech-acts as commands and promises clearly indicate that the biblical text can be clear without the need of an intuitive work of the Spirit to clarify the meaning of the text. Most speech-act theorists would agree that the meaning of the statement is apparent in the contextualized textual statement, rather than through an evangelical appeal to illumination behind the text in the mind of the author producing the text.[60] Such a condition of knowing the author's mind is philosophically impossible unless the author communicates it. Such communication would supersede this illuminational aid and place it back into the trajectory of the communication, which is the text.

Additionally, the absence of such an illumination aid makes more sense of two hermeneutical conditions. The first is that rather repeatedly *godly commentators disagree* with features which other godly commentators may say are within the meaning of a text. If godly Christians were given this illumination aid, then it would unify Christian commentaries but we find that the Bultmannian ones continue to emphasize John's disciples are Hellenistically writing to engage Gnosticism while those influenced by early Judaism (such as Craig Keener) reflect on John's engagement emerging from his Jewish background.[61] The reason for this disagreement is not that some of these commentators are not listening to the illumination of the Spirit but rather each commentator has his own sensitivities to context, grammar, authorial thought forms, context, and theological construct. Perhaps they are fusing the text to a theological model that allows the secondary authority of tradition to be primarily determinative over the primary authority of the biblical text. Some allow tradition to determine meaning rather than textual meaning challenging and modifying a growing and developing tradition. However, even within the same tradition there is still disagreement. Here their sensitivity to these textual features identifies why their interpretations differ.

Secondly, if such an illumination aid occurred for Christians then they would always be able to produce superior commentaries, *but sometimes non-Christians in fact have produced the best commentaries on a book of the Bible*. For example, the best commentary on Leviticus 1–16 is by Jacob Milgrom,[62] who as a Jew is very sensitive to the textual and contextual features within that book. Milgrom accurately and passionately embraces his interpretation; he is not merely working on the level of intellectual assent. Thus, such illumination is an impotent aid or no aid at all if merely attention

---

60. Barr, *The Semantics of Biblical Language*.

61. Bultmann, *John*; Keener, *John*.

62. Milgrom, *Leviticus 1–16*. Of course with the completion of Milgrom's third volume this case could be expanded for Milgrom has the best commentary on the whole of Leviticus.

to text in context produces a superior product of understanding. Anything that God does not promise to give and is not effective in demonstrating its ability to provide superior interpretation, accuracy, and unity should not be depended upon as coming from God. Thus claims from illumination as authority are not properly warranted.

When it comes to interpretation, Paul places Christians under a rubric that we should study to show ourselves approved as a workman rightly handling the Word of God (2 Tim 2:15). Interpretation is our responsibility. Likewise, Peter identified that abuse of the Biblical text is also our responsibility (2 Pet 3:16). The Holy Spirit neither takes the credit nor the blame for our interpretations.

John wrote expecting all the apostles to bear witness of the things of Jesus Christ. An example of this witness is the encouragement and command by Jesus to Peter to "feed my lambs" (John 21:16–23). The other apostles also bear witness along with John (John 20:30–31; 21:24–25; 1 John 1:1–2).

John Writes Within an Early Jewish Perspective

With the Qumran discoveries, some commentators concluded that the Gospel of John was composed within a common background of the thought of Qumran.[63] In fact, James Charlesworth concluded that John utilized literary dependence upon 1QS for his development of dualism in his writings.[64] Most do not tie John to literary dependence but do see that there is a common perspective out of which they both write. Marianne Thompson considers that such perspectivalism is in harmony with historical accuracy of the gospel of John.[65] The rest of this chapter examines the similar passages among the *Charter of a Jewish Sectarian Association* (1QS, 4Q255–264a, 5Q11) and "The Gospel of John." The *Charter of a Jewish Sectarian Association* (hereafter referred to as 1QS) was produced by an early Jewish community living in multiple groups throughout the land of Israel and having a concentration at Qumran.[66] This document in its versions establishes a community

---

63. Beasley-Murray, *John*, lxi–lxiii; Brown, *John i–xii*, lxiii–lxv; Hunter, *John*, 27; Kummel, *Introduction to the New Testament*, 158; Keener, *John*, 1:241; Aune, "Dualism in the Fourth Gospel and the Dead Sea Scrolls," In *Neotestamentica et Philonica*. ed. Aune, Seland, and Ulrichsen, 289–303 and in *Jesus, Gospel Tradition and Paul in the Context of Jewish and Greco-Roman Antiquity*, 130–48.

64. Charlesworth, "A Critical Comparison of the Dualism in 1QS 3.13–4.26," In *John and the Dead Sea Scrolls*, 101.

65. Thompson, "The 'Spirit Gospel,'" In *John, Jesus, and History*. ed. Anderson, Just, and Thatcher, 103–108.

66. *The Dead Sea Scrolls*. trans. Wise, Abegg, and Cook, 113; Multiple groups are

rule for the variety of Essene communities and their unified gatherings. I recognize that these different genre documents are produced by different authors and from different Jewish and Christian communities. However, similarity between John and 1QS argue for interpreting John from a Jewish informed context where the author has embraced Christianity, rather than a Gnostic or Hellenistic philosophical context or mystery religion context. 1QS emerged from the Essene community to identify how these Jewish men order their community. The Gospel of John emerged from a disciple of Jesus describing the Judean narrative of Jesus' ministry. However, 1QS and John have common aspects of a worldview, and at other times the overlap is superficial (similar motifs but reflective of different worldviews). This chapter will explore the material that each document presents that has similarity of perspective with the other.

Both documents position themselves within a heritage that considers dualistic motifs of light and darkness (John 1:4–9; 3:19–21; 5:35; 6:17, 19; 8:12; 9:5; 11:9–10; 12:35–6, 46).[67] Such dualism is grounded upon the Old Testament hope that Yahweh is the archetypical light, "The LORD is my light and my salvation, whom shall I fear?" (Ps. 27:1). This revelational light metaphor is balanced by 1QS and John insisting on the invisibility of God present among Jewish monotheism (John 1:18; 6:46).[68] However, God reveals Himself as light in *Shekinah* and fire.[69] Extending this revelation of divine light, Jesus is the true light entering the world to enlighten any human with the divine glory (John 1:4, 9, 14). Jesus in John has both seen the Father and reveals Him to the Christian community. The fact that Yahweh epitomizes this light identifies Him from Old Testament and second Temple sources (including 1QS) as the Orderer among chaos in a manner where He

---

apparent in diverse liturgical roles and an established liturgy able to be unified at multiple locations for thousands of participants (1QS 1.21–25; 2.1, 11, 18–22; 3.20, 25; 5.1, 3–10, 20–24; 6.8; 8.1; 9.3); 'elders' perhaps officials at synagogues (1QS 6.8; Acts 4:5, 8); novices presumably at various locations (1QS 6.21); 4QSd ellipses concerning priests; mixed Essene communities are discussed by: Philo (*Quod Omnis Probus Liber Sit* 12–13; *Hypothetica* 11.1–18) and Josephus (*J. W.* 2.8.2–13; *Ant.* 18.1.2, 5; *Life* 1.2).

67. 1QS 3.17–4.1; cf. 1QM 13.5–6, 14–15.

68. 1QS 11.20; 2 *En.* 48.5; *'Abot R. Nat.* 2, 39 A; *Sipra VDDen. Pq.* 2.2.3.2–3; *Tg. Ps.-J* on Gen 16:13; *Tg. Neof.* On Ex. 33:23; *Tg. Onq.* On Ex. 33:20, 23.

69. Exod 13:22; 40:34–48; Pss 27:1; 104:1–2; Rev 21:23; 1QH 7.24–25; 4 *Bar.* 9.3; *L.A.E.* 28.2; *T. Zeb.* 9.8 (paraphrasing Mal 4:2); *PGM* 4.1219–1222; perhaps 4Q451 frg. 24, line 7; *Sib. Or.* 3.285; *b. Menaḥ.* 88b; *Gen. Rab.* 3.4 (citing Ps 104:2); 59.5 (citing Isa 60:19); *Ex. Rab.* 50.1 (citing Ps 104:2); *Num. Rab.* 15.2; *Pesiq. Rab.* 8.5 (citing Pss 27:1; 119:105); 21.5 (citing Isa 60:19); *Shekinah* glory (Wis 17; 18.1–3; *b. Menaḥ.* 86b; *Ex. Rab.* 14.3; *Sipre Num.* 41.1.1; *b. Ber.* 60b).

continues to penetrate the threatening chaos with light: to create,[70] to enable visibility in the creation,[71] to enlighten in understanding,[72] to provide good moral guidance,[73] also to protect (the point of the synonymous parallelism of Ps 27:1), and ultimately to bring about kingdom salvation of His making.[74] Such an experience of this divine light prompts the believers to call themselves "sons of light" (John 12:36).[75]

This light metaphor extends to the forms in which the message is carried, namely Torah (Ps 119:105, 130),[76] and wisdom (Prov 4:18; 6:23; Eccl 2:13).[77] This light role extends to outstanding individuals as spokesmen of the message in Yahweh's service (such as Abraham,[78] Moses,[79] David,[80] and John the Baptist [John 5:33–35]) and ultimately to Yahweh's Messianic servant as a light to the nations by which he establishes a covenant relationship with them (Isa 9:1–2, 6–7; 42:6; 49:6).[81]

70. Some second Temple sources see light as a primeval light before creation (*2 En.* 24.4; *Ex. Rab.* 50.1) while others identify early in the creation light is used by God to limit chaos (Gen 1:3–5; *Gen. Rab.* 42.3; *b. Ḥag.* 12a).

71. *3 En.* 5.3; *b. Ḥag.* 12a; *p. Ber.* 8.6 section 5; *Gen Rab.* 42.3; *Lev. Rab.* 11.7; *Num. Rab.* 13.5; *Ruth Rab.* Proem 7; *Pesiq. Rab.* 23.6.

72. Sir 31.17; 4Q392 frg. 1; Aune, "Dualism in the Fourth Gospel," In *Neotestamentica et Philonica*. ed. Aune, Seland, and Ulrichsen, 290.

73. 1QS 3.3; also 1Q27 1.5–6; 4Q183 2.4–8; 1Q185 1–2 2.6–8; *T. Job* 43.6/4; *Sib. Or.* frg. 1.26–27; *1 En.* 108.12–14.

74. Job 30:26; Ps 35:8–10; Isa 9:2–7; 45:7; 60:1–11; Matt 13:43; Rev 18:1; 21:23; 22:5; *1 En.* 1.8; 5.7; 108.11–14; 1QM541 9 1.4–5; *Sib. Or.* 2.316; *'Abot R. Nat.* 37. 95 B; *b. Ḥag.* 12b; *Pesaḥ.* 50a; *Ta'an.* 15a; *Pesiq. Rab Kah.* 21.3–5; *Pesiq. Rab Kah.* Sup. 5.1; *Ex. Rab.* 14.3; 18.11; *Lev. Rab.* 6.6; *Song Rab.* 1.3, section 3; *Eccl. Rab.* 11.7.1; *Pesiq. Rab.*36.1; 42.4. This includes the restoration of light after this present era of sin affect (*h. Ḥag.* 12a; *Gen Rab.* 11.2; 42.3; *Ex. Rab.* 18.11; *Lev. Rab.* 11.7; *Num. Rab.* 13.5; *Pesiq. Rab.* 23.6 42.4).

75. 1QS 1.9; 2.16; 3.13, 14, 25; 1QM 1.1, 3, 9, 11, 13; Aune, "Dualism in the Fourth Gospel and the Dead Sea Scrolls," In *Neotestamentica et Philonica*. ed. Aune, Seland, and Ulrichsen, 289.

76. 1QS 5.8, 16; 8.22; 9.23; 4Q256 9.2, 6; 4Q258 1.2, 6; Bar 4.2; 4Q511 frg. 1, lines 7–8; frg. 18, lines 7–8; *CIJ* 1.409, section 554 (Hebrew on bronze lamp in Italy); *L.A.B.* 9.8; 11.1–2; 15.6; 19.4; , 6; 23.10; 33.3 end 51.3; *2 Bar.* 17.4; 18.1–2; 59.2; *Sipre Num.* 41.1.2; *p. B. Meši'a* 2.5; section 2; *Hor.* 3.1, section 2; *Sukkah* 5.1, section 7; *Gen. Rab.* 26.7; *Pesiq. Rab.* 8.4–5; 17.7; 46.3; *L.A.B.* 37.3; *Sipre Deut.* 343.7.1; *Gen. Rab.* 3.5; *Ex. Rab.* 14.10; *Deut. Rab.* 4.4; 7.3; *Eccl. Rab.* 11.7, section 1.

77. 1QS 2.3; 11.5–6; 1QM 1.8; Wis 6.12; 7.26, 29–30; *4 Ezra* 14.20–21; Sir 22.11; Tatian 13; Philo, *Alleg. Interp.* 3.45.

78. *T. Ab.* 7.14B; *Gen. Rab.* 2.3; 30.10; *Pesiq. Rab.* 20.2.

79. *Sipre Num.* 93.1.3; *b. Soṭah* 12a, 13a; *Ex. Rab.* 1.20, 22, 24; *Pesiq. Rab.* 15.4.

80. 11Q5 27.2.

81. *1 En.* 48.4 (alluding to Isa 42:6; 49:6); 1QSb 4.27; *Pesiq. Rab Kah.* Sup. 6.5; *Gen.*

John picks up part of this light metaphor as centered on Messiah Jesus. Jesus identifies Himself as revelationally the Light of the world while He is here in the world (John 8:12; 9:5). Thus Jesus is the True Light available to enlighten any of the humans who are to be enlightened (John 1:9). In this light role Jesus provides humans with a way to follow that will provide everlasting life to those who follow in faith (John 8:12; 12:46).

1 John continues with this light dualism but more grounded within a Jewish monotheism in which Father God is the light (1 John 1:5). To be in fellowship with God is to walk in the light and reflect the characteristics of the light (1 John 1:6–7).

Stepping back, K. G. Kuhn proposed that Qumran dualism is indebted to Iranian Zoroastrianism but Leon Morris and David Aune disagreed, claiming that both spirits of this dualism remain created and under the sovereignty of the Jewish monotheistic God.[82] For example, Morris developed that the angel of darkness is ascribed full responsibility for all evil, including that which the sons of light perform.[83] In 1QS the good and evil spirits have a balanced struggle for and in humanity much like the *Testaments of the Twelve Patriarchs*.[84] Cyrus Gordon additionally argued that this dualism of light and darkness is framed by the Hebrew emphasis of opposites, like day and night, to represent the whole.[85] Whereas, contrasting further with Zoroastrian dualism, the Gospel of John has a clear inequality between opposing spirits, in which the Holy Spirit is fully divine and more powerful than Satan. John utilized symbols like light and healing from blindness to indicate that a person is coming to know, whereas darkness and remaining in blindness indicates the truly ignorant person.[86]

Sectarian Judaism had a heavy predestination root but this included human responsibility.[87] This meant that the chosen of Israel was the righteous remnant.[88] John and early Christianity extended the elect covenant

---

Rab. 1.6; 85.1; *Pesiq. Rab.* 36.1–2; 37.2; *Tg.1 Chr.* 8.33.

82. Morris, *Studies in the Fourth Gospel*, 325–8; Aune, "Dualism in the Fourth Gospel and the Dead Sea Scrolls," In *Neotestamentica et Philonica*. ed. Aune, Seland, and Ulrichsen, 289–303 and In *Jesus, Gospel Tradition and Paul in the Context of Jewish and Greco-Roman Antiquity*, 130–48.

83. Morris, *Studies in the Fourth Gospel*, 325.

84. 1QS 3.18–22; 4.21–23; 1QM 13.5–6, 14–15; *Test. Jud.* 20.1–5; *Test. Ash.* 1.1–5; *Test. Ben.* 6.1; Sidebottom, *The Christ of the Fourth Gospel*, 20.

85. Gordon, *The Ancient Near East*, 35, n. 3.

86. Painter, "Johannine Symbols," *JTSA* 27(1979): 26–41.

87. 1QS 1.9–10; 10.1–5; 4Q180 frg. 1 line 2; *1 En.* 1.1–3, 8; 5.7–8; 25.5; 38.4; 48.1, 9; 50.1; 58.1; 61.4, 12; 93.2; *Jub.* 11.17; *T. Job* 4.11/9.

88. Deut 4:37; 10:15; Neh 9:7; Jer. 33:24; Sir 46.1; 2 Macc 1.25; *Jub.* 1.29; 22.9–10;

community to Gentiles as well as Jews who believed in Jesus (John 10:16, 29).[89] Though the sons of light belong to and are resourced by the spirit of light, they can still sin prompted by the spirit of darkness (1 John 1:9; 2:1).[90]

Both documents also identify in this dualism: day with light and night with darkness (John 3:2; 9:4; 13:30; 19:39).[91] In 1QS 10.1-3, the night is controlled and dissipates with the surging of the empirically observable celestial light sources: sun, moon, and stars. Whereas, John draws these night and day images more deeply into the dualism to dramatize the truth of Jesus and the responses others have to Him. Darkness signifying an epistemic deficiency whereas light presents revelatory clarity.[92] In a darkened time of confusion, Nicodemus comes to Jesus and Jesus opens for him a kingdom salvation message to penetrate his darkness (John 3:2; 19:39). During the dark of the night, the disciples were terrorized by a ferocious storm on the sea as Jesus comes walking to them visibly on the water (John 6:17–19). Later, Jesus encourages his disciples that as long as the time permits, works that bring glory to God are to be done (John 9:4). Using light and darkness as metaphors for day and night, those in unbelief depart to the night and subsequent perdition (John 3:19–20; 11:10; 12:35, 46–48). An extension of this with ominous foreboding is conveyed as Judas leaves the disciple band to enter the night on his way to betray Jesus into the hands of the religious leaders (John 13:30).

Both documents identify that their respective communities are "children of light" (John 1:9–12).[93] 1QS identifies that the revelation of the laws of God into a covenant of mercy marks out a distinctive believing community aligned with God against the rebellious "children of darkness" destined for covenant curse.[94] Likewise, the "children of light" are the blessed elect ones of God in contrast to the "children of flesh" who "walk in darkness" (John 1:13; 1 John 1:6–7).[95] The sectarian Jews consider that

---

1QS 1.10; 2.5; 9.14; 11.7; 1QM 10.9–10; 12.1, 4; 15.1–2; 17.7; 1QpHab 5.3; 9.12; 10.13; 4QpPs 37 frag. 1; *Mek. Pisha* 1.135–7; Sir *9.118*–30; *Gen. Rab.* 1.4.

89. Col 3:12; 2 Thess 2:13; *1 Clem.* 50.7.

90. 1QS 3.18–22; 4.21–23; 1QM 13.5–6, 14–15; *Test. Jud.* 20.1–5; *Test. Ash.* 1.1–5; *Test. Ben.* 6.1.

91. 1QS 10.1–3.

92. Keener, *John*, 381–7, 371–74; Bennema, "Christ, the Spirit and the Knowledge of God," In *The Bible and Epistemology.* ed. Healy and Parry, 110–14.

93. 1QS 1.9–10; 2.16; 3.13.

94. 1QS 1.9–10; 2.16.

95. 1QS 11.7–10; Ruzer, "Reading 1QS 1 and 1QS 11 as Backdrop to the Johannine Prologue," Paper given at SBL meeting, Nov. 20, 2010.

this instruction of light entails mysteries hidden from others.[96] The sons of light receive their instruction from especially "the Instructor, who is to enlighten and teach" them concerning the different spiritual levels, eras, and outcomes.[97] Somewhat like this increased perceptual enlightenment, John positions the personified Light, Jesus Christ as entering the world (John 1:5; 3:19; 12:35–36). John uses the imagery of light in the Temple as an evident parallel to communicate the definitive "Light of the world" (John 8:12).[98] This imagery of Jesus being the "Light of the world" is pressed home vividly through the miraculous account and imagery of blind receiving sight, while the religious leaders remain spiritually blind in their rejection of Him (John 9:1–5). However, Jesus is the personified Light of the world itself rather than a mere human instructing His group in the light teachings (John 1:5, 9; 9:4). When Jesus leaves the disciples they no longer are bathed in the Light and run some risk of being overwhelmed by darkness (John 12:35–36). So John encourages believing Jesus' message which develops His followers as a distinct community with light characteristics (John 1:5, 12; 3:16, 19). Such faith is broadly described as faithfully practicing the truth (John 3:21). This habituation in the Truth draws close to Jesus and God as the light and shows that they have the light character of "children of light" because their deeds evidence divine creative activity (John 3:21; 8:12; 1 John 1:5–6). To be broadly characterized by other than this divinely wrought lifestyle shows oneself not to be of the family of light and to instead be condemned in the judgment on darkness. While 1QS conceives of becoming "children of light" by a Jewish covenantal means, John presents faith historically beginning by obeying a personal presence of Jesus (John 3:17–19).[99] The predestined are born to the children of light from the truth, a fountain of light (John 3:19).[100] 1QS identifies that the children of light are enlightened about the character and fate of humans, and about the path of righteousness and fear of Laws of God.[101] Both texts provide a strong confidence that God is sovereign and that He determines everything, especially the initial drawing of those into the children of light (John 6:37; 10:29).[102] Whereas in John, enlightenment

---

96. 1QS 5.11–12; 8.1–2, 12; 9.13, 17–19; 11.3–5; 1QpHab 7.4–5, 13–14; 1QH 2.13–14; 9.23–24; 11.9–10, 16–17; 12.11–13; 1QM 3.9; 17.9; 4 *Ezra* 14.45–47.

97. 1QS 3.13.

98. Countering Bultmann's Gnostic background for this image (*John*, 342 n. 5), O'Day argues for a Jewish background ("John," In the *New Interpreter's Bible*, 9:632, n. 206); phrase occurs 4Q451 frg. 24, line 7; frg. 9 1.3–4.

99. 1QS 1.9–10; 2.16–18.

100. 1QS 3.19.

101. 1QS 3.13; 4.2–3.

102. 1QS 3.15–17.

is a metaphor of increasing communication to and knowing among the children of light. Which means that John the Baptist is a lamp providing light available for all humans, but the overwhelming True Light is Jesus Christ (John 1:4-12; 5:35-37; 8:12; 9:5; 10:16, 27-29; 12:35-36, 46). However, this light of Christ is only received among those who believe Jesus (John 1:4-12; 8:12; 10:16, 27-29; 11:9; 12:35-36, 46).

This imagery of children of light is similar to the Palestinian Jewish texts of "children of God," wherein God is described as forming a covenant community of His people.[103] In such a Jewish context, teaching a person *Torah* begets them as children of God.[104] This identifies the Qumran community as viewing themselves as in the continuing heritage of Moses,[105] whereas in John there is a contrast that Jesus is superior to Moses by providing direct access to divine revelation, grace, miraculous provision, and life sustenance (John 1:17; 6:32; 7:19). In John, reception of Jesus as the Light by faith initiated Jews and Gentiles into Jesus' new covenant people, the children of God (John 1:12; 11:52).

The most similar passage to the Johannine perspective is the discussion in 1QS 3.17-4.1 concerning the rival human communities of light and darkness.

> Col. 3.17 He created humankind to rule over 18 the world, appointing for them two spirits in which to walk until the time ordained for His visitation. These are the two spirits 19 of truth and falsehood. Upright character and fate originate with the Habitation of Light; perverse, with the Fountain of Darkness. 20 The authority of the Prince of Light extends to the governance of all righteous people; therefore they walk in the paths of light. Correspondingly, the authority of the Angel 21 of Darkness embraces the governance of all wicked people, so they walk in the paths of darkness.
>
> The authority of the Angel of Darkness further extends to the corruption 22 of all the righteous. All their sins, iniquities, shameful and rebellious deeds are at his prompting, 23 a situation God in His mysteries allows to continue until His era dawns. Moreover, all the afflictions of the righteous, and every trial in its season, occur because of this Angel's diabolic rule. 24 All the spirits allied with him share but a single resolve: to cause the Sons of Light to stumble.

103. Wis 11.10; *Pss. Sol.* 17.27; 4QDibrê ham-Meʾorôt 3.4-10; 1QH 9.35-36; *Jub.* 1.25; 2.20; 19.29; *b. Ber.* 7a, 19a; *Sukkah* 45b; *b. Taʿan.* 23b.

104. *M. ʾAbot* 3.15; *b. Sanh.* 19b; *Pesiq. Rab.* 21.21.

105. 1QS 1.3.

Yet the God of Israel (and the Angel of His Truth) assist all 25 the Sons of Light. It is actually He who created the spirits of light and darkness, making them the cornerstone of every deed, 26 their impulses the premise of every action. God's love for one spirit Col. 4.1 lasts forever.[106]

Those of the darkness hate the light and reject the light because their deeds are evil (John 3:19-21). In 1QS and Qumran darkness currently holds the upper hand in the battle for control.[107] This is mirrored in John by the persistent rejections of Christ by the darkened world (John 1:11; 3:19-20). Ultimately, the conflict will be resolved in favor of the Light and the sons of light at the final battle (John 3:18; Rev 14:14-16; 19).[108]

In John, Jesus embodies the revelational and salvific Light (John 1:4-12; 5:35-37; 8:12; 9:5; 10:16, 27-29; 12:35-36, 46), whereas, in 1QS the Prince of Light governs all the righteous in the light.[109] Such a prince in 1QS was identified as an angel or messenger of Truth assisting the sons of light.[110] At Qumran, in opposition to this angel of light stands a dualistic angel of darkness attempting to corrupt the righteous to depart into the children of darkness.[111]

Both communities of light have their habitation as of light (1 John 1:5; 2:8-10).[112] Such a habitation of light is further developed as indicated by "walking" in the path of light (John 3:20; 12:35-36; 1 John 1:7).[113] This habitation goes deeper than reception of communication and a transformed lifestyle, the life in the light deepens into an everlasting fellowship with God, Christ, the Holy Spirit, and one's comrades in the light (John 14:6-7, 17; 1 John 1:3-7).[114]

The true temple at Qumran is the community.[115] The true worship at Qumran is through a *merkabah* mysticism in which the worshippers in the spirit join the heavenly chorus in worship.[116] C. H. Dodd and Alan Rich-

---

106. 1QS 3.17-4.1 from *The Dead Sea Scrolls.* trans. Wise, Abegg, and Cook, 120 and checked by *The Dead Sea Scrolls.* trans. Martinez and Tigchelaar, 78-79.

107. 1QS 11.10; 1QM 13.11-12.

108. 1QM 1.7; *1 En.* 58.5-6; *Gen. Rab.* 89.1.

109. 1QS 3.20; CD 5.18; 1QM 13.10.

110. 1QS 3.24-25.

111. 1QS 1.18; 2.19; 3.20-24; 1QM 1.1, 5, 13; 4.2; 11.8; 17.5-6; *Jub.* 17.6; 18.9, 12; 48.2, 9, 12, 15; 49.2; *Pesiq. Rab.* 20.2; 53.2.

112. 1QS 3.19.

113. 1QS 3:20.

114. 1QS 2.25.

115. 1QS 8.5, 8-9; 9.6; CD 3.19A; 2.10, 13B; 4Q511 frg. 35, lines 2-3.

116. Isa 6; Rev 4-5; 1QS 11.8; 1QM 12.1-2; 4QShirShab; *Jub.* 30.18; 31.14; *Sipre Deut.* 306.31.1; *Pr. Man.* 15; *Apoc. Ab.* 17.

ardson claim that John 2:21 "the temple of His body" presupposes that the Christian community is a temple in John, as Paul develops (Rom 12:4-6; 1 Cor 12:12).[117] However, this Johannine discussion of Jesus' body refers in the context to the destruction of His earthly physical body through His death and the actual resurrection from the grave of Jesus resurrection body. There is no community body of Christ development in this section of John.

The dualism also functions through the metaphor of life. Jewish texts promise life as a continued life in Deuteronomic *Torah* blessings (Deut 30:6, 15-16, 19)[118] or creation blessings through wisdom (Prov 3:18; 13:14),[119] until early Judaism deepens this blessing into everlasting life and personal resurrection where the dead will awake from their sleep among the dust to either everlasting life or everlasting contempt (Dan 12:2-3).[120] Such everlasting life cannot be merely realized eschatology for it continues without end as an expression of kingdom (Dan 12:2-3; John 3:15-17; 1 John 5:11-13).[121] This sort of eschatological resurrection hope becomes common in early Judaism.[122] That is, when the faithful in the Mosaic Covenant die

---

117. Dodd, *Historical Tradition in the Fourth Gospel*, 161; Richardson, *An Introduction to the Theology of the New Testament*, 255, 261; 1 *Clem.* 37.5; Origen, *Comm. Jo.* 10.228-232.

118. Bar 3.9; 4.1-2; *Pss. Sol.* 14.1-2; *L.A.B.* 23.10; 2 *Bar.* 38.2; *m. 'Abot* 2.7; *b. 'Abot* 6.7, bar.; *'Abot R. Nat.* 34A; 35B; *Sipre Deut.* 306.22.1; 336.1.1; *b. Ḥag.* 3b; *Roš Haš.* 18a; *p. Ber.* 2.2, section 9; *Ex. Rab.* 41.1; *Lev. Rab.* 29.5; *Num. Rab.* 5.8; 10.1; 16.24; *Deut. Rab.* 7.1, 3, 9; *Tg. Eccl.* 6.12.

119. Wis 8.13, 17; Sir 4.12; 17.11; 1 *En.* 98.10, 14; 2 *Bar.* 38.2.

120. 1QS 4.6-8; CD 3.20; 4Q181 3-4; 1 *En.* 37.4; 40.4; 58.3; 4 Macc 15.3; *Ps. Sol.* 3.12; *Sib. Or.* 3.49 frag. 3; Baldwin, *Daniel*, 204-206; Wright, *Resurrection*, 108-110.

121. 1QS 4.6-8; CD 3.20-21; 1QH 3.10-22; 6.34; 11.12; 1QM 12.1-4.; 2 Macc 7.9-14, 22-23.

122. 1 *En.* 58.3; 62.14-16; 91.10; 92.2; 108.11-14; 2 *Bar.* [Syriac] 30.1-5; 2 Macc 7.9-14, 22-23; 14.43-46; 4 Macc 7.19; 16.25; 4 *Ezra* 7.32; *Sib. Or.* 4.180; *T. of Ben.* 10.6-8; *T. Levi* 18; *T. Jud.* 24; *T. of Hos.* 6:2 interprets this text to be resurrection whereas the text speaks of the reviving of Israel on the third day; *Tg. Jon.* on Isa 27:12f describes salvation as being accomplished on the third day; *b. Sanh.* 90b where Gamaliel claims that God would give the resurrected patriarchs land, not merely their descendants and Johanan Numbers 18:28 the portion of YHWH given to Aaron is taken that he will be alive again, likewise Num 15:31 is claimed that the remaining guilt of the offender will be accountable in the world to come; 91b-92a; *B. Ta'an.* 2a; *B. Ket.* 111; *m. Sanh.* 10.1, 3; *T. Mos.* 10.8-10; *Gen. Rab.* 14.5; 28.3; *Lev. Rab.* 14.9; *Messianic Apocalypse* adds resurrection to a modification of Psalm 146:5-9 as a Messianic expectation to be done to others; *T. Jud.* 25.4 claims this Messianic resurrection would begin with Abraham, Isaac, and Jacob; *T. Benj.* claims that after these are raised the whole of Israel will be raised; *Ps. of Sol.* 3.11-12; 4Q521 frag. 2, col. 2.1-13; frags. 7 and 5, col. 2.1-7; 1QH 14.29-35; 19.10-14; *Targum Songs* 8.5; the benediction in the *Amidah*, the *Shemoneh Esre*. However, Wis 3.1; 8.19-20; 9.15 and Josephus' description of the Pharisees (*Ant.* 17.152-154; 18.1.3-5; *J. W.* 2.151-153; 2.8.14; *Ap.* 2.217-8) follow more a Platonic

they continue as blessed on into the afterlife with bodily resurrection unto Paradise. For example, some Qumran manuscripts speak of the afterlife as everlasting life,[123] and others develop intimate bodily resurrection for the faithful.[124]

Going beyond early Judaism, John develops a climactic sign miracle to be that of raising Lazarus from the dead to elucidate Jesus' teaching that He is the resurrection and the life (John 11:25). Lazarus was on his death bed when friends sent for Jesus. However, Jesus delayed in coming because as He said, "This sickness is not unto death[125] but for the glory of God, that the Son of God may be glorified by it" (John 11:4). That is, the outcome will be a miracle that brings forth glory to Jesus and God. After two days, Jesus announced to His disciples that they were going to Judea at Martha and Mary's request for their brother Lazarus. The disciples were alarmed knowing that the Jewish leadership was seeking Jesus' life. Jesus reassured His disciples that missteps do not have to be devastating, but Lazarus is dead so let us go to him (John 11:7-16). Thomas pessimistically concluded that they were all going to go and die with Lazarus.

This miracle takes the Jewish idea of a resurrection as foreshadowing the general Jewish resurrection[126] and specifically applies it to Jesus who is the resurrection source for eschatological life. As Jesus was coming to Bethany, Martha met Him with an expression of faith, "Lord, if you had been here, my brother would not have died. Even now I know that whatever You ask of God, God will give You" (John 11:21-22). She was hoping for resurrection as Jesus had done for others (Matt 9:18, 23-25; Mark 5:35-42; Luke 7:12-16; 8:49-56). However, Jews had little hope of the spirit remain-

---

immortality of the soul view, but even here the soul eventually is given a body to match (Wis 9.15; Josephus, *J. W.* 2.163). Also the Biblical authors (Matt 22:23-33; Mark 12:18-27; Acts 23:6-7) and the *Eighteen Benedictions* present the Pharisees as believing the bodily resurrection of the dead; cf. Gillman, *The Death of Death*, 101-142; Wright, *Resurrection*, 129-206 for the post-Biblical Jewish view. The early church from patristic through medieval eras embraced bodily resurrection instead of Platonic immortality of the soul with regard to personal eschatology (Bynum, *The Resurrection of the Body in Western Christianity*, 200-1336; Wright, *Resurrection*, 480-552).

123. 1QS 4.6-8; CD 3.20; 4Q181 3-4; *1 En.* 37.4; 40.4; 58.3; 4 Macc 15.3; *Ps. Sol.* 3.12; *Sib. Or.* 3.49 frag. 3.

124. 1QH 3.10-22; 6.34; 11.12; 1QM 12.1-4.

125. This phrase is used in 1 John 5:16-17 regarding sin that leads to death, namely condemnation. Morris (*John*, 538-540) conjectures that Lazarus is already dead when the friends make the appeal to Jesus, with Bethany a one day's journey away and Jesus staying two more days and then traveling the one day to Bethany, thus Lazarus being dead for four days.

126. *Pesiq. Rab Kah.* 9.4; *1 En.* 62.14-15 identify that when the Son of Man resurrects, the elect will resurrect also.

ing near the body for four days. Jesus responds with "Your brother shall rise again." Martha took this statement as an affirmation of the Pharisaic view of final resurrection in the last days. Jesus responded to her, "*I am the resurrection and the life*; he who believes in Me shall live even if he dies, and everyone who lives and believes in Me shall never die" (John 11:25-26). The minority Pharisaic view of resurrection life has the faithful Jew resurrecting upon death, thus retaining the monotheistic God as the God of the living Abraham, Isaac, and Jacob (Exod 3:6; Luke 16:19-30; 20:39).[127] *Jesus as the embodiment of resurrection life is bringing her a present power to meet her need*. In verse 26, one article governs the two participles: "lives and believes," indicating that they are intimately connected on the same plain; a realized eschatology both now and everlasting. That is, the one who believes, lives with everlasting life already (John 3:16; 11:26). In Johannine writing, this everlasting life is a mystical reality that is already true of the one who believes (John 3:16-18). Jesus then asked her if she believes, to which she responded that she believes that He is the Messiah the Son of God. So Martha called Mary to come to meet Jesus.

Mary greeted Jesus much as Martha had done. Jesus asked where Lazarus had been laid. Upon showing Him, Jesus wept. Then He was deeply angry with the ravages death brings. Jesus asked for the stone to be removed. Martha protested that by this time he will stink. Jesus asked, "Did I not say to you, if you believe, you will see the glory of God." So the stone was removed. Jesus then prayed thanking the Father for hearing Him but that the miracle which was about to be accomplished was for those standing there so that they might believe that the Father had sent Him. Following this prayer He shouted "Lazarus come forth." And Lazarus came walking out of the tomb bound in his burial wrappings. Jesus said "Unbind him and let him go." Many of the Jews who saw this believed in Him but some told the religious leaders who then plotted to kill Lazarus along with Jesus (John 11:45-57).

Since Jesus Himself is the resurrection life, this miracle of resurrection for Lazarus hints at the subsequent miracle which would take place in the next few weeks, that of Jesus' own resurrection. This affirmation Jesus made of being the resurrection and the life is like Peter's statement that Jesus is the "Prince of Life" which indicates that it was completely incongruous for the "Prince of Life" to be killed, so God vindicated Him by raising Him from the dead (Acts 3:15-16).

127. Jesus view (Luke 16:19-31) is consistent with Jewish tradition (*Abr.* 50-55; 4 Macc 7:18-19; 13.17; 16:25; Philo, *Sacr. CA* 1.5; *T. Abr.* 20.8-14; *Qoh. Rab.* 9.5.1; *b. Sanh* 90b; *Ex. Rab.* 1.8; *Deut. Rab.* 3.15; *LAB* 4.11; *T. Isaac* 2.1-5; *T. Benj.* 10.6; *Apoc. Sed.* 14.3; *3 En.* 44.7). The sages could also read "living God" as "God of the living" (*Pesiq. R.* 1.2).

There are a variety of titles for the rival angels or spirits in 1QS: the holy spirit, the prince of light, the spirit of truth, the angel of truth. John will add the role of Jesus as divine messenger come from God, thus not an equal dualism. Whereas, the opposition in 1QS is identified as the spirit of Belial, Mastemoth, the spirit of error, a spirit of confusion, and the angel of darkness.[128] This adversary (*Satan* in Hebrew) is seen as ensnaring the rest of Israel beyond the sectarian Jews.[129] John will add to these roles multiple levels of evil, namely: the devil, antichrist, and antichrists as leaders among this opposition (John 8:44; 1 John 2:18, 22).

God loves the spirit of truth in his birthing and establishment of the children of light (John 3:6–8; 1 John 4:2–6; 5:7–8).[130] With a birthing by the spirit, the child of the spirit takes upon himself the character of the spirit (John 3:6–8).[131] Such a spirit is one of holiness, humility, patience, love, goodness, and wisdom (1 John 1:5–2:11; 4:2–15).[132]

Leon Morris recognized that salvation at Qumran is by keeping the Law within a covenant nomism but he holds that for John salvation is by faith in the person Jesus as the Messiah (John 3:16).[133] Therefore, both documents present covenant nomism as early Jewish perspective, wherein those: 1) faithful in the Mosaic Covenant should expect blessing and everlasting life,[134] and 2) the rebel to Mosaic Covenant should expect death (John 7:49).[135] Such covenant nomism contemplates living unto eschatological justification.[136] Reflecting this perspective, both documents present disciplinary exclusion from synagogue and community if a Jew violates the community standards (John 9:22, 34; 16:2).[137]

---

128. 1QS 1.18, 21; 2.19; 3.18–19, 21; 4.12; *Mastemoth* appears in 3.23 and 4QAmaram b.

129. 1QS 1.18, 23–24; 2.19; 3.20–21; 1QM 13.11–12.

130. 1QS 3:26; 9:3–4.

131. 1QS 3.15–4.26.

132. 1QS 2.3; 4.3, 211 *En.* 49.3; 4 *Ezra* 5.22; *Jos. Asen.* 19.11; LXX: Exod 28:3; 31:3; 35:31; Deut 34:9; Isa 11:2; Eph 1:17; Gal 5:22–6:1.

133. Morris, *Studies in the Fourth Gospel*, 330–1.

134. *Bar* 3.9; 4.1–2; *Pss. Sol.* 14.1–2; *L.A.B.* 23.10; 2 *Bar.* 38.2; *m. 'Abot* 2.7; *b. 'Abot* 6.7, bar.; *'Abot R. Nat.* 34A; 35B; *Sipre Deut.* 306.22.1; 336.1.1; *b. Ḥag.* 3b; *Roš Haš.* 18a; *p. Ber.* 2.2, section 9; *Ex. Rab.* 41.1; *Lev. Rab.* 29.5; *Num. Rab.* 5.8; 10.1; 16.24; *Deut. Rab.* 7.1, 3, 9; *Tg. Eccl.* 6.12.

135. *B. Šabb.* 88b; *Ex. Rab.* 5.9; *Lev. Rab.* 1.11; *Deut. Rab.* 1.6; *Song Rab.* 5.16, section 3.

136. 1QS 3.6–8.

137. 1QS 6.247.25; 4Q265 1 1–2; 4Q266 18 4–5; 4Q284a.

The phrase "all flesh" in both documents means "all humanity" (John 17:2).[138] The human body's mortality and finiteness meant such flesh lacked moral perfection and was susceptible to sin (1 John 2:16).[139]

Qumran considered that the uninformed and the religious leaders are under covenant curse (John 7:49; Deut 27:15-26).[140] Both frameworks recognize that among Judaism covenantal curses and damnation are for those who apostatize from the way of the Law (John 7:49).[141]

At Qumran, atonement is caused by God,[142] but consistent as a blessing of compliance to the Law.[143] For Qumran, remaining consistent in the narrow way of the Law obtains everlasting life,[144] whereas, the Gospel of John recognizes that Moses provided the Law establishing covenantal curse and blessings for the Jewish community (John 7:49). In contrast to this, John sees salvation as graciously provided by faith in Christ (John 1:17; 3:16). 1 John 1:7-2:2 identifies that Christ is the active agent to graciously bring about atoning propitiation and forgiveness. However, both 1QS and John anticipate that the Law will continue to be the dominant framework governing Israel until the Prophet, and Messiah of Aaron and Israel comes to bring in the new kingdom era (John 1:17).[145]

The phrase "keeping my word" is used among O.T. and early Judaism as obeying God's Law and the subsequent echo of the prophets.[146] In John the phrase shifts to that of the authoritative Messiah Jesus; Jesus' word extends and replaces the Law as authority in the believer's life (John 8:51-52, 55; 14:23-24; 15:20; 17:6; 1 John 2:5; Rev 3:8, 10).

---

138. Gen 6:3, 12-13; Num 16:22; Pss 78:39; 145:21; Isa 40:5-6; 49:26; Jer 25:31; 45:5; Ezek 20:48; 21:4-5; Rom 3:20; *Jub.* 25.22; 1QS 11.9; CD 1.2; 2:20; 1QH 13.13, 16; 1QM 12.12; 4Q511 frg. 35; line 1; *Sir.* 28.5; *T. Jud.* 19.4; *T. Zeb.* 9.7; *T. Ab.* 7.16B; *T. Job* 27.2/3; It can also include animals (Gen 9:16; Num 18:15; Ps 136:25; *Jub.* 5.2).

139. 1QS 11.9, 12; 1QH 9.14-16.

140. 1QS 10:19-21; *Midr. Sam.* 5.9.

141. 1QS 2.11-18; 8.22.

142. 1QS 1.24; 2.16; 4.22; 5.5-6, 21-22.

143. 1QS 5.2, 6; 8.22.

144. 1QS 4.7; *Ps. Sol.* 14.3 repeated with argument from 5.15; and 6.18; *T. Joseph* 18.1; *Jub.* 5.10; 10.17; 22.22; *2 Bar.* 48.22b; CD 3.11-16, 20-21; 7.5, 9; 13.11; 20.17-20, 25-27; 4Q228 frag. 1 1.9; 4Q266, frag. 11; 4QMMT C; 1QS 3.7-12; additionally CD col. 7, 6 refers to the result of obedience to the Law as living for 1000 generations; Gathercole, "Torah, Life and Salvation," In *From Prophecy to Testament.* ed. Evans and Sanders, 126-45; Gathercole, *Where is Boasting?*, 66-67; Neusner, *Handbook of Rabbinic Theology*, 559-99; contrary to Dunn, *The Theology of the Apostle Paul*, 152-3.

145. 1QS 9.9-11.

146. Deut 4:2; 33:9; 1 Chr 10:13; Ps 119:9, 17, 67, 101, 158; *Jub.* 2.28; CD 6.18; 10.14, 16; 20.17; 1QS 5.9; 8.3; 10.21; *Sib. Or.* 1.52-53.

The phrase "works of God" are often the mighty miracles that God accomplishes (John 4:34; 9:3; 17:4; Rev 15:3).[147] However, in John and 1QS "works" more often stand for ethically complying with the commandments of God (John 3:19-21; 7:7; 8:39, 41; 1 John 3:8, 12; 2 John 11; 3 John 10; Rev 2:2, 5-6, 19, 22-23, 26; 3:1-2; 8, 15; 9:20; 14:13; 16:1; 18:6; 20:12-13; 22:12).[148]

Knowledge is especially that of God's will and contains a relational and moral component as Eduard Lohse develops.

God, without whose will nothing takes place, teaches all understanding (1QS 11.17f; 3.15). He reveals what is hidden and makes his mysteries known (1QpHab 11.1; 1QS 5.11; 1QH 4.27; etc.). The will of God is made known to the members of the covenant community in the covenant, that is the legal statutes given by God (1QS 3.1; 8.9f). This knowledge includes the obligation to do the will of God (1QS 1.5; 9.13; etc.) and to conduct one's life according to the will of God.[149]

However, beneath this relational and moral knowledge is the actual relationship of knowing God in an intimate and covenantal manner (John 17:3; 1 John 5:20).[150] This could be identified with Paul Moser's filial knowledge of God.[151] John embraces such a view and way of knowledge grounded

---

147. 1QS 4.4; 1QM 13.9; CD 13.7-8; Tob 12.6.

148. Several different Hebrew phrases translate as 'works of the Law' (ἔργων νόμου) from either 'works' (מַעֲשֵׂה) or 'faithfulness' (לְםֹ חֶסֶד); 1QS 5.21, 23-24; 6.18; 4Q394 frag. 3-7 col. 1-2.1-3; 4Q398=4QMMT frag. 14 col. 2.3; 4QFlor. 1.1-7; *2 Bar.* 57.2; Lohmeyer, *Probleme paulinischer Theologie*, 3174; Christianson, *The Covenant in Judaism and Paul*; Watson, *Paul and the Hermeneutics of Faith*, 334-5; Hofius, "'Werke des Gesetzes,'" In *Paulus und Johannes*. ed. Sänger and Mell, 271-310; Dunn, *The New Perspective on Paul*, especially chapters 1, 8, 10, 14, 17, 19 which were articles from 1992-2008 on works of the Law which nicely provides a trajectory for how the view grew; de Roo, "The Concept of 'Works of the Law' in Jewish and Christian Literature," In *Christian-Jewish Relations Through the Centuries*. ed. Porter and Pearson, 116-47; Cranfield, "'The Works of the Law' in the Epistle to the Romans," *JSNT* 43(1991): 89-101; these contrast with Dunn, *Romans 1-8*, 1:159; Sanders, *Paul and Palestinian Judaism*, 118; of reformation view: Moo, *Romans 1-8*, 216-7; "'Law', 'Works of the Law', and Legalism in Paul," *WTJ* 45(1983): 82; Bachmann, "Rechtfertigung und Gesetzeswerke bei Paulus," *TZ* 49(1993): 1-33; "4QMMT und Galaterbrief, *ma'ase hatorah* und *ERGA NOMOU*," *ZNW* 89(1998): 91-113, both reprinted in *Antijudaismus im Galaterbrief*, 1-33, 33-56; or English translation: *Anti-Judaism in Galatians?*, 15. In spite of Dunn's identification of the concept with the "palisades and iron walls to prevent mixing with any other peoples" *Letter of Aristeas* 139-42 (*The New Perspective on Paul*, 8-9), even though the phrase "works of the Law" is not in the *Letter of Aristeas*; Hogeterp, "4QMMT and Paradigms of Second Temple Judaism," *Dead Sea Discoveries* 15(2008): 359-379.

149. Lohse, *Colossians and Philemon*, 25.

150. Driver, *The Judean Scrolls*, 545 compares this with 1QS 2.3.

151. Moser, *The Elusive God*, 46-7, 98, 113-123.

in God's self-revelation (John 1:14). There is a personal component to this knowledge in knowing God and Jesus. This knowledge cannot be separated from faith in the historical Jesus (1 John 4:1-6). Likewise, this knowledge is evident in the believer's life through the appropriate virtues that evidence consistency of life; one knows Him as evident in obedience (1 John 2:3; 3:6; 5:2, 18), walks in love (3:14; 4:7-8, 13; 5:2), adheres to the truth (1 John 4:6; 5:13; 3 John 12) and blesses with peace (2 John 10-11; Matt. 10:12).[152] Unfortunately such life-changing wisdom went forth among humanity but found no dwelling place, being rejected by humans (John 1:10).[153]

The O.T. and early Judaism developed a narrow way of light for righteousness and wisdom (Rev 15:3).[154] To reflect this "way" in the desert of Isaiah 40, the Qumran community referred to itself as "the way."[155] To bring this life transformation about in 1QS the spirit of truth fosters life transformation to include the following virtues: love the brotherhood of light, hate darkness, humility, patience, abundant compassion, perpetual goodness, insight, understanding, wisdom, faithfulness, and zeal for Law.[156] Such a transformed character identifies the children of light as in the status of being righteous, where such righteousness is recognizable through righteous works.[157] John proposes a similar divinely caused transformed life producing the following virtues: faith and love of Jesus as the One embodied from God, love of Christian brothers, truthfulness, freedom in this truth, obedience to Jesus commandments and lifestyle, consistent maturity not dominated or characterized by sin, responsiveness to publicly acknowledge personal sin, answered prayer, and joy (John 3:16, 21; 8:32, 34, 42; 15:10-12, 14-17; 16:8-10; 17:17, 19; 18:37; 1 John 1:5-10; 2:3, 5, 10-11, 21; 3:3-11, 23-24; 4:2, 6-8, 12, 16-17, 20-21; 5:3, 10-11, 13-16). There is significant overlap of virtue lists but they are not identical. For example, both ban the hatred of spiritual brothers (1 John 4:7-8, 16, 20-21).[158] Such a commitment to virtues produced a physical and moral separation for God[159] from outsid-

---

152. 1QS 2.9; Tob 12.17.

153. *1 En.* 42.2.

154. Exod 18:20; 32:8; Deut 8:6; 9:16; 10:12; 11:22, 28; Isa 55:7-9; 56:11; 59:8; 66:3; Tob 1.3; *1 En.* 91.19; 94.1; *Jub.* 20.2; 21.2; 23.20-21; 25.10; 1QS 3.9, 18; 4.6, 12; 5.10; 6.2; 9.8, 19; CD 2.15-16; 7.4, 6-7; 8.9; 4Q400 frg. 1 col. 1 line 14; *Sib. Or.* 3.233.

155. 1QS 8.14; 9.17-20; 10.21; CD 1.13;2.3; 4Q403 1 1.22; 4Q405 frg. 23, col. 1.11; 4Q185 frg. 1-2, col. 2.1-2; 4Q400 frg. 1, col. 1.14; 4Q473 frg. 1; *Jub.* 23.20-21.

156. 1QS 1.9-11; 4.3-4; 9.21.

157. 1QS 3.19; 4.10, 20; also "God's sons" are referred to as "righteous" in Sir 4.10; Wis 2.18; *Jub.* 1.24-25; 4QFlor 1.6-7; 1QSa 2.11-14.

158. 1QS 5.25.

159. *Jub.* 22.29; 30.8; 1QS 8.21; 9.6; 1QM 9.8-10; 14.12; Wis 18.9; 3 Macc 6.3; *Ex.*

ers[160] (John 17:14; Rev 12:6). Within such a two-ways salvation framework, those who by divine transformation manifest these virtues consistently are seen as atoned for by God and thus justified (1 John 1:7–2:2).[161]

In contrast, the phrase "walking in darkness" became identified as describing humanity in sin (John 8:12)[162] ushering in a blind condition of not knowing where they are going (John 9:4; 11:9; 12:35).[163] These damned partook of the character of darkness such that they could be called children of darkness.[164] In this framework, to complete the idea of house codes, Geza Vermes identifies that 1QS 4.10–11 catalogs the following vice list: greed, slackness in search for righteousness, wickedness and lies, haughtiness and pride, falseness and deceit, cruelty and abundant evil, ill temper and much temper and brazen insolence, abominable deeds [committed] in a spirit of lust, ways of lewdness in the service of uncleanness, a blaspheming tongue, blindness of eye and dullness of ear, and stiffness of neck and heaviness of heart.[165]

Apostasy is referred by both documents as "stumbling," which indicates a damning judgment (John 6:61; 1 John 2:10).[166] 1QS views such apostasy as unpardonable sin.[167] John's development of unpardonable sin is by using the phrase "sin unto death" (1 John 5:16). In response to this, both 1QS and John identify that the believers are not to show hospitality to such false teachers (2 John 8–11).[168] Instead, covenant curse and God's intended vengeance comes upon the sons of darkness, and thus serves as the basis for 1QS calling the children of light to hate the wicked people.[169]

Rab. 15.24; 1 Cor 1;2; 1 Clem. 1.1.

160. 1QS 5.18; 9.8–9; CD 13.14–15.

161. Isa 1:27; 56:1; 58:8; 1QS 10.11; 11.2–3, 5, 9, 12–15; 1QH 4.29–32, 36–37; Gen. Rab. 33.1; Ruth Rab. proem 1.

162. Eccl 2:14; 1QS 3.21; 4.11; 11.10; Pesiq. Rab. 8.5; t. 'Ed. 2.3; Bennema, "Christ, the Spirit, and the Knowledge of God," In The Bible and Epistemology. ed. Healy and Parry, 110–14.

163. Prov 4:19; Gen. Rab. 60.1.

164. 1QS 2.16; 3.13, 24–25; 1QM 1.1, 9, 11, 13; 3.6; 13.14–15; 4Q176 frg. 12–13, col.1, lines 12, 16; frg. 10–11, 7–9, 20, 26, line 7.

165. Vermes, The Complete Dead Sea Scrolls, 102; 1QS 4.10–11.

166. 1QS 2.11–12; 3.24; 1QpHab 11.7–8; 4Q174 3.7–9; Sir 9.5; 25.21; 34.7, 17; 35.15; 39.24; Rom 11:11; 1 Cor 8:9; James 2:10; 3:2; b. Soṭ. 22a; T. Reu. 4.7.

167. 1QS 7.15–17, 22–23; 1Q22; 4Q163 frg. 6–7; CD 8.8; 10.3; Jub. 15.34; p. Ḥag. 2.1, section 9; p. Šebu. 1.6, section 5.

168. 1QS 7.24–25; Sipre Deut. 1.10.1; p. Giṭ. 5.10 section 2; Matt 10:14; Sir 11.29, 34; Did. 11.5.

169. 1QS 1.4, 9–11; Ps 139:21; Sir 27.24.

In early Judaism, most sinners endure hell temporarily where they are either annihilated[170] or released.[171] John sketches out a more permanent horror of everlasting punishment reflective of Daniel's resurrection parallel (John 3:16–18 parallel of everlasting life and judgment similar to Dan 12:2; Rev 20:10; Matt 25:41, 46). However, both John and 1QS include these ideas as hell.

In John, the question "Are you Elijah?" refers to the promise to send Elijah before the Day of the Lord so that Israel might join kingdom blessing instead of covenant curse (John 1:21; Mal 3:1–2; 4:5–6).[172] John the Baptist refuses to identify himself as this definitive Elijah figure (John 1:21) but instead defines himself by Isaiah 40:3 as a voice crying in the wilderness "Make straight the way of the Lord" (John 1:23). This same Isaianic text and orientation is how 1QS defines the role of the Qumran community.[173] Qumran's narrow desert way reflects the Law of Moses[174] and the continuing revelation from the holy spirit and the prophets. Whereas, John the Baptist narrow desert way focuses especially on embracing and following Jesus as Messiah (John 1:6–8, 29–34).

As a metaphor, cleansing is developed as that which is brought about by the holy spirit[175] but this cleansing is also described as occurring through cleansing waters.[176] Such cleansing brings about a morally pure lifestyle free of iniquity. However, these cleansing waters are clarified to not be ritual washings.[177] Craig Keener takes this washing water in 1QS as a metaphor for the holy spirit.[178] Drawing the two sources together, Keener also sees the Johaninne phrase "born of water and the Spirit" as equivalent to "born from above" and thus in his opinion completely a divinely accomplished activity (John 3:3, 5).[179] Perhaps Raymond Brown's view that the "water" is an allusion to the initiation rite of baptism like that of John the Baptist, or sectarian Jews practiced (identifying Jews with kingdom) fits better as the external evidence for the internal transformation wrought by God and is also similar

---

170. 1QS 4.13–14; *Gen. Rab.* 6.6; t. Sanh. 13.3, 4; *Pesiq. Rab Kah.* 10.4; *Pesiq. Rab.* 11.5; 2 Macc 12.43–45.

171. *Num. Rab.* 18.20; b. Šabb. 33b; *Lam. Rab.* 1.11–12, section 40.

172. Sir 48.10.

173. 1QS 8.12–16; 9.19–20; 4Q176 1–2 1.4–9; *Targum Pseudo-Jonathan* as presented by Taylor, *The Immerser*, 26.

174. 1QS 8.15–16.

175. 1QS 3.7; 4.21.

176. 1QS 3.8–9.

177. 1QS 3.4.

178. Keener, *John*, 1:351.

179. Keener, *John*, 1:547.

to the baptismal practice in 1QS (John 1:1:23; 3:3, 5; Matt 3:2).[180] The contextual way to show the wind/spirit moving is through the external evidence of the believer's commitment in baptism (John 3:8).

Qumran's transformational role[181] is argued by Shafaat and Keener to be analogous to the Johannine role of the *paraklete* (John 15:15; 16:13; 1 John 2:1).[182] This is unlikely since the Johannine concept is more complex than this. The concept includes Jesus as *paraklete* in His ascension as a personal comforter to apply atonement when the Christian sins and is transparent in acknowledging his sin (1 John 1:7–2:2). The Johannine concept also entails that the Holy Spirit is *paraklete* during Jesus ascension, so that the Spirit will convict the world of sin, righteousness and judgment (John 16:7–11). This role is not necessarily transformational since the world could remain unresponsive to this convicting ministry. However, the Spirit's role of *paraklete* will include an abiding ministry of the spirit of truth in and encouraging believers in a manner that the world cannot receive (John 14:16–17).

1QS 9.11 maintain the coming of eschatological figures to include three separate individuals: the Prophet,[183] a priestly messiah of Aaron,[184] and a Davidic kingly messiah of Israel.[185] John combines the role of the Mosaic Prophet and Messianic King into the one person Jesus, Who is beyond both (John 1:41, 48–49; 4:19; 6:31–40; 18:37; 19:19). Perhaps, the priestly Messiah is also seen as a description of Jesus on the basis that He propitiates for the sin of His people using a word only appropriate with reference to either

---

180. 1QS 3.4–9; 6.14–23; b. *Yeban* 2; T. *Levi* 14.6; *Sib. Or.* 4.165; Brown, *John I–XII*, 142–3; afterlife is known as kingdom (11QTemple 51.15–16; Philo, *Spec.* 4.164).

181. 1QS 4.20–23; 1QH 3.8–10.

182. Shafaat, "Geber of the Qumran Scrolls," *NTS* 26(1980–1): 263–69; Keener, *John*, 2:956.

183. 1QS 9.11; Deut. 18:15–21 echoed in 4Q175 1.5–8; 4QTest. 1–20; CD 2.12; 6.1; 1QH 18.14–15; 11QMelch.; *Gen. Rab.* 100.10; *Deut. Rab.* 9.9; *Pesiq. Rab Kah.* 5.8.

184. 1QS 9.11; 1QSa 2.11–17; CD 12:23–13:1; 14:19; 19:10–11; 20:1; *Charter of a Jewish Sectarian Association* 9.11; text 7 19; 4Q171 3.15; 4Q175 1.14; 4Q521 frag. 8 9. Some also argue that 4Q174 3.11–12 "interpreter of the Law" should be identified as the priestly Messiah because it's close proximity to the blessing of Levi of Deuteronomy 33 in this text, a blessing that in the earlier 4QTestimonia probably refers to the eschatological priest. A priestly Messiah is also supported by: T. *of the Twelve Patriarchs*, T. *Levi* 4.2; 17.2; 18.6–7.

185. 1QS 9.11; 2 Sam 7:12–15; *Pss. of Sol.* 17.32; 18.57; *Shemoneh 'Esreh* 14; Sir 47.11, 22; 1 Macc 2.57; CD 7.20; 12.23–13.1; 14.19 (=4Q266 frag. 18, 3.12); 19.10–11; 20.1; 1QSa 2.11–12, 14–15, 20–21; 1QSb 5.20; 1QM 5.1; 4Q161; 4Q252 frag. 1 5.3–4; 4Q381 frag. 15.7; 4Q382 frag. 16.2; 4Q458 frag. 2, 2.6; 4Q521 frag. 2 4, 2.1; 4Q521 frag. 7.3; 4QFlor 1.10–13; 4QPat 3–4; b. '*Erub.* 43a; *Yoma* 10a; *Sukk.* 52a; 52b; *Meg.* 17b; *Hagiga* 16a; *Yebam.* 62a; *Ketab* 1126; *Soṭah.* 48b; *Sanh.* 38a; *Gen. Rab.* 97 on Gen 49:10; *Ex. Rab.* 25.12 on Exod 16:29; *Num. Rab.* 14.1 on Num 7:48.

God or the high priest at the Day of Atonement (1 John 2:2; 4:10). Perhaps Jesus as priest is also hinted at through Him being identified by John the Baptist as the "lamb of God, Who takes away the sin of the world" and Jesus' own reference that He is the Temple, where such atonement would be thought to take place through the death of the sacrifice (John 1:29, 36; 2:19–22). Clearly John develops Jesus as Messiah as the center of his gospel. Such a unified and focused emphasis on Messiah Jesus is very foreign to 1QS presentation of diverse Messianic roles.

In summary, 1QS and John share a significant overlap of second Temple thought forms and phraseology. Though the genre and purpose of each document is different there is a commonality of a similar early Jewish heritage, worldview, and language.

Conclusion

Johannine Epistemology retains a substantial role for empiricism and the corporate testimony that confirms the voice and presence of Jesus. John adds a distinctive voice expressing Jesus Christ as sent from the Father in His humanity to know, to say and to do what the Father has for Him. As Jesus ascends, He leaves the Holy Spirit to reveal to the apostles what they need to know including reminders of what Jesus had said and predictions for the future as well. Much of the perspective that John reflects in this inspired empirical presentation of Jesus reflects a perspectivalism that is also apparent in early Judaism, especially strongly instanced by 1QS.

7

James' Wisdom Epistemology of Empiricism and Evidence

THESIS: JAMES JOINS OLD Testament and ancient Near Eastern wisdom literature in developing an empirical and evidential epistemology that informs a virtue ethic of wisdom within the way creation works, which is pragmatically vindicated through consistent good deeds.

Jesus' brother, James the Just, was a leading pillar for the Church in Jerusalem (Jas 1:1; Acts 12:17; 15:13; 21:18; 1 Cor 15:7; Gal 1:19; 2:9, 12).[1] In this capacity, James provided wise counsel for the Jewish Christian diaspora scattered throughout the Roman Empire (James 1:1).[2] Tradition presented James as a Nazarite, persistently praying for Israel to be forgiven, who was martyred by the high priest Ananus before Vespasian's siege of Jerusalem.[3]

There are three Greek words for knowledge utilized in James (γινώσκω, ἐπισταμαι, and οἴδα). All the words emphasize an experiential knowing that leads to practice (Jas 2:20; 3:13; 4:17). This would position James concept of knowledge within a collective basic belief form of empiricism.[4] In James, ἐπισταμαι emphasized more the idea of "recognize" than the other two words (Jas 1:3; 2:20; 5:20). The word οἴδα maintains within its semantic field more of an emphasis of knowing that there are consequences, such that one

---

1. Eusebius, *Hist. eccl.* 2.23.15; Wis 2.15.

2. Origen, *Hom. In Gen.* 13.2; *Hom. In Jos.* 7.1; *Comm. In Ps.* 30, 65, 118; *Sel. Exod.* 15; *Comm. In Joh.* frag 6, 126; *P. Oxy.* 10.1229; 11.1171; Eusebius, *Hist. eccl.* 2.23.24–25; Thirty-ninth Easter letter; Council of Rome (382 A.D.), Synod of Hippo (A.D. 393) and Third Council of Carthage (A.D. 397, 419).

3. Eusebius, *Hist. eccl.* 2.23.4–8 [Hegesippus]; Josephus, *Ant.* 20.200; Wis 3.5–6.

4. Gericke, "A Comprehensive Philosophical Approach to Qohelet's Epistemology," *HvTSt* 71:1(2015): 3, 7–8; Plantinga, *Warrant and Proper Function*, 6; *Knowledge and Christian Belief*, 25–44; Locke, *Concerning Human Understanding* 1.1.15; 2.11.8–9; 2.32.6; 3.3.6–8; pre-modern empiricism is apparent in Lactanius, *Workmanship of God*, 9–10.

reaps what she sows (Jas 3:1; 4:4). In fact, as one's responsibility increases so do the consequences (Jas 3:1). Whereas, ἐπισταμαι includes the idea of being agnostic about the future which then prompts proposing and humbly implementing pragmatic plans to realize a hoped for future (Jas 4:14).[5]

Jaco Gericke raised a series of arbitrary issues about knowledge in Qohelet that show Gericke operated in a Platonic concept of knowledge as *justified true belief* in contemporary empiricism.[6] For example, within Platonic knowledge Gettier problems present themselves in which one's belief may be justified and true yet fail to count as knowledge.[7] However, Gericke proposed three ways to resolve Gettier problems all of which James and ANE wisdom could appeal. 1) The first escape from Gettier is to recognize a causal approach championed by Alvin Goldman that something is known only if the truth of a belief has caused the subject to have that belief in the appropriate way.[8] 2) A second manner to escape Gettier problems is to follow Keith Lehrer and Thomas Paxton in adding an additional defeasibility condition, that is that knowledge is redefined as undefeated justified true belief.[9] In James 2:14-26 faith working in pragmatic ways vindicates the authenticity of knowledge using either a Goldman causality strategy or a Peircean defeasibility condition. 3) However, neither Qohelet, nor James are engage empirical knowledge within such modern nuance. Rather, James and Qohelet define knowledge to operate more within a basic belief with a broader empirical semantic field than does Platonism, so in James' concept of knowledge Gettier problems would never emerge.[10] So the fact

---

5. Frydrych, *Living Under the Sun*, 15–53; Gericke, "A Comprehensive Philosophical Approach to Qohelet's Epistemology," *HvTSt* 71:1(2015): 4–5; Peirce, *Collected Papers*. Hartshorne and Weiss, vol. 5 paragraph 9; "The Fixation of Belief," *Popular Science Monthly* 12(Nov., 1877): 1–15; "How to Make Our Ideas Clear," *Popular Science Monthly* 12(Jan., 1878): 286–302.

6. Gericke, "A Comprehensive Philosophical Approach to Qohelet's Epistemology," *HvTSt* 71:1(2015): 5–6; Plato, *Theaetetus* 151, 186.

7. Gericke, "A Comprehensive Philosophical Approach to Qohelet's Epistemology," *HvTSt* 71:1(2015): 5–6; Gettier, "Is Justified True Belief Knowledge?," *Analysis* 23(1963): 121–23.

8. Gericke, "A Comprehensive Philosophical Approach to Qohelet's Epistemology," *HvTSt* 71:1(2015): 6; Goldman, "A Causal Theory of Knowing," *The Journal of Philosophy* 64(1967): 357–72.

9. Gericke, "A Comprehensive Philosophical Approach to Qohelet's Epistemology," *HvTSt* 71:1(2015): 6; Lehrer and Paxson, "Knowledge: Undefeated Justified True Belief," *The Journal of Philosophy* 66(1969): 225–37.

10. Gericke, "A Comprehensive Philosophical Approach to Qohelet's Epistemology," *HvTSt* 71:1(2015): 6; Plantinga, *Warrant and Proper Function*, 6; *Knowledge and Christian Belief*, 25–44; Locke, *Concerning Human Understanding* 1.1.15; 2.11.8–9; 2.32.6; 3.3.6–8; pre-modern empiricism is apparent in Lactanius, *Workmanship of God*, 9–10.

that Gericke raised the Gettier issue shows that he is exploring a modern understanding of Qohelet rather than Qohelet's biblical semantic thought forms themselves.

Additionally, Jaco Gericke raised categories championed by Bertrand Russell such as "knowing that" (כִּי) clauses in Eccl 3:12, 14; 4:17; 7:22; 8:12; 9:5; 11:9 which are parallel to ὅτι clauses in Jas 1:3; 2:20; 3:1; 5:20) and "knowing how" (ל) clauses in Eccl 6:8 and 10:15 which are broadly parallel to the verb expressing knowledge in Jas 4:14 and 17).[11] Such analysis with wisdom literature presents versions of overlapping empirical experience. Gericke concludes this analysis with "the above refers to experiential knowledge and skill"[12] which locates all these arbitrary divisions of knowledge within empiricism.

Many commentaries recognize that James is written in a form of paraenesis. Dibelius clarifies that "by paraenesis we mean a wisdom text which strings together admonitions of general ethical content."[13] Such paraenesis often has an eclectic shift of topics within ancient Near Eastern wisdom from the vantage of a creation theology perspective.

O.T. wisdom books do not seem to fit within the dominant Old Testament covenant strategy for Israel, as do the Law and the prophets. W. G. Lambert reminds us that the piety of O.T. wisdom "is completely detached from the law and ritual, which gives it a distinctive place in the Hebrew Bible."[14]

There is no indication that the Old Testament wisdom books themselves are positioned conceptually within the Mosaic covenant. For example, the use of *berit* or "covenant" within wisdom is best seen as referring to other kinds of relationships, like a marriage covenant that an adulteress spurns even though it is from God (Prov 2:17). Eliphaz uses *berit* as a metaphor of peace in a synonymous parallel relationship to *shalom* (Job 5:23). Job confesses that he has covenanted with his eyes not to gaze on a virgin in lust (Job 31:1). God also barrages Job with questions like "Will you covenant with Leviathan to make him your servant?" (Job 41:4). Furthermore, *torah* in Job is a reference from Eliphaz that his own instruction is viewed by him as God's (Job 22:22). However, the dominant pattern of *torah* in Proverbs is that of parental instruction, that especially a boy's father tells his son, and

---

11. Gericke, "A Comprehensive Philosophical Approach to Qohelet's Epistemology," *HvTSt* 71:1(2015): 3; Russell, "Knowledge by Acquaintance and Knowledge by Description," *Proceedings of the Aristotelian Society* 11(1910–11):108–128.

12. Gericke, "A Comprehensive Philosophical Approach to Qohelet's Epistemology," *HvTSt* 71:1(2015): 3.

13. Dibelius, *James*, 3, 5–6 following Wendland, *Anaximenes von Lampsakos*, 81ff; Vetschera, *Zur griechischen Paränese*.

14. Lambert, *Babylonian Wisdom Literature*, 1.

the son must obey (Prov 1:8; 3:1; 4:2; 6:20, 23; 7:2; 23:14; 28:4, 7, 9; 29:18; 31:26).[15] This of course positions Proverbs as within the emphasis of ancient Near East wisdom as it communicates broadly observable instruction for how creation works communicated from father to the son who would become king.[16]

However, within wisdom psalms and early Jewish wisdom texts after the Babylonian captivity, the Mosaic covenant strategy as *torah* and Law blend with wisdom to inform and direct the meditation of wise people (Pss 1:2; 37:31).[17] James continues in this early Jewish mixing of wisdom and Law traditions (Jas 2:8–12).[18] The Mosaic Law is the royal Law from the divine King (Jas 2:8).[19] James' experience in synagogue exposed him to authoritative *mishnahic* method in which apodictic laws are grouped in lists such as the Decalogue to aid memorization. Instances of central Law texts specifically include some of these memorized obligatory *torah* or *halakhah* such as the Decalogue and loving one's neighbor as one loves oneself (Jas 2:8–11; Exod 20:13–14; Lev 19:18; Deut 5:17–18). This appeal works within *pesher* (contemporizing the *torah* to new issues)[20] supporting James' command to not provide preferential treatment to wealthy but to honor the poor in their midst or God will judge (Jas 2:1–13). However, James primarily utilized a *midrashic* method utilizing narrative story to provide a biblical reason for

---

15. Bullock has produced a nice volume in *An Introduction to the Old Testament Poetic Books* but in this volume p. 31 he alludes to overlapping and borrowing of wisdom from Law and in two Evangelical Theological Society papers he defends this view. He seems to follow von Rad, *Old Testament Theology*, 1:433–34 and Scott, "Priesthood, Prophecy, Wisdom, and the Knowledge of God," *JBL* 80 (1961): 1–15 in this view. However, the evidence of these terms in the wisdom books contexts seems to go otherwise than to connect wisdom with Law. In the O.T., Wisdom and Law only seem to get connected in Psalms 1, 19, 111, and 119, and the second Temple works of Sir and the Wis, showing that wisdom and Law are not opposed to each other, even though neither seems to show evidence of being dependent on the other. Within the New Testament wisdom and Law are intimately connected in the ministries of Jesus as sage and new Moses, and echoed in wisdom books like James. All this shows that wisdom and Law are harmonious but are grounded in different strategies.

16. The forum of wisdom being communicated in the ancient near East as from father to son is broadly exampled by the following few samples: Sumerian *Instructions of Suruppak*, Babylonian *Counsels of Wisdom*, Ugaritic *Counsels of Shubeawilum*, Egyptian *Instruction of Merikare*, *Instruction of Ptahhotep*, and *Instruction of Any*.

17. Sir 35.1ff; 38.24–39:11.

18. Corroborated by *The Letter of Peter to James* 2.5.

19. 4 Macc 14.2.

20. Ellis, "A Note on Pauline Hermeneutics," *NTS* 2(1955–6): 131–2; Sanders, "Habakkuk in Qumran, Paul, and the Old Testament," In *Paul and the Scriptures of Israel*. ed. Evans and Sanders, 107–8.

action.²¹ For example, James makes *halakhah* appeals to show faith through practical works by utilizing narrative accounts of Abraham's near-sacrificing of Isaac and Rahab's hiding the spies (Jas 2:14–26). These *halakhah* appeals reflect warrant and obligation from *torah* narrative, rather than Aristotelian logic.²² An additional appeal is made by James for his readers to be righteous and pray based on the narrative account of Elijah's effective prayer for draught and rain (Jas 5:13–18), which is grounded in Mosaic covenant curse and blessing (Deut 28:12, 24). Because God provides such Law, no interpreter is in a position to judge and disregard God's Law, for the divine Judge will destroy those who are so disobedient (Jas 4:11–12).²³ Instead, for these Jewish Christians the Mosaic Law should be taken intensely to heart in practical ways (Jas 1:26–27). As such the Mosaic Law becomes a perfect Law of freedom, providing real guidance for life (Jas 1:26–27; Pss 19:7; 119).²⁴ This form of knowing informs the right thing to do so that the informed might do it in their practice (James 4:17).

In the few places that lady wisdom speaks she brings revelation (Prov 1:20–33; 8–9). Because wisdom was present with the creation process (Prov 3:19; 8:22–31; Ps 104:24; Job 28:26–28),²⁵ Thomas Frydrych argued that wisdom provides a correct mediator revelational perspective of creation which offers a favorable relation with Yahweh.²⁶ However, in James, wisdom

---

21. Josephus, *Ag. Ap.* 2.175–81; Jerusalem synagogue Theodotus inscription; Philo, *Embassy* 311–3; *Megillat Ta'anit*; *y. Hor.* 3.5 (48c); *b. Tem.* 14b; *b. B. Meṣ.* 59a–b; *Sifre Deut.* 351; *Iggeret Rav Sherira Gaon* 1–2; Hays utilizes an appeal from authority to explain Paul's argument in "Psalm 143 and the Logic of Romans 3," *JBL* 99:1(1980): 107–15; Meeks provides a Pauline example of rabbinic *midrash* (story and exhortation) following *m. 'Abot* 5.4 sins and plagues of the Exodus in "'And Rose up to Play,'" *JSNT* 16(1982): 64–78, following the lead of Weiss, *Der erste Korintherbrief*, 250; Zeitlin, "Midrash: A Historical Study" *JQR* 44(1953): 21–36; Wright, *Midrash*, 52–59, 64–67; Ellis, "Midrash, Targum and New Testament Quotations," In *Neotestamentica et Semitica*. ed. Ellis and Wilcox, 61–69; le Déaut, "Apropos a Definition of Midrash" *Int* 25(1971): 259–82; Miller, "Targum, Midrash and the Use of the Old Testament in the New Testament" *JSJ* 2(1971): 29–82; Bloch, "Midrash," In *Approaches to Ancient Judaism*. ed. Green, 29–50; Porton, "Defining Midrash," In *The Study of Ancient Judaism*. ed. Neusner, 1:55–95; McNamara, "Some Issues and Recent Writings on Judaism and the New Testament" *IBS* 9(1987): 136–49.

22. Ellis, *Paul's Use of the Old Testament*, 11; Gooch, "Paul, the Mind of Christ, and Philosophy," In *Jesus and Philosophy*. ed. Moser, 89.

23. Sir 1.1–10.

24. Philo, *Prob.* 43–48 describes Mosaic law in this manner; Stoics describe a law of nature in this manner (Epictetus, *Diatr.* 4.1.158; Seneca, *Vit. Beat.* 15.7) but natural law does not fit James' use of "law" (νόμον) because he quotes Exod 20:13–14; Lev 19:18; Deut 5:17–18 from Law in James 2:8–11.

25. Sir 1.1, 4; Wis 7.21; 9.1–4, 9.

26. Frydrych, *Living Under the Sun*, 57–59, 218 "God is an important part of the

comes more directly from God as direct revelation provided to those who ask (Jas 1:5; 3:15). As such, this wisdom reflect divine characteristics (such as: purity, peace, gentleness, reasonableness, mercy, goodness, and integrity) into the lives which embrace it (Jas 3:15–18).

The strategy of ancient Near Eastern wisdom draws upon the common wisdom available from empirically observing the way creation works as from the Creator (Jas 1:11, 17–18; Job 38–41; Prov 3:19–20; 20:12; 22:2; 30:14).[27] James continues this creation theology perspective to argue for why it is not appropriate to blame the generous Creator for suffering, nor to curse fellow humans made by the Creator in His image (Jas 1:17–18; 3:9). Michael Fox summarized that wisdom obtained from observing creation is accessed throughout the ancient Near East wisdom context as follows:

> The similarities in form and content between Israelite and Egyptian didactic wisdom literature have been so well established that there can be no doubt that Israelite Wisdom is part of an international genre (which includes Mesopotamian wisdom) and cannot be properly studied in isolation.[28]

The similarities penetrate deeper than structure to the fundamental concepts. The integrity of wisdom in Proverbs, Qoheleth, Job and James is the same, reflecting what Thomas Frydrych identified as "epistemological implications" of coherence and empirical observations that reflect the order of creation.[29] As such wisdom does not provide absolute and precise truths but paradigmatic reasonable approximations of reality that are sufficient to fund life purposes.[30]

For example, Crenshaw develops the foundational role for justice in wisdom literature.

> The fundamental concept which underlies these instructions is *ma'at*, which may be translated as justice, order, truth. No distinction exists between secular and religious truth for this

---

epistemological process."

27. Johnson, "The Seeds of Epistemology and Ontology in Genesis 1" *Proceedings EGU & MWBS* 18(1998): 1–2 develops empirical creation theology before getting distracted with psychological self-awareness categories. Westermann retains the empirical observation and experience focus in his book, *Roots of Wisdom*, 6–38. Gericke discussed Qohelet's creation perspective as "folk-epistemological analysis" in "A Comprehensive Philosophical Approach to Qohelet's Epistemology," *HvTSt* 71:1(2015): 2–3.

28. Fox, "Two Decades of Research in Egyptian *Wisdom* Literature," *ZAS* 107(1980): 120.

29. Frydrych, *Living Under the Sun*, 69.

30. Frydrych, *Living Under the Sun*, 217.

literature. God's will can be read from the natural order, social relations and political events. Life in accordance with the principle of order paid off in tangible blessings, just as conduct at variance with *ma'at* brought adversity.³¹

This concern for justice continues into James. The virtue of righteousness is an important life quality empowering effective prayer (Jas 5:6, 16). Such a virtue needs to be translated into a right act in practical situations projecting a proposal for actual behavior (Jas 4:17).³² By working out one's faith in doing the virtuous proposal such a good deed pragmatically vindicates one's righteous character in the manner of Peircean pragmatism (Jas 2:21, 24–25; 3:13; 4:17).³³

Michael Fox has written for and against the empirical quality of Jewish wisdom literature. In 1987 Fox wrote optimistically that wisdom literature is essentially empirical with experience being the primary source for knowledge.³⁴ At this point he did not clarify whether such wisdom was naively assumed direct knowledge as in Thomas Reid's common sense realism (though Jaco Gericke considers there are instances of this)³⁵ or more nuanced Lockean induction within an epistemological dualism entailing an inference made about reality within empiricism which is then confirmed by further experience with this reality.³⁶ Jaco Gericke considered that Qohelet's knowledge is mostly of a Lockean type of empiricism in that it involves inference, memory, reasoning, and testimony to others. Fox concurs, further explaining that empirical argumentation proceeds from sensory experience to form testimony much as Locke claimed.³⁷ The book of James reflects this

---

31. Crenshaw, *Old Testament Wisdom*, 214.

32. Frydrych, *Living Under the Sun*, 11.

33. Frydrych, *Living Under the Sun*, 15–53; Gericke, "A Comprehensive Philosophical Approach to Qohelet's Epistemology," *HvTSt* 71:1(2015): 4–5; Peirce, *Collected Papers*. Hartshorne and Weiss, vol. 5 paragraph 9; "The Fixation of Belief," *Popular Science Monthly* 12(Nov., 1877): 1–15; "How to Make Our Ideas Clear," *Popular Science Monthly* 12(Jan., 1878): 286–302.

34. Fox, "Qohelet's Epistemology," *HUCA* 58(1987): 137–41; This optimism mirrors Fox's commentary *Qohelet and His Contradictions* whereas his skeptical turn mirrors his post-modern commentary *A Time to Tear Down & A Time to Build Up*.

35. Gericke, "A Comprehensive Philosophical Approach to Qohelet's Epistemology," *HvTSt* 71:1(2015): 7 "direct knowledge"; Reid, *Thomas Reid*. ed. Brookes; Abraham, "The Epistemology of Jesus," In *Jesus and Philosophy*. ed. Moser, 158–9; Brueggemann, *A Pathway of Interpretation*, 115.

36. Gericke, "A Comprehensive Philosophical Approach to Qohelet's Epistemology," *HvTSt* 71:1(2015): 7; Locke, *Concerning Human Understanding* 1.1.15; 2.11.8–9; 2.32.6; 3.3.6–8; pre-modern empiricism is apparent in Lactanius, *Workmanship of God*, 9–10.

37. Fox, "Qohelet's Epistemology," *HUCA* 58(1987): 143–44.

Lockean emphasis. Fox then concluded that the collective experience went through a validation process whereby "propositions as publicly observable facts" provided validation further confirming proper understanding.[38] Such an approach remains communally naïve (like common sense realism or Reformed epistemology noticing consequences) without articulating a proposal to be tested (as in Peircean pragmatism)[39] which then confirms that humans reap what they sow (Jas 2:20; 3:1, 13; 4:4, 17).

In 2007 Michael Fox skeptically attacked and distanced empiricism from wisdom literature.[40] Fox seemed to especially be distancing wisdom literature from the naïve confidence within a Thomas Reid common sense empiricism because Fox follows Von Rad in recognizing that experience does not directly translate to wisdom.[41] Neither Fox, nor von Rad, recognize that Locke provided a nuanced form of empiricism that often involves an active inference and confirmation permitting the wise and the fool to have similar experiences but each taking away very different lessons to make sense of their experience. Ultimately, Fox placed this epistemic statement upon the coherence theory of truth in which the lessons learned are dependent upon one's basic belief.[42] However, along the way to this conclusion Fox denied that this view was internally rationally self-contained as would be the case in the coherence theory of truth.[43] Instead, Fox identified that one's statements of faith are evidenced by experiential data (Prov 10:3; 12:21; 16:7) and consequences (Prov 20:22).[44] This evidentialism identifies that Fox wished wisdom literature to remain in externalism permitting experience to inform an empiricism. A more consistent manner to make

---

38. Fox, "Qohelet's Epistemology," *HUCA* 58(1987): 144, 154; Fox utilized Sir 34.9–12 to demonstrate observations prompt conclusions (Fox, "Qohelet's Epistemology," 146). Frydrych argued that the experience is one of collective experience (*Living Under the Sun*, 57).

39. Frydrych, *Living Under the Sun*, 15–53; Gericke, "A Comprehensive Philosophical Approach to Qohelet's Epistemology," *HvTSt* 71:1(2015): 4–5; Peirce, *Collected Papers*. Hartshorne and Weiss, vol. 5 paragraph 9; "The Fixation of Belief," *Popular Science Monthly* 12(Nov., 1877): 1–15; "How to Make Our Ideas Clear," *Popular Science Monthly* 12(Jan., 1878): 286–302.

40. Fox, "The Epistemology of the Book of Proverbs," *JBL* 162:4(2007): 670.

41. Fox, "The Epistemology of the Book of Proverbs," *JBL* 162:4(2007): 670; Gericke raised a similar positivist problem under the open ended "structure of knowledge and the regress problem" before proposing "basic belief" was a way Qohelet could escape such skepticism ("A Comprehensive Philosophical Approach to Qohelet's Epistemology," *HvTSt* 71:1[2015]: 7–8).

42. Fox, "The Epistemology of the Book of Proverbs," *JBL* 162:4(2007): 671, 675–84.

43. Fox, "The Epistemology of the Book of Proverbs," *JBL* 162:4(2007): 671, 675–84.

44. Fox, "The Epistemology of the Book of Proverbs," *JBL* 162:4(2007): 671, 675–84.

Fox's point is to recognize that within Lockean empiricism there is an active inference to interpret raw data and thus it is possible for different interpreters (the wise and the fool) to infer different conclusions and to take away different lessons from the same experience. That is, there is an inference beyond the experience that permits a skeptical element to be overwritten by an interpreter to permit an optimistic conclusion which can be confirmed by further experience of this same interpreter. Thus permitting that the naïve person or the fool might not learn any lesson from that same experience. It seems to me that Fox wished to position ancient wisdom in this nuance of Lockean empiricism without having the philosophical language to do so. From this vantage point, Fox advocates "favoring the empirical interpretation" expressed by Tomáš Frydrych in his commentary and thus positions wisdom literature within nuanced empiricism.[45]

A wisdom perspective operates within empiricism or at times a common sense realism.[46] The most prevalent reminder of this empirical focus is in Qohelet's evaluation of the works "under the sun" in horizontal observation (Eccl 1:3, 9, 14; 2:11, 17–22; 3:16; 4:1, 3, 7, 15; 5:13, 18; 6:1, 12; 8:9, 15, 17; 9:3, 6, 9–13; 10:5). Occasionally, the observational perspective is also encouraged by the counsel of "go to the ant and observe" (Prov 6:6–11; 24:30–34) leaving the observer open to infer a variety of lessons dependent upon her experience and worldview. Thomas Frydrych argued on the bases of examining the extensive empirical activity in Prov 30:18–31 that usually these empirical observations were not superficial observations but those that spanned several seasons prompting inferences of significant insight into behavior and consequences.[47] However, more often life concerns are simply described in the literature of wisdom as simply observed. For example, James 1:11 describes that "the sun rises with a scorching wind, and withers the grass; and its flower falls off, and the beauty of its appearance is destroyed; so too the rich man in the midst of his pursuits will fade away." Not only are nature occurrences noticeable but also the decline of human

---

45. Fox, "The Epistemology of the Book of Proverbs," *JBL* 162:4(2007): 672; Frydrych, *Living Under the Sun*, 54; Such a balanced view is proposed also by Gericke, "A Comprehensive Philosophical Approach to Qohelet's Epistemology," *HvTSt* 71:1(2015): 1–9.

46. Locke, *Concerning Human Understanding* 1.1.15; 2.11.8–9; 2.32.6; 3.3.6–8; "A Discourse of Miracles," In *Works*, 9:256–65; "The Reasonableness of Christianity," In *Works*. vol. 6; pre-modern empiricism is apparent in Lactanius, *Workmanship of God* 9–10; Reid, *Thomas Reid*. ed. Brookes; Abraham, "The Epistemology of Jesus," In *Jesus and Philosophy*. ed. Moser, 158–9.

47. Frydrych, *Living Under the Sun*, 56.

welfare.[48] In fact, observational consistency in nature serve as a basis for moral instruction (Jas 3:10-12).[49]

However, the empirical observations about morality and human welfare mean that such wisdom is not merely empirical but reflexive.[50] So the process of thinking through wisdom requires a reflective stage where the believer considers the relevance and application of what she sees. For example, the believer should consider the endurance of Job and reflect on the compassion and mercy of God throughout the experience (Jas 5:11). If she lacks wisdom then it is a primary opportunity to ask God for this wisdom because He provides abundantly (Jas 1:5).

This moral instruction expresses a two ways framework to fit desirable wisdom in contrast to foolishness.[51] The encouraged way is that of a wise person would pragmatically vindicate their wisdom by right action (Jas 3:13).[52] In fact, James describes faith vividly as dead without good works to vindicate it (Jas 2:17). Whereas, the alternative way is that of the fool who will be destroyed in God's judgment (Jas 4:12; 5:1-3). That is, instead of the normal creation framework of one "reaping what was sown" (Prov 1:18-19; 26-28, 31; 11:18; 22:8; Eccl 3:16-18; Job 4:8 and the retribution principle of Job's counselors), there is a more divine active impending eschatological judgment in some wisdom statements (Jas 4:12; 5:1-3; Prov 16:2; 17:3; 21:2; 29:26). Biblical wisdom also includes a positive benefit grounded in God's favor toward the wise (Jas 4:12; Prov 24:12; 10:3, 22, 24; 12:2; 16:7; 25:21-22).

With the possibility of negative consequences from either creation or God's judgment, wisdom begins with the fear of the Lord (Prov 1:7, 29; 3:7; 8:13; 9:10; 10:27; 14:26-27; 15:16, 33; 16:6; 19:23; 22:4; 23:17; 24:21; Job 6:14; 22:4; 28:28; Matt 10:28; Heb 10:31; Jas 5:1-7, 9).[53] This is not merely reverence but a recognition that God and creation bring judgment consequences upon those who ignore what those future consequences might

---

48. Observations echoed in wisdom texts: Job 13:28; 15.30; 27.21 LXX; Prov 27:1; Eccl 12:6; Wis 2.8; Sir 11:20; Josephus, *J. W.* 6.274.

49. Observations echoed in wisdom texts: Marcus Antoninus 4.6.1; 8.15, 46; 10.8.6; Seneca, *Ep.* 87.25; *Ira.* 2.10.6; Plutarch, *Trana.* 13; Epictetus, *Diatr.* 2.10.18-19.

50. O'Dowd, "A Chord of Three Strands," In *The Bible and Epistemology.* ed. Healy and Parry, 67.

51. Dibelius, *James,* 4; similar to *Did.* 1; *Barn.* 19-20.

52. Frydrych, *Living Under the Sun,* 15-53; Peirce, *Collected Papers.* Hartshorne and Weiss, vol. 5 paragraph 9; "The Fixation of Belief," *Popular Science Monthly* 12(Nov., 1877): 1-15; "How to Make Our Ideas Clear," *Popular Science Monthly* 12(Jan., 1878): 286-302.

53. Gericke, "The Beginning of Wisdom is Paranoia," *Scriptura* 111(2012): 440-51.

hold. The wise choose to align themselves with positive consequences and thus reducing reasons to fear God, such as disobedience (Jas 2:12–13). Fearing God motivates obedience. Those who do not morally change, such as the demons, remain within fear for a good reason, judgment is coming (Jas 2:19; 5:1–7, 9).

Within *midrashic* narrative proverbs, the enticing adulteress enters the square to corrupt, opposed by lady wisdom as a compelling rival metaphor to motivate young men to choose to live wisely.[54] Will the reader submit to a sovereign God in spite of the difficulties of suffering in this life (Jas 1:13–18; Job). Perhaps metaphors like these are designed to provoke right action in a wisdom direction.

James used vivid imagery that has taken on a level of evocative symbols to illustrate his points from the creation.[55] For example, many dangers emerge from the tongue as a wild beast or rudder (Jas 3:3–12; Prov 6:17; 10:31; 17:4; 18:21; 21:6; 26:28).[56] In suffering there is no place for blaming God even though He is sovereign (Jas 1:13–18; Job).[57] The life of the poor is often oppressed by the rich (Jas 2:2–3; 5:1–6; Prov 14:31; 17:5; 22:7, 16, 22; 28:15).[58] Wealthy should be humble and generous while the poor should celebrate in God's pleasure (Jas 1:9–10; 4:4; Prov 14:21; 19:17; 22:9; 31:20).[59] Prayer is effective from a righteous life and not from a wicked or divided heart (Jas 1:5–7; 5:16; Prov 15:8, 29; 28:9).[60]

Similarities extend to narrative wisdom as well. For example Job has slight similarities to the Indian legend of Haris-candra in *The Mārkaṇḍeya Purāṇa* though Haris-candra brings his sufferings upon himself by giving his wealth away, while Job is struck down under the sovereignty of God and the adversary in His court.[61] The Ugaritic *Story of Keret* affirms the retribution principle[62] by following the placating of the gods through ritual

---

54. At this point Perdue (*Wisdom and Creation*, 88–100) is too oversensitive to the extra-biblical context as he sees lady wisdom through goddess imagery, for the biblical texts monotheism limits the range of acceptable options, excluding any queen of heaven as not properly biblical. Also Perdue, *Wisdom in Revolt*. reflects a polytheistic post Babylonian context for its metaphors of theology.

55. Kennard, *A Critical Realist's*, 177–80; Ricoeur, *The Symbolism of Evil*.

56. Sir 19.6–12; 20.5–8, 18–20; 22.27; 28.13–2635.7–9.

57. Sir 15.11–20; Wis 3.4–6.

58. Sir 13.19–20; Wis 2.10–20.

59. Wis 5.8; Sir 18.15.

60. Sir 1.27.

61. Pargiter, *The Mārkaṇḍeya Purāṇa*.

62. A nice discussion of the retribution principle and its corollaries is carried on by my previous colleague Walton, in *Ancient Israelite Literature in its Cultural Context*,

prayers which Job's counselors encourage (Job 11). The use of speeches and appeals in the course of narrative wisdom is common in Job, *The Babylonian Theodicy*,[63] and the Egyptian *The Protest of the Eloquent Peasant*.[64] Even Qoheleth has a high degree of similarity to Babylonian *Dialogue of Pessimism*[65] and Egyptian works, like *The Harper's Song* and *The Dispute Between a Man and His Ba* (soul).[66] This does not require that everything is the same in these expressions of wisdom. K. van der Torn reminds us that the antithetic mode of expression between wise and fool is most emphasized within Hebrew wisdom and largely absent from Mesopotamian and Ugaritic wisdom.[67] James provides such narrative accounts in miniature to help the wise to negotiate suffering (Jas 1:12–18; 2:1–6). James is also salted with empirical Jewish parables so there is no need to appeal to Hellenistic rhetoric to make sense of them (Jas 3:2–5).[68]

There are however clear differences with the biblical wisdom when compared to the broader ancient Near Eastern wisdom. Unlike other ancient Near Eastern wisdom, James, Qoheleth and Proverbs incorporate occasional vertical refrains of God's generosity (Jas 1:13, 17, 2:5, 23; 4:6–8; 5:15; Eccl. 2:24–26; 3:12–15, 22; 7:14; 8:15; 12:9–14; Prov 15:9; 3:11–12; 18:10) amid the common skeptical human perspective "under the sun." In the nineteen eighties the upbeat refrains were emphasized in biblical theology but as post-modernism continued to develop, within a contemporary biblical theology of Qoheleth the pessimism of the vanity of vanities tended to predominate.[69] Likewise in the book of Job, *El Shadday*'s dominance of the created order to overwhelm the retribution principle sets the book of Job apart as superior to other ancient Near Eastern theodicy texts. Of all the Old Testament wisdom texts Proverbs is actually the closest parallel to ancient near Eastern wisdom but even here there is a greater emphasis of an

---

179–89; document is contained in Watson and Wyatt, *Handbook of Ugaritic Studies*.

63. Lambert, *Babylonian Wisdom Literature*, 68–69; Pritchard, *Ancient Near Eastern Texts*, 438–40, 601–4.

64. Foster, *Ancient Egyptian Literature*.

65. Lambert, *Babylonian Wisdom Literature*, 142; Pritchard, *Ancient Near Eastern Texts*, 437–8.

66. Foster, *Ancient Egyptian Literature*.

67. Van der Toorn, *Sin and Sanction in Israel and Mesopotamia*, 101.

68. McArthur and Johnston, *They also Taught in Parables* nicely collects many of the rabbinic parables; so there is no need to position parables into Aristotelian rhetoric such as Anderson does (*Glossary of Greek Rhetorical Terms Connected to Methods of Argumentation*, 86–87; Aristotle, *Rhet.* 2.20).

69. This point is illustrated in some of the recent works that show increasing effect of post-modernism such as Fox, *A Time to Tear Down & A Time to Build Up* in contrast to Fox *Qohelet and His Contradictions*. Anderson *Qoheleth and Its Pessimistic Theology*.

orientation toward God than other ancient Near Eastern wisdom's nearly exclusive social orientation (Prov 3:11–12; 10:3, 22, 24; 12:2; 16:2, 4, 7; 17:3; 21:1–2, 30–31; 19:21; 25:21–22; 29:26). James continues with this encouraging vertical dimension (Jas 1:13, 17, 2:5, 23; 4:6–8; 5:15). This means that in a biblical theology of wisdom there must be a clear divine intrusion that the revelational canonical context brings rather than merely identifying biblical wisdom as identical to ancient Near Eastern wisdom.[70]

The nesting of the wisdom program seems to best fit conceptually within creation theology. That is, the sovereign God through wisdom has effortlessly brought the universe into existence out of the waters of chaos (Gen 1:2–26; 8; Prov 3:19–20; 20:12; 22:2; 30:14; Job 38:1–41; Jas 1:17–18). The order that God brought to the chaos (as indicated by separation (Gen 1:4–7, 10), and by designed purposefulness *tob*, and the governance of time by the heavenly objects (Gen 1:14–18; 8:22) serves to provide humans with obligation to fit within this order as a player within creation. The role for human as image of God serves to set all humans as God's representative on the scene as we minutely picture God's creating and sovereignty at work. Some of this obligation comes with the blessing of God to be fruitful, multiply, fill, subdue and rule the earth (Gen 1:28; 9:1–7). Other obligation comes by God's fiat framing specific obligations within this purposeful order (Gen 1:26; 2:15–17, 24; 9:2–6). There are significant benefits to be obtained in living rightly to this order (Gen 6:8–9; 8:1). However, so often mankind departs from this righteousness and plunges the creation order into a chaos of his own doing, which God responds with curse or a return to chaos within the created order, fighting chaos with chaos (Gen 3:6–21; 4:8–15; 6:2–7:24; 9:21–25; 11:1–9; Job 41:1–11; Eccl 3:19–21). The order of the creation that remains after these judgments preserves the order but marred by frustrating futility. However, the believer should not accuse the good Creator for such chaos or evil, twisted order emerges from within the human himself (Jas 1:13–18). In fact, God provides wisdom for the believer who asks for it in their circumstances (Prov 8:22–31; Jas 1:5).

This application of creation theology is made more vivid by the wisdom texts. If humans are to negotiate one's way around creation staying within those ways that bring success and staying clear of the pits of futility, then such a person needs wisdom. The retribution principle of "you reap what you sow" is part of this wise perspective. Proverbs joins in at this point to provide a variety of specific wise stepping stones, which strengthen both mind and will. For example, with regard to the specific issue of love and marriage there are many practical guidelines within the book of Proverbs

---

70. Contrary to Westermann, *Roots of Wisdom*.

ranging from the adulteress to avoid, to the ideal wife praised by all her family, and a host of scattered comments between. None of these quite has the same poetic passion of Adam's recognition of Eve's embodiment and the implications to become one flesh in marriage (Gen 2:23–24). However, Proverbs develops further counsel within this context of marriage that helps complement the Genesis pattern. Here is where the Song of Songs encourages the love passion (which Adam briefly poetically expressed) but it comes within a context that is also tainted by tension, conflict and pain (Gen 3:16). Therefore, the Song of Songs reflects these elements of relationship within a narrative including frustrating futility as well. This futility within the divine order is acutely driven home by the experimental nature of Qoheleth with periodic reminders that the divine order is still there when one takes into account the vertical blessings that come from God. The recognition of these blessings should motivate the wise person to enjoy the blessings and limit the range of one's own futile experimentation. However, sometimes futility overwhelms the servant of God in excruciating suffering. Here, Job and James display God's sovereignty because the whole process of extreme suffering is in the crucible of futility (Job; Jas 1:12–18). While many judgments are brought on by our reaping the consequences of sin and foolishness, there are times when no explanation is given and we must still worship God and serve Him righteously; Job and James remind us of this struggle. Wisdom nests in creation theology and conceptually develops an alternative universal revelatory program for the whole of humankind, which continues to stand as applicable to all humankind. As such, it provides a complementary voice to the profoundly Jewish program of Law and prophets.

The messages of wisdom books can be summarized in inductive generalizations. Old Testament wisdom as a whole can be summarized as: the wise man will hear, fear and obey Yahweh and live life well according to the framework of how creation works (including the joys of love), understanding that apparent futility and suffering should not dissuade from faithfulness to God. The various components of Old Testament wisdom's message are seen as coming from respective books. For example, Proverbs can be summarized as: the wise man will hear, fear and obey Yahweh, and live life well according to the framework of how creation works, whereas many others will be destroyed in their wicked plans. Additionally, the Song of Songs narratively and poetically illustrates the joys and pains of love while affirming erotic expressions of physical beauty. Furthermore, the message of Job is that the righteous sometimes suffer for sin, sometimes for purification and sometimes for reasons which they may never know under God's sovereignty, so that they need to remain faithful to God in whatever circumstances they find themselves. Likewise, in Qoheleth life appears to be futile in its aimless wanderings and problems under the sun, but life, work and food are gifts from God to be enjoyed to the fullest and God is to be obeyed, since He will eventually judge all men. In the New Testament, James exhorts Jewish believers in dispersion to maintain a consistent allegiance to God, while God matures us, through the endurance of purifying trials. In these the believer should readily care for the needs of the vulnerable, receive and apply the Law, properly control oneself (especially one's tongue), and humbly submit to God's wisdom.

8

Hebrews Epistemology of Prophecy as Rhetorical Proclamation that Christ is Supreme

THESIS: THE PRIMARY EPISTEMOLOGY in the book of Hebrews is that prophecy is utilized as *midrashic* rhetoric to support the theme of the book that Christ is supreme over all other options. The narrative discussions are approached with a common sense realist point of view except where miracles develop a Lockean epistemic dualism and act as confirming evidence. There is also Edwardsian empirical evidence of a cleansed conscience to demonstrate the transformative nature of the initiation of the new covenant, which the author utilized in a Peircean pragmatic manner.

The author of the book of Hebrews is unknown. The book does not identify the author. The early church is familiar with the book and encouraged by its spiritual content and high Christology.[1] Origen claimed that it was not written by Paul and that only God knows the author.[2]

The book is written to Hebrew Christians. The title "to the Hebrews" was affixed to the book before the end of the second century much like several N. T. letters had titles added.[3] Hartwig Thyen defended that Hebrews was similarly positioned as a Jewish Christian homily with several other volumes of its era.[4] Old Testament citations and allusions permeate the book implying that the readership has familiarity with them, however with

---

1. Clement of Rome, *Cor.* 12 with Heb 1:3–4; Hermas, *Vis.* 2.3.2 with Heb 3:12; *Sim.* 1.1–2 with Heb 11:13–15 and 13:14; Justin Martyr, *Apol.* 1.12.63 with Heb 3:1 and *Dial.* 96.113 with Heb 1:13; 5:6; 7:17, 21.

2. Origen quoted by Eusebius, *Hist. eccl.* 6.25.11–14.

3. Rom and the Cor epistles also have the same superscription phenomena; Lane, *Hebrews 1–8*, lxix; Koester, *Hebrews*, 46.

4. Thyen, *Der Stil des jüdish-hellenistischen Homile*; similar to: *1 Clement*; parts of 1 Macc; parts of 3 Macc; 4 Macc; *Did.*; *Barn.*; *Shep. Herm.*; parts of Tob.; Wis.

a high Christology of Jesus' deity. The temptation for the readers in the book is to depart from Christ and return to disobedience under the Mosaic Law and Judaism (Heb 2:2–4; 3:7–4:13; 10:26–31). This temptation is not what Gentile Christians were dealing with in the first century so they do not seem to be the primary audience.

Hebrews is framed by repeated quotations[5] and allusions to the Old Testament. These prophecies present themselves as revealed by the testimony from the Holy Spirit (Heb 2:4; 3:7; probably 6:4; 9:8; 10:15, probably 29).[6] Such O.T. quotes are engaged through a *pesher* application to the new context agenda within a Christian Pharisaic appreciation of the authoritative books of the O.T.[7] For example, Psalm 95:7–10 combines with a *midrash* or re-telling of the Exodus journey toward the promised land to provide a call to join a persistent faith toward kingdom rest (Heb 3:7–4:13).[8] Such rabbinic use of example also adds rhetorical persuasion beyond a Jewish audience.[9] Even the author's re-appropriation of Psalm 110 fits within *midrash* patterns to support

---

5. The quotations are close to LXX and MT but two thirds have slight differences from both showing that the author is operating within the canons of rabbinic *pesher*; Howard, "Hebrews and the Old Testament Quotation," *NovT* 10(1968): 211.

6. These patristics also support the same epistemic diligence that the prophets operated under inspiration (Ignatius, *Magn.* 8.2; *Barn.* 5.6; *Herm. Sim.* 9.12.1–2; *2 Clem.* 17.4; Justin Martyr, *1 Apol.* 31–53; 62.4; *Dial.* 56–7; Irenaeus, *Haer.* 4.20.4; Origen, *Prin.* 3.12).

7. Josephus, *Ant.* 13. 171–3, 297; 18.12–15; *J. W.* 2.119, 162–3; 4 Macc 5:16–27; Philo, *Dreams* 1.124–5; *m. Yad.* 4.6–8; *B. Qidd.* 66a; Resurrection: 2 Macc 7.9–14, 22–23; 14.43–46; *1 En.* 22; 58.3; 62.14–16; 91.10; 92.2; 104; 108.11–14; *Jub.* 5.10; 10.17; 22.22; *L.A.B.*; CD 3.11–16, 20–21; 7.5, 9; 13.11; 20.17–20, 25–27; 1QH 11.19–23 [3.18–22]; 19.10–14 [11.7–11]; 1QS 3.7–12; 4.7; 4Q228 frag. 1 1.9; 4Q266, frag. 11; 4Q385 2; 4Q386 1–2; 4QMMT C; 4Q521 2.2.12; 5.2.5–6; *2 Bar.*[Syriac] 30.1–5; 49–51; 4 Macc 7.19; 16.25; *4 Ezra* 7.26–44; *Sib. Or.* 4.180; *T. Benj.* 10.6–8; *T. Levi* 18; *T. Jud.* 24; Lim, *Pesharim*, 44–53..

8. Buchanan (*Hebrews*, xxiii–xxiv) explains Hebrews' discussion of the exodus within Hillel's first rule as a strong *a fortiori* argument: what applies in a minor case also applies in a major case; Josephus, *Ag. Ap.* 2.175–81; Jerusalem synagogue Theodotus inscription; Philo, *Embassy* 311–3; *Megillat Ta'anit*; *y. Hor.* 3.5 (48c); *b. Tem.* 14b; *b. B. Meş.* 59a–b; *Sifre Deut.* 351; *Sifra* 193.1.1–11; *Iggeret Rav Sherira Gaon* 1–2; Zeitlin, "Midrash: A Historical Study," *JQR* 44(1953): 21–36; Wright, *Midrash*, 52–59, 64–67; Ellis, "Midrash, Targum and New Testament Quotations," In *Neotestamentica et Semitica*. ed. Ellis and Wilcox, 61–69; le Déaut, "Apropos a Definition of Midrash," *Int* 25(1971): 259–82; Miller, "Targum, Midrash and the Use of the Old Testament in the New Testament," *JSJ* 2(1971): 29–82; Bloch, "Midrash," In *Approaches to Ancient Judaism*. ed. Green, 29–50; Porton, "Defining Midrash," In *The Study of Ancient Judaism*. ed. Neusner, 1:55–95; McNamara, "Some Issues and Recent Writings on Judaism and the New Testament," *IBS* 9(1987): 136–49.

9. Aristotle, *Rhet.* 1.2.8; especially vivid examples 4.49.62; Quintilian, *Inst.* 5.11.9; Lausberg, *Handbook of Literary Rhetoric*, sect. 410–26; Koester, *Hebrews*, 93.

the grand theme of Christ's supremacy (Heb 1:13; 5:6; 7:17, 21).[10] George Buchanan explains the *midrash* process for this rabbinic analogy for a text like Psalm 110 applying to the Messiah that originally referenced the lesser Davidic king (an appropriation of the first Hillel logical rule).[11]

> Midrashic composers were resourceful apologists with amazing skill in manipulating words, phrases, and passages to suit their own needs in ways that were far removed from the original meaning of the text. The reason such a method was necessary was the official interpreter had to relate an ancient text that was considered sacred to the needs of a worshiping community in a different period of time and under situations that differed from those that prompted the writing of the scripture on which they depended. Authors of midrashim were not free to ignore the text and present their ideas on the basis of contemporary need and normal logic. The scripture gave them their authority to speak. Their use of scripture represents their skill in presenting their own views on the basis of the sacred text. Rabbis had numerous, well-established rules for doing this and some of them were employed by the author of Hebrews.[12]

The author quoting these authoritative testimonies of revelation fitted them into his agenda for the supremacy of Christ (Heb 2:6; 10:15).[13] Peter O'Brien considers that this biblical foundation for the argument frames the book after a pattern of a synagogue homily.[14]

Rhetorical critics identify the book of Hebrews as mostly within the Hellenistic category of deliberative rhetoric[15] by offering the readers future rewards for considering to remain within the new covenant and with Jesus (Heb 4:11; 6:18; 10:36; 12:1–2). So evidence of high style is incorporated within the book to increase the readiness of the listeners.[16]

10. Buchanan, *Hebrews*, xxi.

11. Hillel rule number one: What applies in a minor case also applies in a major case; *Sipra* intr 1; *'Abot R. Nat.* 37; *Gen. Rab.* 92.7; *Pesaḥ.* 18b; *Yoma* 43a; Pool, *The Traditional Prayer Book*, 128–30.

12. Buchanan, *Hebrews*, xxi–xxii.

13. See previous note on *midrash*; Bock, *Proclamation from Prophecy and Pattern*; Ricoeur, "The Hermeneutics of Testimony" cited in David Ford, "Paul Ricoeur," In *Jesus and Philosophy*. ed. Moser, 190; Bruce, *Hebrews*, xix–xxii.

14. O'Brien, *Hebrews*, 20.

15. Aristotle, *Rhet.* 1.2.8; 3.7.1–2; Quintilian, *Inst.* 8.3.5.

16. Quintilian, *Inst.* 8.3.5; Garuti, *Alle origini*, 33–184; Attridge, *Hebrews*, 20–21; Cosby, "The Rhetorical Composition of Hebrews 11," *JBL* 107(1988): 257–73; *The Rhetorical Composition and Function of Hebrews 11*; Koester, *Hebrews*, 92–96; deSilva, *Despising Shame*, 30, 33.

The author of Hebrews also utilized transitional warnings to refocus and regain the attention of his readers (Heb 2:1–4; 3:12–4:13; 6:1–20; 10:26–39; 12:1–13) as is common enough in ancient prolonged arguments of *epideictic* rhetoric.[17] Within this form of rhetoric there are often appeals to hold fast to a goal within one's previous commitments (Heb 3:6; 4:14; 10:23, 35–39; 11:11). This is balanced by warnings of impending shame to threatened damnation if the readers leave Christ and the new covenant to return to the Mosaic covenant. The last of the warnings (Heb 12:1–13) is relaxed a bit to encourage the readers to consider that damnation is unlikely in their faithfulness but discipline might still be utilized to make them stronger.

Several interpreters wish to position themselves rhetorically as advocates for a hybrid rhetoric. O'Brien summarized this position as, "for those who remain committed to God and Christ, Hebrews is epideictic. But for those tending to drift away from the faith, it is deliberative."[18] Such analysis connects with classical Greek patterns but may not be that helpful since the book fits into both categories and the subsequent analysis of the book leaves a number of parts of a speech absent.[19]

The author of Hebrews considered that the character of those, described in the book, who have lived faithfully without making it to the final goal served as embodied testimony for both author and readers to continue in faith (Heb 11:1–3 [first person present plural verbs "we understand" νοοῦμεν]–12:1).[20] The statement and lives of the great cloud of witnesses testify so that believers would continue to endure the race by focusing our attention on the example of Christ as the goal (Heb 12:1–2). So that ultimately these previous believers point to Jesus' life lived in suffering as testifying the example of suffering faith for the believer to live. So there are several levels of testimony occurring in the book. These testimonies press the reader through content to the life implications to imitate Christ or fellow believers who have gone before the readers.

---

17. Quintilian, *Inst.* 4.3.12–17; Cicero, *De oratore* 3.53. section 203; deSilva, *Despising Shame*, 42–46; Eisenbaum, *The Jewish Heroes*, 136–7; Koester, *Hebrews*, 89.

18. O'Brien, *Hebrews*, 26; Koester, *Hebrews*, 82; Lane, *Hebrews 1–8*, lxxix; deSilva, *Hebrews*, 46; Johnsson, *Defilement and Purgation*, 13.

19. Koester, *Hebrews*, 82; deSilva, *Hebrews*, 46; Lane, *Hebrews 1–8*, lxxix–lxxx; Westfall, *A Discourse Analysis*, 6–7; O'Brien, *Hebrews*, 26.

20. Character is an important facet in increasing persuasion of a witness (Origen, *Prin.* 3.12; Aristotle, *Rhet.* 1.2.3–4, 13; Quintilian, *Inst.* 4.1.7; 5.14.24–25; Lausberg, *Handbook of Literary Rhetoric*, sect. 371) and interpreters recognize our author utilized this aspect in his argument (Mitchel, "The Use of πρεπειν and Rhetorical Propriety in Hebrews 2:10," *CBQ* 54(1992): 681–701; Eisenbaum, "Heroes and History in Hebrews 11," In *Early Christian Interpretation of the Scriptures of Israel*, 380–96; Craig Koester, *Hebrews*, 91–92, 94.

The author joins Christ and the previous speakers, heard by his audience, by pointing to Christ. In this manner, all these testifiers confirm Christ's message (Heb 1:2; 2:3).[21] Such corporate voice reflects a corporate memory of the accounts of the past (Heb 12:17). These spokesmen join together as authoritative confirmation over time within a Pharisaic worldview, and thus increase the reader's confidence in the message.[22]

This approach is an externalism of a practical realistic non-foundational empiricism similar to Thomas Reid's common sense realism.[23] Though when miracles are involved as divine miraculous testimonies, then the epistemic framework is better understood as Lockean supernatural evidence of God vindicating the speaker (Heb 2:4 "signs," "wonders," and "gifts"; probably 6:4).[24] Thus the confirming divine miracle provides a greater confidence to those who experienced them in the context of receiving the message. Gottlieb Lünemann and Wilhelm Linss claim that experiential ownership of these signs prompt the author to utilize terms of logical conclusion that reflect "inner necessity."[25]

Jesus obtaining answered prayer also supports a Lockean argument for why the readers should affiliate with Jesus as their high priest (Heb 5:7). That is, unlike the Jewish priests who are frail and sin, Jesus is pious and is "heard" as a yes answer to His Gethsemane prayer that death would pass from Him so that resurrection would occur (Heb 5:7; Pss 4:2 LXX; 6:8–9; 10:17; 18:6; 19:3; 22:24; 28:6; 31:22; 34:6; 40:1; 61:5; 66:19; 78:21, 59; 106:44; 1 John 5:14–15).[26] There is a real appeal to associate with Jesus as our high priest who in His piety can source the believer's everlasting salvation (Heb 5:9).

21. Examples of such claims include: Papius recounted in Eusebius, *Hist. eccl.* 5.20.4–7; Irenaeus, *Letter to Florinus*; Clement of Alexandria, *Strom.* 7.106.4; Eusebius, *Hist. eccl.* 2.1.4; Kelber, "The Case of the Gospels," *Oral Tradition* 17(2002): 65; Dunn, *Jesus Remembered*, 239–243; Ricoeur, *Memory, History, Forgetting*; Bauckham, *Jesus and the Eyewitnesses*, 295–6, 310–57.

22. Seneca, *Controversiae*, preface 3–4; Bauckham, *Jesus and the Eyewitnesses*, 295–6.

23. Reid, *Thomas Reid.* ed. Brookes; Abraham, "The Epistemology of Jesus," In *Jesus and Philosophy.* ed. Moser, 158–9; Brueggeman, *A Pathway of Interpretation*, 115.

24. Locke, *Concerning Human Understanding* 1.1.15; 2.11.8–9; 2.32.6; 3.3.6–8; "A Discourse of Miracles," In *Works*, 9:256–65; "The Reasonableness of Christianity," In *Works*, vol. 6; pre-modern empiricism is apparent in Lactanius, *Workmanship of God* 9–10; Keener, *Miracles*, 1:35–208.

25. Lünemann, *Critical and Exegetical Hand-Book to the Hebrews*, 422; Linss, "Logical Terminology in the Epistle to the Hebrews," *CTM* 37:6(1966): 365–6.

26. Kennard, *Messiah Jesus*, 360–2; Blaising, "Gethsemane a Prayer of Faith," *JETS* 22(1979): 333–43; this view is not sufficiently countered by the disjunction (contra Gundry, *Mark*, 870).

In the new covenant relationship the believer obtains a filial knowledge of the Lord who is the eschatological Judge (Heb 8:11; 10:30, 34).[27] This relationship reassures the believer that she is authentically His child rather than illegitimate (Heb 12:8). Thus any discipline from God is designed to mature rather than destroy under His wrath.

Christians also have a once for all corporate atonement that is provided by Jesus Christ's sacrificial death after the pattern of a Day of Atonement (Heb 9:1–10:12). This framework was especially understood to operate within a Platonic metaphysic by the philosophical side of the early church and the classical commentators of the nineteenth century (with similar Platonic phrases present within Heb 8:5; 9:23–24; 10:1; 12:27–28).[28] For example, the author of Hebrews identified that Jesus *transcended* a *shadow* existence of *lower dualistic* earthly tabernacle in order to enter the *heavenly* drawing the believer toward *perfection* where she can *perceive things unseen*.[29] If such a view were Platonic it would have implications toward an anti-realist epistemology that would denigrate faith and knowledge below intuition and discursive reasoning.[30] However, more recent comparisons with religious Platonism and Jewish Christian mysticism denies this claimed Platonic heritage for the book of Hebrews. For example, Ronald Williamson concludes that Hebrews and Philo belonged "to two entirely different schools of exegesis."[31] For example, in Platonism only the heavenly realm of the forms is unchangeable truth and the goal is to perceive this truth while earthly expressions are derivative shadows reflecting the forms. However, in Hebrews and in *merkabah* (throne/chariot) mysticism both the heavenly and the earthly realms are real changeable creations by the personal God Who occupies both realms simultaneously and is perceived through the biblical text, faith and occasional mystical experiences, all prompting the believer toward a future kingdom goal (Exod 40:34–38; Isa 6:1–8; Ezek 1:24–28; 10:4, 18–20; Heb 9:19–24).[32] The framework, goals, and methodol-

---

27. Origen, *Prin.* 3.12; Moser, *The Elusive God*, 46–7, 98, 113–123.

28. Origen's reading the O.T. through a spiritual lens of Hebrews (*Princ.* 4.2.4, 6, 9; *Biblia Patristics*, 3:453–5; also Clement of Alexandria, *Strom.* 1.5, 9; 6.7–11; 7.16).

29. Each of the italicized words were taken by some in a Platonic sense (Plato, *Resp.* 514A–515D; Plotinus, *Enneads* 5.3.6.17; Clement of Alexandria, *Strom.* 1.6, 11; 2.2, 4, 13; 4.20; 7.1; Origen, *Princ.* 2.11.6–7; *Fathers of the Church*, 89.319; *Die griechische Schriftsteller*, 38.238–390.

30. Plato, *Resp.* 5.511d–e; *Tim.* 29c; Philo permits a larger role for faith (*Rewards* 28).

31. Williamson, *Philo*, 576–9; Lane, *Hebrews 1–8*, cvii–cviii; Hurst, *Hebrews*, 7–42.

32. *1 En.* 14; 37–71; *2 En.* 15–17; *Asc. Isa.* 9; *Adam and Eve* 37; *Apoc. Ab.* 29; *Exod. Rab.* 43.8; *m. Hag.* 2.1; *b. Hag.* 14a; 15a; *Hek. Rab.* 20.1; *b. Sanh.* 38b; Pate and Kennard, *Deliverance Now and Not Yet*, 98–103; Sholem, *Jewish Gnosticism*; Dean-Otting, *Heavenly Journeys*; Itamar Gruenwald, *Apocalyptic and Merkavah Mysticism*, 29–72; Schafer,

ogy of Hebrews and Platonism are very different. In fact, Hebrews is much closer to that of the nuanced realism of *merkabah* mysticism which occupies a place within sectarian early Judaism, Pauline and Johannine theology.

Christ's atonement accomplished in the heavenly temple is a superior atonement to that which the high priest would perform in the earthly tabernacle. Not only is Christ's atonement accomplished by a superior priest in a superior place but it accomplishes everlasting forgiveness for all who believe. This finished everlasting forgiveness is superior over the real repeated year-by-year forgiveness available for Jews during the Day of Atonement. However, this truth of everlasting forgiveness is not itself evidentially noticeable as another aspect of the new covenant, namely, the cleansed conscience as an internal evidential aspect confirming a believer's authenticity as participating within the new covenant (Heb 8:10, 12; 9:13–14, 23, 28; 10:3–4, 14–18). That is, the internal transformation of a believer's conscience toward responsiveness to God's laws and maturely obeying God provides internal warrant as Lockean evidence within an epistemic dualism to confirm a new covenant believer with everlasting forgiveness, much like Edwards sixth sense does in his construct of the Spirit's religious affections.[33] Furthermore, if one was looking for this evidence to reassure whether those who identify with Christ are authentic Christians, as the author of Hebrews does, then this transformed conscience and consistency of life reflecting such a responsive conscience operate as a Peircean pragmatic verification principle of the fact that his readers are authentic believers in Christ unto kingdom (Heb 6:9–12; 10:32–39).[34]

The primary epistemology that the book of Hebrews demonstrates is that prophecy is utilized as *midrashic* rhetoric to support the theme of the book that the real Christ is supreme over all other options. Multigenerational communal testimony and confirming miracles support this theme within a Lockean epistemic dualism. However, the Lockean evidence is extended into Edwardsian empirical evidence of a cleansed conscience demonstrating authentic transformed new covenant nature. Furthermore, the author occasionally utilized this Edwardsian cleansed conscience as a Peircean pragmatic verifying principle to reassure himself that his readers were believers in Christ.

Kehhalot-Studien; Chernus, "Visions of God in Merkabah Mysticism," *JSJ* 13(1982): 123–46; Koester, *Hebrews*, 97–100.

33. Edwards, *Religious Affections*; *Freedom of the Will*, 4:1:337–42; YE6:342–3; *Miscellanies*, number 267; Jenson, *America's Theologian*, 30; Locke, *Concerning Human Understanding* 1.1.15; 2.11.8–9; 2.32.6; 3.3.6–8.

34. Peirce, *Collected Papers*. Hartshorne and Weiss, vol. 5 paragraph 9; "The Fixation of Belief," *Popular Science Monthly* 12(Nov., 1877): 1–15; "How to Make Our Ideas Clear," *Popular Science Monthly* 12(Jan., 1878): 286–302.

9

Putting the N. T. Epistemology Together

EACH OF THE BIBLICAL contributors provide a vivid testimony similar to Paul Ricoeur's treatment of testimony. Each chapter appreciates that this material is engaged reflecting rabbinic language and thought forms, especially the chapters on Jesus, Paul, and Hebrews. All the chapters explore aspects of Jewish-Christian *midrash*, re-appropriating Old Testament quotes and narrative in a new performative *pesher* manner to present Jesus as the Christ. The rhetorical emphasis reflects the heritage of rabbinic rhetoric (reflecting the heritage of Weiser, Schweitzer, Davies, Sanders, and Dunn). Therefore there are prominent roles for inspired biblical revelation, mystical vision, dream or audible divine voice, which all possessed a significant authoritative place in Pharisaic-rabbinic Judaism. Biblical epistemologists were extensively engaged in this book but they tend to approach the field though word studies of "knowledge" rather than philosophical categories or approaches. The treatment in this book attempted to accomplish both to foster the conversation between philosopher and exegete.

Perhaps the thought forms of William Alston help the philosopher to engage the mystical aspects, especially in Jesus, Paul and John. That is, emerging from a Jewish root the thought forms tend to be more Jewish than Hellenistic. However, the Lukan historiography extensively engages Hellenistic Greco-Roman historiographic method and the concept of "witness" to explain the historical precision and why writing began mid-first century instead of upon Jesus' departure.

The biblical contributors express an oral stage of engaging Christianity from within a Wittgenstein communal language game or Plantinga properly basic communal faith system of a Christian-rabbinic worldview. This approach includes a communal application of Thomas Reid's more individual common sense realism. This non-foundational realism was carried on in communal oral tradition as was practiced among synagogue and the rabbinics, communally resilient tradition over generations. When multiple interpretations occur concerning miracles and with close rivals, the epistemology shows nuance as in an epistemic dualistic non-foundational Lockean epistemology where which miraculous signs contribute to the meaning and authority of the testimony conveyed by the individual or group. Occasionally, this Lockean epistemic dualism also adds an internal transformation much as Jonathan Edwards modified Locke to set forth his religious affections. These religious affections are often caused by God to fund a divine virtue ethic but in the synoptic gospels the emphasis is more on responsibility so the virtue ethic is presented there as the responsibility of the disciple traveling on the narrow way unto kingdom. These two compatibilist strands come together especially in Peter, Paul, and Hebrews. At times these authors try to confirm whether their readers are authentic in the narrow way and when this occurs the Edwardsian religious affection is appropriated through a Peircean pragmatic move. Occasionally, Peircean pragmatism occurs elsewhere to increase the credibility of the Lockean evidence, as in how Peter takes Christ's transfiguration to pragmatically increase his confidence for the coming kingdom. This internal knowledge with its self-referential confirmation for a personal relationship participates within the range of filial knowledge or relationship with God as developed by Paul Moser.

None of the biblical contributors studied adds a critical realist or a post-modern aspect in the wake of Kant and Kierkegaard, so they are all pre-modern thinkers in ways that the realist moderns, like Locke, sometimes reflect. So none of the biblical authors develop the fullness of my critical realist epistemology.

Much has happened since these authors utilized their epistemologies, so that they might not be the last word for the reader's consideration and crafting of one's own epistemology. However, in the same manner as biblical authors fund much of the content of the Christian faith, this book has attempted to suggest aspects of epistemology to be considered for inclusion within a reader's own epistemology. Further, since most of these biblical authors also are perspectival in their epistemology, the development of the emphasis of their perspectives provides the surrounding contexts that may also orient the reader to a deeper engagement, contextualization, and worldview perspective. A Christian-rabbinic-Judaism provides the perspectival framework for Matthew's Jesus, Paul, Peter, and Hebrews. These are mostly in patterns from Hillite Phaisaic Judaism re-appropriated within Christian commitments. However, Luke is a Christian hybrid of this rabbinic Judaism as filtered through Greco-Roman historical canons. Qumran sectarian Judaism provides a closer perspectival framework for John to reflect Christ. Finally, James expressed a Christian appropriation of creation theology within an ancient Near Eastern wisdom tradition.

Most of the biblical authors develop an aspect of virtue epistemology which also funds a disposition and ethic that can be transferrable onto the reader's own epistemology and ethic. However, rarely are the biblical authors strictly expressing epistemology or ethics, so often this virtue epistemology expresses a facet of the narrow way unto kingdom salvation within a two ways salvation.

So when a concept of a narrow way unto kingdom is described the reader should consider deepening these virtues beyond epistemology to a level of filial relationship with Father, Christ and the Spirit. One's existential relationship could also be cultivated on a N. T. mystical level, which is not philosophical mysticism (beyond a human's ability to know). Rather, biblical mysticism is a personal intimate relationship in close proximity or internally penetrated (as in *perichorises*) with divine persons. Such biblical mysticism cultivates the relationship of being in Christ and allowing the Spirit to empower our corporate and personal life from inside out. In fact, Paul and John urge their readers to be fully within each of the Trinitarian members in such a manner that these persons of God are also within each of us and our community as well. So for these epistemologies to be implemented an intimate personal relationship with each of the persons of the Trinity should also be cultivated with a vibrant prayer life and an attempt to reflect the character and commitments of these Trinitarian persons beyond each of us, beyond each of our believing communities to include the vulnerable persons who They are concerned about. Thus, the filial knowledge reflects a person's whole being and community life. Enjoy the journey as we travel with God and others. In such a journey the conversation has begun but is never complete provided we are traveling with each other.

Select Bibliography

Abrahams, Israel. *Studies in Pharisaism and the Gospels.* New York: KTAV, 1967.
Agus, Jacob. *Judaism and Christianity.* New York: Arno Press, 1973.
Alexander, P. S. "The Rabbinic Hermeneutical Rules and the Definition of Midrash," *PIBA* 8(1984): 96–125.
———. "Quid Athens et Hierosolymis? Rabbinic Midrash and Hermeneutics in the Graeco-Roman World" in *A Tribute to Geza Vermes: Essays on Jewish and Christian Literature and History.* JSOT 100. edited by P. Davies and R. White. Sheffield: Sheffield Academic Press, 1990, 153–66.
Allen, C. Leonard. "Baconianism and the Bible in the Disciples of Christ: James S. Lamar and *"The Organon of Scripture,"* *CH* 55:1(1986): 65–80.
Allen, Diogenes. *Philosophy for Understanding Theology.* Atlanta: John Knox Press, 1985.
Alston, William. *Perceiving God: The Epistemology of Religious Experience.* Ithaca: Cornell University Press, 1991.
Anderson, Paul, Felix Just, and Tom Thatcher. *John, Jesus, and History. Volume 2 Aspects of Historicity in the Fourth Gospel.* Atlanta: Society of Biblical Literature, 2009.
Anderson, R. Dean. *Glossary of Greek Rhetorical Terms Connected to Methods of Argumentation, Figures and Tropes from Anaximenes to Quintilian.* Leuven: Peeters, 2000.
Anderson, William. *Qoheleth and Its Pessimistic Theology: Hermeneutical Struggles in Wisdom Literature.* Lampeter: Edwin Mellen, 1997.
Appold, Mark. "Jesus' Bethesaida Disciples: A Study in Johannine Origins." In *John, Jesus, and History, Volume 2: Aspects of Historicity in the Fourth Gospel.* edited by Paul Anderson, Felix Just, and Tom Thatcher. Atlanta: Society of Biblical Literature, 2009, 2:27–34
Ariel, Donald. "Survey of Coin Finds in Jerusalem (until the End of the Byzantine Period)," *Liber Annus* 32(1982): 284–314.
Armstrong, Claude. "St. Paul's Theory of Knowledge," *The Church Quarterly Review* 154:313(Oct-Dec 1953): 438–52.
Aslan, Reza. *Zealot: The Life and Times of Jesus of Nazareth.* New York: Random House, 2014.
Assmann, Jan. *Das kulturelle Gedächtnis: Schrift, Erinnerung und politische Identität in frühen Hochkulturen.* Munich: C. H. Beck, 1992.
Attridge, H. W. *The Epistle to the Hebrews: A Commentary on the Epistle to the Hebrews.* Philadelphia: Fortress, 1989.

Audi, Robert and William Wainwright. *Rationality, Religious Belief, and Moral Commitment*. Ithaca: Cornell University Press, 1986.

Aune, David. "Dualism in the Fourth Gospel and the Dead Sea Scrolls: A Reassessment of the Problem." In *Neotestamentica et Philonica*. edited by David Aune, Torrey Seland, and Jarl Ulrichsen, Leiden: Brill, 2003, 289–303 and In *Jesus, Gospel Tradition and Paul in the Context of Jewish and Greco-Roman Antiquity*. Tübingen: Mohr Siebeck, 2013, 130–48.

Austin, John. *How to Do Things with Words*. Cambridge: Harvard University Press, 1975.

Bachmann, Michael. "4QMMT und Galaterbrief, *ma'ase hatorah* und ERGA NOMOU," *ZNW* 89(1998): 91–113.

———. *Anti-Judaism in Galatians? Exegetical Studies on a Polemical Letter and on Paul's Theology*. Grand Rapids: Eerdmans, 2008.

———. *Antijudaismus im Galaterbrief: Exegetische Studien zu einem polemischen Schreibenund zur Theologie des Apostels Paulus*. NTOA 40. Freiburg: Universitätsverlag, 1999.

———. "Rechtfertigung und Gesetzeswerke bei Paulus," *TZ* 49(1993): 1–33.

Back, Sven-Olav. *Jesus of Nazareth and the Sabbath Commandment*. Åbo: Åbo Akademi University Press, 1995.

Bacon, Francis. *Advancement of Learning* in vol. 30 *Great Books of the Western World*. Chicago: Encyclopaedia Britannica, 1977.

Bahr, G. J. "The Seder of Passover and the Eucharistic Words." *NovT* 12 (1970): 181–202.

Bailey, K. E. "Informal Controlled Oral Tradition and the Synoptic Gospels," *AJT* 5 (1991): 34–54.

———. "Middle Eastern Oral Tradition and the Synoptic Gospels," *ExpTim* 106(1995): 363–67.

Balch, D. L. "The Areopagus Speech: An Appeal to the Stoic Historian Posidonius against Later Stoics and the Epicureans." In *Greeks, Romans, and Christians*. edited by D. L. Balch. Minneapolis: Fortress, 1990, 52–79.

Baldwin, Joyce. *Daniel: An Introduction & Commentary*. Downers Grove: Inter Varsity, 1978.

Bammel, Ernst. "Markus 10:11f und das jüdische Eherecht" *ZNW* 61(1970): 95–101.

Barnes, J. *The Presocratic Philosophers*. London: Routledge & Kegan Paul, 1979.

Barr, James. *The Semantics of Biblical Language*. Oxford: Oxford University Press, 1961.

Barret, C. K. "Paul's Speech on the Areopagus." In *New Testament Christianity for Africa and the World: Essays in Honor of Harry Sawyer*, edited by M. E. Glasswell and E. W. Fashole-Luke. London: SPCK, 1974, 69–77.

———. *The First Epistle to the Corinthians*. New York: Harper and Row, 1968.

Barth, Karl. *A Shorter Commentary on Romans*. Richmond: John Knox, 1963.

———. *Church Dogmatics IV/3.2: The Doctrine of Reconciliation*. Edinburgh: T & T Clark, 1956.

Barton, Stephen, Loren Stuckenbruck and Benjamin Wold. *Memory in the Bible and Antiquity: The Fifth Durham-Tubingen Research Symposium (Durham, September 2004)*. Tübingen: Mohr Siebeck, 2007.

Bates, Matthew. *The Hermeneutics of the Apostolic Proclamation: The Center of Paul's Method of Scriptural Interpretation*. Waco: Baylor Press, 2012.

Bauckham, Richard. *Gospel of Glory: Major Themes in Johannine Theology*. Grand Rapids: Baker, 2015.
———. *Jesus and the Eyewitnesses: The Gospels as Eyewitness Testimony*. Grand Rapids: Eerdmans, 2006.
———. *Jude, 2 Peter*. Waco: Word Books, 1983.
———. "The Gospel of John and the Synoptic Problem." In *New Studies in the Synoptic Problem: Oxford Conference, April 2008*. edited by P. Foster, et. al. Leuven: Utigeveru Peeters, 2011, 658–85.
Bauer, Walter, Robert Kraft and Gerhard Krodel. *Orthodoxy and Heresy in Earliest Christianity*. Philadelphia: Fortress, 1971.
Beasley-Murray, G. R. *John*. Waco: Word, 1987.
Becker, Jürgen. *Paul: Apostle to the Gentiles*. Louisville: Westminster John Knox, 1993.
———. *Paulus: Der Apostel der Völker*. Tübingen: Mohr Siebeck, 1989.
Bekken, Per Jarle. *The Word is Near You: A Study of Deuteronomy 30:12–14 in Paul's Letter to the Romans in a Jewish Context*. Berlin: de Gruyter, 2007.
Bennema, Cornelis. "A Theory of Character in the Fourth Gospel with Reference to Ancient and Modern Literature," *BibInt* 17(2009): 375–421.
———. *Encountering Jesus: Character Studies in the Gospel of John*. Milton Keyes: Paternoster, 2009..
Berger, Peter and Thomas Luckmann, *The Social Construction of Reality: A Treatise in the Sociology of Knowledge*. Garden City: Doubleday, 1966.
Berkowitz, Luci, Karl Squiter and William Johnson. *Thesaurus Linguae Graecae Canon of Greek Authors and Works*. New York: Oxford Press, 1990.
Bernard, J. H. *A Critical and Exegetical Commentary on the Gospel According to St. John*. Edinburgh: T & T Clark, 1928.
Betz, Hans. *Galatians: A Commentary on Paul's Letter to the Church in Galatia*. Philadelphia: Fortress, 1984.
Bialoblocki, S. "Hermeneutik," In *Encyclopaedia Judaica: Das Judentum in Galentum in Geshichte und Gegenwart*. Berlin: Eschkol Verlag, 1972, 7:1181–94.
Biblia Patristics: Index des citation et allusions bibliques dans la litterérature patristique. Paris: Éditions du Centre national de la recherché scientifique, 1975.
Bietenhard. "Natürliche Goetteserkenntnis der Heiden? Eine Erwägung zu Röm 1," *ThZ* 12(1956): 275–88.
Bird, Michael. *The Gospel of the Lord: How the Early Church Wrote the Story of Jesus*. Grand Rapids: Eerdmans, 2014.
Black, David Alan. *New Testament Textual Criticism: A Concise Guide*. Grand Rapids: Baker Books, 1994.
Black, Robert. "The Conversion Stories in the Acts of the Apostles," PhD dissertation Emory University, 1985.
Blaising, Craig. "Gethsemane a Prayer of Faith," *JETS* 22(1979): 333–43.
Blanton, Thomas R. "Spirit and Covenant Renewal: A Theologoumenon of Paul's Opponents in 2 Corinthians" *JBL* 129(2010): 129–51.
Bloch, R. "Midrash." In *Approaches to Ancient Judaism: Theory and Practice*, ed. W. S. Green. Callaway: Scholars Press, 1978, 29–50.
Blomberg, Craig. *The Historical Reliability of the Gospels*. Downers Grove: InterVarsity, 1987.
Bock, Darrel. *Luke*. Grand Rapids: Baker, 1996.

———. *Proclamation from Prophecy and Pattern: Lukan Old Testament Christology.* Sheffield: JSOT, 1987.
Bokzer, B. Z. *Judaism and the Christian Predicament.* New York: Alfred Knopf, 1967.
Bond, "Renewing the Mind: The Role of Cognition Language in Pauline Theology and Ethics," *TynB* 58:2(Jan, 2007): 317–20.
Bonhoeffer, Dietrich. *Life Together.* New York: Harper & Row, 1954.
Bonhoffer, A. *Epiketet und das Neue Testament.* Giessen: Alfred Töpelmann, 1911.
Bonneau, Normand. "The Logic of Paul's Argument on the Curse of the Law in Galatians 3:10–14," *Nov Test* 39(1997): 60–80.
———. "The Logic of Paul's Argument on the Resurrection Body in 1 Cor 15:35–44a," *Science et Esprit* 45:1(1993): 79–92.
Bonsirven, Joseph. *Exégèse rabbinique et Exégèse paulinienne.* Paris: Beauchesne et ses fils, 1938.
Boomershine, Thomas. "Epistemology at the Turn of the Ages in Paul, Jesus, and Mark: Rhetoric and Dialectic in Apocalyptic and the New Testament." In *Apocalyptic and the New Testament.* edited by Joel Marcus and Marion Soards. Sheffield: Sheffield Academic, 1989.
Borg, Marcus. *Jesus in Contemporary Scholarship.* Valley Forge: Trinity, 1994.
Borgen, Peder. "God's Agent in the Fourth Gospel." In *Religion in Antiquity.* edited by Jacob Neusner. Leiden: Brill, 1968, 137–48.
Bourke, M. "The Literary Genus of Matthew 1–2," *CBQ* 22(1960): 160–75.
Bousset, Wilhelm. *Kyrios Christos: A History of Belief in Christ from the Beginnings of Christianity to Irenaeus.* Nashville: Abingdon, 1970.
Bouttier, Michel. *En Christ: E'tude d'exe'gese et de the'ologie Pauliniennes E'tudes d'historie et de philosophie religieuses 54.* Paris: Presses universitaires de France, 1962.
Bovon, Francis. "The Role of the Scriptures in the Composition of the Gospel Accounts: The Temptations of Jesus (Lk. 4.1–13 par.) and the Multiplication of the Loaves (Lk. 9.10–17 par.)." In *Luke and Acts.* edited by Gerald O'Collins and Gilberto Marconi. New York: Paulist, 1991, 27–28.
Boyarin, Daniel. *A Radical Jew: Paul and the Politics of Identity.* Berkley: University of California Press, 1994.
Bray, Gerald. *Romans: Crossway Classic Commentaries.* Downers Grove: InterVarsity, 1995.
Brooke, G. J. *Exegesis at Qumran: 4QFlorilegium in its Jewish Context.* Sheffield: JSOT, 1985.
Brown, Colin. *Quests for the Historical Jesus.* Edinburgh: T. & T. Clark, 2015.
Brown, Raymond. *The Gospel According to John i–xii*, vol. 29. Garden City: Doubleday, 1966.
———. *John xiii–xxi*, vol. 29A. Garden City: Doubleday, 1966.
———. *The Epistles of John.* Garden City: Doubleday, 1982.
Brown, Robert. "Edwards, Locke, and the Bible," *JR* 79:3(1999): 361–84.
Bruce, F. F. *1 and 2 Corinthians.* Grand Rapids: Eerdmans, 1971.
———. *Commentary on the Book of Acts.* Grand Rapids: Eerdmans, 1979.
———. *The Epistle of Paul to the Romans: An Introduction and Commentary.* Grand Rapids: Eerdmans, 1985.
———. *The Epistle to the Hebrews.* Grand Rapids: Eerdmans, 1964.
———. *The Speeches in the Book of Acts the Apostles.* London: Tyndale, 1942.

———. "The Speeches in Acts-Thirty Years After." In *Reconciliation and Hope. New Testament Essays on Atonement and Eschatology presented to L. L. Morris on his 60th Birthday.* Exeter: The Paternoster Press, 1974, 53–68.

Brueggemann, Walter. *A Pathway of Interpretation: The Old Testament for Pastors and Students.* Eugene: Cascade, 2008.

———. "Impossibility and Epistemology in the Faith Tradition of Abraham and Sarah (Gen 18:1–15)" *ZAW* 94:4(1982): 615–34.

Buchanan, George. *To the Hebrews.* Garden City: Doubleday, 1972.

Bullock, Hassell. *An Introduction to the Old Testament Poetic Books.* Chicago: Moody Press, 1988.

Bultmann, Rudolf. *Der Stil der paulischen Predigt und die kynisch-stoische Diatribe.* Göttingen: Vandenhoeck & Ruprecht, 1910.

———. *Jesus Christ and Mythology.* New York: Scribner, 1958.

———. *The Gospel of John: A Commentary.* Oxford: Blackwell, 1971.

———. "The History of Religions Background of the Prologue to the Gospel of John." In *The Interpretation of John,* edited by J. Ashton. Edinburgh: T & T Clark, 1997, 27–46.

———. *Theology of the New Testament.* London: SCM, 1952.

Bultmann, Rudolf, Hans Bartsch, Reginald Fuller. *Kerygma and Myth: A Theological Debate.* New York: Harper & Row, 1961.

Burnett, Andrew. *Roman Provincial Coinage.* London: British Museum Press, 1992.

Bynum, Caroline Walker. *The Resurrection of the Body in Western Christianity, 200–1336.* New York: Columbia University Press, 1995.

Byrskog, Samuel. *Story as History-History as Story: The Gospel Tradition in the Context of Ancient Oral History.* Tübingen: Mohr, 2000 and Leiden: Brill, 2002.

Calvin, John. *Commentaries on the Epistle of Paul the Apostle to the Romans.* Grand Rapids: Baker, 1979.

Campbell, Constantine. *Paul and Union with Christ: An Exegetical and Theological Study.* Grand Rapids: Zondervan, 2012.

Caputo, John and Linda Alcoff. *St Paul Among the Philosophers.* Bloomington: Indiana University Press, 2009.

Carson, D. A. "Matthew." In *The Expositor's Bible Commentary,* Grand Rapids: Zondervan, 1984.

———. *The Gospel According to John.* Leicester: InterVarsity, 1991.

Charlesworth, James H. *Jesus' Jewishness: Exploring the Place of Jesus in Early Judaism.* New York: Crossroad, 1991.

———. *Jesus Within Judaism.* Anchor Bible Reference. Garden City: Doubleday, 1988.

———. *John and the Dead Sea Scrolls.* New York: Crossroad, 1990.

Charlesworth, James H. with Petr Pokorny. *Jesus Research: An International Perspective: The First Princeton-Prague Symposium on Jesus Research, Prague 2005.* Grand Rapids: Eerdmans, 2009.

Charlesworth, James H. and Walter P. Weaver. *Images of Jesus Today.* Valley Forge: Trinity, 1994.

Chernus, Ira. "Visions of God in Merkabah Mysticism," *JSJ* 13(1982): 123–46.

Chilton, Bruce. *Rabbi Paul: An Intellectual Biography.* New York: Doubleday, 2004.

Christianson, Ellen Juhl. *The Covenant in Judaism and Paul: A Study of Ritual Boundaries as Identity Markers.* Leiden: Brill, 1995.

Ciampa, Roy and Brian Rosner. *The First Letter to the Corinthians*. Grand Rapids: Eerdmans, 2010.
Cohon, Samuel. "The Place of Jesus in the Religious Life of His Day," *JBL* 48(1929): 82–108.
Collins, Adela Yarbro. *Mark: A Commentary*. Minneapolis: Fortress, 2007.
Collins, J. J. "The Works of the Messiah," *DSD* 1(1994): 98–112.
Collins, John and Daniel Harlow. *The Eerdmans Dictionary of Early Judaism*. Grand Rapids: Eerdmans, 2010.
Conzelmann, Hans. *A Commentary on the First Epistle to the Corinthians*. Philadelphia: Fortress, 1975.
———. *Acts of the Apostles*. Hermenia. Philadelphia: Fortress, 1987, 2nd edition 1972.
———. *The Theology of St. Luke*. Philadelphia: Fortress, 1961.
Cook, W. Robert. *The Theology of John*. Chicago: Moody, 1979.
Cooper, Craig. *Politics of Orality*. vol. 6 *Orality and Literacy in Ancient Greece*. Leiden: Brill, 2007.
Cosby, M. R. *The Rhetorical Composition and Function of Hebrews 11: In Light of Example Lists in Antiquity*. Macon: Mercer University Press, 1988.
———. "The Rhetorical Composition of Hebrews 11" *JBL* 107(1988): 257–73.
Cothenet, Eduard, et al. "Imitation du Christ," *Dictionnaire de Spiritualité* 7(1971): 1536–1601.
Cowley, A. E. *Aramaic Papyri of the Fifth Century B.C. Edited with Translation and Notes*. Oxford: Clarendon, 1923.
Cox, Harvey. *The Secular City*. New York: Macmillan, 1965.
Cranfield, C. E. B. *A Critical and Exegetical Commentary on the Epistle to the Romans*. Edinburgh: Clark, 1975–79.
———. "'The Works of the Law' in the Epistle to the Romans," *JSNT* 43(1991): 89–101.
Creed, J. M. *The Gospel According to St. Luke*. London: Macmillian, 1930.
Crenshaw, James. *Old Testament Wisdom*. Atlanta: John Knox, 1981.
Crook, Zeba. *Reconceptualizing Conversion: Patronage, Loyalty, and Conversion in the Religion of the Ancient Mediterranean*. Berlin: deGruyter, 2004.
Crossan, John Dominic. *Jesus: A Revolutionary Biography*. San Francisco: Harper San Francisco, 1994.
———. *The Historical Jesus: The Life of a Mediterranean Jewish Peasant*. San Francisco: Harper, 1991.
Crouzel, Henri. "L'imitation et la 'suite' de Dieu et du Christ dans les premiers siècles chrétiens, ansi que leurs sources gréco-romaines et hébraiques," *JAC* 21(1978): 7–41.
Cullmann, Oscar. *The Christology of the New Testament*. London: SCM, 1963.
Cunningham, Scott and Darrell Bock. "Is Matthew Midrash?," *BSac* 144(1987): 157–80.
Dabney, Lyle. "'Justified by the Spirit': Soteriological Reflections on the Resurrection," *International Journal of Systematic Theology* 3:1(Mar. 2001): 50.
Danker, Frederick. "Under Contract: A Form-Critical Study of Linguistic Adaptation in Romans." In *Festchrift to Honor F. Wilbur Gingrich, Lexicographer, Scholar, Teacher, and Committed Christian Layman*. edited by E. M. Barth and R. E. Concroft. Leiden: Brill, 1972.
Das, Andrew. *Paul, the Law and the Covenant*. Peabody: Hendrickson, 2001.
Daube, David. *The New Testament and Rabbinic Judaism*. London: University of London Press, 1956.

———. "Rabbinic Methods of Interpretation and Hellenistic Rhetoric," *HUCA* 22(1949): 239–264.
Davids, Peter. *A Theology of James, Peter, and Jude*. Grand Rapids: Zondervan, 2014.
Davies, W. D. *Paul and Rabbinic Judaism: Some Rabbinic Elements in Pauline Theology*. Mifflintown: Sigler Press, 1998.
Davies, W. D. and Dale Allison, *The Gospel According to Saint Matthew*. Edinburgh: T & T Clark, 1988.
Dawes, Gregory. "But if you can Gain your Freedom," *CBQ* 52[1990]: 681–97.
Dean-Otting, Mary. *Heavenly Journeys: A Study of the Motif in Hellenistic Jewish Literature*. New York: Peter Lang, 1984.
de Boer, Willis P. *The Imitation of Paul: An Exegetical Study*. Kampen: J. H. Kok, 1962.
Deismann, Adolf. *Light from the Ancient East: The NT Illustrated by Recently Discovered Texts of Graeco-Roman World*. translated by Lionel Strachan. New York: George Daron, 1927.
de Jonge, Irene, René Nünlist, and Angus Bowie. *Narrators, Narratees, and Narratives in Ancient Greek Literature*. Leiden: Brill, 2004.
de Roo, Jacqueline C. R. "The Concept of 'Works of the Law' in Jewish and Christian Literature." In *Christian-Jewish Relations Through the Centuries*. JSNTSup 192. Rochampton Papers 6. edited by Stanley Porter and Brook Pearson. Sheffield: Sheffield Academic, 2000, 116–47.
Descartes, René. *Meditations on First Philosophy* in *Great Books of the Western World*. number 31. ed. Mortimer Adler. Chicago: Encyclopedia Britannica, 1952.
deSilva, David. *Despising Shame: Honor Discourse and Community Maintenance in the Epistle to the Hebrews*. Atlanta: Scholars Press, 1995.
———. *Epistle to the Hebrews*. Atlanta: Scholars Press, 1995.
Dever, William. "Archeology, Texts, and History-Writing: Toward an Epistemology." In *Uncovering Ancient Stones*. edited by Lewis Hopfe. Winona Lake: Eisenbrauns, 1994, 105–17.
Dewey, Joanna. "From Storytelling to Written Text: The Loss of Early Christian Women's Voices," *BTB* 26(1996): 71–78.
———. *Orality and Textuality in Early Christian Literature*. Semia Studies. Atlanta: Scholars, 1995.
Dibelius, Martin. *James: A Commentary on the Epistle of James*. Philadelphia: Fortress, 1976.
———. "Paul on Areopagus." In *Studies in the Acts of the Apostles*. edited by H. Greeven. New York: Charles Scribner's Sons, 1956, 26–77.
———. "The Speeches in Acts and Ancient Historiography." In *Studies in the Acts of the Apostles*. edited by H. Greeven. New York: Charles Scribner's Sons, 1956, 138–85.
Dibelius, M., Heinrich Greenan, and Mary Ling. *Studies in the Acts of the Apostles*. London: SCM, 1973.
Dickens, Charles. *A Christmas Carol and Other Stories*. Roslyn: Walter J. Black, 1932.
Die griechische Schriftsteller der ersten Jahrhunderte. Berlin: Akademie Verlag and Leipzig: Hinrichs, 1899.
Diels, H. *Die Fragmente der Vorsokratiker*. Berlin: Wiedmannsche Buchhandlung, 1912.
Diller, Kevin. *Theology's Epistemological Dilemma: How Karl Barth and Alvin Plantinga Provide a Unified Response*. Downers Grove: InterVarsity, 2014.
Dodd, C. H. *According to the Scriptures: The Sub-Structure of New Testament Theology*. London: Nisbet, 1952 and New York: Scribner's, 1953.

———. *Historical Tradition in the Fourth Gospel*. Cambridge: Cambridge University Press, 1965.
———. *The Apostolic Preaching and Its Developments*. London: Hodder, 1936.
———. "The Framework of the Gospel Narrative," *ExpTim* 43(1931–32): 396–400.
Draper, Jonathan. *Orality, Literacy, and Colonialism in Antiquity. Semia Studies*. Atlanta: Society of Biblical Literature, 2004.
Driver, G. R. *The Judean Scrolls: The Problem and a Solution*. Oxford: Blackwell, 1965.
Dunn, James. *Christology in the Making*. Grand Rapids: Eerdmans, 1980.
———. *Jesus Remembered*. Grand Rapids: Eerdmans, 2003.
———. *Jesus, Paul and the Law: Studies in Mark and Galatians*. Louisville: Westminster/John Knox, 1990.
———. *Jews and Christians: The Parting of the Ways, A.D. 70 to 135*. Grand Rapids: Eerdmans, 1992.
———. *Paul and the Mosaic Law*. Grand Rapids: Eerdmans, 1996.
———. "Q as oral tradition." In *The Written Gospel*. edited by Markus Bockmuehl and Donald Hagner. Cambridge: Cambridge University Press, 2005, 45–69.
———. *Romans 1–8* and *Romans 9–16*. Dallas: Word, 1988.
———. *The Christ & the Spirit, Volume 1 Christology*. Grand Rapids: Eerdmans, 1998.
———. *The New Perspective on Paul*. Grand Rapids: Eerdmans, 2005, 2008.
———. *The Theology of Paul the Apostle*. Grand Rapids: Eerdmans, 1998.
———. "Works of the Law and the Curse of the Law (Galatians 3:10–14)," *NTS* 31(1983): 523–42.
Dunn, James and Alan Suggate. *The Justice of God*. Grand Rapids: Eerdmans, 1993.
Dunn, James and Scot McKnight. *The Historical Jesus in Recent Research*. Winona Lake: Eisenbrauns, 2005.
Dupont, Jaques. "Conversion in the Acts of the Apostles." In *The Salvation of the Gentiles: Studies in the Acts of the Apostles*. New York: Paulist, 1979, 61–84.
———. *Gnosis: La Connaissance Religieuse Dans Les Épitres de Saint Paul*. Louvain: E. Nauwelaerts, 1949.
Edwards, Jonathan. *Freedom of the Will*. New Haven: Yale University Press, 1957.
———. *Religious Affections*. New Haven: Yale University Press, 1959.
Ehrman, Bart. *Lost Scriptures: Books that Did Not Make it into the New Testament*. Oxford: Oxford University Press, 2003.
Eisenbaum, P. M. "Heroes and History in Hebrews 11." In *Early Christian Interpretation of the Scriptures of Israel: Investigations and Proposals*. edited by C. Evans and J. A. Sanders. Sheffield: Sheffield Academic, 1997, 380–96.
———. *The Jewish Heroes of Christian History: Hebrews 11 in Literary Context*. Atlanta: Scholars, 1997.
Elliott, John H. *1 Peter. AB*. New York: Doubleday, 2000.
Elliott, Mark Adam. *The Survivors of Israel*. Grand Rapids: Eerdmans, 2000.
———. "La Conversion dans les Actes des Apôtres," *LumVie* 47(1960): 47–70.
Ellis, E. Earle. "A Note on Pauline Hermeneutics," *NTS* 2(1955-6): 127–33.
———. "Midrash, Targum and New Testament Quotations." In *Neotestamentica et Semitica*. edited by E. E. Ellis and M. Wilcox. Edinburgh: Clark, 1969, 61–69.
———. *Paul's Use of the Old Testament*. Edinburgh: Oliver and Boyd, 1957.
———. *The Old Testament in Early Christianity: Canon and Interpretation in the Light of Modern Research*. Grand Rapids: Baker, 1991.

Elman, Yaakov and Israel Gershoni. *Transmitting Jewish Traditions: Orality, Textuality, and Cultural Diffusion*. New Haven: Yale University Press, 2000.
Ely [later Lyman], Mary Redington. *Knowledge of God in Johannine Thought*. New York: The Macmillan Co., 1925.
Etheridge, J. W. *The Targums of Onkelos and Jonathan ben Uzziel on the Pentateuch, with fragments of the Jerusalem Targum from the Chaldee*. New York: Ktav Pub. House, 1968.
Evans, Craig. *Life of Jesus Research: An Annotated Bibliography*. New Testament Tools and Studies 13. Leiden: Brill, 1989.
———. "Luke and the Rewritten Bible: Aspects of Lukan Hagiography." In *The Pseudepigrapha and Early Biblical Interpretation*. edited by James Charlesworth and Craig Evans. Sheffield: Sheffield Academic, 1993, 170–201.
———. *To See and Not Perceive: Isaiah 6:9–10 in Early Jewish and Christian Interpretation*. JSOT 64. Sheffield: Sheffield Academic, 1989.
———. *Word and Glory: On the Exegetical and Theological Background of John's Prologue*. Sheffield: JSOT, 1993.
Evans, Craig and James Sanders. *Paul and the Scriptures of Israel*. Sheffield: Sheffield Academic, 1993.
———. "The Gospels and Midrash: An Introduction to Luke and Scripture." In *Luke and Scripture: The Function of Sacred Tradition in Luke-Acts*. edited by Craig Evans and James Sanders. Minneapolis: Fortress, 1993, 1–13.
Evans, Craig and Stanley Porter. *Dictionary of New Testament Background*. Downers Grove: InterVarsity, 2000.
Farrar, Frederic. *The Life and Work of St. Paul*. New York: Dutton, 1879.
Fathers of the Church. Washington D.C.: Catholic University of America, 1947.
Fee, Gordon. *The First Epistle to the Corinthians*. Grand Rapids: Eerdmans, 1987.
Finkel, Asher. *The Pharisees and the Teacher of Nazareth: A Study of their Background, their Halachic and Midrashic Teachings, the Similarities and Differences*. Leiden: E. J. Brill, 1964.
Fiore, Benjamin. "Paul, Exemplification, and Imitation." In *Paul in the Greco-Roman World: A Handbook*. edited by Paul Sampley. Harrisburg: Trinity Press International, 2003, 228–57.
———. *The Function of Personal Example in the Socratic and Pastoral Epistles*. An. Bib. 105. Rome: Biblical Institute Press, 1986.
Fisher, John. "Jesus Through Jewish Eyes: A Rabbi examples the Life and Teachings of Jesus," a paper presented at the Evangelical Theological Society, Nov. 2003.
Fitzmyer, Joseph. "A Re-Study of an Elephantine Aramaic Marriage Contract (AP 15)." In *Near Eastern Studies in Honor of William Foxwell Albright*. edited by H. Goedicke. Baltimore: Johns Hopkins University Press, 1971, 137–68.
———. *Romans: A New Translation with Introduction and Commentary*. AB 33. New York: Doubleday, 1993.
———. "The Matthean Divorce Texts and Some New Palestinian Evidence" *TS* 37(1976): 197–226.
Flusser, David. *Judaism and the Origins of Christianity*. Jerusalem: Magnes, 1988.
Fornara, Charles William. *The Nature of History in Ancient Greece and Rome. Eidos Studies in Classical Kinds*. Berkeley: University of California Press, 1983.
Fortna, R. *The Gospel of Signs: A Reconstruction of the Narrative Source Underlying the Fourth Gospel*. Cambridge: Cambridge University Press, 1970.

Foster, John. *Ancient Egyptian Literature: An Anthology.* Austin: University of Texas Press, 2001.

Foster, P., A. Gregory, J. S. Kloppenborg, and J. Verheyden. *New Studies in the Synoptic Problem, Oxford Conference, April 2008.* Leuven: Uitgeverij Peeters, 2011.

Fox, Michael. *A Time to Tear Down & A Time to Build up: A Rereading of Ecclesiastes.* Grand Rapids: Eerdmans, 1999.

———. *Qohelet and His Contradictions.* Sheffield: Almond, 1989.

———. "Qohelet's Epistemology," *HUCA* 58(1987): 137–41.

———. "The Epistemology of the Book of Proverbs," *JBL* 162:4(2007): 669–84.

———. "Two Decades of Research in Egyptian *Wisdom* Literature," *ZAS* 107(1980): 120–35.

France, R. T. *Jesus and the Old Testament.* London: The Tyndale, 1971.

Franke, August Hermann. *Praelectiones Hermeneuticae, ad Exponendi Sensvm Scripturae S. Theologiae Stvdiosis Ostendendam Adjiecta est in Fine Brevis et Lvcvlenta Scriptvram S. cvm Frvtv Legendi Institvtio.* Halle: Waisenhaus, 1710.

Frydrych, Thomas. *Living Under the Sun: Examination of Proverbs and Qoheleth.* Leiden: Brill, 2002.

Gadamer, Hans. *Truth and Method.* New York: Crossroad, 1984.

Gaffin, Richard. *The Centrality of the Resurrection: A Study in Paul's Soteriology.* Grand Rapids: Baker, 1978.

Gaffney, James. "Believing and Knowing in the Fourth Gospel," *TS* 26(1965): 215–41.

Gärtner, Bertil. *The Areopagus Speech and Natural Revelation.* Lund: C. W. K. Gleerup, 1955.

———. "The Pauline and Johannine Idea of 'To Know God' against the Hellenistic Background: The Greek Philosophical Principle 'Like by Like' in Paul and John," *NTS* 14(1968): 217–20.

Gathercole, Simon. "Torah, Life, and Salvation: Leviticus 18:5 in Early Judaism and the New Testament." In *From Prophecy to Testament: The Function of the Old Testament in the New.* ed. Craig Evans. Peabody: Hendrickson, 2004, 126–139.

———. "Torah, Life and Salvation: The Use of Lev. 18.5 in Early Judaism and Christianity." In *From Prophecy to Testament: The Function of the Old Testament in the New,* edited by C. A. Evans and J. A. Sanders. Peabody: Hendrickson, 2005, 126–45.

Gaventa, Beverly. *From Darkness to Light: Aspects of Conversion in the New Testament.* Philadelphia: Fortress, 1986.

Gentry, Peter. "The Septuagint and the Text of the Old Testament," *BBR* 16(2006): 193–218.

Gerhardsson, B. *Memory and Manuscript: Oral Tradition and the Written Transmission in Rabbinic Judaism and Early Christianity.* Lund: Gleerup, 1961, 1998.

———. *The Gospel Tradition.* Lund: Gleerup, 1986.

Gericke, Jaco. "A Comprehensive Philosophical Approach to Qohelet's Epistemology," *HvTSt* 71:1(2015): 1–9.

———. "The Beginning of Wisdom is Paranoia: An Overlooked Aspect of the 'Fear of YHWH' in the Context of Lacanian Psych-Epistemology," *Scriptura* 111(2012): 440–51.

Gettier, E. "Is Justified True Belief Knowledge?," *Analysis* 23(1963): 121–23.

Gillman, Neil. *The Death of Death: Resurrection and Immortality in Jewish Thought.* Woodstock: Jewish Lights Publishing, 2000.

Godet, Frederic. *Commentary on John's Gospel.* Grand Rapids: Kregel, 1978.
———. *Commentary on Romans.* Grand Rapids: Kregel, 1977.
Goldman, Alvin. "A Causal Theory of Knowing," *The Journal of Philosophy* 64(1967): 357–72.
Gooch, Paul. *Partial Knowledge: Philosophical Studies in Paul.* Notre Dame: University of Notre Dame Press, 1987.
Goodenough, Erwin. *Jewish Symbols in the Greco-Roman World.* Princeton: Princeton University Press, 1992.
Gordon, Cyrus. *The Ancient Near East.* New York: W. W. Norton, 1965.
Gorman, Michael. *Inhabiting the Cruciform God: Kenosis, Justification, and Theosis in Paul's Narrative Soteriology.* Grand Rapids: Eerdmans, 2009.
Grave, S. A. *The Scottish Philosophy of Common Sense.* Oxford: Clarendon Press, 1960.
Graver, Margaret. *Stoicism and Emotion.* Chicago: University of Chicago, 2007.
Green, Joel B. *Conversion in Luke-Acts: Divine Action, Human Cognition, and the People of God.* Grand Rapids: Baker, 2015.
———. *The Theology of the Gospel of Luke.* Cambridge: Cambridge University Press, 1995.
Green, Joel B., Scot McKnight and I. Howard Marshall. *Dictionary of Jesus and the Gospels.* Downers Grove: InterVarsity Press, 1992.
Gregerman, Adam. "Critique of *Short Stories by Jesus*" a paper presented at the Society for Biblical Literature, Nov. 22, 2015.
Grenz, Stanley. *Beyond Foundationalism.* Louisville: Westminster John Knox Press, 2001.
Grice, H. Paul. "Meaning," *Philosophical Review* 66(1957): 377–88.
———. "Utterer's Meaning and Intentions," *Philosophical Review* 78(1969): 147–77.
———. "Utterer's Meaning, Sentence-Meaning, Word-Meaning." In *The Philosophy of Language.* edited by J. R. Searle. Oxford: Oxford University Press, 1977, 54–70.
Grosheide, F. W. *Commentary on the First Epistle to the Corinthians.* Grand Rapids: Eerdmans, 1953.
Gruenwald, Itamar. *Apocalyptic and Merkavah Mysticism.* Leiden: Brill, 1980.
Gundry, Robert. *Mark: A Commentary on His Apology for the Cross.* Grand Rapids: Eerdmans, 1993.
———. *Matthew: A Commentary on His Literary and Theological Art.* Grand Rapids: Eerdmans, 1982.
Gundry, Stanley. *Four Views on the Role of Works at the Final Judgment.* Grand Rapids: Zondervan, 2013.
Gutierrez, Pedro. *La Paternité spirituelle selon S. Paul.* Paris: Gabalda, 1968.
Haacker, Klaus. *The Theology of Paul's Letter to the Romans.* Cambridge: Cambridge University Press, 2003.
Hadot, Pierre. *Philosophy as a Way of Life.* Oxford: Blackwell, 1995.
Halbwachs, Maurice. *Les cadres sociaux de la mémoire.* Paris: Alcan, 1925 translated as *On Collective Memory.* edited by Lewis Coser. Chicago: University of Chicago Press, 1992.
Harnack, Adolf. *Acts of the Apostles.* translated by John Richard Wilkenson. New York: G. P. Putnam's Sons, 1909.
———. *The Mission and Expansion of Christianity in the First Three Centuries.* translated and edited by James Moffatt. Gloucester: Peter Smith, 1972.

Harrington, Wilfrid. *Luke: Gracious Theologian: The Jesus of Luke*. Blackrock: Columbia, 1977.
Harris, J. Rendel. *Testimonies*. Cambridge: Cambridge University Press, 1916.
Hawthorne, Gerald, Ralph Martin and Daniel Reid. *Dictionary of Paul and His Letters*. Downers Grove: InterVarsity, 1993.
Hays, J. Daniel. "The Persecuted Prophet and Judgment on Jerusalem: The Use of LXX Jeremiah in the Gospel of Luke," *BBR* 25:4(2015): 453–75.
Hays, Richard. *Echoes of Scripture in the Letters of Paul*. New Haven: Yale University Press, 1989.
———. "Psalm 143 and the Logic of Romans 3," *JBL* 99:1(1980): 107–15.
———. *The Faith of Jesus Christ: The Narrative Substructure of Galatians 3:1–4:11*. Grand Rapids: Eerdmans, 2002.
Healy, Mary and Robin Parry. *The Bible and Epistemology: Biblical Soundings on the Knowledge of God*. Milton Keynes: Paternoster, 2007.
Heinemann, Joseph. *Prayer in the Talmud*. Berlin: Walter de Gruyter, 1977.
Hemer, C. J. *The Book of Acts in the Setting of Hellenistic History*. Winona Lake: Eisenbrauns, 1990.
———. "The Speeches in Acts II: The Areopagus Address," *TynB* 40(1989): 239–59.
Hengel, Martin. "Eye-witness memory and the writing of the Gospels: Form criticism, community tradition and the authority of the authors." In *The Written Gospel*. edited by Markus Bockmuehl and Donald Hagner. Cambridge: Cambridge University Press, 2005, 70–96.
———. *Judaism and Hellenism*. Translated by John Bowden. Philadelphia: Fortress Press, 1974.
———. *The Hellenization of Judaea in the First Century after Christ*. London: SCM, 1989.
———. *The Septuagint as Christian Scripture: Its Prehistory and the Problem of its Canon*. New York: T & T Clark, 2002.
Hennecke, Edward and Wilhelm Schneemelcher. *The New Testament Apocrypha*. Philadelphia: Westminster, 1965.
Henningsson, Jan. "Faith, Obedience, Understanding and Liberation: Reflections on Biblical Epistemology in Honor of Revd. Dr. D. W. Jesudoss Gurukul," *Swedish Missiological Themes* 88:2(2000): 179–91.
Henry, Matthew. *Matthew Henry's Commentary on the Whole Bible*. Peabody: Hendrickson, 1991.
Hess, Johann Jakob. *Geschichte der drey letzten Lebensjahre Jesu (The History of the Three Last Years of the Life of Jesus)*. Leipzig-Zürich, Orell, Gesner, 1768–72, 1776.
Hicks, Robert Drew. *Epicurus Principle Doctrines*, 23 accessed April 16, 2014, http://Classics.mit.edu/Epicurus/princdoc.html.
Hildesheimer, Azriel. *Halakbot G'dolot*. Berlin: Mekize Nirdamim, 1888.
Hirsch, E. D. *Validity in Interpretation*. New Haven: Yale University Press, 1967.
Hirsch, Emmanuel. *Geschichte der neuen Evangelische Theologie in Zusammenhang mit den allgemein Bewegung des Europäischen Denkens*. Gütersloh: Bertelsmann, 1951.
Hodge, Charles. *Romans*. Grand Rapids: Eerdmans, 1950 of 1886 edition.
Hofius, Olfried. "'Werke des Gesetzes': untersuchunger zu der paulinischer Rede von den ἔργων νόμου." In *Paulus und Johannes: Exegetische Studien zur paulinishen und johanneischen Theologie und Literatur. Wissenschaftliche Untersuchungen zum*

Neuen Testament 198. edited by Dieter Sänger and Ulrich Mell. Tübingen: Mohr Siebeck, 2006, 271–310.

Hogeterp, Albert. "4QMMT and Paradigms of Second Temple Judaism," *Dead Sea Discoveries* 15(2008): 359–379.

Hollaz, David. *Examen Theologicum Acroamaticum* published in 1707 is available as *Acromaticum Universam Theologiam Thetico-Polemicam Complectens.* Lipsiae: B.C. Breitkopfii, 1763.

Horsley, G. H. R. "Speeches and Dialogue in Acts," *NTS* 32(1986): 609–14.

Horsley, Richard. *Oral Performance, Popular Tradition, and Hidden Transcript in Q. Semia Studies.* Atlanta: Society of Biblical Literature, 2007.

Horsley, Richard, Jonathan Draper, and John Miles Foley. *Performing the Gospel: Orality, Memory, and Mark.* Minneapolis: Fortress, 2006.

Howard, G. "Hebrews and the Old Testament Quotation," *NovT* 10(1968): 208–16.

Hübner, Hans. *The Law in Paul's Thought.* Edinburgh: T. & T. Clark, 1984.

Hunter, A. M. *According to John: A New Look at the Fourth Gospel.* London: SCM, 1968.

Hurst, L. D. *The Epistle to the Hebrews: Its Background of Thought.* Cambridge: Cambridge University Press, 1990.

Immanuel, Babu. *Repent and Turn to God: Recounting Acts.* Perth: HIM International Ministries, 2004.

Instone-Brewer, David. *Feasts and Sabbaths: Passover and Atonement.* Grand Rapids: Eerdmans, 2011.

Isaac, Jules. *Jesus and Israel.* New York: Holt, Rinehart and Winston, 1971.

Jackson, J. Foakes and Kirsopp Lake. *The Beginnings of Christianity: Part 1 The Acts of the Apostles.* Grand Rapids: Baker, 1979.

———. *The Acts of the Apostles. Vol 4 Translation and Commentary.* Grand Rapids: Baker, 1979.

Jacobs, Joseph. "Jesus of Nazareth in History." In *Jewish Encyclopedia.* New York: Funk and Wagnalls, 1916, 7:160–63.

Jacobs, L. "Hermeneutics." In *Encyclopedia Judica.* Jerusalem: Keter, 1971, 8:366–72.

Jacomb, Thomas. *Sermons on the Eighth Chapter to the Epistle to the Romans (Verses 1–4).* Edinburgh: The Banner of Truth Trust, 1996.

Jenson, Robert. *America's Theologian: A Recommendation of Jonathan Edwards.* New York: Oxford University Press, 1988.

Jeremias, J. *New Testament Theology: The Proclamation of Jesus.* New York: Scribner's, 1971.

———. *The Eucharistic Words of Jesus.* London: SCM, 1966.

———. *The Sermon on the Mount.* Philadelphia: FBBS, 1963.

Jervell, Jacob. *Die Apostelgeschichte.* Göttingen: Vandenhoeck & Ruprecht, 1998.

———. *The Theology of the Acts of the Apostles.* Cambridge: Cambridge University Press, 1996.

Jewett, Robert. *Romans: A Commentary.* Minneapolis: Fortress, 2007.

Jobes, Karen. "When God Spoke Greek: The Place of the Greek Bible in Evangelical Scholarship," *BBR* 16(2006): 219–236.

Johnson, Luke Timothy. "Critique of *Short Stories by Jesus*" a paper presented at the Society for Biblical Literature, Nov. 22, 2015.

———. *The Gospel of Luke.* Collegeville, MN: Liturgical, 1991.

———. *The Real Jesus. The Misguided Quest for the Historical Jesus and the Truth of the Traditional Gospels.* San Francisco: Harper Collins, 1996.

Johnson, Michael. "The Seeds of Epistemology and Ontology in Genesis 1" *Proceedings EGU & MWBS* 18(1998): 1–10.

Jones, Olin McKendree. *Empiricism and Intuitionism in Reid's Common Sense Philosophy*. Princeton: Princeton University Press, 1927.

Jung, Volker. *Das Ganze der Heiligen Schrift. Hermeneutik und Schriftauslegung bei Abrham Calov*. Stuttgart: Calwer Verlag, 1999.

Karis, Robert. *Luke: Artist and Theologian*. New York: Paulist, 1985.

Käsemann, Ernest. "The Problem of the Historical Jesus," translated by W. J. Montague. *SBT* 41. Allenson/London: SCM, 1964, Original title, "Das Problem des historischen Jesus." *ZTK* 51 (1954): 125–53.

———. "The Structure and Purpose of the Prologue to John's Gospel." In *New Testament Questions of Today*. Philadelphia: Fortress Press, 1969, 138–67.

Kautzsch, A. F. *De Veteris Testamenti Locis Paulo Apostolo Allegatis*. Leipzig: Metzger und Wittig, 1869.

Keck, Leander. "Paul as Thinker," *Int* 47(1993): 27–33.

———. "The Law and 'the Law of Sin and Death' (Rom 8:1–4): Reflection on the Spirit and Ethics in Paul." In *The Divine Helmsman: Studies on God's Control of Human Events, Presented to Lou H. Silberman*. edited by James L. Crenshaw and Samuel Sandmel. New York: KTAV, 1980.

Kee, Howard Clark. *Good News to the Ends of the Earth: The Theology of Acts*. London: SCM, 1990.

———. "Knowing the Truth: Epistemology and Community in the Fourth Gospel." In *Neotestamentica et Philonica: Studies in Honor of Pedro Borgen*. edited by David Aune, Torrey Seland, and Jarl Ulrichsen. Leiden: Brill, 2003.

Keener, Craig. *A Commentary on the Gospel of Matthew*. Grand Rapids: Eerdmans, 1999.

———. *Acts: An Exegetical Commentary*. Grand Rapids: Baker, 2012–15.

———. "Miracle Reports and the Argument from Analogy," *BBR* 25:4(2015): 475–95.

———. *Miracles: The Credibility of the New Testament Accounts*. Grand Rapids: Baker, 2011.

———. *The Gospel of John: A Commentary*. Peabody: Hendrickson Publishers, 2003.

———. "We Beheld His Glory! (John 1:14." In *John, Jesus, and History, Volume 2: Aspects of Historicity in the Fourth Gospel*. edited by Paul Anderson, Felix Just, and Tom Thatcher. Atlanta: Society of Biblical Literature, 2009, 2:15–25.

Kelber, Werner H. "The Case of the Gospels: Memory's Desire and the Limits of Historical Criticism," *Oral Tradition* 17(2002): 55–86.

———. "The Generative Force of Memory: Early Christian Traditions as a Process of Remembering," *BTB* 36(2006): 15–22.

Kelber, Werner and Samuel Byrsog. *Jesus in Memory: Traditions in Oral and Scribal Perspectives*. Waco: Baylor University Press, 2009.

Kennard, Douglas W. *A Critical Realist's Theological Method: Returning the Bible and Biblical Theology to be the Framer for Theology and Science*. Eugene: Wipf and Stock, 2013.

———. *Biblical Covenantalism in Prophets, Psalms, Early Judaism, Gospels, and Acts. Volume Two Judaism, Covenant Nomism, and Kingdom Hope*. Eugene: Wipf and Stock, 2015.

———. *Biblical Covenantalism: Engagement with Judaism, Law, Atonement, the New Perspective, and Kingdom Hope. Volume One Biblical Covenantalism in Torah: Judaism, Covenant Nomism, and Atonement.* Eugene: Wipf and Stock, 2015.

———. *Biblical Covenantalism: Engaging the New Perspective and New Covenant Atonement. Volume Three Biblical Covenantalism in New Testament Epistles.* Eugene: Wipf and Stock, 2015.

———. "Evangelical Views of Illumination of Scripture and Critique," *JETS* 49(Dec. 2006): 797–806.

———. "Jeremiah and Hebrews: Mosaic, Davidic, and New," paper presented at ETS, Mar. 1994.

———. *Messiah Jesus: Christology in His Day and Ours.* New York: Peter Lang, 2008.

———. "Paul and the Law" a paper presented at ETS Mid-West regional meeting in March, 1996.

———. "Petrine Redemption: Its Meaning and Extent." *JETS* 30 (1987): 399–405.

———. *The Classical Christian God.* Lewiston: Edwin Mellen, 2002.

———. "The Doctrine of God in Petrine Theology." ThD diss. Dallas Theological Seminary, 1986.

———. "The Law in James" a paper presented at ETS Mid-West regional meeting in March, 1993.

———. "The Reef of the O.T.: A Method for Doing Biblical Theology that Makes Sense for Wisdom Literature." *SwJT* 56:1(2013): 227–57

———. *The Relationship Between Epistemology, Hermeneutics, Biblical Theology and Contextualization.* Lewiston: Edwin Mellen, 1999.

———. "The Way to Kingdom Salvation: Synoptics and the Law" a paper presented at ETS Mid-West regional meeting in March, 1992.

Kennard, J. Spencer. *Render to God: A Study of the Tribute Passage.* New York: Oxford University Press, 1950.

Kennedy, George. *New Testament Interpretation through Rhetorical Criticism.* Chapel Hill: University of North Carolina Press, 1984.

Kierkegaard, Soren. *Fear and Trembling.* Princeton: Princeton University Press, 1983.

Kilgallen, J. J. "Acts 13, 38–39: Culmination of Paul's Speech in Psidia," *Bib* 69(1988): 480–506.

Kim, Seyoon. *The Origin of Paul's Gospel.* Grand Rapids: Eerdmans, 1982.

Kirk, Alan and Tom Thatcher. *Memory, Tradition, and Text: Uses of the Past in Early Christianity.* Atlanta: Society of Biblical Literature, 2005.

Kistemacher, Simon. *Exposition of the Acts of the Apostles.* Grand Rapids: Baker, 1990.

Klijn, A. F. J. "The Study of Jewish Christianity," *NTS* 20 (1973–74): 419–31.

Klijn, A. F. J. and G. J. Reinink. *Patristic Evidence for Jewish-Christian Sects.* Leiden: Brill, 1973.

Koch, Dietrich-Alex. *Die Schrift als Zeuge des Evangeliums: Untersuchungen zur Verwendung und zum Verständnis der Schrift bei Paulus.* Tübingen: Mohr Siebeck, 1986.

Koester, *Hebrews.* New York: Doubleday, 2001.

Kraeling, E. G. *The Brooklyn Museum Aramaic Papyri: New Documents of the Fifth Century B.C. from the Jewish Colony at Elephantine.* New Haven: Yale University Press, 1953.

Kruse, Thomas. "Kantakkrima-Strafzahlung oder Steuer?," *Zeitschrift für Papyrologie und Epigraphik*, 124(1999): 166–90.

Kummel, W. G. *Introduction to the New Testament.* London: SCM, 1975.
Kung, Hans. *Signposts for the Future.* New York: Doubleday, 1978.
Kurz, William. "Narrative Models for Imitation in Luke-Acts." In *Greeks, Romans, and Christians,* edited by D. L. Balch. Minneapolis: Fortress Press, 1990, 171–189.
Kvanvig, Jonathan. *Intellectual Virtues and the Life of the Mind.* Savage: Rowman & Littlefield, 1992.
Lachs, Montefiore, Finkel, Friedlander, *The Jewish Sources of the Sermon on the Mount.* New York: KTAV, 1991.
Lambert, W. G. *Babylonian Wisdom Literature.* Oxford: Clarendon Press, 1960.
Landau, Brent. "The Epistle of James to Quadrantus: An Apocryphon with Jewish-Christian Traditions," a paper presented at Society for Biblical Literature, Nov. 22, 2015.
Lane, William. *Hebrews 1–8.* Dallas: Word, 1991.
Lapham, F. *Peter: The Myth, the Man and the Writings: A Study of Early Petrine Texts and Tradition.* Sheffield: Sheffield Academic, 2003.
Lapide Phihas. *The Sermon on the Mount.* Maryknoll: Orbis, 1986.
Lausberg, Heinrich. *Handbook of Literary Rhetoric: A Foundation for Literary Study.* Leiden: Brill, 1998.
Law, George. "The Law of the New Covenant in Matthew," *American Theological Inquiry* [online] 5:2[July 15, 2012]: 27–29.
Law, Robert. *The Tests of Life: A Study of the First Epistle of St. John.* Edinburgh: T & T Clark, 1914.
le Déaut, R. "Apropos a Definition of Midrash," *Int* 25(1971): 259–82.
Lee, Bernard. *The Galilean Jewishness of Jesus.* New York: Paulist, 1988.
Lehrer, Keith and Thomas Paxson, "Knowledge: Undefeated Justified True Belief," *The Journal of Philosophy* 66(1969): 225–37.
Leisengang, Hans. *Der Apostel Paulus als Denker.* Leipzig: J. C. Himrichs'sche Buchhandlung, 1923.
Levine, Amy-Jill. *The Social and Ethical Dimensions of Matthean Salvation History: "Go nowhere among the Gentiles. . ." (Matt. 10:5b). Studies in the Bible and Early Christianity, Vol. 14.* Lewiston: Edwin Mellen, 1988.
———. *Short Stories by Jesus: The Enigmatic Parables of a Controversial Rabbi.* New York, Harper One, 2014.
Lieberman, Saul. *Greek in Jewish Palestine.* New York: Jewish Theological Seminary, 1942.
———. "Rabbinic Interpretation of Scripture." In *Hellenism in Jewish Palestine.* New York: Jewish Theological Seminary, 1962, 47–82.
Lightfoot, John. *A Commentary on the New Testament from the Talmud and Hebraica.* Grand Rapids: Baker, 1979.
Lim, Timothy. *Pesharim.* London: Sheffield, 2002.
Lindars, Barnabus. *New Testament Apologetic.* Philadelphia: Westminster, 1961.
———. *The Gospel of John.* Grand Rapids: Eerdmans, 1972.
Lindberg, Carter. *The Pietist Theologians: An Introduction to Theology in the Seventeenth Centuries.* Malden: Blackwell, 2005.
Linss, Wilhelm. "Logical Terminology in the Epistle to the Hebrews," *CTM* 37:6(1966): 365–69.
Litfin, Duane. *St. Paul's Theology of Proclamation: 1 Cor 1–4 and Greco-Roman Rhetoric.* Cambridge: Cambridge University Press, 1994.

Lloyd, G. E. R. *Polarity and Analogy: Two Types of Argumentation in Early Greek Thought*. Cambridge: Cambridge University Press, 1966.
Lloyd-Jones, D. M. *Romans: An Exposition of Chapters 7:1–8:4: The Law: Its Functions and Limits*. Edinburgh: Banner of Truth, 1973.
Loader, William. *Jesus' Attitude Towards the Law: A Study of the Gospels*. Grand Rapids: Eerdmans, 1997.
Locke, John. *A Letter Concerning Toleration*. translated by William Popple, edited by James Tully. Indianapolis: Hackett, 1983.
———. *Concerning Human Understanding* in vol. 35 *Great Books of the Western World*. Chicago: Encyclopaedia Britannica, 1977.
———. *The Works of John Locke*. London: C. & J. Rivington, 1824.
Lohmeyer,E. *Probleme paulinischer Theologie*. Stuttgart: Kohlhammer, 1954.
Lohse, Eduard. *Colossians and Philemon*. Philadelphia: Fortress, 1971.
Long, A. A. *Hellenistic Philosophy: Stoics, Epicureans, Skeptics*. London: Duckworth, 1986.
Longenecker, Richard. *The Epistle to the Romans: A Commentary on the Greek Text*. Grand Rapids: Eerdmans, 2016.
Lundbom, Jack. *Deuteronomy: A Commentary*. Grand Rapids: Eerdmans, 2013.
Lünemann, Gottlieb. *Critical and Exegetical Hand-Book to the Hebrews*. New York: Funk & Wagnalls, 1885.
Luther, Martin. *Luther's Works*. ed. E. Theodore Bachman. Philadelphia/Minneapolis: Fortress, 1960.
Maass, F. "Von den Ursprüngen der rabbinischen Schriftauslegung," *ZThK* 52(1955): 129–61.
Mack, Burton. *A Myth of Innocence. Mark and Christian Origins*. Philadelphia: Fortress, 1988.
Mackay, Anne. *Signs of Orality: The Oral Tradition and Its Influence in the Greek and Roman World*. Leiden: Brill, 1999.
Malherbe, Abraham. "ΜΗ ΓΕΝΟΙΤΟ in the Diatribe and Paul," *HTR* 73(1980): 231–40.
Manson, T. W. *On Paul and John: Some Selected Theological Themes*. London: SCM, 1963.
Marcus, Joel. "Mark 4:10–12 and Marcan Epistemology," *JBL* 103:4(1984): 558–63.
———. *The Way of the Lord. Christological Exegesis of the Old Testament in the Gospel of Mark.*. Louisville: Westminster/John Knox, 1992.
Marshall, I. H. *I Believe in the Historical Jesus*. Grand Rapids: Eerdmans, 1977.
———. *Luke: Historian and Theologian*. Grand Rapids: Zondervan, 1971.
———. *The Gospel of Luke: A Commentary on the Greek Text*. International Greek Testament Commentary. Grand Rapids: Eerdmans, 1978.
———. "The Divine Sonship of Jesus," *Int* 21(1967): 87–103.
———. "The Synoptic Son of Man Sayings in Recent Discussion," *NTS* 12 (1965–66): 327–51.
Marshall, I. H. and David Peterson. *Witness to the Gospel: The Theology of Acts*. Grand Rapids: Eerdmans, 1998.
Marshall, L. H. *The Challenge of New Testament Ethics*. New York: Macmillan, 1947.
Martinez, Florentino and Eibert Tigchelaar. *The Dead Sea Scrolls: Study Edition*. Leiden: Brill, 1997.
Martley, Raoul. "The Mirror and 1 Cor 13:12 in the Epistemology of Clement of Alexandria," *VC* 30(1976): 109–20.

Mathies, David Kratz. "Reading the Moral Law: A Hermeneutical Approach to Religious Moral Epistemology," *The Conrad Grebel Review* 23:3(2005): 74–84.

Matthews, John F. "The Tax Law of Palmyria: Evidence for Economic History in a City of the Roman East," *JRS* 74(1984): 157–80.

Mayer-Haas, Andrea. *"Geschenk aus Gottes Schatzkammer (bSchab 10b)": Jesus und der Sabbat im Spiegel der neutestamentlichen Schriften.* Neutestamentliche Abhandlungen 43. Münster: Aschendorff, 2003.

Mayordomo, Moisés. *Argumentiert Paulus logisch? Eine Analyse vor dem Hintergrund antiker Logik.* Tübingen: Mohr Siebeck, 2005.

McArthur, Harvey and Robert Johnston, *They also Taught in Parables.* Grand Rapids: Zondervan, 1990.

McFadden, Kevin W. "The Fulfillment of the Law's DIKAIŌMA: Another Look at Romans 8:1–4" *JETS* 52(2009): 483–97.

McNamara, M. "Some Issues and Recent Writings on Judaism and the New Testament" *IBS* 9(1987): 136–49.

Meeks, Wayne. "'And Rose up to Play': Midrash and Paraenesis in 1 Corinthians 10:1–22," *JSNT* 16(1982): 64–78.

Meier, John. *A Marginal Jew: Rethinking the Historical Jesus. Vol. 1. The Roots of the Problem and the Person.* New York: Doubleday, 1991.

———. *A Marginal Jew: Rethinking the Historical Jesus. Vol. 2. Mentor, Message, and Miracles.* New York: Doubleday, 1994.

———. *A Marginal Jew: Rethinking the Historical Jesus. Vol. 3. Companions and Competitors.* New York: Doubleday, 2001.

———. *A Marginal Jew: Rethinking the Historical Jesus. Vol. 4. Law and Love.* New Haven: Yale University Press, 2009.

———. *A Marginal Jew: Rethinking the Historical Jesus. Vol. 5 Parables.* New Haven: Yale University Press, 2016.

Melancthon, Philip. *Commentary on Romans.* St. Louis: Concordia, 1992.

———. *Loci communes von 1521. Melancthons Werke 2.1.* ed. Hans Engelland. Gütersloh: Bertelsmann Verlag, 1952.

Metzger, Bruce. *A Textual Commentary on the Greek New Testament.* Stuttgart: Deutsche Bibelgesellschaft, 2002.

Meyer, Ben. *The Aims of Jesus.* London: SCM, 1979.

Michael, Otto. *Paulus und Seine Bibel.* Gütersloh: Bertelsmann, 1929 reprinted Darmstadt: Wissenschaftliche Buchgesellschaft, 1972.

Miegge, Giovanni. *Gospel and Myth in the Thought of Rudolf Bultmann.* Richmond: John Knox, 1960.

Milgrom, Jacob. *Leviticus 1–16.* New York: Doubleday, 1991.

Miller, M. P. "Targum, Midrash and the Use of the Old Testament in the New Testament," *JSJ* 2(1971): 29–82.

Miller, Nicholas. "Divided by Visions of the Truth: The Bible, Epistemology, and the Adventist Community," *AUSS* 47:2(2009): 241–62.

Mitchel, A. C. "The Use of πρεπειν and Rhetorical Propriety in Hebrews 2:10," *CBQ* 54(1992): 681–701.

Mitchell, Margaret. *Paul and the Rhetoric of Reconciliation: An Exegetical Investigation of the Language and Composition of 1 Corinthians.* Tübingen: Mohr Siebeck, 1991.

———. *The Heavenly Trumpet: John Chrysosto and the Art of Pauline Interpretation.* Tübingen: Mohr Siebeck, 2000.

Moessner, David. "Triadic Synergy of Hellenistic Poetics in the Narrative Epistemology of Dionysius of Halicarnassus and the Authorial Intent of the Evangelist Luke (Luke 1:1-4; Acts 1:1-8)," *Neot* 42:2(2008): 289-303.

Molina, Bruce and J. Neyrey, *Calling Jesus Names: The Social Value of Labels in Matthew*. Sonoma: Polebridge, 1988.

Montague, G. T. "Paul and Athens," *TBT* 49(1970): 14-23.

Montefiore, C. G. *Rabbinic Literature and Gospel Teachings*. New York: KTAV, 1970.

Moo, Douglas. "'Law', 'Works of the Law', and Legalism in Paul," *WTJ* 45(1983): 73-100.

———. *The Epistle to the Romans*. Grand Rapids: Eerdmans, 1996.

———. *The Wycliffe Exegetical Commentary: Romans 1-8*. Chicago: Moody, 1991.

Moody, Dale. "God's only Son: the translation of John 3:16 in the Revised Standard Version," *JBL* 72(1953): 213-19.

Morissette, Rodolphe. "La condition de ressuscité, 1 Cor 15, 35-49: Structure littéraire de la periscope," *Bib* 53(1972): 208-28.

Morris, Leon. *Studies in the Fourth Gospel*. Grand Rapids: Eerdmans, 1969.

———. *The First Epistle of Paul to the Corinthians*. Grand Rapids: Eerdmans, 1958.

———. *The Gospel According to John*. Grand Rapids: Eerdmans, 1971.

Moser, Paul. *Empirical Knowledge*. New York: Rowman & Littlefield, 1986.

———. "Gethsemane Epistemology Volitional and Evidential," *Philosophia Christi* 14(2012): 263-74.

———. *Jesus and Philosophy*. New York: Cambridge University Press, 2009.

———. *The Elusive God: Reorienting Religious Epistemology*. Cambridge: Cambridge University Press, 2008.

Moser, Paul and Michael McFall. *The Wisdom of the Christian Faith*. Cambridge: Cambridge University Press, 2012.

Moule, C. F. D. "A Neglected Factor in the Interpretation of Johannine Eschatology." In *Studies in John: Presented to Professor Dr. J. N. Sevenster on the Occasion of His Seventieth Birthday*. edited by M. C. Rientsma. Leiden: Brill, 1999, 155-60.

———. *Essays in New Testament Interpretation*. Cambridge: Cambridge University Press, 1982.

———. "The Individualism of the Fourth Gospel," *NovT* 5(1962): 171-90.

———. *The Origin of Christology*. Cambridge: Cambridge University Press, 1977.

Mouw, Richard. "John Locke's Christian Individualism," *Faith and Philosophy* 8:4(1991): 448-60.

Murray, John. *Redemption-Accomplished and Applied*. Grand Rapids: Eerdmans, 1955.

———. *The Epistle to the Romans*. Grand Rapids: Eerdmans, 1959, 1965.

Myers, Alicia. *Characterizing Jesus: A Rhetorical Analysis on the Fourth Gospel's Use of Scripture in its Presentation of Jesus*. London: T & T Clark, 2012.

Neder, Adam. *Participation in Christ: An Entry into Karl Barth's Church Dogmatics*. Louisville: Westminster John Knox, 2009.

Neusner, Jacob. *Handbook of Rabbinic Theology: Language, System, Structure*. Boston: Brill Academic, 2002.

———. *Judaism When Christianity Began: A Survey of Belief and Practice*. Louisville: Westminster John Knox, 2002.

Newman, Cardinal John Henry. *An Essay in Aid of A Grammar of Assent*. London: Longmans, Green & Co., 1870, 1903.

Neyrey, Jerome H. "Acts 17, Epicureans, and Theodicy: A Study in Stereotypes." In *Greeks, Romans, and Christians*. edited by D. L. Balch. Minneapolis: Fortress, 1990, 118–134.

———. "John III-A Debate Over Johannine Epistemology and Christology," *NovT* 23:2(1981): 119–23.

Norden, Eduard. *Agnostos Theos: Untersuchungen zur formengeschichte religiöser Rede*. Leipzig: Teubner, 1913.

———. *Die antike Kunstprosa vom VI. Jahrundert V. Chr. Bis in die Zeit der Renaissance*. Stuttgart: Teubner, 1958.

Nygren, Anders. *Agape and Eros*. London: SCPK, 1957.

O'Brien, Peter. *The Letter to the Hebrews*. Grand Rapids: Eerdmans, 2010.

Ochs, Peter. *Peirce, Pragmatism and the Logic of Scripture*. Cambridge: Cambridge University Press, 1998.

O'Day, Gail. "John" in *New Interpreter's Bible: A Commentary in Twelve Volumes*. Nashville: Abingdon, 1995.

Oecolampadius, Johannes. *In Hieremiam prophetam commentariorum libri tres Ioannis Oecolampadii*. Argentinae: n. p., 1533.

O'Grady, John F. "Individualism and the Johannine Ecclesiology," *BTB* 5(1975): 235–45.

Ollenburger, Ben, Elmer Martens, Gerhard Hasel. *The Flowering of O. T. Theology*. Winona Lake: Eisenbrauns, 1992.

Orr, William and James Walther. *1 Corinthians*. Garden City: Doubleday, 1976.

Osborne, Grant. *The Hermeneutical Spiral*. Downers Grove: InterVarsity, 1991.

O'Toole, Robert. *The Unity Luke's Theology: An Analysis of Luke-Acts*. Wilmington: Michael Glazier, 1984.

Overman, Andrew. *Matthew's Gospel and Formative Judaism: The Social World of the Matthean Community*. Minneapolis: Fortress, 1990.

Owen-Ball, David. "Rabbinic Rhetoric and the Tribute Passage (Matt 22:15–22; Mark 12:13–17; Luke 20:20–26)," *Nov. Test.* 35(1993): 1–14.

Painter, John. "Johannine Symbols: A Case Study in Epistemology," *JTSA* 27(1979): 26–41.

———. "Memory Holds the Key: The Transfiguration of Memory in the Interface of History and Theology." In *John, Jesus, and History, Volume 1: Critical Appraisal of Critical Views*. edited by Paul Anderson, Felix Just, and Tom Thatcher. Atlanta: Society of Biblical Literature, 2007, 1:229–48.

Pargiter, F. E. *The Mārkaṇḍeya Purāṇa*. Delhi: Indological Book House, 1969.

Park, Eugene Eung-Chun. "Covenant Nomism and the Gospel of Matthew," *CBQ* 77:4(2015): 668–85.

Pate, C. Marvin and Douglas W. Kennard. *Deliverance Now and Not Yet: The New Testament and the Great Tribulation*. New York: Peter Lang, 2003, 2005.

Patte, D. *Paul's Faith and the Power of the Gospel*. Philadelphia: Fortress, 1983.

Payne, Phillip. "Midrash and History in the Gospel with Special Reference to R. H. Gundry's *Matthew*." In *Studies in Midrash and Historiography*. edited by R. T. France and David Wenham. Sheffield: JSOT, 1983, 3:177–215.

Pedersen, T. Engberg. *Paul in his Hellenistic Context*. Minneapolis: Fortress, 1995.

Peirce, Charles Sanders. "How to Make Our Ideas Clear," *Popular Science Monthly* 12(Jan., 1878): 286–302.

———. *The Collected Papers of Charles Sanders Peirce*. edited by Charles Hartshorne and Paul Weiss. Cambridge: Harvard University Press, 1966.

———. "The Fixation of Belief," *Popular Science Monthly* 12(Nov., 1877): 1-15.
Perdue, Leo. *Wisdom and Creation: The Theology of Wisdom Literature*. Nashville: Abingdon, 1994.
———. *Wisdom in Revolt: Creation Theology in the Book of Job*. JSOT 121. Sheffield: JSOT/Almond, 1991.
Pervo, Richard. *Acts: A Commentary*. Minneapolis: Fortress, 2009.
Pesch, Rudolf. *Die Apostelgeschichte*. Zurich: Benzinger, 1986.
Pines, S. "The Jewish Christians of the Early Centuries of Christianities According to a New Source," *The Israeli Academy of Sciences and Humanities Proceedings* [Jerusalem], 2(1966): 237-309.
Plantinga, Alvin. *Knowledge and Christian Belief*. Grand Rapids: Eerdmans, 2015.
———. *Warrant and Proper Function*. New York: Oxford University Press, 1993.
———. *Warranted Christian Belief*. New York: Oxford University Press, 2000.
———. *Warrant: The Current Debate*. New York: Oxford University Press, 1993.
Plantinga, Alvin and Nicholas Woltersdorf. *Faith and Rationality: Reason and Belief in God*. Notre Dame: University of Notre Dame Press, 1983.
Plummer, A. *A Critical and Exegetical Commentary on the Gospel According to St. Luke*. International Critical Commentary. Edinburgh: T & T Clark, 1896.
Pokorny, Petr. *From the Gospel to the Gospels: History, Theology and Impact of the Biblical Term "euangelion."* Berlin: De Gruyter, 2013.
Polanyi, Michael. *The Tacit Dimension*. Garden City: Doubleday, 1966.
Pool, David de Sola. *The Traditional Prayer Book for Sabbath and Festivals*. New Hyde Park: University Books, 1960.
Popkin, Richard. "Fideism." In *The Encyclopedia of Philosophy*. edited by Paul Edwards. New York: Macmillan, 1967, 3:201-203.
Porter, Stanley. *John, His Gospel, and Jesus: In Pursuit of the Johannine Voice*. Grand Rapids: Eerdmans, 2015.
———. *Paul in Acts*. Peabody: Hendrickson, 2001.
———. *The Criterion for Authenticity in Historical-Jesus Research: Previous Discussion and New Proposals*. Sheffield: Sheffield Academic, 2000.
———. "Thucydides 1.22.1 and Speeches in Acts: Is There a Thucydidean View?," *NovT* 2(1990): 121-42.
Porter, Stanley and Andrew Pitts. *Christian Origins and Greco-Roman Culture: Social and Literary Contexts for the New Testament*. Leiden: Brill, 2013.
Porton, G. G. "Defining Midrash." In *The Study of Ancient Judaism*. edited by J. Neusner. New York: KTAV, 1981, 1:55-95.
Pritchard, James. *Ancient Near Eastern Texts: Relating to the Old Testament*. Princeton: Princeton University Press, 1969.
Puech, E. "Une Apocalypse messianique (4Q521)," *RevQ* 15(1992): 475-519.
Quenstedt, Johann Andreas. *Theologia Didactico-Polemica*. Wittenberg: Johanne Ludolph Quenstedt, 1685.
———. *The Nature and Character of Theology: An Introduction to the Thought of J. A. Quenstedt from THEOLOGIA DIDACTIO-POLEMICA SIVE SYSTEMA THEOLOGICUM*. abridged, edited and translated by Luther Poellot. St. Louis: Concordia, 1986.
Radmacher, Earl and Robert Preus. *Hermeneutics, Inerrancy, and the Bible*. Grand Rapids: Zondervan, 1984.
Räisänen, Heikii. *Paul and the Law*. Tübingen: Mohr Siebeck, 1983.

Reid, Thomas. *Essays on the Intellectual Powers of Man.* ed. Baruch Brody. Cambridge: MIT Press, 1969.

———. *Thomas Reid, An Inquiry into the Human Mind on the Principles of Common Mind.* edited by Derek Brookes. Edinburgh: Edinburgh University Press, 1997.

Reimarus, Hermann Samuel. "Von dem Zwecke Jesu und seiner Junger: Noch ein Fragment des Wolfenbuttelschen ungenannten fragment?" or translated as "On the Intentions of Jesus and His Disciples." In *Reimarus: Fragments.* Translated by Ralph Fraser and edited by Charles Talbert. Philadelphia: Fortress Press, 1970.

Renan, E. *The Life of Jesus.* translated by C. E. Wilbour. London: Trübner, 1864, Original title: *La Vie de Jésus.* Paris: Michel Lévy Frères, 1863.

Resch, D. Alfred. *Der Paulinismus und die Logia Jesu in ihrem gegenseitigen Verhältnis.* Leipzig: J. C. Hinrichs, 1904.

Richards, E. Randolph. "Silvanus Was Not Peter's Secretary: Theological Bias in Reading Bias in Interpreting διὰ Σιλουανοῦ ἔγραψα in 1 Pet 5:12," *JETS* 43(2000): 417-32.

Richardson, Alan. *An Introduction to the Theology of the New Testament.* New York: Harper & Brothers, 1958.

Ricoeur, Paul. *Essays on Biblical Interpretation.* Philadelphia: Fortress, 1980.

———. *Figuring the Sacred: Religion, Narrative, and Imagination.* Minneapolis: Fortress, 1995.

———. *Hermeneutics & the Human Sciences.* Cambridge: Cambridge University Press, 1981.

———. *Interpretation Theory: Discourse and the Surplus of Meaning.* Fort Worth: The Texas Christian University Press, 1976.

———. *Memory, History, Forgetting.* Chicago: University of Chicago Press, 2004.

———. *Oneself as Another.* Chicago: The University of Chicago Press, 1992.

———. *The Conflict of Interpretations.* Evanston: Northwestern University Press, 1974.

———. *The Symbolism of Evil.* Boston: Beacon, 1967.

———. *Time and Narrative.* Chicago: University of Chicago Press, three volumes: 1984, 1985, 1988.

———. "Toward a Hermeneutics of the Idea of Revelation." In *Essays on Biblical Interpretation.* London: SPCK, 1981, 73-118.

Ridderbos, H. N. *The Speeches of Peter in the Acts of the Apostles.* Cambridge: The Tyndale Press, 1962.

Ritschl, A. B. *The Christian Doctrine of Justification and Reconciliation.* 3 vols. Edinburgh: Edmonston and Douglas, 1872.

Roberts, R. C. and W. Jay Wood. *Intellectual Virtues: An Essay in Regulative Epistemology.* Oxford: Clarendon Press, 2007.

Robertson, Archibald and Alfred Plummer. *First Epistle of St. Paul to the Corinthians.* Edinburgh: T. & T. Clark, 1911.

Robinson, J. M. "The Johannine Trajectory." In *Trajectories Through Early Christianity.* edited by J. M. Robinson and H. Koester. Philadelphia: Fortress, 1971, 232-66.

Roepe, G. *De Veteris Testamenti locrum in apostolorum libris allegation.* n.p., 1827.

Russell, Bertrand. "Knowledge by Acquaintance and Knowledge by Description," *Proceedings of the Aristotelian Society* 11(1910-11): 108-128.

Ruzer, Serge. "Reading 1QS 1 and 1QS 11 as Backdrop to the Johannine Prologue," Paper given at SBL meeting, Nov. 20, 2010.

Sacks, Oliver. *The Man Who Mistook his Wife for a Hat.* New York: Harper and Row, 1985.

Safrai, S. "The Rechov Inscription," *Immanuel* 8(1978): 48-57.
Safri, S. and M. Stern. *The Jewish People in the First Century*. Philadelphia: Fortress, 1976.
Saldarini, Anthony. *Matthew's Christian-Jewish Community*. Chicago: University of Chicago, 1994.
Sandbach, F. H. *The Stoics*. London: Chatto & Windus, 1975.
Sanders. E. P. "Habakkuk in Qumran, Paul, and the Old Testament." In *Paul and the Scriptures of Israel*. edited by Craig Evans and James Sanders. Sheffield: Sheffield Academic, 1993.
———. *Jesus and Judaism*. Philadelphia: Fortress, 1985.
———. *Jewish Law from Jesus to the Mishnah*. London: SCM, 1990.
———. *Judaism: Practice and Belief 63B.C.E.–66 C.E*. London: SCM, 1992.
———. *New Testament Christological Hymns*. Cambridge: Cambridge University Press, 1971.
———. *Paul and Palestinian Judaism: A Comparison of Patterns of Religion*. London: SCM, 1977.
———. *Paul, the Law, and the Jewish People*. Minneapolis: Fortress, 1983.
———. *The Historical Figure of Jesus*. London: Penquin, 1993.
Sanders, Jack. *The Jews in Luke-Acts*. Philadelphia: Fortress, 1987.
Sandmel, David. "Critique of *Short Stories by Jesus*" a paper presented at the Society for Biblical Literature, Nov. 22, 2015.
Sandys-Wunsch, John and Laurence Eldredge. "J. P. Gabler and the Distinction Between Biblical and Dogmatic Theology: Translation, Commentary, and Discussion of his Originality," *SJT* 33(1980): 133-58.
Schafer, Peter. *Kehhalot-Studien*. Tübingen: Mohr [Paul Siebeck], 1988.
Schaff, P. *Creeds of Christendom*. New York: Harpers, 1877.
Schiffman, Lawrence and James VanderKam. *Encyclopedia of the Dead Sea Scrolls*. New York: Oxford University Press, 2000.
Schlatter, Adolf. *Die Geschichte des Christus*. Stuttgart: Calwer Vereinsbuchhandlung, 1923 translated by Andreas Köstenberger as *The History of the Christ: The Foundation for New Testament Theology*. Grand Rapids: Baker, 1997.
———. "Der Zweifel an der Messianität Jesu." In *Zur Theologie des Neuen Testaments and zur Dogmatik*. Munich: C. Kaiser, 1969, 151-202.
Schleiermacher, F. E. D. *The Life of Jesus*. translated by S. M. Gilmour. edited by J. C. Verhegden. Lives of Jesus Series. Philadelphia: Fortress, 1975, Original title: *Das Leben Jesu*. Edited by K. A. Rutenk Berlin: Reimer, 1868.
Schmeiler, Thomas. *Paulus und die "Diatribe": Eine Vergeichende Stilinterpretation*. Münster: Aschendorff, 1987.
Schnabel, Eckhard J. *Law and Wisdom from Ben Sira to Paul: A Tradition Historical Enquiry into the Relation of Law, Wisdom, and Ethics*. Tübingen: J. C. B. Mohr [Paul Siebeck], 1985.
Schnackenburg, Rudolf. *The Gospel According to St. John*. London: Burns & Oates, 1968.
Schoeps, Hans-Joachim. *Jewish Christianity: Factual Disputes in the Early Church*. Philadelphia: Fortress, 1969.
———. *Theologie und Geschichte des Judenchristentums*. Tübingen: Mohr, 1949.
Schrage, Wolfgang. "Leig, Kreuz und Eschaton: Die Peristasenkataloge als Merkmale paulinischer *theologia crucis* und Eschatologie." In *Kreuzestheologie und Ethik*

im Neuen Testament: Gesammelte Studien. Göttingen: Vandenhoeck & Ruprecht, 2004, 23–57.

Schreiner, Thomas. *Romans.* Grand Rapids: Baker, 1998.

———. *The Law and Its Fulfillment.* Grand Rapids: Baker Books, 1993.

Schubert, P. "The Final Cycle of Speeches in the Book of Acts," *JBL* 87(1968): 1–16.

———. "The Place of the Areopagus Speech in the Composition of Acts." In *Transitions in Biblical Scholarship.* edited by J. Coert Rylaarsdam. Chicago: University of Chicago Press, 1968, 235–61.

Schutter, W. L. "1 Peter 4.17, Ezekiel 9.6, and Apocalyptic Hermeneutics." In *SBL Seminar Papers.* SBLSP 26. Atlanta: Scholars, 1987, 276–84.

———. *Hermeneutical Composition in First Peter.* Tübingen: Mohr [Siebeck], 1989.

Schweitzer, Albert. *The Kingdom of God and Primitive Christianity.* New York: Seabury, 1968.

———. *The Mystery of the Kingdom of God.* New York: Macmillan, 1950.

———. *The Mysticism of Paul the Apostle.* Baltimore: John Hopkins University Press, 1998.

———. *The Quest of the Historical Jesus.* translated by W. Montgomery. London: Adam and Charles Black, 1948.

Schweizer E. "Concerning the Speeches in Acts." In *Studies in Luke–Acts,* edited by L. E. Keck and J. L. Martyn. London: SPCK, 1968, 208–16.

Scott, E. F. *The Ethical Teaching of Jesus.* New York: Macmillan, 1924.

Scott, Ian. *Paul's Way of Knowing: Story, Experience, and the Spirit.* Grand Rapids: Baker, 2009, previously published as *Implicit Epistemology in the Letters of Paul: Story, Experience and the Spirit.* Tübingen: Mohr Siebeck, 2006.

Scott, R. B. Y. "Priesthood, Prophecy, Wisdom, and the Knowledge of God," *JBL* 80 (1961): 1–15.

Scroggs, Robin. "New Being: Renewed Mind: New Perception Paul's View of the Source of Ethical Insight," *The Chicago Theological Seminary Register* 72:1(1982): 1–12.

Seifrid, Mark. *Christ, Our Righteousness: Paul's Theology of Justification.* Downers Grove: InterVarsity, 2000.

Selby, Rosalind. *The Comical Doctrine: An Epistemology of New Testament Hermeneutics.* Milton Keynes: Paternoster, 2006.

Selwyn, Edward. *The First Epistle of St. Peter.* New York: Macmillan, 1947.

Shafaat, Ahmed. "Geber of the Qumran Scrolls and the Spirit-Paraclete of the Gospel of John," *NTS* 26(1980–1): 263–69.

Sheeley, Steven. *Narrative Asides in Luke-Acts.* Sheffield: Sheffield Academic, 1992.

Shields, B. E. "The Areopagus Sermon and Romans 1.18ff: A Study in Creation Theology," *ResQ* 20(1977): 23–40.

Shiell, David. *Reading Acts: The Lector and the Early Christian Audience.* Boston: Brill, 2004.

Sholem, Gershom *Jewish Gnosticism, Merkabah Mysticism, and Talmudic Tradition.* New York: The Jewish Publication Society of America, 1960.

Shumate, Nancy. *Crises and Conversion in Apuleius' Metamorphoses.* Ann Arbor: University of Michigan Press, 1996.

Sidebottom, E. M. *The Christ of the Fourth Gospel.* London: SPCK, 1961.

Silberman, Lou. *Orality, Aurality and Biblical Narrative.* Semia Studies. Atlanta: Scholars, 1987.

Sisson, Russel. "Abductive Logic and Rhetorical Structure in 1 Corinthians 9," *Proceedings* 26(2006): 93–100.
Smalley, Stephen. *1, 2, 3 John*. Dallas: Word, 1984.
Soards, M. *The Speeches in Acts: Their Content, Context, and Concerns*. Louisville: Westminster/John Knox, 1994.
Spener, Philipp Jakob. *Consilia Et Judicia Theologia*. Frankfurt a.M., 1709.
Stanley, Christopher. *Arguing with Scripture: The Rhetoric of Quotations in the Letters of Paul*. London: T & T Clark, 2004.
———. *Paul and the Language of Scripture: Citation Technique in the Pauline Epistles and Contemporary Literature*. Cambridge: Cambridge University Press, 1992.
———. "'Pearls Before Swine?' Did Paul's Audience Understand His Biblical Quotations?" *NovT* 41(1999): 124–44.
Stiver, Dan. *Theology After Ricoeur: New Directions in Hermeneutical Theology*. Louisville: Westminster John Knox, 2001.
Stowers, Stanley. *Diatribe and Paul's Letter to the Romans*. Chico: Scholars, 1981.
Stowers, "Paul on the Use and Abuse of Reason." In *Greeks, Romans, and Christians*. edited by David Balch, Everett Ferguson, Wayne Meeks. Minneapolis: Fortress, 1990.
Strauss, D. F. *The Life of Jesus Critically Examined*. 3 vols. trans. G. Eliot. London: Chapman, 1846, Original title: *Das Leben Jesu Kritisch bearbeitet*. 2 vols. Tübingen: Osiander, 1835–36.
Strecker, Georg. *Das Judenchristentum in den Pseudoklementinen, TU 70, no. 2*. Berlin: Akademie, 1958, revised edition 1981.
Stuhlmacher, Peter. *Paul's Letter to the Romans*. Louisville: Westminster/John Knox, 1994.
———. "The Pauline Gospel." In *The Gospel and the Gospels*. edited by Peter Stuhnmacher. Grand Rapids: Eerdmans, 1991, 149–72.
Talbert, Charles. "Biographies of Philosophers and Rulers as Instruments of Religious Propaganda in Mediterranean Antiquity," *ANRW* 2.16.2 (1978): 1619–51.
———. *Literary Pattern, Theological Themes, and the Genre of Luke-Acts*. Missoula: Scholars Press, 1974.
Tasker, R. V. G. *The Gospel According to St. John*. Grand Rapids: Eerdmans, 1960.
Tavard, George. *Holy Writ or Holy Church: The Crisis of the Protestant Reformation*. New York: Harper & Brothers, 1959.
Taylor, J. E. "The Phenomenon of Early Jewish Christianity: Reality or Scholarly Invention," *VC* 44 (1990): 313–34.
Taylor, Joan. *The Immerser: John the Baptist within Second Temple Judaism*. Grand Rapids: Eerdmans, 1997.
Teeter, David. *Scribal Laws: Exegetical Variation in the Textual Transmission of Biblical Law in the Late Second Temple Period*. Tübingen: Mohr Siebeck, 2014.
Thatcher, Tom. *Jesus, The Voice, and the Text: Beyond the Oral and Written Gospel*. Waco: Baylor University Press, 2008.
———. *Why John Wrote a Gospel: Jesus-Memory-History*. Louisville: Westminster John Knox, 2006.
Thielman, Frank. *Paul & the Law: A Contextual Approach*. Downers Grove: InterVarsity, 1994.
Thiselton, Anthony. *New Horizons in Hermeneutics: The Theory and Practice of Transforming Biblical Reading*. Grand Rapids: Zondervan, 1992.

———. *The First Epistle to the Corinthians.* Grand Rapids: Eerdmans, 2000.

———. *The Two Horizons: New Testament Hermeneutics and Philosophical Description.* Grand Rapids: Eerdmans, 1980.

Thompson, Marianne Meye. "The 'Spirit Gospel': How John the Theologian writes History." In *John, Jesus, and History. Volume 1 Critical Appraisals of Critical Views.* edited by Paul Anderson, Felix Just, and Tom Thatcher. Atlanta: Society of Biblical Literature, 2002, 103–108.

Thompson, Richard and Thomas Phillips. *Literary Studies in Luke-Acts.* Macon: Mercer University Press, 1998.

Thyen, Hartwig. *Der Stil des jüdish-hellenistischen Homile.* Göttingen: Vandenhoeck & Ruprecht, 1955.

Tobin, Thomas. *Paul's Rhetoric in its Contexts: The Argument of Romans.* Peabody: Hendrickson, 2004.

Tosato, Angelo. "The Law of Leviticus 18:18: A Reexamination," *CBQ* 46(1984): 199–214.

Treggiari, Susan. *Roman Marriage: Iusti coniures from the Time of Cicero to the Time of Ulpian.* Oxford: Clarendon, 1991.

Trites, Allison. *The New Testament Concept of Witness.* Cambridge: Cambridge University Press, 1977.

Trompf, G. W. *The Idea of Historical Recurrence in Western Thought: From Antiquity to the Reformation.* Berkeley: University of California Press, 1979.

Uytanlet, Samson. *Luke-Acts and Jewish Historiography: A Study on the Theology, Litterature, and Ideology of Luke-Acts.* Tübingen: Mohr Siebeck, 2014.

van der Toorn, K. *Sin and Sanction in Israel and Mesopotamia.* Assen: Van Gorcum, 1986.

Vanhoozer, Kevin. *Biblical Narrative in the Philosophy of Paul Ricoeur: A Study in Hermeneutics and Theology.* Cambridge: Cambridge University Press, 1990.

———. *Is There Meaning in this Text?* Grand Rapids: Zondervan, 1998.

Vanier, Jean. *Community and Growth.* New York: Paulist, 1989.

van Voorst, Robert E. *The Ascents of James: History and Theology of a Jewish-Christian Community,* SBLDS 112. Atlanta: Scholars, 1989.

Velasco, Jesus Maria and Leopold Sabourin. "Jewish Christianity of the First Centuries," *BTB* 6 (1976): 5–26.

Vermes, Geza. "A Summary of the Law by Flavius Josephus," *NT* 24(1982): 289–303.

———. *Jesus and the World of Judaism.* Philadelphia/London: Fortress/SCM, 1984.

———. *Jesus the Jew: A Historian's Reading of the Gospels.* New York: MacMillan/Collins, 1973, 1983.

———. *The Complete Dead Sea Scrolls in English.* New York: Lane/Penguin, 1997.

———. *The Religion of Jesus the Jew.* Minneapolis: Fortress, 1993.

Vetschera, Rudolf. *Zur griechischen Paränese.* Smichow: Rohliček & Sievers, 1912.

Volf, Miroslav. *Captive to the Word of God: Engaging the Scriptures for Contemporary Theological Reflection.* Grand Rapids: Eerdmans, 2010.

Vollmer, Hans. *Die altestamentlichen Citate bei Paulus.* Freiburg: Mohr Siebeck, 1895.

von Harnack, Adolf. *Das Wesen des Christentums.* Leipzig: Hinrichs, 1913, translated as *What is Christianity.* New York: Harper, 1957.

von Rad, Gerhard. *Old Testament Theology.* New York: Harper and Row, 1962.

Wacholder, B. Z. "The Calendar of Sabbatical Cycles during the Second Temple and Early Rabbinic Period," *HUCA* 44(1973): 98–116.

Wagner, Ross. *Heralds of the Good News: Paul and Isaiah in Concert in the Letter to the Romans*. Leiden: Brill, 2002.
Wallmann, Johannes. *Philipp Jakob Spener und die Aufänge des Pietismus*. Tübingen: Mohr, 1970.
Walton, John. *Ancient Israelite Literature in its Cultural Context*. Grand Rapids: Zondervan, 1989.
Walton, John and Brent Sandy, *The Lost World of Scripture: Ancient Literary Culture and Biblical Authority*. Downers Grove: InterVarsity, 2013.
Wainwright, A. W. *A Paraphrase and Notes on the Epistles of St. Paul*. Oxford: Clarendon, 1987.
Wainwright, William. *Reason and the Heart*. Ithaca: Cornell University Press, 1995.
Watson, Francis. *Paul and the Hermeneutics of Faith*. London: T & T Clark/Continuum, 2004.
Watson, Wilfred G. E. and N. Wyatt, *Handbook of Ugaritic Studies*. Boston: Brill, 1999.
Weiss, Johannes. *Der erste Korintherbrief*. Göttingen: Vandenhoeck & Ruprecht, 1910.
Wendland, Paul. *Anaximenes von Lampsakos: Studien zur ältesten Geschichte der Rhetorik*. Berlin: Weidmann, 1905.
Westcott, B. F. *The Gospel According to St. John*. Grand Rapids: Eerdmans, 1978.
Westermann, Claus. *Roots of Wisdom: The Oldest Proverbs of Israel and Other Peoples*. Louisville: Westminster John Knox, 1995.
Westfall, C. I. *A Discourse Analysis of the Letter to the Hebrews: The Relationship between Form and Meaning*. London: T & T Clark, 2005.
Westphal, Merold. "Taking St. Paul Seriously: Sin as an Epistemological Category." In *Christian Philosophy*. edited by Thomas Flint. Notre Dame: University of Notre Dame, 1990, 200–226.
Whiston, William. *An Essay Towards Restoring the True Text of the Old Testament*. London: J. Senex, 1722.
Wikenhauser, Alfred. *Pauline Mysticism: Christ in the Mystical Teaching of St. Paul*. New York: Herder and Herder, 1960.
Wilckens, Ulrich. *Der Brief an die Römer*. Zurich: Benzinger, 1978, 1980, 1982.
Wilk, Florin. *Die Bedeutung des Jesajabuches für Paulus*. Göttingen: Vandenhoeck & Ruprecht, 1998.
Wilkinson, Michael F. and J. P. Moreland. *Jesus Under Fire*. Grand Rapids: Zondervan, 1995.
Willard, Dallas. *The Divine Conspiracy: Rediscovering our Hidden Life in God*. San Francisco: HarperSanFrancisco, 1998.
Williams, David. *Acts*. NIBCNT. Peabody: Hendrickson, 1990.
Williamson, Ronald. *Philo and the Epistle to the Hebrews*. Leiden: Brill, 1970.
Willis, Wendell Lee. *Idol Meat in Corinth: The Pauline Argument in 1 Corinthians 8 and 10*. Chico: Scholar's, 1985.
Winter, Bruce. *Philo and Paul among the Sophists*. Cambridge: Cambridge University Press, 1997.
Wise, Michael, Martin Abegg, and Edward Cook. *The Dead Sea Scrolls: A New Translation*. San Francisco: HarperSanFrancisco, 1996, 2005.
Witherington III, Ben. *The Jesus Quest: The Third Search for the Jew of Nazareth*. Downers Grove: InterVarsity, 1995.
Wittgenstein, Ludwig. *Philosophical Investigations*. translated by G. E. M. Anscombe. New York: Macmillan, 1953.

Wood, W. Jay. *Epistemology: Becoming Intellectually Virtuous.* Downers Grove: InterVarsity, 1998.
Wrede, William. *The Messianic Secret.* Cambridge: Clarke, 1971.
Wright, A. G. *Midrash: The Literary Genre.* Staten Island: Alba House, 1968.
Wright, N. T. *Jesus and the Victory of God.* vol. 2 of *Christian Origins and the Question of God* Minneapolis: Fortress, 1996.
———. *The Climax of the Covenant: Christ and the Law in Pauline Theology.* Minneapolis: Fortress, 1993.
———. "The Lord's Prayer as a Paradigm of Christian Prayer." In *Into God's Presence: Prayer in the N. T.* edited by R. N. Longenecker. Grand Rapids: Eerdmans, 2001.
———. *The New Testament and the People of God.* vol. 1 of *Christian Origins and the Question of God.* Minneapolis: Fortress, 1992.
———. *The Resurrection of the Son of God.* Minneapolis: Fortress, 2003.
———. "Toward a Synthesis of Pauline Theology (1 and 2 Thessalonians, Philippians, and Philemon)." In *Pauline Theology I: Thessalonians, Philippians, Galatians and Philemon.* edited by J. M. Bassler. Minneapolis: Fortress, 1991.
———. *What Saint Paul Really Said: Was Paul of Tarsus the Real Founder of Christianity?* Grand Rapids: Eerdmans, 1997.
Yinger. Kent. *Paul, Judaism, and Judgment According to Deeds.* Cambridge: Cambridge University Press, 1999.
Yitzhaq of Berdichev, Levi. *Imre Tzaddiqim,* ed. Tz'vi Hasid. Zhitomir: n. p., 1899.
Young, Brad. *Meet the Rabbis: Rabbinic Thought and the Teachings of Jesus.* Peabody: Hendrickson, 2007.
Zagzebski, Linda. *Virtues of the Mind.* Cambridge: Cambridge University Press, 1996.
Zehnle, R. F. *Peter's Pentecost Discourse.* Nashville: Abingdon, 1971.
Zeitlin, S. "Midrash: A Historical Study," *JQR* 44(1953): 21–36.

Author Index

Abegg, M, 181, 188
Abraham, W, 5, 20, 23, 96, 126, 148, 208, 219
Adams, R, 6, 25, 43, 126, 157
Aeschylus, 130
Akiba, 43, 82, 157
Alexander, L, 97
Alexander, P, 18, 142, 146
Alighieri, D, 140
Allen, C, 5
Allen, D, 129
Allison, D, 22–24, 30, 32, 35, 37–38, 41, 44, 46, 54, 57–60, 66, 76, 79, 82
Alston, W, 4–5, 20, 23, 124, 141, 148, 150, 152, 173, 222
Anaximenes, 148
Ambroisiater, 141, 159
Ambrose, 8
Anderson, R, 84, 146–48, 211
Anselm, 139
Antonius, M, 209
Appold, M, 167
Aquinas, T, 137, 139
Aratus Soli, 129–30
Ariel, D, 79
Aristeas, 81
Aristophanes, 54
Aristotle, 11, 84, 91, 96, 99, 101, 114, 117, 129–30, 142, 144–47, 149–50, 161–62, 211, 216–18
Armstrong, C, 151
Arrian, 97, 150, 166
Aslan, R, 79
Assman, J, 92
Athanasius, 8
Athenaeus, 144
Athenagoras, 44, 158
Attridge, H, 217
Audi, R, 6
Augustine, 5, 8, 18, 24, 141, 159
Augustus, 97
Aune, D, 181, 183–84
Aurelius, M, 52
Austin, J, 18, 57, 104, 109, 124, 152, 162, 175
Azulai, 19, 33

Bachmann, M, 194
Bacon, F, 5
Bahr, G, 83
Bailey, K, 4, 11, 88, 93
Balch, D, 104, 118, 130
Bammel, E, 48
Barr, J, 135, 180
Barrett, C, 104, 118, 135, 178
Barth, K, 19, 132, 151, 156
Barton, S, 82, 162
Bartsch, H, 124, 131
Basil, 175
Bates, M, 136
Bauckham, R, 3–4, 11, 88, 92–95, 122, 124, 163, 165, 166, 219
Bauer, F, 132
Beasley-Murray, G 172, 177, 181
Becker, J, 138
Bekken, P, 136, 143
Belleville, L, 144
Bennema, C, 165, 185, 196
Berger, P, 103
Berkowitz, L, 121

Betz, H, 150
Bialoblocki, S, 18, 142
Bietenhard, H, 115, 123, 129
Black, R, 12
Blaising, C, 57, 219
Blanton, T, 155–56
Bloch, R, 142, 204, 216
Blomberg, C, 98
Bock, D, 63, 98, 110, 118, 123–24, 217
Boethius, 56
Bokzer, B, 32, 42
Bond, L, 154
Bonhoeffer, A, 144, 151
Bonneau, N, 144–45, 161–62
Bonsirven, J, 143
Boomershine, T, 11, 85, 93, 151
Borg, M, 87
Borgen, P, 173
Borin, M, 87
Bourke, M, 98
Bousset, W, 151
Bouttier, M, 151
Bovon, F, 104
Boyarin, D, 136
Bray, G, 159
Breech, J, 87
Brody, B, 5
Brooke, G, 110
Brookes, D, 5, 20
Brown, R, 6, 87–88, 172, 177–79, 181, 197–98
Bruce, F, 105, 135, 217
Brueggeman, W, 5, 20, 96, 126, 150, 219
Buchanan, G, 216–17
Bullock, H, 203
Bultmann, R, 1, 4, 90, 98–99, 124, 131, 144, 151, 168, 170, 173, 180, 186
Bunyan, J, 9
Burnett, A, 79
Bynum, C, 190
Byrskog, S, 3, 95

Cadbury, H, 97, 105–6
Calvin, J, 9, 158
Campbell, C, 152
Carson, D, 45, 163, 170, 172
Cassian, J, 8
Charlesworth, J, 87–89, 181

Chernus, I, 221
Chicago Bib Herm, 134, 178
Chilton, B, 142
Christianson, E, 194
Chrysippus, 129
Chrysostom, J, 61, 94, 130, 141–42, 144, 175
Ciampa, R, 135
Cicero, M, 52, 86, 93–94, 97, 99, 120, 128–30, 145, 161, 218
Clement Alex, 3, 8, 30, 52, 66, 92, 99, 124, 130, 162, 219–20
Clement Rome, 8, 121, 123, 126, 158, 185, 215
Climacus, J, 8
Cohon, S, 72
Collins, A, 79, 110
Conzelmann, H, 4, 95, 98, 103, 133
Cook, E, 181, 188
Cook, W, 179
Cosby, M, 217
Cothenet, E, 100, 106
Cowley, A, 49
Cox, H, 24
Cranfield, C, 159, 194
Creed, J, 63
Crenshaw, J, 205–6
Crook, Z, 103
Crossan, J, 79, 89
Crouzel, H, 100, 106
Cullmann, O, 115, 123
Cunningham, S, 98
Cyprian, 8, 21
Cyril, 8

Dabney, D, 159
Danker, F, 158
Das, A, 159
Daube, D, 42, 75, 77
Davids, P, 122
Davies, W, 1, 4, 18, 22–24, 30, 32, 35, 37, 41, 44, 46, 54, 57–60, 66, 76, 79, 82, 144, 149–51, 222
Dawes, G, 145, 162
Dean-Otting, M, 220
de Boer, W, 100, 106
Deisman, A, 115, 123, 150, 158
Demetrius, 146

AUTHOR INDEX

Demosthenes, 91, 93
de Roo, J, 194
Descartes, 139
de Silva, 217–18
Dever, W, 89
Dewey, Joanna, 3, 93
Dewey, John, 7, 91
Dibelius, M, 97, 102, 105, 118, 202, 209
Didymus, 175
Dickens, C, 64
Diels, H, 168
Diller, K, 19
Dionysius Alex, 8
Dionysius Hal., 10, 96–97, 99–101, 131, 144, 166, 170, 175
Dittenberger, 78
Dodd, C, 42, 105, 135, 188–89
Downing, F, 97
Draper, J, 3, 92
Driver, G, 194
Dunn, J, 1, 3–4, 9–10, 14–15, 26, 39, 88, 90, 92–93, 124, 135, 159, 161, 168, 178, 193–94, 219, 222
Dupont, J, 12, 130–31, 138, 149

Edwards, J, 6–7, 159, 221, 223
Ehrman, B, 84, 132
Eisenbaum, P, 218
Elliott, M, 15, 33, 89, 124, 126
Ellis, E, 65, 70–71, 81, 136–37, 142–43, 152, 203–4, 216
Ely, M, 170–71
Epictetus, 52, 104, 129, 144, 152, 174, 204, 209
Epicurus, 128
Epimenides, 130
Epiphanius, 18, 45, 52
Etheridge, J, 152
Euripides, 99, 129
Eusebius, 3, 8, 18, 44, 52, 68, 91, 94–95, 99, 121, 124, 130, 152, 163, 200, 215, 219
Evans, C, 21, 42, 70, 87, 89, 104, 169–70

Fee, G, 135, 178
Finkel, F, 38, 59, 73
Fiore, B, 100, 106, 145, 162
Fisher, J, 42, 70–73, 75

Fitzmyer, J, 49, 129, 143
Flannery, F, 4, 20, 149
Flusser, D, 45
Foley, J, 82
Ford, D, 115, 154, 217
Fornara, C, 100
Fortna, R, 170
Foster, J, 211
Fox, M, 205–9, 211
Franke, A, 134, 178
Friedlander, G, 38
Frydrych, T, 201, 204–9
Fuller, R, 124, 131

Gabler, J, 90
Gadamer, H, 2
Gaffin, R, 151–52
Gaffney, J, 171
Gamaliel, 20, 141, 145–49, 189
Gärtner, B, 105, 118, 133
Garuti, P, 217
Gathercole, S, 136, 193
Gaventa, B, 103
Gerhardsson, B, 10, 93
Gericke, J, 200–2, 205–6, 208–9
Gettier, E, 201–2, 205
Gillman, N, 190
Godet, F, 159, 178
Goldman, A, 201
Gooch, P, 18, 156, 158, 162, 204
Gordon, C, 184
Gorgias, 91, 93
Gorman, M, 151–52
Grave, S, 5
Green, J, 98, 103, 140
Gregerman, A, 84
Grenz, S, 134
Grice, H, 18, 57, 82, 108
Grosheide, F, 135, 179
Gruenwald, I, 220
Gundry, R, 98, 219
Gutierrez, P, 100

Haacker, K, 143–44
Halbwachs, M, 3, 92, 124
Harnack, A, 87, 99
Harrington, W, 98
Harris, J, 135

AUTHOR INDEX

Hays, D, 104, 118, 136–37, 142, 143–44, 204
Healy, M, 3, 133, 137, 148, 158, 160
Hegel, G, 132
Heidegger, M, 154
Heinemann, J, 58
Hemer, C, 97, 105, 118, 129–30
Hengel, M, 88, 92, 143
Henningsson, J, 150, 163
Henry, M, 159
Heraclitus, 168
Hermas, 215
Herodotus, 96
Hesiod, 28, 44
Hess, J, 87
Hicks, R, 128
Hilary Pointers, 8, 175
Hildesheimer, A, 33
Hillel, 37, 65, 68, 70–71, 132, 141, 145–48, 216–17, 223
Hippolytus, 21, 136, 175
Hirsch, E, 134, 178
Hodge, C, 158
Hodot, 22
Hoener, H, 77
Hofius, O, 194
Hoggerterp, A, 194
Hollanz, D, 134, 178
Holmén, T, 75
Horace, 15, 69, 98
Horsley, R, 92, 105
Howard, G, 216
Hübner, H, 159
Huna, 36
Hunter, A, 181
Hurst, L, 220
Hus, J, 134

Iamblichus, 52
Ignatius, 31, 94, 123, 136, 168, 216
Immanuel, B, 12
Instone-Brewer, 69–71
Irenaeus, 18, 44, 92, 94–95, 99, 121, 123, 136, 158, 163, 216, 219
Ishmael, 22, 146

Jackson, F, 99
Jacobs, L, 18, 57

Jaffee, M, 93
James, W, 7
Jenson, R, 6
Jeremias, 54, 57–58, 83
Jerome, 18
Jervell, J, 98–99
Jewett, R, 129
Jobes, K, 143
Johanan, 21, 189
Johnson, L, 82–84, 87, 104, 118
Johnson, M, 205
Johnson, W, 121
Johnsson, W, 218
Johnston, R, 84, 146, 211
Jones, O, 5
Josephus, 12, 14–15, 17, 23, 27–29, 31–34, 43, 46–49, 52, 56, 58, 62, 69, 72, 77–78, 81, 91, 96–100, 104, 108, 141, 152, 157, 166, 182, 190, 200, 204, 209, 216
Jung, V, 178
Justin, 21, 44, 52, 78, 80–81, 94, 121, 123, 136, 158, 168, 215–6

Kant, I, , 7, 154, 223
Kaplan, M, 7
Karis, R, 98
Käsemann, E, 88, 170
Kautzsch, A, 135
Keck, L, 138, 159
Kee, H, 98, 163, 166
Keener, C, 12, 81, 95, 97–100, 102, 104, 107, 110, 114, 116, 122, 125, 166–70, 172–73, 177–78, 180–81, 185, 197–98
Kelber, W, 3, 92, 124, 219
Kennard, D, 1–2, 5, 7, 13, 16, 18–19, 21, 32, 34, 57, 60, 74–76, 82–86, 103, 105, 106, 109, 112, 116, 129, 132, 134–36, 139–40, 143, 146–48, 152, 159, 168, 177–78, 210, 219–20
Kennard, J, 79
Kennedy, G, 105
Kierkegaard, S, 7, 120, 126, 149–50, 223
Kilgallen, J, 105, 118–19
Kim, S, 120, 149, 152–53
Kirk, A, 92, 96

Kistemacher, S, 102
Klijn, A, 39
Koch, D, 135, 143
Koester, C, 215–18, 221
Kraeling, E, 49
Kruse, T, 158
Kuhn, K, 105, 184
Kummel, W, 181
Kurz, W, 100, 106

Lachs, S, 38
Lactanius, 6, 12, 104, 107, 116, 122, 167, 173, 200–1, 206, 208–9, 219
Laertius, D, 31, 52, 129, 168
Lake, K, 99
Lambert, W, 202, 211
Landau, B, 149
Lane, W, 215, 218
Lapham, F, 121
Lapide, P, 41
Lausberg, H, 23, 145, 216, 218
Law, G, 19, 167
Leclerc, J, 98
Le Déaut, R, 142, 204, 216
Lehrer, K, 201
Leisengang, H, 133
Levine, A, 18, 33, 84
Lieberman, S, 18, 52
Lightfoot, G, 36, 98
Lim, T, 104, 110, 123
Lindars, B, 135, 172, 177–78
Linss, W, 219
Litfin, D, 132
Lloyd, G, 145
Loader, W, 32
Locke, J, 6–7, 12, 32, 104, 107, 110, 114, 116, 122, 125, 131, 139, 159, 166–67, 173, 200–1, 206, 208–9, 219, 221–23
Lohse, E, 194
Lohmeyer, E, 194
Loisy, A, 87
Long, A, 168
Longenecker, R, 132, 144
Lucian, 27, 82, 96
Luckman, T, 103
Lucretius, 130
Lünemann, G, 219

Luther, M, 103, 159

Maass, F, 18, 142
MacDonald, D, 99
Mack, B, 89
Mackay, R, 92
Maier, P, 97
Malherbe, A, 132, 144
Marcus, J, 11, 19, 21, 23–24, 123, 170
Marshall, I, 83, 88, 97
Marshall, L, 24
Martin, F, 5
Martley, R, 162
Mathies, D, 2
Matthews, G, 5, 17, 19, 22, 141, 148
Matthews, J, 79
Matthias, M, 134, 177–78
Maximus Tyre, 144
Mayordomo, M, 129, 132, 145–47, 150
McArthur, H, 84, 146, 211
McElenry, N, 87
McFadden, K, 159
McKnight, S, 87
McNamara, M, 204, 216
Meeks, W, 142, 204
Meier, J, 12, 18, 84, 87, 89, 112
Melanchthon, P, 159
Metzger, B, 98, 175–76
Meyer, B, 89
Michael, O, 143
Miegge, G, 131
Milgrom, J, 137, 180–81
Miller, M, 142, 204
Miller, N, 2
Milligan, G, 158
Mitchel, A, 218
Mitchell, M, 142–43
Moessner, 97
Molina, B, 77
Montague, G, 105, 118
Montefiore, C, 38, 46
Moo, D, 158, 194
Moody, D, 172
Morissette, R, 162
Morris, L, 135, 154, 172, 177–79, 184, 190, 192

Moser, P, 5, 9, 20–21, 23, 43, 57, 108, 120, 122, 130, 163, 165, 169, 179, 194, 220
Moule, C, 88, 163, 165
Moulton, J, 158
Murray, J, 151, 159
Myers, A, 96

Nahum, 78
Naziznzen, G, 8, 95, 153
Neder, A, 151
Neusner, J, 143, 162
Newman, J, 134, 178
Neyrey, J, 77, 105, 118, 169–70, 173
Noland, J, 95
Norden, E, 140, 170
Novation, 175
Nygren, A, 6, 25, 43, 126, 157
Nyssa, G, 8

Ochs, P, 7
O'Brien, P, 217–18
O'Day, G, 186
O'Dowd, R, 13, 34, 143, 209
Oecolampadius 159
O'Grady, J, 165
Oliver, I, 70
Origen, 21, 39, 47, 95, 121, 136, 175, 189, 200, 215–16, 218, 220
Orr, W, 135, 179
Osborne, G, 2
O'Toole, R, 98
Overman, J, 18, 33
Owen-Ball, D, 81

Painter, J, 166, 184
Papias, 92, 121, 124
Pargiter, F, 210
Park, E, 33
Parry, R, 3
Pate, C, 1, 5, 60, 86, 106, 112, 116, 220–21
Patte, D, 144
Pausanins, 129
Paxton, T, 201
Payne, P, 98
Peirce, C, 7, 124, 126, 161, 174, 201, 206–7, 209, 221–23

Pelagius, 159
Perdue, L, 210
Pervo, R, 99
Pesch, R, 99
Philo, 6, 14–18, 21–22, 27–29, 44–45, 48, 52, 61, 63, 69, 71, 80–81, 91, 96, 100, 104, 123, 132, 136, 141, 143, 157, 168, 182–83, 191, 204, 216
Philosttus, 129
Pines, S, 73
Plantinga, A, 5, 19, 22, 129, 148, 200
Plato, 27, 29, 44, 91, 93, 129, 145, 152, 154, 162, 168, 189–90, 201
Pliny Elder, 31, 97–98
Pliny Younger, 121, 161
Plotinus, 120
Plummer, A, 83, 135, 179
Plutarch, 52, 91, 93, 96, 100–1, 130, 145, 161, 166, 209
Pokorny, P, 3, 92
Polanyi, M, 134, 178
Polkow, D, 87
Polybius, 95
Polycarp, 28, 30, 44, 61, 81, 158
Pool, D, 53, 146–48, 217
Popkin, R, 156
Porter, S, 102, 105, 118, 163, 167, 170
Porton, G, 142, 204, 216
Pritchard, J, 211
Pseudo-Isocrates, 82
Puech, E, 110

Quintilian, 10, 96–97, 99–101, 145, 162, 170, 216–18
Quenstedt, J, 134, 178

Rae, M, 5, 19, 158, 160
Räisänen, H, 159
Reid, T, 5, 7, 20, 23, 96, 122, 148, 206–9, 219, 222
Reimarus, H, 87
Reinink, G, 39
Renan, E, 87
Resch, D, 144
Richards, E, 121
Richardson, A, 188–89

AUTHOR INDEX

Ricoeur, P, 2-3, 57, 82, 92, 107, 109, 115-16, 120, 122, 124-25, 130, 166, 210, 217, 219
Ridderbos, H, 105
Ritschl, A, 87
Roberts, R, 126
Robertson, A, 135, 179
Robinson, J, 168
Roepe, G, 135
Rood, T, 99
Rosner, B, 135
Russell, B, 202
Ruzer, S, 185

Sabourin, L, 39
Sacks, O, 5
Safrai, S, 65, 72
Saldarini, A, 18, 32, 39
Sanders, E, 1, 4, 15, 33, 39, 89, 104, 112, 143, 151, 159, 170, 203, 222
Sandmel, D, 84
Sandy, B, 11, 88-89, 93
Schafer, P, 220
Schechter, S, 42
Schellenberg, R, 140-43
Schlatter, A, 87
Schleiermacher, F, 87, 134
Schnabel, E, 159
Schnackenburg, R, 170, 179
Schrage, W, 141
Schreiner, T, 9, 159
Schoeps, H, 39
Schubert, P, 105, 118
Schutter, W, 123
Schweitzer, A, 1, 4, 7, 24, 87-88, 103, 151-52, 222
Schweizer, E, 103, 105
Scoggs, R, 160
Scott, E, 24, 203
Scott, I, 3, 129, 133, 138-40, 148, 150, 154, 159-60
Seifrid, M, 159
Selby, R, 2
Selwyn, E, 102
Seneca, 92, 124, 126-27, 162, 204, 209, 219
Sextus, E, 67, 81, 140
Shafaat, A, 198

Shammai, 71-72
Sheeley, S, 99
Shields, B, 105, 118
Shiell, D, 98
Sholem, G, 220
Shumate, N, 111
Sidebottom, E, 184
Silberman, L, 3, 92
Silius Italicus, 96
Simai, 80
Simeon, 46, 65
Sisson, R, 161
Smalley, S, 172
Snodgrass, K, 84
Soads, M, 105-6
Solon, 44
Sophocles, 52, 91
Spener, P, 134, 177
Squiter, K, 121
Stanley, C, 136, 138, 143
Stecker, G, 39
Stegman, T, 95, 104, 118, 133, 137
Stein, R, 87, 134, 177
Stiver, D, 2
Stoaeus, 52
Stowers, S, 132, 144
Strabo, 128, 141
Strauss, D, 87
Stuhlmacher, P, 115, 159
Suetonius, 61, 98, 115, 123
Suggate, A, 14

Tacitus, 44, 78, 96
Talbert, C, 97, 100, 111
Tanhuma, 36
Tasker, R, 178
Tatian, 168, 183
Tavard, G, 134, 178
Taylor, J, 197
Taylor, J. E., 39
Teeter, D, 142
Tertullian, 21, 59, 80-81, 94, 99, 121, 156, 167
Thatcher, T, 3, 92, 96, 166-67, 179
Theodoret, 175
Theon, 96, 99
Thielman, F, 159
Thiselton, A, 2, 133, 135, 162, 179

Thomas a Kempis, 8
Thompson, M, 181
Thucydides, 10, 95–96, 101, 105
Thyen, H, 215
Tobin, T, 132, 135–37, 142
Tosato, A, 48
Treggiari, S, 48
Trites, A, 91
Trompf, G, 100, 106

Uytanlet, 100

Valerius Max, 100
Vall, G, 13, 34
Vander Kam, J, 155–56
Van der Toorn, K, 211
Vanhoozer, K, 2
Vanier, J, 151
Van Voorst, R, 39
Velasco, J, 39
Vermes, G, 45–46, 58, 80, 89, 196
Vetschera, R, 202
Vincent Lerins, 8
Vital, 33
Vitruvius, 97
Volf, M, 22
Vollmer, H, 135
Von Harnack, A, 24
von Rad, G, 203, 207

Wacholder, B, 65
Wagner, R, 137, 143
Wainwright, W, 6, 25, 43, 126, 157
Wise, M, 181
Walke, W, 87
Wallman, J, 134, 177
Walther, J, 135, 179
Walton, J, 11, 88–89, 93, 210
Watson, F, 135, 137, 194, 211

Weaver, W, 87
Weiser, A, 4, 222
Weiss, J, 142, 204
Wendland, P, 202
Westcott, B, 172, 177–78
Westermann, C, 205, 212
Westfall, C, 218
Westphal, M, 127, 154, 156
Whiston, W, 135
White, R, 18
Wikenhauser, A, 151
Wilckens, U, 143
Wilk, F, 137
Willard, D, 9
Williams, D, 102
Williamson, R, 220
Winter, B, 132
Wise, M, 181, 188
Witherington, B, 87
Wittgenstein, L, 17, 19, 22, 141, 148, 222
Woltersdorf, N, 19
Wood, R, 6, 126–27, 153
Wrede, W, 87
Wright, N, 1, 13, 40, 58, 87, 89–90, 102, 108, 142, 150, 159, 161, 189–90, 204, 216
Wyatt, N, 211

Xenophon, 95

Yinger, K, 9
Yitzhaq, 19, 33
Yohannan, 75, 80
Young, B, 32, 33

Zagzebski, L, 6
Zehnle, R, 105
Zeitlin, S, 142, 204, 216

Subject Index

Abduction, 161
Adultery, 46–47
Allegiance, 104, 113, 152–53
Authority, 76–82, 107, 145

Basic Belief, 5, 22–68, 127, 200, 222–23
Bath Qol, 20, 173

Coherence, 205
Conscience, 127
Cosmological Arg, 128–30
Covenant Nomism, 13–19, 32–76

Dependence on God, 59, 61
Design Priority, 49
Divorce, 48–51

Empiricism, 6–7, 12, 91–102, 104, 107, 110, 113–16, 122, 125, 131, 139, 158–59, 173–74, 179, 200–202, 205–10, 219–23
Essene, 181–99
Evidence, 104, 107

Faith, 107
Fasting, 61–62
Filial Knowledge, 5, 20–21, 120, 122, 163
Forgiveness, 59–60

Generous, 54–56, 59
Gentleness, 27–28
Gnosticism, 170–71
Good works, 31–32
Grieving, 26–27

Haggadah, 18, 22–82, 142–45
Hallakah, 18, 32–68, 82–85, 141–42, 203–4
Hellenistic Rhetoric, 132, 145–46, 149, 161–62, 211, 216, 218
Historiographic method 5, 86–120
Honesty, 52–53

Illumination, 133–39, 177–81
Imitation of Christ, 113
Integrity, 29, 47, 56, 205
Intention, 55
Inspiration, 176–81, 204–5
Intuition, 133–39

Jesus reveals, 173–76

Law, 13–19, 145–50, 202–4, 216
Love, 43–45
Loyalty to God, 62–64
Lust, 46–47

Mercy, 28–29
Merkabah mysticism, 5, 220–21, 224
Midrash, 115, 216–17, 222
Murder, 45–46
Mysticism, 4–5, 124, 152–61, 167–68, 220–21, 224
Myth, 98–99, 131

Natural Knowledge of God 128–30
New Covenant, 42–43, 154–55
Nonjudgmental, 69–74

Oaths, 52–53

SUBJECT INDEX

Obedience, 158
Oral Tradition, 3–4, 6–7, 10–88, 91–93, 124

Peacemaker, 29–30, 46
Performative, 109–10, 115–16, 124, 162, 174–75
Perseverance, 30–31
Persistence, 61
Pesher, 104, 141–42, 216
Pharisaic, 3–4, 6–7, 10–85, 91–93, 132, 141–50, 222–23
Platonism, 27, 29, 44, 91, 93, 129, 145, 152, 154, 162, 168, 189–90, 201, 220
Poverty, 25–26
Pragmatism, 6–7, 124–26, 158–62, 174, 201, 206–10, 221–23
Prayers, 56–59
Purity, 55

Qumran, 181–99

Rabbinic, 3–4, 6–7, 10–88, 91–93, 132, 141–50, 161–62, 216, 222–23
Reconciliation, 46
Repentance, 108
Renew Mind, 154–60
Revelation, 204–5
Right Affections, 28

Sabbath, 69–74
Scribal Authority, 76–82

Testimony, 5, 92–93, 107, 125, 174
Two ways salvation, 8–9, 22–24

Virtue Epistemology, 8–9, 22–32, 41–68, 126–27, 153–60, 224
Volition, 130

Wisdom , 8, 200–214

Zoroastrianism, 184

Scripture Index

GENESIS

1	212
2	49, 212–13
3	212–13
4	212
6	212
7	212
8	212
9	48, 53, 212
11	212
15	53
42	48

EXODUS

3:6	80–81, 191
16	59, 72, 74, 160
20	45–46, 48, 52, 58, 69, 203
21	54
22	54
23	69
24:8	83
28	48
31	69
34	69, 72
35	69
40	220

LEVITICUS

1–16	180
1–7	46, 74
11–15	74
16	61
17	74
18	48, 50, 74, 160
19	25, 44, 50, 52, 58, 72, 157, 203
20	48, 74
22	44, 74
23	72
24	54, 73

NUMBERS

15	69
19	74
21	176
28	73
30:2	52

DEUTERONOMY

5	45–46, 69, 91, 203
6	38, 43, 157
8:3	38
9:7	16
10:16	43
14–16	55, 69
17	91
19	52, 54, 91
23–24	48, 52, 54, 59, 72, 74
25:5	79
27	53, 193

DEUTERONOMY (continued)

28:12—30:20	16, 204
30:6	189
32:6	58

1 SAMUEL

16:7	56
17:43	68
21:6	73

2 SAMUEL

7:12–13	115, 123

1 KINGS

6	160

2 KINGS

4:33–34	57
8:13	68
17:23	16

1 CHRONICLES

23:31	73

NEHEMIAH

1:4	61
9:32	16
13:15–22	69

ESTHER

4	14, 61

JOB

	210, 213
4:8	67, 209
5	67, 202
6	209
18:5–6	23
22	209
28	204, 209
29:2–3	23
30:1	68
31	202
38–41	205, 212
38:15	23
42	202

PSALMS

1:2	203
4	23, 219
6	219
10	219
18	23, 219
19	204, 219
22	219
27:1	23, 182–83
28	219
31	219
34	219
37:31	203
40	219
48:3	23
51:16–17	55
56:13	23
61	219
66	219
78	219
95:7–10	216
103:13	58
104	204
106	219
119	183, 204
126:2–6	26
104:2	23
110	115, 123, 216–17
127:2	65

PROVERBS

	213
1	203–4, 209
2	202

3	189, 203, 205, 209, 211	10	26, 51
4	183, 203	26:6–8	26, 58
6	183, 203, 208, 210	32:17	65
7	203	35:5–6	11
8–9	204, 209	42	119, 183
10	207, 209–10	49	119, 183
11	67, 209	52:6	58
12	207, 209	53	75, 83, 116
13	189	54	51
14	209–10	58:13	70, 74
15	209–11	61:1–2	11–12, 26, 110, 112
16	207, 209	63:16	58
17	209–10	66:10	26
18	210–11		
19	209–10		
20	160, 205, 207		
21	209–10		
22	67, 205, 209–10		
23	23, 203, 209		
24	208, 209		
26	210		
28	23, 203, 210		
29	203, 209		
30	205		
31	210		

JEREMIAH

17	69
31:13–34	13, 16, 19, 26, 33, 83, 155
44	160

EZEKIEL

1	220
5	160
10	220
21:3	16
20:31	16
22	74
34	155
36.23—37:28	13, 58, 155

ECCLESIASTES 213

1	208
2	183, 208
3	202, 208–9, 212
4	202, 208
5	208
6	202, 208
7	202
8	202, 208
9	208
10	202, 208
11	202

DANIEL

6:10	56
7:13–14	175
9:3	61
12:2–3	78, 189, 197

ISAIAH

1:23	51
2:5	23
4:1	58
6	220
9	16, 183

HOSEA

6:6	71
10:12	23

JOEL

2	56, 62, 155

AMOS

8:5	69

MICAH

5:3-4	16

HAGGAI

2	74

ZECHARIAH

7	61
8:19	61

MALACHI

3	197
4	197

MATTHEW 10-85

1:20	20
1:25	20
2:13	20
3	20, 152, 198
4:1-11	20, 38, 60
4:18-25	45, 67, 100
5	18-36, 41-55, 101
5:3-12	16, 21-32, 66, 67
5:20	19, 33
6	20, 23-24, 41, 46, 55-58, 60, 62-67, 101
7:1-12	56-57, 61, 66-68, 101
7:13-27	21-23, 63
8	12, 75, 91
9:2-13	20, 66, 94, 113
9:14-25	41, 62, 75, 190
9:27-35	12, 100
10	94, 195, 209
11	12, 57
12	12, 70-74
13	46-47, 64
15	12, 47
16	12, 20, 47
17:5	20
18	46-47, 84, 91
19	12, 18, 39-41, 44, 49-51
20:30	12
21-23	76-79
21:9	12
22	40, 43, 77-82, 157
23	19, 33, 38, 52-53, 55
24	47, 60
25	36, 197
26:20-29	83
26:59-75	41, 53, 77, 125
28	69, 116

MARK

1	57, 69, 75, 95, 100, 152
2:18-28	61-62, 70-74
3:4-11	12, 70-72, 77
5:7	12
5:35-42	75, 190
6	57
7	50
8	12, 100
10	12, 39-40, 48-51
11:9-25	12, 60
12	43, 55-56, 77-82, 157
13	100
14	83, 100
14:32-56	41, 57, 95
16:1	69

LUKE 11-12, 86-120

1	20, 86, 93, 95-97, 100-101, 108-9
2	20, 109
3:2-18	22, 77, 109, 152
3:22-38	20, 100, 109

SCRIPTURE INDEX

4:1–13	20, 60	6	169–70, 173–75, 182, 185–87, 196, 198
4:17–22	11–12, 18, 59, 110		
4:38–41	12, 69	7	169–70, 173–74, 187, 192, 194
5	57, 61–62, 75, 113		
6:5–28	16, 22–32, 39, 44, 55, 57, 72, 74, 100–101	8	41, 56, 164, 169–70, 173, 182, 184, 186–88, 192–96
6:37–49	23, 66–67, 101		
7	11, 66, 73, 75–76, 112–13, 171, 190	9	12, 169, 182, 185, 188, 192, 194, 196
8	12, 75, 99, 112–13, 171, 190	10	169, 173, 185–88
		11	57, 99, 165, 169, 182, 185, 187, 190–91, 196
9	20, 57, 99, 113–14		
10:9–16	114	12	12, 38, 169–70, 173, 182, 184–88, 196
10:25–37	40, 43–44, 66, 157		
11:1–29	12, 57, 59–61, 114	13–16	83, 169–70
11:34–46	23, 55	14	61, 134, 169–70, 173, 176–79, 188, 198
12	64–66, 113		
13	22, 69–71, 108, 112–13	15	61, 95, 166, 169, 173, 176, 193, 195, 198
14	113		
15	66, 84	16	61, 134, 170, 173, 176–79, 192, 195, 198
16	26, 35–36, 50–51, 62–64, 80, 191	17	57, 164, 170, 173, 193–96
18:1–8	61		
18:9–39	12, 39–40, 57, 59, 61, 66, 141	18	41, 164–65, 169, 195, 198
19	12, 113	19	185, 198
20	12, 55, 77–82, 191	20	101, 165, 167, 177, 181
21	56, 113	21	94, 165, 167, 169, 181
22	83, 125		
23:8	12	**ACTS**	
23:34	44		
23:40—24:11	69, 93, 112	1	86, 91, 94–97, 100, 119, 125, 177
24:44–48	38, 91, 108, 114		
		2	99, 104, 107–8, 114–15, 122–25, 177
JOHN			
		3	56, 94, 102, 107, 114–15, 122, 124–25, 191
1	12, 38, 152, 164–65, 168–75, 182, 184–88, 193, 195, 197–99	4	77, 99–100, 108, 114, 122, 124
2	12, 152, 189, 199	5	99, 107–8, 149
3	165, 169–72, 174–76, 182, 185–86, 188–89, 191–95, 197–98	6	99
		7	98
		8	104, 108, 116–17
4	165, 169–70, 194–95, 198	9	94, 104, 108, 119–20, 128, 149, 153
5	71–72, 169–70, 173, 182–83, 195	10	56, 102, 104, 107, 114–16, 122, 124–25

ACTS (continued)

11	104, 107, 114, 122, 128
12	200
13	94, 104, 108, 118–19, 141
14	117
15	107, 114, 117, 122, 200
16	94–96, 104, 108, 117, 119
17	108, 117–18, 119, 128–30
18	104, 108, 117, 141
19	104, 107, 117, 152
20–21	94–95, 102, 104, 107, 117, 119, 128, 141, 200
22	104, 119–20, 128, 132, 141, 149, 153
23:6–10	77–78, 132, 141, 145
24	104, 119, 145
25	145
26	107, 118–20, 132, 141, 145
27	94–95
28	94–95, 118

ROMANS

1	129, 140
2	149
3	102, 146, 149, 152, 156
4	139, 142, 146, 158
5	146, 152, 154, 157, 162
6	120, 149, 152–55, 159
7	140, 153, 156, 159–60
8	146, 153, 155–62
9	146, 149
11	140, 146
12	146, 162, 189
13	142, 155
14	148, 152, 156
15	102, 146, 148, 157, 162

1 CORINTHIANS 148

1	102, 130, 133, 137–38, 147, 152
2	131–34, 137–39, 160, 177
3	145
4	147
5	153
6	146, 156
7	142, 144–45
8	102, 148, 162
9	144, 146–48, 161–62
10	102, 139, 148
11	83, 96, 145, 147, 162
12	102, 146, 149, 189
13	140, 157, 162
14	102
15	99, 131, 144, 153, 162, 200

2 CORINTHIANS 148

1	157
3	140, 146–47
5	157
6	147, 156
9	160
12	141

GALATIANS 137

1	200
2	154, 157, 161, 200
3	146, 152–53, 156
4	102, 120, 147
5	145, 156–57, 159–60
6	142, 156

EPHESIANS

1	160
3	161
4	153–54, 161

PHILIPPIANS

1	139, 156
2	146, 158, 161
3	132, 141, 145, 158, 162
4	157

COLOSSIANS 94

1	161–62
2	130
3	153–54

1 THESSALONIANS

1	145, 162
2	145
5	102, 162

1 TIMOTHY

1:4	99, 131
4	131
5	142, 146–47

2 TIMOTHY

2	157, 181
4	131

TITUS

1	131, 157, 162
2	157

PHILEMON 146

HEBREWS 215–21

1	217, 219
2	216–19
3	216, 218
4	59, 216–18
5	57, 217, 219
6	216, 218, 219, 221
7	217
8	220–21
9	216, 220–21
10	209, 216, 217–18, 220–21
11	171, 218
12	217–20

JAMES 200–214

1	51, 200, 202, 204–5, 210–13
2	200–204, 207, 210–12
3	200–202, 205–7, 209, 211
4	200–201, 204, 206–7, 209, 211–12
5	200, 202, 204, 206, 209–12

1 PETER

1	102, 121, 125–26
2	127
3	125, 127
4	102, 125
5	121

2 PETER

1	86, 95, 99, 121–22, 124–27, 131
2	102, 123, 125, 127
3	123–24, 181

1 JOHN

1:1–10	23–24, 86, 94, 97, 163, 166–67, 181, 184–86, 188, 192–93, 195–96, 198
2	134, 167, 169, 177, 179, 185, 188, 192–93, 195–96, 198–99

1 JOHN (continued)

3	169, 194–95
4	169–72, 192, 195, 199
5	167, 169, 189, 194–96, 219

2 JOHN

8–11	194–96

3 JOHN

10	194

REVELATION

168, 188, 193–97

www.ingramcontent.com/pod-product-compliance
Lightning Source LLC
Chambersburg PA
CBHW050342230426
43663CB00010B/1955